THE PUB IN

MANCHESTER
UNIVERSITY PRESS

THE PUB IN LITERATURE

England's altered state

STEVEN EARNSHAW

Manchester University Press
Manchester and New York

distributed exclusively in the USA by St. Martin's Press

Copyright © Steven Earnshaw 2000

The right of Steven Earnshaw to be identified as the author of this work has been asserted by him in accordance with the Copyright, Designs and Patents Act 1988.

Published by Manchester University Press
Oxford Road, Manchester M13 9NR, UK
and Room 400, 175 Fifth Avenue, New York, NY 10010, USA
http://www.manchesteruniversitypress.co.uk

Distributed exclusively in the USA by
St. Martin's Press, Inc., 175 Fifth Avenue, New York, NY10010, USA

Distributed exclusively in Canada by
UBC Press, University of British Columbia, 2029 West Mall,
Vancouver, BC, Canada V6T 1Z2

British Library Cataloguing-in-Publication Data
A catalogue record for this book is available from the British Library.

Library of Congress Cataloging-in-Publication Data applied for

ISBN 0 7190 5304 8 hardback
       0 7190 5305 6 paperback

First published 2000

07 06 05 04 03 02 01 00   10 9 8 7 6 5 4 3 2 1

Typeset in Sabon with Frutiger
by Northern Phototypesetting Co Ltd, Bolton
Printed in Great Britain
by Bookcraft (Bath) Ltd, Midsomer Norton

FOR LIZ

This moment in the public house, this pub moment, I'm going to have to keep on coming back to it.

Martin Amis, *London Fields*

Contents

	Acknowledgements	*page* viii
1	Introduction	1
2	Early doors	18
3	The Falstaffian state	45
4	Wonderfull yeares	69
5	Pepys pissed	90
6	'Jovial, brutal, vulgar, graphic Ned Ward'	110
7	Scene, *An Inn*? And horrible gin	133
8	Where did the Romantics drink?	160
9	Dickens	188
10	Of Rainbows and Fingers	208
11	Our mutual wasteland	234
12	Kegged	257
	Bibliography	274
	Index	288

Acknowledgements

Many people have helped in providing contexts, references and ideas for this book. I have relied upon two founts of knowledge in particular: Phil Cox has been stalwart in fielding all the half-formed queries I waylaid him with, quickly giving them coherence, providing material and suggesting other people I might contact; Lisa Hopkins has likewise been consistently generous and forthcoming in her responses to all questions. They have both enabled me to cut through great swathes of unfamiliar territory with less trepidation and more enthusiasm than would otherwise have been possible.

Across the five years in which I have been researching the book Peter Smith has kept his eye on all possibly relevant (and irreverent) material, and his detailed comments on an earlier version of the Shakespeare section have been invaluable, as have his comments on the completed manuscript.

Ian Baker has allowed rambling, free-associative conversations to take place. Thanks to his reading of the manuscript many errors have been avoided, and his insights into *1* and *2 Henry IV* and *Henry V* inform those sections.

Al Clayton, to be found at the Porter's Cottage, Sharrowvale Road, gave me several sheets of A4 with a list of all literature that might contain pub references. On more than one occasion I have turned to this when faced with no idea of where to go to next. Tim Price, the landlord there, put some key novels my way, as well as undoing the mythology surrounding 'mine Host'.

Alison Findlay's paper 'Theatres of Truth: Drinking and Drama in Early Modern England' opened up the world of drinking places in literature that did not include Shakespeare, and so set me off on many mazy paths.

The 'Drink, Drinkers and Drinking Places' conference at Sheffield University, organised by Sue Owen and James Nicholls, and the 'Intoxicating Images' strand of the 'Consumption' conference at Liverpool John Moores University, arranged by James Nicholls, demonstrated that there is a dissipated community of scholars interested in swapping anecdotes and arcane knowledge about all forms of addiction. Of those I remember talking to I would like to thank Kevin McCarron, James Nicholls (and for a copy of his paper on Hemingway), Alan Girvin (comments on 'national time'), Sue Owen (and for a copy of her paper on the Restoration and drink), Alison Findlay (on 'time' in the Renaissance), and Julie Barmazel for a copy of her paper.

I was fortunate early on in finding Matthew Frost as an editor. He has been genuinely interested in the topic, and felt that simply writing a good book was the most important thing. The comments he elicited from the three readers for Manchester University Press were helpful in getting me to realise that what I was really interested in is 'pubs' and literature rather than 'drink' in general, and that my original idea of treating a set number of texts thematically was not the best approach. The criticisms of the one sceptical reader kept me mindful throughout of the need for rigour.

One of the many joys of researching the book has been that most people have something to offer on the subject of pubs, since most people in Britain have had experience of them. One who has reflected on his own more than passing acquaintance with pub culture is Jon Begley, and his comments have informed my own thinking on pub life. Jon is also to be thanked for his pithy understanding of what the book might look like, and for his discussions of 1980s' Britain. The Redmonds and other Liverpool acquaintances have been equally informative on pub culture and heritage.

I have been lucky in being able to draw on the expertise and support of colleagues: Phil Cox, Ian Baker and Lisa Hopkins I have already mentioned; Robert Miles has greatly helped me in thinking through both conceptual problems and the organisation of my research; Chris Hopkins endured with good grace a barrage of questions about minor twentieth-century novelists and Anglo-Saxon literature. Dave Hurry gave me Flann O'Brien's 'Myles'; Emma Clery discussed the coffee-houses and the 'public sphere'; Sara Mills raised pertinent difficulties with the original structure; Keith Green gave me leads; Frances Dann put me on to 'Dr Syntax' and *Drinking with Dickens*; Jill LeBihan helped make sense of the decline of brewsters; Danny Broderick talked Patrick Hamilton.

From History, Mick Worboys has always shown great willingness in answering questions on medicine, and in showing me where to look for information. Mark Harrison, Tony Taylor and Peter Cain have also given historical aid. Of those who have now left the English department, Glenn Dibert-Himes showed me how to use the web as a research tool, Judy Simons highlighted strengths and weaknesses in the initial proposal and has always been very supportive, and Alison Chapman e-mailed sundry references.

Elsewhere, Mark Rawlinson offered perceptive comments on the book's first outline, and suggested areas to look into. Julian North discussed nineteenth-century addiction and let me see a copy of her paper on the same. Greg Walker set me right on Skelton and Hoccleve. Any legal queries went to Steve Robinson and Julie Cox, psychiatric queries on schizophrenia and alcoholism to Simon Mullens, physiology to Liz Wragg, philosophy to

Douglas Burnham, food to Catherine Burgass, religion to Debra Tuckett. Martin Greenough helped with absinthe and Amis.

When in London I was accommodated by Paul Tarpey and Christian Duffin. The former also assisted through his memory and enthusiasm for Dickens's novels, and the latter in an uncanny knack for choosing pubs with literary associations. Thanks also to Penny, James and Danny for my time down there.

Rather late in the day I hit upon the idea of offering an acknowledgement to anyone I met who could come up with a new lead to chase. So thanks to Patrick Duffin, who managed it, and hard luck to Mike, who never did, yet continues to proffer Sherlock Holmes in the hope he'll be acknowledged.

Deborah Madsen, Steven Connor and Vince Newey have kindly supported my applications for funds, and I am also grateful to Vince Newey for pushing Anya Taylor's *Bacchus in Romantic England* in my direction just at the right time. Gary Day gave a big boost to the project by accepting a chapter on *The Mayor of Casterbridge* for his edited volume *Varieties of Victorianism*. John Williams deserves credit for inadvertently making me think about such an adventure when he suggested I give a paper at the British Sociological Annual Conference in 1995.

I would like to thank the library staff at Sheffield Hallam University, particularly Paul Stewart, and staff at Sheffield University Library and the British Library.

If I have forgotten to thank anyone, I hope they will accept the drinker's usual excuse for memory loss. If they seek me out, and can convince me I have met them before, they have the right to claim the tipple of their choice.

Steven Earnshaw

1

Introduction

The pub is an oasis. It offers warmth, friendship, jokes, gossip, food, pint-pot philosophy and a pleasant release from the daily grind. On a lazy summer's afternoon it is possible to wile away the hours outside a country pub, drifting into a soporific haze beneath the benign gaze of Albion's gently undulating hills. In the winter months a pub provides the perfect refuge from the elements, with a blazing fire, beer and idle banter, all comfort against the dark hours.

The pub is good for business – a place to seal a deal, purchase illegal substances, or buy cheap goods from the back of a lorry. Drink is the social lubricant, breaking down barriers of age, gender, race and class. Travel to any part of England and you know that there is respite for you wherever there is a pub sign. It is the place to lose the everyday, careworn self, and replace it with unthinking contentment. The 'public house' is just that: a home from home available to everyone.

But the pub is a trap. It is the place to drink away your wages or your dole money. It is the playground of dangerous liaisons, a neutral and anonymous space. As a refuge it allows you to abscond from each and every problem. When you're low, it doesn't judge, but draws you on into a deeper indifference. Just one drink, you say, but that drink saps your will power so that you take a second drink, and then, why not?, a third, a fourth, until you can't remember why you were ever out of the pub in the first place. The next day's hangover adds to your depression. And there's only one way out of that despondency – back to the pub at the earliest opportunity, to drink the hair of the dog that bit you.

And the pub is frightening. It's where the lads get beered up before a football match, oiling their aggression. The pub at the weekend is the site of random violence – you must avoid catching someone's eye, saying the wrong word, being the wrong colour or having the wrong accent. Women go into a pub expecting visual harassment at the very least. And then you must always be on the lookout for the pub-goer who is a maniac.

The pub is a home from home …

> Bifil that in that seson on a day,
> In Southwerk at the Tabard as I lay…
>
> *Canterbury Tales*[1]

> With al the wo of this worlde, his wyf and his wenche
> Baren hym home to his bedde and broughte hym therinne;
> And after al this excesse he had an accidie.
> That he slepe Saterday and Sonday til sonne yede to reste.
> Thanne waked he of his wynkyng and wiped his eyghen;
> The fyrste word that he warpe was, 'Where is the bolle?'
>
> *Piers the Plowman*[2]

English literature begins in a pub, an 'inn' to be precise, The Tabard in Chaucer's *Canterbury Tales* (1372–1400). It is here that a group of pilgrims meet before setting off on their journey. The host, Harry Bailly, is a goodfellow who offers to travel with them. He holds out the prize of a free feast on their return for the pilgrim who can tell the best tale. It is something of a challenge to literature itself, since what follows is a collection of vastly different stories – from high-class courtly romance to low-class ribaldry, from poetry to prose – held together purely by the host's desire to be entertained by a good narrative. The host of the inn is therefore someone not unlike the connoisseur of literature, eager to find the best story there is, told in the best way possible. But the host is also like the author, the overseer and organiser of the material at his disposal.

The inn is a good place for English literature to set out from, because drinking places and literature have both been significant and pervasive in the development of the English nation and English consciousness. Tourists coming to England will have a number of cultural signposts telling them what makes England 'England': high on the list will be 'the pub' as a must-see and 'English beer' as a must-drink, together with the knowledge that England's literary heritage is an essential part of its identity, often simply short-circuited to 'Shakespeare'. They will find it strange that the English allow themselves to be ejected out of one of their most vaunted institutions at twenty past eleven. In other parts of the world bars can stay open until the early hours of the morning, and so 'last orders' also becomes a characteristic of 'Englishness'.

What this book attempts to do is weave a pattern out of the strands of 'pub', English literature and England. It is curious that as far as I am aware no one before has chosen to put the three elements together in book form. This volume proceeds chronologically, taking in a number of interdependent histories. The rhetoric surrounding what it is to be English involves the summoning up of different discourses: the English legal system and the English constitution; national 'characteristics' and habits; England's changing economic system, infrastructure and religious affiliations. It also involves histories less specifically national: changes in science which have affected the way the human world is perceived, psychology and medicine in particular.

But this book is also a crawl through the drinking places of English literary history. It raids the 'canon', taking as read that this has been one of the major features in determining an English tradition and a sense of 'Englishness'. In making 'pubs' the focal point it provides what some might think is a distorted view. Jane Austen has virtually nothing to say about drinking places (although she wrote and revised *Pride and Prejudice* in the Rutland Arms, Bakewell, Derbyshire[3]) and so only gets this marginal mention, despite her centrality for the (current) canon. On the other hand, certain writers who have been consigned to those dregs known as 'footnotes' are granted what might seem a disproportionate amount of space. Ned Ward, the 'Grub Street hack', becomes one of the book's central concerns. He writes scatologically of the seamier side of London at the end of the seventeenth century and the beginning of the eighteenth: his milieu is taverns and alehouses, his language is vibrant and excessive and not what critics have thought to be good literature, yet some of the descriptive passages in *The London Spy* (1698–1700) are the best to be found on the subject. *The Pub in Literature* therefore veers in and out of the three elements according to what appears most pertinent and most interesting. It does not make the claim that there is an unerring or necessary connection between the three strands, or an undiscovered, continuous generic line of English literature dealing with drinking places, as it can be argued for 'drinking songs' or 'Anacreontics' (verse in praise of love or wine). The importance of literature to the formation of national consciousness has long been recognised, the importance of drinking places less so, but the notion that these two elements are themselves indissolubly linked would be debatable. The idea of the book is to trace the role of drinking places in literature, to see how and to what purposes these are used, and to examine these imaginative formations as they mesh with the history of England.

To make such a pattern has meant that other histories have had to be left to one side. The book's rubric means that there is, sadly, no space for Robert Burns, James Joyce and Dylan Thomas, for the book is about the fashioning of all things English, and those writers have their own national and literary contexts. Similarly, the book is not about writers who drank, but about literature that represents alehouses, taverns, inns and pubs between its pages: the history of authors inspired or drowned by the god Bacchus is a different history. And so, contrary to what many have surmised, this book is not simply an arbitrary coupling of the author's hobbies, or a cunning means to redeem misspent hours, but rather a pattern that has some interest for others outside my own immediate concerns.

Even though there is not the space to make a comparative literary study, it is perhaps pertinent to sketch in other traditions. Some of these would have been familiar to the writers discussed later, and so set up relevant contexts, others are interesting in themselves and open up avenues of enquiry I have not had the leisure to pursue. In European literature there is a long tradition of 'bacchic' verse, characterised by the praise of wine's powers of inspiration and transformation. Its roots lie in the Greek myth of Dionysus and its 'composite idea of abandon, fertility and drunkenness'. Anya Taylor has followed the Dionysian element through from Euripides' *The Bacchae* to Virgil and Ovid and their use of Dionysus' followers Silenus and Dypsas; and from there to the Italian Renaissance, and on to Rabelais' *Gargantua and Pantagruel*. In England it can be found in Falstaff, and 'in Ben Jonson's drinking-songs and masques, in cavalier drinking-songs by Herrick, Cowley and Rochester, and in John Gay's "A Ballad. On Ale"'.[4] Philip F. Kennedy notes the same constituent elements of love and wine in the independent Arabic wine poem (*khamriyya*), particularly in the writings of Abū Nuwās (d. 813/15). 'Whenever a man kisses [the wine], the pleasure of embrace intoxicates him', is a typical line from the *khamriyya*.[5] Also fond of the interrelation between wine, love and life, were the European poets later known as the Goliards.[6] However, there is perhaps more of an emphasis on the virtues of tavern sodality in the Goliards, than the qualities of wine and love, than Kennedy's schema allows for. Writing in Latin between the 10th and the 13th centuries, a flavour of Goliardic poetry is given in the following verse from the writer known as 'The Archpoet of Cologne', composing sometime around the 1160s:

> My intention is to die
> In the tavern drinking;
> Wine must be at hand, for I
> Want it when I'm sinking.
> Angels when they come shall cry,
> At my frailties winking:
> 'Spare this drunkard, God, he's high,
> Absolutely stinking!'[7]

With these traditions – Greek, Arabic, Goliardic – each has its own particular slant with specific social, cultural and economic influences moulding the bacchic literary genre to its own ends. I can only sketch these other cultural literary traditions to hint at what a comparative history might take into account, and note also that there is an era of Hebrew verse much given to drink in tenth- to twelfth-century Spain.[8] The English literary tradition also has many examples of bacchic verse, with obvious overlaps in the praise of wine and its properties, its various relationships with 'love' and 'death' (conflation, juxtaposition, opposition), and its problematic relationship with religion: these slot easily into the lineage or family resemblances already suggested. The current study is focused primarily on the English pub and its precursors, rather than bacchic literature and its cognates.

Good taste: of inns and alehouses, Pope and Ward

> Thou most beauteous inn,
> Why should hard-favoured grief be lodged in thee
> When triumph is become an alehouse guest?
>
> *Richard II*[9]

In the Anglo-Saxon period there were three main types of drinking establishment: the *eala-hus*, *win-hus* and *cumen-hus*,[10] which, from the medieval period onwards are recognisable to us as alehouse, tavern and inn respectively. These had different functions in the eyes of the law, and had cultural distinctions readily understood by the general public, as the epigram to this section shows. Isabella uses the social differences between two types of hostelry in order to give King Richard dignity: Bolingbroke, the pretender to Richard's crown, is an alehouse in comparison to Richard's stately inn-like qualities. Inns were socially at the top of the hierarchy of drinking places, taverns somewhere in the middle, and alehouses at the bottom attracting the lower orders of society. The distinctions held well into the eighteenth century, although the term 'alehouse' starts to lose out to the term 'public house' after the Restoration.[11] It is true that nomenclature was not particularly stable, as a comment by a judge at the beginning of the eighteenth century makes clear when ruling on the legislation of 1604 'against inordinate haunting and tippling', one of the first of many Jacobean Acts aimed at drink and drinking places. Justice Salkeld states: 'this statute extends not to inns, for they are for lodging of travellers; but if an inn degenerate to an alehouse, by suffering disorderly tippling & c. it shall be deemed as such'.[12] This indicates that drinking-house space had some latitude with respect to its social and legal status, not entirely bound either to its architecture or ultimately to its function (inns, strictly speaking, were for the lodging of travellers). The emphasis on 'order' as the distinguishing feature gives a good insight into the main concern of the state and the law, and the apparent fluidity underlines the fact that drinking establishments were differentiated in the popular mind according to social respectability, and that social respectability itself was to do with legitimate enterprises such as travel rather than simply passing the time. Pope's pithy description of the inn where Buckingham died in 1687 is a notable exception to the hierarchy of drinking places: 'In the worst inn's worst room, with mat half-hung, / The floors of plaster, and the walls of dung, / On once a flock-bed, but repaired with straw, / With tape-tied curtains, never meant to draw, / The George and garter dangling from that bed / Where tawdry yellow strove with dirty red, / Great Villers lies.'[13] But this inn was somewhere in farthest-flung Yorkshire, and a southerner like Pope might have presumed that normal categories did not apply to northern establishments.[14]

To begin English literature in Chaucer's The Tabard and leave it at that is a conceit that would make for a pleasant, romanticised journey through

English literature and history, but it would also leave out those hostelries with lower social status, such as the tavern and, especially, the alehouse. Books about inns are usually littered with literary references as part of the mythology that has grown up around them: inns in many ways are already literary creations. Alehouses, on the other hand, catering for the lower end of the social scale, were not purpose-built, but were usually houses where someone sold an occasional brew. As a consequence they do not have the architectural presence or history that inns and taverns have, and their literary history is to be found in folk-lore, moral tracts and ballads. It is also quite fair to say that until Peter Clark's book *The English Alehouse: A Social History 1200–1830*, published in 1983, no one took more than a desultory interest in the existence of the humble alehouse.

Part of the pattern of this book, then, is to incorporate this more neglected story into literary history. And here we find that the canon of English literature has another starting point, coeval with *The Canterbury Tales*: William Langland's *Piers the Plowman* (1360–87). Chaucer's work is devised as entertainment, a collation of tales performed by distinctive characters. The host gets annoyed with those tale-tellers (including Chaucer himself) who are boring and lack 'wit'. Langland's work on the other hand sets off a different train of writing: like *The Canterbury Tales* it gives us a particular view of England at the end of the fourteenth century, but Langland's mode is primarily didactic and moral. Chaucer's work begins with the conviviality of drink; Langland's begins with a warning against drunkenness. The contrast between the two pieces – between Chaucer's high-class inn providing food, company, accommodation and drink in a convivial setting, and Langland's diatribe against drunkenness in Book 1, and lusty description of an alehouse in Book 5, where the customers are prey to excesses of all sorts – is one that is repeated throughout our history in different ways.

More than this, literature itself begins to take on the aspects of these particular settings. Chaucer can readily talk about an inn because it does not carry too many disreputable overtones. Inns had a religious background, emerging from the hospitality provided by monasteries which managed such places for the benefit of travellers (the still extant George at Glastonbury, for instance). But the alehouse is a different matter altogether, and *Piers the Plowman* only talks of it in disparaging terms. Where writing aspires to be literature, this attitude persists through the following centuries: to praise an alehouse is to lower the literature itself to that base level and run the risk of becoming 'subliterary'. And so this leads us to look at a third tradition, writing that has remained outside the roll-call of 'quality': ballads such as 'John Barleycorn' with its roots in Anglo-Saxon literature; hack writing – where 'literary quality' is sacrificed in preference to pleasing an audience's baser tastes; and minor figures whose stars waxed and waned quickly, such as Patrick Hamilton and Arthur Morrison. To find alehouses and taverns in English literature it is also necessary to visit these pages.

Thus the history of English literature and drinking places is one that has also traced the tension between what is to be regarded as literature and what, it has been maintained, is unsuitable. Originating in the works of classical writers, the idea of literary decorum states that high literature requires elevated subjects. It is an idea that has remained central to discussions of literature. Consequently, to set a scene in anything below an inn is automatically to plunge it into low comedy. This may be one of the reasons why no one has attempted a history that would range across not just inns, but those socially blighted spaces, taverns and alehouses; there may have been a feeling with literary critics that somehow it would not be quite 'proper' to put literature in the company of ale.

One of the first attempts to place Shakespeare's drink and drinkers in context, taken from a lecture in 1926, is a good example of the unease felt in mixing these two ingredients together:

> I hope I shall not be accused of disrespect to the greatest of English poets by inviting you to examine for an hour's time what place he made on his stage to drinking and drinkers. There are so many loftier aspects by which his works appeal to the world that it may well seem unpardonable to call the attention of such a distinguished audience to that which appears to be the mere scum and froth of his genius.[15]

Emile Legouis has been in good company. That self-proclaimed arbiter of literary taste and upholder of literary values, Alexander Pope, dismisses at least two writers on the grounds that they or their literature were associated with drinking places at the wrong end of the social scale. He calls John Skelton 'beastly', and the main reason appears to be Skelton's poem 'The Tunnyng of Elynour Rummyng' (*c.* 1517), about an alehouse full of drunken women. Pope's second target, Ned Ward, has already been mentioned. Pope attacked him in *The Dunciad* for being the owner of an 'alehouse'. But Pope would have known that Ned Ward owned a tavern, a more socially respectable place, not an alehouse. He would have known this because he drank there himself: hardly fair play from the most admired writer of his generation (although, of course, merely owning a tavern gains no one automatic access to the pantheon of literature). To even the score, it might be noted that Pope himself was accused of unbecoming behaviour, pouring half a pint of canary into his hat in the parlour of an Oxford hostelry,[16] and that after a drinking session with Addison in the Lion at Hampton-on-Thames he had 'so bad a headache he went about for months denouncing the great essayist as a terrible and confirmed drunkard'.[17]

England and drinking places

Just as this book is not a romanticised trip to the great and good of literature's most notable inns, neither is it simply an inverse romanticising in the name of those who have been ignored or damned by literary history. It would be most pleasing to agree with R. F. Bretherton when he says that:

> in the steady refusal to submit to the dictates of authority in matters of drunkenness, gambling, and Sabbath-breaking, the sturdy independence of the common Englishman was vindicated and strengthened, and Kings and governments were taught that their decrees were vain unless they had the approval of the people behind them. In the evolution of national character and national life the humble village inns and alehouses played a part which the historian may occasionally deplore, but which he cannot afford altogether to neglect.[18]

But alehouses and taverns have more often than not been a refuge from authority rather than the occasion for challenging it, despite the anxieties of successive governments and monarchies. The festival revels of medieval England may have provided days of misrule when the social world was turned upside down, and their survival in various forms into post-agrarian England was undoubtedly a source of conflict with a modernising nation that demanded more sobriety and consistent work-patterns. But resistance to dictates infringing upon the right to drink when and where people desired, and at what cost, has usually taken the form of subterfuge, of illicit brewing and distilling, and, when opening-hours legislation has been in force, of 'lock-ins'. Outright hostility to anti-drink legislation has never quite reached national rebellion, although there have been some close shaves. In the run-up to the increase of duty on gin in 1736, a tax which would immediately have taken this drink out of the reach of the lower orders, the government feared riots throughout the nation and had representatives of law and order on stand-by in major cities on the eve of the legislation coming into force. They had some justification in fearing such an event – there had been mock funeral processions through the streets, with effigies of 'Madam Geneva' (gin) going to her death. In the end, the nation drank so much of the spirit as a last salute to one of its favourite routes to oblivion that by the time the Act was in force it was too drunk to further its objections. On the other hand, hardly anybody purchased the requisite £50 licence to retail when the Act came into force, and the nation continued to drink at low prices via various ruses – a free tumbler of gin on payment of a penny to see the pig – and the Act had to be repealed because it was unworkable. A similar event on a lesser scale occurred thirty years later with the threatened introduction of a tax on cider. Debates in the House of Commons on the Cider Bill led to agitation from the Cider Counties in 1763, including 'mournful processions leading apple trees and empty cider hogsheads decorated with black streamers through the streets'.[19] But in the practice of everyday life, drinking places have fulfilled those needs outlined at the start of this chapter.

Whatever the reality, it has not prevented the perception that drinking places are hotbeds of social unrest, in Restoration England and in Georgian

England especially, and governments have acted accordingly, sending spies out to gather tavern gossip. It is true that the Radical movement, from 1790 to 1820, made great use of the taverns for meeting places. But the very same taverns were also to be cast by Radical leaders and spokesmen as a drain on the working man's financial and intellectual resources: 'I look upon drunkenness as the root of much more than half the mischief, misery and crimes with which society is afflicted,' wrote William Cobbett in *The Political Register* in 1821, although he also campaigned against the costly price of beer for the labourer, and Richard Carlile, another working-class Radical, remembered: 'I was a regular, active, and industrious man, working early and late ... and when out of the workshop never so happy anywhere as at home with my wife and two children. The alehouse I always detested ... I had a notion that a man ... was a fool not to make a right application of every Shilling.'[20] If the underground movement existed thanks to sympathetic tavern-keepers, it was also the case that publicans were involved in the massacre at Peterloo in 1819. The public house has been the working man's sanctuary, or it has been his downfall – such opposite judgements can emerge equally from religious zealouts, the middle class, or working-class Radicals.

The plebs, the middling sort and women

This book covers a period from medieval England to the end of the twentieth century, and so some holding, historical narrative needs to be deployed, along with some recognition that social groupings have not been static. The first stirrings of modern England, as distinct from 'ye olde' medieval England, are usually placed somewhere at the beginning of the sixteenth century. The key elements are the introduction of Protestantism, the subsequent (possibly consequent) growth of legal, economic and administrative systems that form the basis of those we have today, and the emergence of capitalism (mercantile and industrial) as the dominant economic mode.[21] The ensuing tensions in the society of modern England are described by historians in different ways, but I have drawn on two models in particular in order to understand the representation of various groups throughout English literary history.

The first model sees a shift from the medieval world which was feudal and all-inclusive (Chaucer's and Langland's world), to a society that split into two conflicting groups. The polarisation has been tagged 'patrician versus plebeian, respectable versus rough, or polite versus vulgar'.[22] The polarisation also translates into an understanding of culture as divided between 'elite' and 'popular'. 'Elite culture' is literary, modern and sophisticated, whereas 'popular culture' is oral, traditional and rustic. One of the connotations of this polarisation is that 'popular culture' provides a continuity with pre-Industrial England, and that 'elite culture' is what is modern about England.[23]

The second historical model I am using is tripartite, and views the society of early modern England as divided into lower, middling and upper orders.[24] Roughly defined, the lower orders encompass the labouring classes, the middling classes incorporate skilled artisans and professionals, and the upper ranks include the aristocracy and gentry. I have not seen the two models as mutually exclusive but rather as overlapping, since the same person might have viewed him or herself as part of the cultural elite, whilst an emphasis on sobriety and hard work would have distanced him or her from the upper and lower orders. With respect to drinking places, the narrative is shaped in the following fashion.

It is not until the sixteenth century that drinking places acquire substantial national significance. According to Peter Clark, it is only in this period that alehouses become widespread.[25] They also form the largest section of drinking places. The 1577 survey, initiated so that a tax could be levied to raise money to repair Dover Harbour,[26] gives alehouses 86 per cent of the national total of drinking establishments, with inns and taverns together only making the remaining 14 per cent.[27] With the decline of the parish church after the Reformation the alehouse begins to take on many of the social roles formerly associated with it and becomes, with certain qualifications, the new social focus.[28]

In the sixteenth century Puritans and Protestants began the vilification of drunkenness, an exhortation which by the seventeenth century has become widespread and unfailingly takes in alehouses as a prime source of evil. The rhetoric is splendid. George Gascoyne, writing in 1576, sets down the general proposition that 'all common Droonkards are Beasts, but even the wysest councellor, the gravest Philosopher, the cooningest Artificer, the skylfullest wryter, and the most perfect of all sortes and Estates, if they chance at any time to bee infected, and contamynate with this Beastly vice, shall be, (in that dooing) very Beastes also'. Although Gascoyne notes that the prevalence of drunkenness is a recent occurrence, 'howe commonlie it is nowe a dayes exercised amongste us', the belief that men are transformed into beasts when they are drunk, with echoes of the story of Circe turning Odysseus' men into swine, was commonplace, and his target is all sections of society.[29] He does mention alehouses later on, but his concern is 'banquets and meryments',[30] that is, binge drinking in halls rather than the 'everyday' drinking of other countries. He also notes that 'Yea, and (that which is more abominable) some of the Clergie which ought to forbid this, doo them selves also constraine many to drink more then is expedient for them,'[31] a complaint not so common in the seventeenth century when the clergy began to frown more consistently on popular customs. Thomas Young, writing in 1617, and plagiarising Gascoyne in parts, is at least acknowledging the words of another – 'a learned mans description' – when he describes the social unrest caused by drunkenness: 'A Drunkard is the annoyance of modestie, the trouble of civilitie, the spoile of wealth, the destruction of Reason, he is onely the Brewars agent, the Alehouse benefactor, the Beggars companion, the Constables trouble, hee is his wives woe, his Childrens sorrow, his Neighbours scoffe, his own shame, in some: hee is a tub of swill, a spirit of sleep, a picture of a Beast, a Monster of a man.'[32] This is the language Hal directs at Falstaff, and it is the language of Jacobean drink-legislation, as we shall see later.

As might be surmised from comments above, after the Reformation the drinking place is positioned differently within culture from its previous role as represented in either Chaucer or Langland, since it is now an alternative to Church ideology, and, as I will show, represents a place inimical to the Protestant work ethic. In addition, control of the alehouse and tavern raises issues of order and governance, issues very much on the minds of those empowered in the sixteenth and early seventeenth centuries. At the other end of the social scale, the inn becomes important in this period because as England becomes more prosperous and the infrastructure becomes crucial, the inns represent the institution which enables the roads to be travelled. And if the alehouse replaced the parish church as the local social focus, the inns replaced the abbeys which had once provided the resting places for travellers.

In choosing to discuss literature and pubs in conjunction it may seem that I have chosen to focus on a mainly male topic. In terms of the literature, it is the case that most of the material is dominated by the masculine outlook, reflecting the access to representation that has been prevalent throughout the ages. Where women have written, they have belonged to that section of society where they were unlikely to venture at any great length into hostelries. Yet women have played a large part in the history of the pub, often as key workers.[33] Alehouses were mainly run by women and these drinking places only came to be predominantly male-run affairs some time in the sixteenth and seventeenth centuries when men viewed them as profit-making ventures rather than as part of the subsistence or supplementary domestic economy.

The main model here is that of Judith M. Bennett's in *Ale, Beer, and Brewsters in England*, which argues that women have always been involved in some way with drinking places, but usually in a position without economic or political power, and without social status. Alehouses were largely run by women because when they became widowed the income they could get from running an alehouse prevented them from becoming dependent upon the parish. Brewing would have been classed as an aspect of cooking, like baking, so they would most likely already have the skills, and most probably have been doing the brewing in any case. Once they lose this role with the commercialisation and industrialisation of drink, where capital outlay and profit are involved, they take up a subsidiary position elsewhere within the drinking environment, usually as a barmaid. Bennett's model is supplemented by that provided by Susan Dwyer Amussen who argues that women's position was one of 'limited subordination' throughout the early modern period. This means that whilst women were viewed as capable people, they were not treated equally.[34]

Merrie England

In talking of the drinking places of the past, especially in the context of England and Englishness, there is the great temptation to view 'merrie England' either as a golden age or as a myth to be dismantled. 'merrie England' exists so far as it was and is a cultural force, but not as a Golden Age.[35] What is referred to throughout the book rather than 'golden age' is what Bob Bushaway describes: 'customary society (that is, where there was a balance between the claims and rights of the lesser members of the community, and the duties and responsibilities of the leading members in reciprocal relationship)', which changed 'to a new form of social order, in which the prime importance was placed upon contract, the cash nexus and where responsiveness to market forces played the major role'.[36] By using the idea of 'customary society', however, I do not mean to reintroduce the 'myth of the happier past'.[37] This kind of 'balance' certainly did not guarantee any better quality of life. But it is from this transitional period onwards, from the sixteenth century, that the book takes its cue, when an older lifestyle that followed the agricultural and religious calendar was challenged by a different idea of work-discipline. A sixteenth-century couplet identifies the introduction of Protestantism, beer and new industry into England as happening simultaneously: 'Hops, Reformation, bays, and beer / Came into England all in one year.'[38] One of the major barriers to this industrial sobriety was social drinking, as enjoyed on special occasions at festival time (and there were many festivals), and as enjoyed in everyday life in the community centres: the alehouses, taverns and inns. It is true that drinking places had always encountered problems with religious and state authority, but the congruence of an incipient national consciousness, a new religion, the growth of a specifically national literature and the beginnings of commercial capitalism, makes for a unique complex of elements.

The idea of 'merrie England' is part of the broader argument surrounding 'Tradition', another idea which has been politically manipulated throughout our period and had an impact upon the representation of drinking houses. When someone or some group appeals to 'tradition' to validate a contemporary argument, they appeal to what they believe has been good in the past and would wish to see continue (or be revived) in the present. But, as with 'merrie England', what constitutes tradition is usually contingent and partial. 'Beer' is an apt and good example.

Few would not think twice about naming beer as the traditional English alcoholic drink, yet its lineage is not as old as this suggests. Up until the sixteenth century the traditional beverage was ale, with its basic ingredients of malt, yeast and water. Beer, which was distinct from ale because it used hops in addition to these materials, came across from Germany. As well as giving the drink a characteristic bitter taste, another benefit of using hops was that they helped stabilise the product, ensuring that it lasted longer than ale and could therefore travel further than the immediate locale. Initially beer was regarded as a lesser drink than ale, an unwanted foreign import, much as lager had been regarded as inferior to beer in England in the twentieth century. The addition of hops was seen as an adulteration of the traditional English ale. Only from the later sixteenth century onwards did beer come to be regarded as the national drink.[39] Thus tradition depends upon how far back you want to go. At a deeper level, a similar problem has existed with arguments surrounding what the true English constitution should be or is: does it arrive with the Magna Carta in 1215, or does it go much further back, seeing the Normans as usurpers of the more proper Anglo-Saxon tradition?

The drinking place in literature

At its most basic, literature has represented features of the drinking place which would be familiar to its audience: the duplicitous alewife, tavern sodality, the attractive barmaid, the sharking landlord, the sottish idler. From there it has been manipulated for religious ends as a den of iniquity, or political ends, as the seed-bed of revolution, and from there on to more general moral purposes: to illustrate its wasteful nature, a repository for sins of idleness, blasphemy, drunkenness, swearing, gluttony and fornication. And conversely drinking places have been used by writers as a convenient means of bringing together different levels of society, as in Jonson's *The New Inn* (1629), either to highlight existing tensions in society, or to project some ideal of social harmony, or to do both. The drinking place then becomes the microcosm of society: in Martin Amis's *London Fields* (1989) to know a London pub is to know London; in Patrick Hamilton's *Hangover Square* (1941) pub life mirrors an enervated nation on the brink of war. When the drinking place is more narrowly defined, as 'An alehouse room. Several shabby fellows, with punch and tobacco' in Goldsmith's *She Stoops to Conquer* (1773), or Macheath's 'tavern near Newgate' in Gay's *The Beggar's Opera* (1728), we know that the space itself is symbolic of low-life, dissipated and immoral.

As well as serving this symbolic purpose, the drinking place has a dominant role in some narrative structures. This is especially so in picaresque novels, such as Fielding's *Tom Jones* (1749) and *Joseph Andrews* (1742), which could hardly exist without the network of inns and taverns dotted about the country, or a version of the picaresque such as Dickens's *Pickwick Papers* (1836–37). Its usefulness to drama as a single social space with symbolic associations, or to narrative structure as offering a variety of adventures for the picaro (as well as the single space) can be seen against its lesser position within poetry, *The Canterbury Tales* perhaps being the notable exception. The narrative or discursive poetic forms might incorporate drinking places (the ballad for the former, a poem such as Cowper's *The Task* (1785) for the latter) in ways similar to drama and prose fiction. But the lyric finds itself more at home with 'drink' itself rather than the social space, hamstrung from this point of view by the tradition of 'wine and love'. The Romantics such as Lamb and Keats may have been great drinkers, and frequented the tavern or inn, but this did not occasion flights of fancy dedicated to the local.

As I have already suggested, literature has often colluded in the denigration of the 'lesser' drinking places and their inhabitants, partly in an attempt to aggrandise itself, partly in an attempt to stay in tune with the ruling social mores. I hope to redress this imbalance without resort to mythologising. I also hope that this book adds enjoyment and awareness to those occasions where readers find themselves drawn into an alehouse, tavern, inn or public house: to know that when Hal and Falstaff drink at the Boar's Head in Eastcheap, the tavern might signify more than just a backdrop, and their drinking relationship more than just the sodality of temporary goodfellows – it has as much to do with England and Englishness as does Hal's speech on the battlefields of France; to know that the jolly picture of 'merrie England' and its inns as represented by Henry Fielding's narrator in *Tom Jones* and *Joseph Andrews* is contemporary with the scathing picture of the drunken lower classes he draws in his role as Henry Fielding the magistrate in *An Enquiry into the Causes of the Late Increase of Robbers* (1751); that to mistake a house for an inn (*She Stoops to Conquer*) is a literary joke that bespeaks not just class anxiety but a literary anxiety; that simply to witness a character enjoying an idle tipple without any moral disapproval is not only a rare thing, it is a triumph in the teeth of many different pressures – social and literary – to see it otherwise.

Notes

1   Geoffrey Chaucer, *The Canterbury Tales*, in *The Complete Works of Geoffrey Chaucer*, ed. F. N. Robinson, 2nd edition (London, Oxford University Press, 1976), General Prologue, ll. 1–2.
2   William Langland, *Piers the Plowman*, in *The Vision of William Concerning Piers the Plowman in Three Parallel Texts*, vol. I, ed. Walter W. Skeat (London, Oxford University Press, 1968 [1886]), ll. 364–9 (B-Text, and hereafter). A modern English version translates this as: 'And after all this dissipation, he fell into a stupor, and slept throughout Saturday and Sunday. Then at sunset on Sunday he woke up, and as he wiped his bleary eyes, the first words he uttered were, "Who's had the tankard?"' – *Piers the Ploughman*, translated into modern

English by J. F. Goodridge, revised edition (Harmondsworth, Penguin, 1966), ll. 5.358–63.

3   Denzil Batchelor, *The English Inn* (London, Batsford, 1964), p. 119.
4   Anya Taylor, *Bacchus in Romantic England: Writers and Drink, 1780–1830* (Houndmills, Basingstoke, Macmillan, 1999), pp. 7–10.
5   Philip F. Kennedy, *The Wine Song in Classical Arabic Poetry: Abū Nuwās and the Literary Tradition* (Oxford, Clarendon Press, 1997), p. 3, n. 5; p. 44.
6   *Ibid.*, p. 3, n. 5.
7   George F. Whicher, *The Goliard Poets: Medieval Latin Songs and Satires* (Westport, Connecticut, Greenwood Press, 1979), p. 111, taken from *The Confession of Golias*. Although Whicher retains the rhyme scheme, his vernacular translation narrows its range to predominantly that of a drinking song. Monica Kendall argues that in addition to this element there were different understandings of it in the Middle Ages, such as allegory, serious confession, shameless confession and satire. (In correspondence; I would also like to thank Monica Kendall for allowing me to see a copy of her MA dissertation 'The Archpoet's "Estuans intrinsecus ira vehementi" and manuscripts in England', History Department, University College, London, 1997.)
8   Raymond Scheindlin, *Wine, Women and Death: Medieval Hebrew Poems on the Good Life* (Philadelphia, Jewish Publication Society, 1986).
9   William Shakespeare, *Richard II (King Richard the Second)*, ed. Stanley Wells (London, Penguin, 1969), 5.1.13–15.
10 Frederick W. Hackwood, *Inns, Ales, and Drinking Customs of Old England* (London, T. Fisher Unwin, 1910), p. 36.
11 Peter Clark, *The English Alehouse: A Social History 1200–1830* (Harlow, Longman, 1983), p. 5.
12 1 Salk 45, ER 91, 'Ale-Houses. Stephens *versus* Watson', Mich. 13 Will. 3, B. R., with reference to 1 Jac. I, c. 9 (1604 Act against inordinate haunting and tipling). Richard Burn, sometime later, is also fairly clear: 'Every Inn is not an alehouse, nor is every alehouse an inn; but if an Inn uses common selling of ale, it is then an alehouse: and if an alehouse lodges and entertains travellers, it is also an inn,' *Justice of the Peace*, 8th edition, 1764, quoted in R. F. Bretherton, 'Country Inns and Alehouses', in *Englishmen at Rest and Play: Some Phases of English Leisure 1558–1714*, ed. Reginald Lennard (Oxford, Clarendon Press, 1931), p. 151.
13 Alexander Pope, 'An Epistle to Bathurst', in *Alexander Pope: A Selection of his Finest Poems*, ed. Pat Rogers (Oxford, Oxford University Press, 1994), ll. 299-305. The image of 'walls of dung' has exercised the imagination of commentators since. See Stuart Gillespie, '"The Worst Inn's Worst Room": Pope's Setting for Buckingham's Death', *Notes and Queries*, 37:3 (1990) 306–8.
14 In England there is a 'North–South divide'. Stereotypically, Northerners view the South – more accurately, the South-East, with London as the centre – as holding the majority of the country's wealth and power, whilst Southerners see the North as a backward, poverty-stricken zone. The belief has persisted until at least the end of the twentieth century.
15 Emile Legouis, 'The Bacchic Element in Shakespeare's Plays', in *Aspects of Shakespeare's Plays* (London, Abercrombie, 1933), p. 84.
16 Batchelor, *Inn*, p. 43.
17 Hackwood, *Inns*, p. 231.

18 Bretherton, 'Inns', pp. 200–1.
19 The Cider Riots remain a little covered area in English history, even though 'Contemporaries were agreed that Sir Francis Dashwood's cider excise was of central importance in the troubled early regnal years of George III. In the words of one reviewer (probably Burke): "no political project since the year 1733, not excepting even the Jew Bill, ever threw the Nation into so high a Ferment"', Patrick Woodland, 'Political Atomization and Regional Interests in the 1761 Parliament: The Impact of the Cider Debates 1763–1766', *Parliamentary History*, 8:1 (1989), 66. Apart from two other essays by Woodland (see Bibliography) there is virtually nothing. Ian Gilmour's *Riot, Risings and Revolution: Governance and Violence in Eighteenth-Century England* (London, Hutchinson, 1992), devotes a couple of pages to the Parliamentary fall-out (pp. 304–5). For contemporary references see also *Annual Register*, 1763, pp. 35–8 (from which Woodland gets his commentary); Cobbett's *Parliamentary History*, 1763, pp. 1307–14; *North Briton*, issues XLI, XLIII and XLVI (1763). Boswell mentions attending a debate upon it and hearing Pitt speak impressively – *Boswell's London Journal 1762–3*, ed. Frederick A. Pottle (London, Heinemann, 1951), 22 March, 1763.
20 E. P. Thompson, *The Making of the English Working Class* (London, Penguin, 1991), p. 814.
21 For a detailed account of how certain texts helped create an idea of the English nation in the sixteenth century, see Richard Helgerson's *Forms of Nationhood: The Elizabethan Writing of England* (Chicago, The University of Chicago Press, 1992). He accepts the traditional view that the change from 'dynasty to nation' occurred in the 1530s with the severance of ties with the Church of Rome, the establishment of the king as head of state and the power of the monarchy over the church, and the definition of England as an 'empire' (p. 4). His book focuses on a generation of Elizabethan writers who came to terms with this and helped define the nation state (p. 15) in different discursive spheres: Spenser's *Faerie Queene*, Coke's *Institutes of the Laws of England*, Camden's *Britannia*, Speed's *Theater of the Empire of Great Britain*, Drayton's *Poly-Olbion*, Hakluyt's *Principal Navigations of the English Nation*, Shakespeare's English history plays and Hooker's *Laws of Ecclesiastical Polity*.
22 For a discussion of this 'polarisation' and related issues, see Tim Harris, ed., *Popular Culture in England, c. 1500–1850* (Houndmills, Basingstoke, Macmillan, 1995), 'Problematising Popular Culture', pp. 1–27.
23 Helgerson notes the contrast between this model, the movement towards 'exclusion' (deriving from Peter Burke's work) and that of Ernest Gellner's model of 'inclusion', which 'links national state formation to an increase in social mobility and a lowering of class barriers' (*Nationhood*, p. 10). In his own book Helgerson does not think they are reconcilable for the works he covers (p. 11). However, for *The Pub in Literature*, the 'exclusion' model is taken as providing the better 'fit'.
24 Harris, *Culture*, 'Problematising Popular Culture', pp. 1–27.
25 Peter Clark, 'The Alehouse and the Alternative Society', in *Puritans and Revolutionaries: Essays in Seventeenth-Century History Presented to Christopher Hill* ed. Donald Pennington and Keith Thomas (Oxford, Oxford University Press, 1976), pp. 49–50.

26 H. A. Monckton, *A History of the English Public House* (London, Bodley Head, 1969), p. 39.
27 Clark, *Alehouse*, pp. 5–6.
28 *Ibid.*, pp. 53ff.
29 George Gascoyne, *A Delicate Diet, for daintie mouthde droonkards. Wherein the fowle abuse of common Carowsing, and Quaffing with hartie draughtes, is honestlie admonished* (London, 1576, reprint, 1789), pp. 5–6.
30 *Ibid.*, p. 18.
31 *Ibid.*, p. 10.
32 Thomas Young, *Englands Bane: or, the Description of Drunkennesse* (London, 1617), n.p.
33 Some taverns would also be primarily brothels.
34 Susan Dwyer Amussen, 'The Gendering of Popular Culture in Early Modern England', in Harris, ed., *Culture*, pp. 48–68.
35 See Raymond Williams, *The Country and the City* (St Albans, Granada/Paladin, 1975), for the prevalence of this belief in English literature and culture, especially chapter four, 'Golden Ages'.
36 Bob Bushaway, *By Rite: Custom, Ceremony and Community in England 1700–1880* (London, Junction Books, 1982), p. 231.
37 Williams, *Country*, p. 54.
38 John Bickerdyke, *The Curiosities of Ale and Beer: An Entertaining History* (London, Swan Sonnenschein, 1889), p. 67.
39 Dating such a change cannot be done with any real precision. According to Pamela Sambrook, 'It is generally reckoned that commercially-produced beer was normally hopped by the sixteenth century, though the time-spread of the introduction can be judged from the date of their first mention in London in 1391, compared with a record made in 1662 in Derbyshire of hopped beer being remembered as an innovation within living memory', *Country House Brewing in England 1500–1900* (London, The Hambledon Press, 1996), p. 133.

2

Early doors

For loue of tales in tauernes to drynke the more, I dyned
Piers the Plowman[1]

He was a janglere and a goliardeys,
And that was moost of synne and harlotries
Canterbury Tales[2]

From The Tabard Inn to Betty's alehouse, and back again

Credit usually goes to the pilgrimage as the means with which Chaucer's *Canterbury Tales* brings together a diverse range of social types, so lending the work a positive distinctiveness.[3] As the social scale ranges from the noble Knight to the disreputable Pardoner and Summoner, *Canterbury Tales* gives us a broad canvas of the folk of late medieval England. Yet it is only because the group gathers at The Tabard in Southwark under the auspices of its jovial Host Harry Bailly that we get the story at all. Further, it is difficult to envisage any setting other than an inn where at least some kind of equal footing between the characters is possible, and there may be something satirical in both the juxtaposition of high and low characters and in the sequential arrangement of the tales (the drunken Miller's follows the worthy Knight's). Yet Chaucer's inn exists for a legitimate purpose: the provision of lodging for a pilgrimage. This representation of an inn therefore replicates its role within society, whilst within the literary work it provides a convenient background for introducing and bringing together a wider mixture of people than might otherwise be possible. With the knitting together of the socially disparate folk by the host, the inn also presents us with a vision of a harmonious world: 'Now, lordynges, trewely, / Ye been to me right welcome, hertely; / For by my trouthe, if that I shal nat lye, / I saugh nat this yeer so myrie a compaignye / Atones in this herberwe as is now.'[4]

The beginning of *Piers the Plowman* likewise gives us a cross-section of social types. When Piers falls asleep he sees 'A faire felde ful of folke' 'Of alle maner of men the mene and the riche'.⁵ However, whereas Chaucer describes his fellow pilgrims in graphic terms, without moral censure, Langland views the folk allegorically from within a strict moral code; they are there to represent vices and virtues. In Book 5 of *Piers*, the dreamer returns to the field of the prologue: 'And thanne saw I moche more than I bifore tolde, / For I say the felde ful of folk that I bifore of seyde, / And how Resoun gan arrayen hym alle the reume to preche'.⁶ With Reason's imprecation, the Seven Deadly Sins offer confessions to Repentance, hoping to be forgiven. It is when we get to Gluttony on his way to Confession that Langland finally drags us into an alehouse. Gluttony is waylaid by Betty the alewife: 'Ac Beton the brewestere bad hym good morwe, / And axed of hym with that whiderward he wolde. / "To holi cherche" quod he, "forto here masse, / And sithen I wil be shryuen, and synne namore." / "I haue good ale, gossib," quod she, "Glotown, wiltow assaye?"'⁷ Once he has ascertained that she has the right spices for the ale, he steps inside and greets his fellow drinkers, including: a shoemaker, a gamekeeper, a tinker, a whore, a parish clerk, a Father, a scavenger, a rope-maker, a trooper, a pewterer and a crew of auctioneers.

Both Chaucer's work and Langland's appear to use a single drinking space to draw together different social orders in order to give some societal overview, yet the social distinctions between an alehouse and an inn ensure that a certain partiality prevails. Although the beginning of *Piers the Plowman* might offer the whole range of society, the alehouse narrows the social make-up to the lower end of the scale. Chaucer's Tabard, despite its much vaunted range of types, omits this very bottom end that Langland includes – there are no whores or scavengers in Chaucer's party – the beggar in The Tabard's yard is an outsider. Although the works in their entirety might (arguably) attempt to be comprehensive in their representations of English folk, when they come to mingling large sections of society within a single drinking space, it is still the case that neither the inn nor the alehouse can encompass the whole of English society. The demands of verisimilitude do not allow for such an organic community.

This recognition of the difference in social status of drinking places occurs in an interesting fashion in *The Canterbury Tales*. Chaucer terms The Tabard a 'gentile hostelrye',⁸ that is, a 'high-class' establishment. The pilgrims are thus under the regime of the 'gentile' at this point, and so, in a sense, is the literature itself. That there is a connection between the type of literature we get and the drinking establishment it hails from is emphasised in the introduction to 'The Pardoner's Tale'. The Pardoner wants to have a drink at an alehouse before he begins his story: 'But right anon thise gentils gonne to crye, / "Nay, lat hum telle us of no ribaudye! / Telle us som moral thyng, that we may leere / Som wit, and thanne wol we gladly heere."'⁹ The set of associations is clear: a tale told in an alehouse will be bawdy, an affront to the 'gentils' and the kind of 'learned' literature such an audience would wish for – in fact the type of courtly audience Chaucer's own work would have entertained. Looking back to The Tabard from this vantage point, it is now apparent that it served to harmonise disparate elements 'upwards', that is, the 'gentile hostelrye' not only enabled the party to cohere, but to cohere according to the prescriptions of society's upper ranks. Once out on the road, the observance of polite codes is under threat, and an alehouse is ever a danger to good (that is, 'moral') literature.

Chaucer thus draws on the ready understanding that the alehouse exists for the lower level of culture, although the narrator does not appear himself to make this moral judgement. It is possible that the description of the Miller as a 'goliardeys' who mainly tells stories of 'synne and harlotries' has something of a tavern connection (see introduction), although as Robinson notes, by the end of the fourteenth century the term 'goliard' had lost its literary association.[10] In Langland the moral disapproval of the alehouse is taken much further, for it is seen purely for the accommodation of excess, the encouragement of gluttony, a visible site for one of the deadly sins. Like Chaucer's inn, Langland's representation of an alehouse suggests a social space taken from everyday life, but its function within the work is primarily a symbolic one rather than one used for scene-setting. Broadly speaking, the opposition between Chaucer's and Langland's depiction of drinking places is maintained throughout literary and social history, an opposition between a respectable place where lodging and refreshment are legitimate ends, and a low place which provides the seed-bed for immoral behaviour.

Whilst this simplified schema is a reasonable guide to the manifestations of drinking places in literature, there remain complications and subtleties. At the beginning of the prologue to *Piers the Plowman*, amongst the motley crowd Piers hears: 'Tauerners vn-til hem tolde the same: / "White wyn of Oseye and red wyn of Gascoigne, / Of the Ryne and of the Rochel, the roste to defye!"'[11] As when Beton the Brewster collars Gluttony, the suggestion is that folk are tempted into drinking places, rather than go voluntarily. The taverner however appears to speak to all ranks as he calls out (although it is unlikely in reality that the clientele of an alehouse would be able to afford the more expensive drink of wine), whereas the alehouse exists only for the lower ranks and dissolute clergy. There is a difference therefore between the casual image of the taverner, disreputable perhaps but appealing to all folk, and the alehouse, enveloping and signifying the worst of gluttony. Even though drunkenness is a sin without social distinction in *Piers the Plowman*, Langland still chooses to make the alehouse, and its associations with the lower orders only, its eternal home.

Further, in the depiction of the alehouse scene in *Piers the Plowman* we have a paradox that is typical of the kind of literature that seeks to denigrate drinking places, yet offers more than mere proselytising. Through its own descriptive powers, through its humour, through its ability to allow Gluttony to speak with his own voice of the life he has led, there is a legitimated enjoyment of base comedy for the audience of *Piers the Plowman*, confronted (supposedly) as its readers are with an artistically licensed 'accurate' portrayal of their own moral failings, a tale designed for their edification. By allowing Gluttony to tell what amounts to a raucous tavern-tale, the audience gets to enjoy it in its full glory with any associated guilt temporarily suspended.

Once inside the alehouse Gluttony is quickly made to feel at home, laughing and singing with the other reprobates into the evening, although when he lets rip an enormous fart it is not so well received: 'His guttis gunne to gothely as two gredy sowes; / He pissed a potel in a *pater-noster*-while, /And blew his rounde ruwet at his rigge-bon ende, / That alle that herde that horne helde her nose after / And wissheden it had be wexed with a wispe of firses.'[12] He becomes too drunk to stand and is carried to bed, not without first being sick on Clement. He sleeps for a couple of days, and his first request on waking is to ask for his tankard: 'And after al this excesse he had an accidie. / That he slepe Saterday and Sonday, till sonne yede to reste. / Thanne waked he of his wynkyng and wiped hise eyghen; / The fyrste word that he warpe was, "Where is the bolle?"'[13] The point about Gluttony's excess could easily be made without such a celebration of his exploits.

The device betrays its origins in the lessons on gluttony (and the other sins) delivered from the medieval pulpit.[14] It is quite probable that as a rhetorical strategy preachers would insert their own knowledge of alehouse drinking practices (or their version of it) into their sermons to give them local piquancy. Because Gluttony has been diverted from his road to mass, the point is made that the alehouse is the Devil's alternative to the Church, a case frequently espoused in sermons of the time. But Langland appears to go further. He presents a particular alehouse boast which is permitted to stand alone for a good while before the voice of the questing Jeremiad begins again, and the force of moral censure once more gets the upper hand. Perhaps because of this ambivalent position of the alehouse scene within *Piers the Plowman* commentaries can argue opposite sides: one, that the alehouse is a 'place of fellowship and good cheer', the other, in response, that such an interpretation is 'hard to reconcile with Langland's graphic description of Glutton's urinating, farting, and vomiting in Betoun's alehouse'.[15] I am inclined to side with the former opinion and agree that Gluttony has a good time in Betty's hostelry, in the belief that an audience sympathetic to the tavern and alehouse would treat Glutton's behaviour indulgently. The fact that the description can still divide critics at the end of the twentieth century suggests that Langland's alehouse continues to be read both as Glutton would have us enjoy ourselves there, and as Piers would have us condemn it.

Of alewives' cunning, alluring and cheating

Langland's image of an alewife who does the devil's work draws upon common cultural perceptions, as Judith Bennett's *Ale, Beer, and Brewsters in England: Women's Work in a Changing World, 1300–1600* shows. Bennett's is the most comprehensive study to date of the social and economic history of women in brewing in early modern England. She argues that the watershed dividing medieval England from modern England is not Richard III's death in 1485 (or, to be more chronologically tidy, 1500), as some historians avow, but the deaths of the first plague in 1348–49, with a possible mortality figure as high as two million.[16] Similarly, therefore, she argues that brewing as a major enterprise is gradually wrested away from brewsters (female brewers) by male hands from the late fourteenth century onwards,[17] although brewing by women continues on a domestic scale, and legislation allows for widows to acquire licences for alehouses. Misogyny is a key issue in the representation of alewives and brewsters, and Bennett follows this line through assiduously. She acknowledges that victuallers in general, whether male or female, came in for criticism, but feels that those against women were particularly virulent.[18] Ralph Hanna has queried some of Bennett's methodological reasoning and, pertinently for what follows, argues that the focus by Bennett upon misogynistic representations of alewives in some instances ignores the wider social context of tavern life and its differently gendered spaces.[19] Yet Hanna's caveat has to be set against what Chappell says in *The Roxburghe Ballads:* 'attacks by [men] on women are in a ratio of one hundred to one upon their own sex'.[20] With these comments in mind, we can turn to the canon of literature on alewives.

As suggested, some of the brewsters encountered in literature before the mid-sixteenth century are no different from their male counterparts and their fraudulent practices, and some alewives are, in their capacity as landladies, no different from other presentations of deceitful or convivial male hosts. These representations can be differentiated from others which evidently do depend upon a gender distinction. Both John Lydgate's 'Ballad on an Ale-Seller' from the early fifteenth century and John Skelton's 'The Tunnyng of Elynour Rummyng' (*c.* 1517)[21] can be classed as misogynistic versions of alewives, although for different reasons. In 'The Prologue' to the *Tale of Beryn*, a 'pseudo-Chaucerian' piece (pre-1600) which takes up the *Canterbury Tales* at the destination point, the story is of how the Pardoner is duped by a female tapster using the promise of sexual favours. The bested Pardoner reflects on his folly, since all those he has met to date have been just as deceitful: 'That he wold trust a tapster of a comon hostry: / ffor comynly for þe most part they been wyly echon.'[22] However, Rose the Regrater in *Piers the Plowman*, like the brewster in the Chester Mystery Play who ends up in hell, is really no different from male alesellers and brewers who engage in the nefarious practices of adulteration and short measures. The alluring alewife, the category that Lydgate's character fits into, is part of a widespread ideological complex related to woman as temptress. The cunning alewife who often cuckolds her husband is part of the more general literature on cuckoldry and the complicated gender issues it invokes. For instance the ballad, 'The Catalogue of Contented Cuckolds', probably seventeenth century, lists ten cuckolded men who meet together in a tavern. Once they have agreed to be content with their miserable lot, they drown 'melancholly in a glass of Nektar'.[23] In the literature of cuckoldry, with its unspoken fear of women who are out of men's control, the target is as much weak men as it is strong women.

Whilst John Skelton's 'The Tunnyng of Elynour Rummyng'[24] draws on a traditional view of the alehouse as wholly disreputable, its twist on Langland's alehouse scene is that Elynour's establishment is graced only by women. Even though her name has been traced to an actual Alianora Romyng who kept the Running Horse near Leatherhead in Surrey,[25] it is highly unlikely that the all-female drinking den is taken from actuality. According to Peter Clark, women would probably have been customers on special festive occasions, but not at other times.[26] This level of the ballad derives from a genre which presents groups of women together as gossips, and the list of names Skelton uses for the drinkers is mostly taken from a fifteenth-century carol, 'The Gossips' Meeting'.[27] Otherwise, the behaviour of the women is no different from men in alehouses as described elsewhere: farting, falling down sick, pissing where they stand, drinking rather than working; and a male version of the steady stream of customers who pawn their belongings for irresistibly good ale occurs in the later ballad 'Joan's Ale is New' (1670).[28]

Skelton divides the work into seven parts (seven *passus*), suggesting the seven Penitential Psalms,[29] or, more simply, the seven deadly sins. The idea of the alehouse as the Devil's Church is reinforced through its inversion of rituals associated with the mass, along with the remark that Elynour and the devil 'be syb', that is, kin.[30] The 'tunnyng' of the title works in a number of ways. 'Tunning' means to pour ale into casks for storage, whilst 'tun' also suggests a particular shape and size when applied to humans. 'The Tunnyng of Elynour Rummyng' therefore increases the figure of the alewife metaphorically – 'a tonnysh gyb';[31] but it might also signify the fact that by 'pouring' her into a poem, Skelton is somehow immortalising her. It is an instance of the double game he intermittently plays throughout the piece, where he is both writing the poem and writing about the poem.

'Elynour Rummyng' begins with a prologue, which aggrandises the as yet unnamed hostess with an extended grotesque description of her looks, of which this is a small part: 'Her face all bowsy, / Comely crynklyd, / Wounder-sly wrynklyd, / Lyke a rost pygges eare / Brystled with here'.[32] Skelton launches into part one by naming Elynour and her location, and then 'But to make up my tale, / She breweth noppy ale', as if in beginning the poem he is brewing up the literature. As in Chaucer and Langland, the narrator feels duty bound to list the characters (a typical feature of literature representing drinking houses as we shall see throughout *The Pub in Literature*, related to its capacity to offer up cross-sections of society). The customers – 'travellars', 'tynkers', 'sweters' (toilers), 'swynkers' (labourers) and 'all good ale drynkers'[33] are described in the same loving detail as Elynour herself. They are poorly dressed, slatternly, some are 'all scurvy with scabbes', some are 'flybytten', and all are characterised as 'such a lewde sorte'.[34] The description of them in the second part evinces even more disgust. They are called swine, and behave like swine, beshitting themselves: '"Fo, ther is a stenche! / Gather up, thou wenche; / Seest thou not what is fall? / Take up dyrt and all / And bere out of the hall!"'[35]

The narrator rounds on Elynour's brewing practice, which includes the blending of hen dung with the ale. Elynour claims that her ale makes women look younger and consequently leads to an improved love life. The third part shows that many of the drinkers pay in kind, with salt, spoons, shoes, pots, wool, wedding rings, often using all their housewifely skills to eke out their measly collateral. Some have to enter the establishment the back way to avoid being seen, whereas others care not what men say. Some even give up their work tools: hatchets, spinning wheels, needles and thimbles. In part four drunken Alice turns up with items of current news, reminding the reader that alehouses were great centres for news gathering. In part five more women arrive, and the simple fact that there is an accumulation of women in one place might have attracted censure from the poem's audience. There may even be specific ironic force since if the poem did appear in 1517 after the Evil May Day riots, contemporary readers would know that proclamations had issued so that 'no women shoulde come together to bable and talke, but all men should kepe their wyves in their houses'.[36] The poem continues to import even more customers at random, and in the sixth part his description of Maude Ruggy is misogynistic in an overtly sexual way: 'Ones hed wold have aked / To se her naked' and 'Such a bedfellaw / Wold make one cast his craw!' (that is, vomit).[37] The narrator's tone of sexual disgust continues when an old woman arrives, only to bark her shin on entering 'And fell so wyde open / That one might se her token'. Part seven adds little to what has gone before, until we are told, unsurprisingly, that 'Suche were there menny / That had not a penny'[38] and so they have to chalk up their debts on the beam or tally. The narrator himself appears exhausted at the end; with itching fingers he claims he has 'wrytten to mytche … Of Elynour Rummynge'.[39] Her power over her customers extends to her power over her chronicler.

Because Skelton draws on a number of different works and genres – gossip's tale, *Piers the Plowman*, mock/tavern masses – and mixes in echoes of pulpit displeasure at the wasteful nature of alehouse tippling, the one-time poet laureate produces something quite unique in his imagining of an all-female drinking space. It is also rendered in his own poetics, now called 'Skeltonics', characterised by short irregular lines and extended use of the same rhyme. It is a poetics that appears particularly suited to the kind of chaotic revel that the poem describes. Rather than viewing alewives as an especially pernicious branch of the female species, the misogyny is drawn from the commonplace. Although Elynour Rummyng is also similar to many literary alewives in that she has affinities with the devil, she is also a woman who, like Betty the Brewster, is skilled in running a bawdy, successful alehouse. The poem's emotional complex is a mixture of fear at one woman's power over others (Elynour as witch), a distaste for all-female groups with their threat to the male world, and (intentionally or not) a celebration of the alewife's hold on society.

Earlier than Skelton's poem is John Lydgate's 'Ballad on an Ale-Seller'. In its portrayal of an alewife who uses her charms to induce men to drink, the poem is not unusual, although Elynour obviously has nothing of this trait, and neither of Langland's alewives is guilty of seduction, for Betty tempts gluttony with good ale, and Avarice's wife simply cheats customers with her deceitful brews by mixing good ale with poor ale: 'I boughte hir barly-malte she brew it to selle, / Peny ale and podyng-ale she poured togideres / For laborers and for low folke; that lay by hym-selue.'[40] And despite Lydgate's title, the poem has little to do with the alehouse or ale. The thrust of the ballad is that the aleseller uses all her charms to get men to fall in love with her in order that they buy her ale. Once in debt she forsakes them. The difference from other pieces on alewives is that the narrator is more concerned with the fact that she gets men to pledge their love and then casts them off, than that she does this to sell ale. Her actions cause men to 'wander in their minds' and walk alone, as the mad do. The only passage specific to drink is in the seventh stanza:

> Gladly ye wil, to gete you acqueyntaunce
> Calle men to drynke, althouhe thei therfor pay
> With your kissyng thouh that ye do pleasaunce
> It shal be derrer, er thei go ther wey,
> Than al ther ale, to them I dar weel saye.
> Thus withe your ale, and withe your cheer so slye,
> Ye them disseyve, that in yow most affye [trust].

The crime of guile in selling ale is secondary to the breaking of men's hearts. Compare it with a later ballad, 'The Ale-wives' Invitation to Married-Men and Batchelors: Shewing, how a Good fellow is slighted when he is brought to Poverty' which sings: 'Therefore take my Counsel, and Ale-Wives don't trust, / For when you have wasted and spent all you have, / Then out of Doors she will you headlong Thrust, / Calling you Rascal and shirking Knave. / But so long as you have money, come early or late, / You shall have her at command, or else her maid Kate,' where the meaning is more overtly to do with alewives using their sexual prowess to gain money, and the hearts of the abandoned males warrant no comment.[41]

But there is a problem in cross-matching an early fifteenth-century lyric with a seventeenth-century ballad. The status of alewives had clearly declined by the seventeenth century and the ballads of this later time, I would speculate, exist because that genre had built up a critical mass. They have little more to offer than the many drink-related songs which fall into stereotypical categories: goodfellows; anti-host/hostess/wife; prodigals both celebratory and rueful; spendthrift husbands; drunken wives. The reliance by social and literary historians on the nine large volumes of *The Roxburghe Ballads* (and other, less voluminous tomes), which consist mainly of material from the seventeenth century, may be a reliance on literature that has embedded within it from earlier centuries a quite different sensibility. The understandable tendency is to read back to older times of popular culture through the vox pop of ballads. This may be useful in that later ballads draw on a certain tradition which is centuries old, but it may also be that they have little bearing on their own period.

The caveat about cross-matching applies to a refrain ('burden') that Bennett uses for one of her chapters, 'These things must be, if we sell Ale'. The lines come from a ballad called 'The Industrious Smith', written by Humfrey Crowch in the reign of Charles I. The haunting refrain ends the majority of the stanzas, as the hard-working smith attempts to supplement his poorly paid job by getting his wife to sell ale (just as Avarice does with his wife Rose in *Piers the Plowman*). The smith is shown to be a weak man (unlike Avarice), unable to do anything without his wife's advice. Instead of getting better, things get worse, because now he is known as a 'host', and even though his wife runs the establishment, he is still called away from his work to join in the drinking. Hardly anybody pays for their drinks, he leaves home, and when he returns he finds 'His Wife kindly sitting on a man's knee'.[42] He looks on helplessly as she openly flirts with another man. The husband manages to grumble a little: '"But," quoth the good wife, "Sweet hart, do not rayl, / These things must be, if we sell Ale."'[43] The second part is similar, until the smith and his helper find themselves working to pay for those who drink at his alehouse. The tale is one of a man made miserable by his faithless and lazy wife, but the smith is portrayed as such a hapless figure that the reader's respect is perhaps for the wife's brazen behaviour. The meaning of the ballad is presented inconsistently, for the framework provided by the short explanation at the beginning indicates that the moral is how an 'idle huswife' will 'work the decay' of her husband, whereas the ending states: 'They might have done better, but they were loth / To fill up their measure with nothing but froth'[44] – they only fail because they refuse to cheat. But here we should be aware of the dates. Bennett indirectly gives the impression that the ballad has its roots in older literature, by not giving the name of the balladeer and by claiming in a footnote that 'These things must be if we sell ale' either derived from a proverb or gave rise to one, as if it taps into ancient wisdom. This blurs the contextual shift that she argues so forcefully for throughout her book. From the context of literary alewives in the fourteenth, fifteenth and early sixteenth centuries, to the context for a seventeenth-century ballad alewife, is perhaps the shift from the integral role played by earlier alewives in the subsistence survival of their family or their own widowhood, to the industrial-capitalist ideas of thrift and disciplined work that were beginning to emerge in the seventeenth. If anything reconciles the ballad's two differing messages it is that they are both pessimistic responses to new pressures. At the beginning and end of the ballad industriousness is called ineffective in a world that consists of so many feckless fellow creatures. By the seventeenth century the alewife has finally had her day in that the connotations of 'alewife' lack the kind of cultural power they previously had. As Bennett claims, women have always been involved in what is often thought of as the man's world of drink and drinking places. However, though their roles have changed, their position has remained consistent with the lower social status of women. Thus they are alewives and brewsters as long as there is no serious profit to be made. When brewing because economically viable on a larger scale, women are ousted. They would not have had access to the substantial capital required to set up a non-domestic brewery, and there would now be a sense that brewing was man's work.[45]

Women's involvement continues, Bennett argues, but they are become barmaids and landlord's appendages. Mistress Quickly in *2 Henry IV* (1598) is a transition figure. Eaten and drunk out of her own establishment, she has to set the law on Falstaff to reclaim her dues. She therefore makes no profit and the only reward for her attractions is that Falstaff breaks his promise to marry her. But dramatic injury is also done to her since she can speak in nothing but unintended innuendo for the amusement of the audience: 'Alas the day, take heed of him [Falstaff] – he stabbed me in mine own house, most beastly, in good faith. 'A cares not what mischief he does, if his weapon be out. He will foin like any devil; he will spare neither man, nor woman, nor child.'[46] The following from John Earle in the seventeenth century confirms Bennett's general contention. According to Earle, a handsome inn hostess

> Is the faire commendation of an Inn, above the fair sign or fair lodgings. She is the loadstone that attracts men of iron, gallants and roarers . . . Her lips are your welcome, and your entertainment her company, which is put into the reckoning too, and is the dearest parcel in it. No Citizens wife is demurer than she at the first greeting, nor draws in her mouth with a chaster simper; but you may be more familiar without distaste, and she does not startle at bawdry.[47]

The role of tempter on to drink is no different from Lydgate's alewife, nor is her overcharging different from previous depictions. But the sense that she is a 'capable person' involved with the brewing process is gone, and her position as a sexual subordinate is more akin to the madam of a brothel. It could easily be a description of Mistress Quickly in *Henry IV*, a character who has little of the 'alewife' about her. At best, Earle's description of a hostess and Falstaff's favourite wench indicate that the essentially medieval role of alewife and brewster are gone. By the end of the seventeenth century the female presence is even further removed from the figure of the alewife and more likely to be that of landlord's daughter or barmaid. In George Farquhar's *The Stage Coach* (1704) the hero's 'man' Fetch arrives at a country inn, and complains about the slow service. Enter Dolly.

DOLLY   D'ye call Sir?
FETCH   Call Sir? What a plague – Egad 'tis a pretty Girl – Heark you Child, Do you serve Travellers upon the Road here?
DOLLY   Yes Sir.
FETCH   Kiss me then.
DOLLY   That's the Chambermaid's Business.[48]

The meaning of drink

As with the 'meaning' of women in such literature, 'drink' in England has always been heavily laden with associations. A drink might be a sign of one or more of the following: social rank, literary tradition, political alignment, religious sympathy, patriotism. All of these elements enter into any discussion of drinking places in literature, and so here I will sketch out some of the resonances 'drink' as a sign can carry.

Wine in England, until the end of the twentieth century, has always been more expensive than beer and ale, and consequently has been associated with the better off. The distinction is a commonplace one in English literature and can be found as early as Saxon times. The Saxons probably drank wine, mead, cider (*appelwin*) and piment (wine, honey and spices), but they mainly drank ale. In an old Anglo-Saxon dialogue, entitled *Alfric's Colloquy*, a lad, on being asked what his drink is, replies, 'Ale, if I have it, water, if I have it not.' To the question why he does not drink wine his answer is, 'I am not so rich that I can buy me wine; and wine is not the drink of children or the weak-minded, but of the elders and the wise.'[49] The notion that wine is for the elderly and wise complements the notion that wine is by far the classiest drink. According to Lydgate wine has nine positive properties. It 'cheers, clears the eyes, glads the heart, heats the stomach, sharpens wits, gives courage, cleanses wounds, makes feasts, and scours the palate'.[50] In Robert Copland's poem 'The Highway to the Spital-House' (1535–36), Copland finds shelter in the doorway of a spital (hospital). The poem concerns his discussion with the Porter about the kind of people who seek help and admittance to the Spital. In describing the 'common women' the porter repeats their claim that 'Wine was not made for every haskard, / But beer and ale for every dastard.'[51]

As well as the social distinction that wine carries, its associations also bring with it a sense of literary quality, whereas the literature surrounding beer and ale always has to stand its ground in the shadow of wine's noble lineage. 'Wine' is intimately linked with 'Bacchus', it is both a physical reality and a spiritual embodiment of inspiration, blood and sublime release, from the Greeks onwards, down through the ages. Ale and beer are ale and beer, what qualities they have are English, down-to-earth, staunch and temperamentally suited to the English. Even though ale can hold its own with wine in terms of antiquity, since it has been traced back to the Egyptians, this has not ensured any form of literary prestige, probably because of the social caste that wine signifies and its associations with (Christ's) blood.

A comic inversion of Bacchus' high literary standing is given in the song 'Nottingham Ale', sung to the tune of 'Lilabolero', which was popular in the eighteenth century. In the lyric itself we are told that 'Bold Bacchus' does not belong to classical myth, as commonly thought, but 'sprang from a barrel of Nottingham Ale, / Nottingham Ale, boys; Nottingham Ale; no liquor / on earth is like Nottingham Ale'.[52] No matter how hard writers have tried, ale and beer do not compete with the literary tradition of Bacchus and the companionate wine. Try substituting 'ale' for 'wine' in the following passage:

> 'Names, deeds, gray legends, dire events, rebellions,
> Majesties, sovran voices, agonies,
> Creations and destroyings, all at once
> Pour into the wide hollows of my brain,
> And deify me, as if some blithe wine
> Or bright elixir peerless I had drunk,
> And so become immortal.'

It does not work because the language is pitched in a 'high' literary mode, and only wine will do. Even the alliteration that 'beer' would provide for 'blithe' would fail to elevate the tone. The fact that wine can be exchanged for any 'bright elixir peerless' shows that this is not wine as a physically real substance, but rather some spiritual liquor known only to the poetic tradition.[53] The association between wine, Bacchus and inspiration is further enhanced because red wine and blood can become interchangeable poetic symbols.

Keats is drawing on the long line of Bacchic verse. But some writers have inspired their own tradition of literary heritage and noble drink. Ben Jonson is foremost: 'Father *Ben*! For thy gentle Assistance I call, Now Toping above in *Apollo's Whitehall*, / Where *Sack*, the true *Nectar*, for ever you drink' begins Richard Ames in *A Search after Wit* (1691).[54] Heywood brings together these elements of literary lineage and Jonson's inspirational drinking in his *A Preparative to Studie: Or, The Vertue of Sack* (1641), which also takes the opportunity to denounce ale as unfit for one as great as Ben:

> Fetch me *Ben Johnson*s Skull, and fill't with Sack,
> Rich as the same he drank, when all the pack

> Of jolly Sisters pledg'd, and did agree,
> It was no Sin to be as drunk as he;
> If there be any Weakness in the Wine,
> There's Virtue in the Cup to make't Divine.
>
> This muddy Drench of Ale does taste too much
> Of Earth[55]

The interplay between the symbolic associations of the three main generic drinks, ale, beer and wine, is contingent upon the context within which they appear. When it relates to hierarchy, social or otherwise, we always descend from the juice of the grape down to malt liquor – hence only wine is good enough for Ben Jonson. In John Grove's *Wine, Beer, Ale, and Tobacco, Contending for Superiority* (1658) 'Water' mediates between the three drinks and judges that wine 'shall be in most request among Courtiers, Gallants, Gentlemen, Poëtical wits', beer 'shall be in most grace with Citizens, as being more staid Liquour', and ale is remitted to the countryside, although this is not meant to be a slur, according to the diplomatic Water.[56] When ale does gather positive connotations they correspond to the traditional English virtues of practical, no-nonsense goodness. A fifteenth-century carol, 'Bryng Us in Good Ale', observes that all victuals bring with them something extra and unwanted – beef has bones, tripe is unclean, eggs have shells and butter has hairs (!) – or else are unsuitable (venison) or too dear (capons).[57] But good ale is what you ask for, and good ale is what you get. A proverbial rhyme on the same theme goes:

> He that buys land buys many stones,
> He that buys flesh buys many bones,
> He that buys eggs buys many shells,
> But he that buys good Ale buys nothing else.[58]

Another set of associations comes in to play when the context is nationalist, and examples of ale being naturally English and the right drink for the English constitution abound. Andrew Boorde's comments in *Regiment of Health* (1542) are unequivocal and often quoted: 'Ale for an englyssheman is a naturall drynke' whereas 'Bere is made of malte, hoppes, and water, it is a naturall drynke for a dutche man. And nowe of late dayes is moche used in Englande to the detryment of many englysshe men, specially it kylleth them the which be troubled with the colycke.'[59] As late as 1651 John Taylor is still peddling the line that beer is the Dutch drink and ale the English one: '*Beere* is a Dutch Boorish Liquor, a thing not knowne in *England*, till of late dayes an Alien to our Nation' whereas A is for Albion, which begins 'Al', and is therefore inextricably linked with ale, an exemplary piece of Taylor logic.[60] The association of beer with the Dutch had really died out by the end of the century, but ale could still be cited as English. In *The Country-Wake* (1696), a popular play from the end of the seventeenth century up to the 1720s, Hob brings ale instead of wine for his friends (after he has drunk their beer), and justifies his deceit with 'Sack Sir, – Od I don't know, I thought you said you had rather have Ale – Ale is indeed much wholsomer now, for your English Stomaches.'⁶¹ But by now beer was in the ascendancy as the national drink.

One context that tends to fade as England becomes more urban-orientated and brewing becomes big business is the proximity and involvement people would have had with the whole process of producing ale and cider. The distance travelled can be seen if we look at how the ballad 'John Barleycorn' treats the whole process of brewing and drinking.

Although the earliest dated record we have of this ballad is from the beginning of the seventeenth century, 'A Pleasant new Ballad to sing both Even and Morne, Of the bloody murther of Sir John-Barleycorn', from which time the use of 'John Barleycorn' as a personification for drink is believed to have started,⁶² the ballad itself is evidently much older. An excellent Scottish version exists which is from the sixteenth century – 'Alan a' Mault',⁶³ but commentators usually claim that the ballad originally hails from the West Country,⁶⁴ and an eleventh-century (perhaps earlier) 'rhyming riddle' from the Saxons has similar features to 'John Barleycorn', clear evidence of its long history.⁶⁵ It also helps account for its allegorical power.

The version in *The Roxburghe Ballads* is a remarkable tale in which an attempt is made by two noblemen to murder Sir John Barleycorn and his kinsmen Thomas Goodale, Richard Beere and Sir William White Wine. It demonstrates the interconnectedness of agriculture, brewing, drunkenness, poverty and release, and how these elements form a primitive, ineluctable cyclical existence.

> Some said 'Kill him,' some said 'Drowne,'
>   others wisht to hang him hie–
> For as many as follow Barley-corne
>   shall surely beggers die.
>
> Then with a plough they plow'd him up,
>   and thus they did devise
> To burie him quicke within the earth,
>   and swore he should not rise.
>
> With harowes strong they combèd him,
>   and burst clods on his head:
> A joyfull banquet then was made
>   when Barly-corne was dead.⁶⁶

The attempted murder continues when John Barleycorn still manages to shoot forth throughout the summer:

> Then he grew till S. James's tide,
>   his countenance was wan;
> For he was growne unto his strength,
>   and thus became a man.

> [Wherefore] with hookes and sickles keene
>   into the field they hied;
> They cut his legs off by the knees,
>   and made him wounds full wide.
>
> Thus bloodily they cut him down
>   from place where he did stand,
> And, like a thiefe, for treachery,
>   They bound him in a band.

The ballad continues in this vein, casting the brewing process in the light of the attempted murder of Sir John Barleycorn. After threshing and steeping, he is then roasted:

> They rubbèd and they stirrèd him,
>   and still they did him turne;
> The malt-man swore that he should die,
>   his body he would burne.
>
> They spightfully tooke him up againe,
>   and threw him on a kill;[67]
> So dried him there with fire hot,
>   and thus they wrought their will.

There is something of the archetypal myth in the ballad, of ritual slaughter and rebirth, but this is inverted by the animosity towards the earth's natural produce rather than a celebration of it. The violent language suggests a fear of ale's power: John Barleycorn makes beggars of each of them, an echo of the common sentiment that drink steals their money and livelihoods; John Barleycorn grows to be a man who has to be cut down, with the implication that Barleycorn's manhood is at the expense of those men who are drawn to him.[68]

The relationship in terms of social hierarchies between Sir John Barleycorn and those out to kill him is unclear (and does not feature in other ballad versions). The original combatants are nobility, as is John Barleycorn himself, but Barleycorn's 'kinsmen' seem to range across the social scale – Richard Beere alongside Sir William White Wine. It may be that all are implicated in Barleycorn's ability to impoverish. At the end of the ballad the drink itself is initially likened to a continuation of Barleycorn's death once he has been 'tunn'd … in a barrell':

> An then they set a tap to him,
>   even thus his death begun;
> They drew out every dram of blood,
>   whilst any drop would run.

People come with weapons to take him away and 'overthrow' him, with the sense maintained of killing him by drinking him. Barleycorn wins the battle in the style to which he is accustomed, making them either 'legless' or 'blind drunk':

> When Sir John Good-ale heard of this,
>   he came with mickle might,
> And there he tooke their tongues away,
>   their legs, or else their sight.
>
> And thus Sir John, in each respect,
>   so paid them all their hire,
> That some lay sleeping by the way,
>   some tumbling in the mire.
>
> Some lay groning by the wals,
>   some in the streets downe right;
> The best of them did scarcely know
>   What they had done ore-night.

The final stanza, which jars a little in its tone from the rest of the ballad and its sudden mention of alewives, switches to an outright plea in the cause of 'good ale', suggesting that the whole attempt to murder John Barleycorn has been half-hearted at best. The injunction of the final two lines however does retain the violence of the rest of the ballad, and thus the importance of drink for the community:

> All you good wives that brew good ale,
>   God turne from you all teene;[69]
> But if you put too much water in,
>   The devill put out your eyne!

The intimate relationship between the people and the drink, involved as they are in its production and consumption, is one of the most telling features of the ballad. The cycle is vicious and inevitable, and makes available the idea that drinking is not some abstract idle activity, but a necessary part of the agricultural year. When *Piers the Plowman* praises honest agricultural work it casts alehouse drinking in a light that is antithetical to such endeavour, and in Book 6 Piers has problems getting some of the workers to help with harvesting, since they would rather drink, as if they could plough the fields by singing 'hey nonny nonny'. But John Barleycorn gives us a different slant: the production and consumption of drink has its dangers, but it is intrinsic to agricultural production. Any attempt to do away with it is, in the ballad, humorously shown to ensure its very existence. By hoeing it into the ground, cutting it down, grinding and drowning it, John Barleycorn is as much created as he is murdered. 'John Barleycorn' is an intense statement about the necessity of drinking, with its roots firmly in popular understanding. It finally refuses the condemnatory moral perception of drink by accepting the inevitability of its life cycle and the people's place and participation in it.

Drunkenness

> The worst of all the deadly sins is in him,
> That beggarly damnation, drunkenness.
>
> *The Revenger's Tragedy*[70]

It will be clear by now that drunkenness was a favourite target of the clergy and other self-appointed moralists. One of the reasons that some may have seen it as the deadliest sin of all was that it often led to other sins, and such an idea had a long history. Thomas Young in *Englands Bane: or, the Description of Drunkennesse* (1617) derives his list of failings related to drunkenness from Plato: '*Drunkennesse is a monster with many heads*: As first, *filthy talke*: Secondly, *Fornication*; Thirdly, *Wrath*; Fourthly, *Murther*; Fiftly *swearing*; Sixtly, *cursing*.'[71]

He amply demonstrates each category with biblical and classical quotations, and these exempla provide the background of authoritative judgements for most literary renditions and statements upon drunkenness.[72] In *Piers the Plowman*, in Book 1, Piers is told that God finds only three things needful for man: clothing, food and drink. The latter is qualified, for drink should only be taken in moderation, enough to quench thirst. The Lady of the Church then reminds him of the story of Lot, whose daughters got him drunk so that they could sleep with him and bear his children.[73] The story of Lot was probably the most cited lesson against the evils of excessive drinking, and is the first example cited by Chaucer's Pardoner in his sermon against drunkenness. He also tells of Herod, who asked for the head of John the Baptist after he had had too much drink.[74] The Pardoner goes on to list the common effects of habitual drinking: it makes a man lecherous, disfigures the face, sours the breath, makes for horrible snoring, takes away the power of speech, makes you fall down like a stuck pig, and it takes away discretion. The stomach of a glutton is 'Fulfilled of dong and corrupcion! / At either ende of thee foul is the sound',[75] which suggests that Glutton's flatulence in *Piers the Plowman* is redolent with moral censure.

Another feature of drunkenness is that, according to Seneca, 'He seith he kan no difference fynde / Bitwix a man that is out of his mynde / And a man which that is dronkelewe' except that depression lasts longer for someone who is drunk.[76] The idea that madness and drunkenness were kin, mainly because of the similarity of symptoms, was an idea that lasted well into the nineteenth century. Yet there is no settled view on drunkenness in *The Canterbury Tales*. Although the Pardoner prefaces his tale with a long diatribe against it, the Pardoner is a self-confessed hypocrite. The further irony is that he believes his story is more likely to please his audience once he has drunk some ale.[77] When the Manciple scolds the cook for his drunkenness, the Host advises him to be wary in case he is found guilty himself of this particular vice.[78] 'The Parson's Tale' is unambiguous in its condemnation of gluttony, but its position and sentiment within *The Canterbury Tales* is atypical (see below), and his idea that drunkenness is the sepulchre of man's wit is virtually identical to the hypocritical Pardoner's idea that drunkenness is the sepulchre of reason.[79] The idea is the same but the sources are morally opposed.

In the pulpit, in addition to the biblical and classical evidence, there was anecdotal support. That the drunken man often saw double was neatly turned into a homily, of which G. R. Owst in *Literature and Pulpit in Medieval England* gives two versions. In the first example some drunks imagine they see two candles when there is only one. Thinking that one is enough, 'they blow out what they fancy to be the other, only to find themselves plunged in darkness'.[80] The second example raises the moral stakes. The drunken husband returns home to his wife, only to see four children in place of the usual two, and 'straightway accuses her of lying and adultery. Having done her to death, and the two sons also in a fit of rage, he recovers later from the effects of intoxication only to hang himself in despair, when the truth has dawned upon his mind.'[81] The innate wrongness of inebriety could not be clearer.

But of course, simply to see these pulpit origins, and to find them migrating into Langland and Chaucer, is not to know how they were received by the majority of people. Gluttony in the end refuses to accede to penitence in *Piers the Plowman*, and the characters in *The Canterbury Tales* cover the whole spectrum of attitudes. No doubt all injunctions to avoid drink and taverns were taken in a practical spirit – an ideal to be broached only intermittently, if at all. The many edicts issued against drunken clergy throughout the middle ages indicate that they were very much given to a lifestyle not so far removed from the lay population, and both priests and nuns were guilty as charged.[82] Wolsey was himself once arrested for drunkenness at a village festival when he was a parish priest.[83] The strategic voices adopted in literature are this mixture of the temperance ideal, an amused distance and seriocomic guilt. A poem such as Hoccleve's *La Male Regle* (1405)[84] rues a life misspent in taverns (the 'ill health' of the title) and looks forward to a more sober and remunerative lifestyle (he begs for payment of his annuity at the end of the poem). But if it is a parody of the penitential lyric form, rather than genuinely penitent, how are we to read it? As M. C. Seymour says: 'Its immediate origin may be a genuine response to a personal illness, though whether this was more than a severe hangover, aggravated by an achingly empty purse, seems doubtful.'[85] Such a mixed attitude is perhaps observable in 'The Tunnyng of Elynour Rummyng' which can be read as a parody of a parody. Skelton was a priest, yet here he is giving full vent to revelry and a mock mass, irreverently mocking Elynour's own irreverent attitude.

If the moral context for drink has been ambivalent when allowed full reign, drunkenness as a national trait has been more straightforward. As early as the eighth century, Boniface suggests to Cuthbert that drunkenness is peculiar to the English.[86] John of Salisbury wrote in the twelfth century to a friend: 'You know that the constant habit of drinking has made the English famous among all foreign nations.'[87] Many have thought the same since, and it becomes a proud boast in *Othello*:

> IAGO   I learned it [the song] in England, where indeed they are most potent in potting. Your Dane, your German, and your swag-bellied Hollander – drink, ho! – are nothing to your English.
> CASSIO   Is your Englishman so expert in his drinking?
> IAGO   Why, he drinks you with facility your Dane dead drunk; he sweats not to overthrow your Almaine; he gives your Hollander a vomit, ere the next pottle can be filled.[88]

But just as Chaucer allows no fixed position on drunkenness, nor does Shakespeare. In *Othello* Iago plies Cassio with drink so that he is undone, yet whilst drunkenness appears to assume its usual homiletic role of moral failing, this is much more to do with character psychology than a simple depiction of drunkenness. The usual idea that man becomes a beast when drunk is given a novel twist because Cassio believes his 'human' being rests upon his reputation: 'O, I have lost my reputation! I have lost the immortal part of myself, and what remains is bestial.' It is not in the act of being drunk that Cassio is (conventionally) bestial, but he is now become a beast regardless of whether he is sober or not. In *Measure for Measure*, Barnardine's refusal to die, a right he can claim because he is drunk, is an absurd affront to the whole project of regulation that the Duke attempts, and is another complicated representation of drunkenness in Shakespeare (see next chapter).[89]

If drunkenness was an English characteristic, in the sixteenth century it was also common knowledge that drunkenness itself was invented by the Dutch, brought back to England after contact with the Low Countries during war: 'a sin that, ever since we have mixed ourselves with the Low Countries, is counted honourable, but, before we knew their lingering wars, was held in the highest degree of hatred that might be'. In Robert Copland's 'The Highway to the Spital-House' (1535–36) the idea is still something of a novelty, for the Porter makes it clear that the English are as much drunkards as the Dutch:

> *Copland.*
> And how say ye by all these great drunkards,
>   That sup all off by pots and tankards,
> Till they be so drunk that they cannot stand?
>   That is but little used in this land,
> Except it be among Dutch folk or Flemings,
>   For Englishmen know not of such reckonings.
>
> *Porter.*
> No do? Yes, yes. I assure you hardily

>   They can do it as well as anybody
> With double beer, be it wine or ale,
>   They cease not till they can tell no right tale.⁹⁰

But by 1608, in Thomas Dekker's *Lantern and Candlelight*, it is accepted that drunkenness has dual nationality: 'What makes a man to loath that mongrel madness, that half English, half Dutch sin, drunkenness, than to see a common drunkard acting his scenes in the open street?'⁹¹

Just as tavern and alehouse clienteles lent themselves to lists, so too did 'drunkenness' and 'drunkards'. Descriptions of the different stages of drunkenness, and the different types of drunkard, amounted to a comprehensive topology of diagnosis, whilst showing how flexible humour psychology could be. At a basic level, the four humours had equivalent types of drunkenness, in which men behaved after the nature of certain animals. The jovial sanguine man was 'ape-drunk', the irascible choleric man 'lion-drunk', the heavy melancholic man 'swine-drunk' and the sleepy phlegmatic man 'mutton-drunk'. Thomas Nashe adds a further four in *Pierce Penniless* (1592): maudlin drunk, martin drunk, goat drunk and fox drunk. The latter, 'crafty drunk', is like Dutchmen, 'that will never bargain but when they are drunk'.⁹² Thomas Young gives a virtually identical list in *Englands Bane*, in a different order, and adds one more for good measure, 'Bat drunke, which are a sort of *Drunkards* that will not openly be seen in such actions, but as the reremowse or Bat, delights in secret places and flies by night.'⁹³ Equally, stages of drunkenness could be listed, as Gascoyne does with his degrees of drink – nine is once more the magic number: 1. quenches thirst; 2. induces mirth; 3. voluptuousness; 4. drunkenness; 5. wrathfulness; 6. contentiousness; 7. furiousness; 8. sluggishness; 9. 'extremitie of sycknesse'.⁹⁴

The frontispiece to Thomas Heywood's *Philocothonista, or, the Drunkard, Opened, Dissected, and Anatomized* (1635) (and the cover for *The Pub in Literature*), shows anthropomorphised animals drinking, fighting, smoking and spewing. As well as describing the different types of drunkard in bestial terms, he gives a possible reason why this should be so. The first age of man, as reckoned in the Bible, up to the deluge, was the Temperate Age. After the flood, Noah planted the vine, and may have moistened the roots with the blood of animals which then filtered through to the wine. Heywood's list of types of drunkard begins to depart from the previous categories in some respects, adding drunken asses, and being dog-drunk and goose-drunk, although he leaves it up to the sober reader's imagination as to what these animal-states might signify.⁹⁵

Although the poisonous allegory of 'The Pardoner's Tale' reads itself as a warning against avarice, it could also be taken as a warning against tavern drunkenness. It begins with three riotous fellows in a tavern who see a corpse go by outside. They are told it is the body of their friend who just the other day was visited by death as he lay drunk on the ale-bench. In their drunken arrogance they decide to take on Death. He fails to present himself at the allotted place, and instead they find there a store of gold. In their attempts to outwit and defraud each other of the treasure, they end up killing one another. Whilst the importance of 'avarice' is clear in their downfall, the curve of the narrative makes of their deaths a moral reckoning for drunken behaviour and tavern life.

Structures and modes, hosts and authors

The drinking place can provide co-ordinating structures for literature in diverse ways. In smaller works, such as the ballads we have looked at, taverns and alehouses can be the central arena for articulating different social conflicts. The enclosed space and the recurrent belief that drinking places harbour sizeable cross-sections of English society make for an easily digested, integrated literary structure, whether the characters are harmonised with each other or not. With pieces like those we have seen from Langland, Chaucer and Skelton, the single space enables analytic descriptions of social types and castes. With such a unifying device in place it then becomes possible to create extended works that hold together normally disparate social elements, such as in Jonson's *The New Inn* (1629). Sometimes it provides an enabling frame, such as in the anonymous *The Taming of a Shrew* (1594), which starts and ends in a tavern, book-ending the main body of the play.

If drinking spaces are useful structuring devices in terms of both narrative and symbolic schemes, they also foreground the issue of modes of writing. For literary history, part of the significance of *The Canterbury Tales* and *Piers the Plowman* are their forays into 'realism', although these two pieces proceed in different ways: Chaucer's *Canterbury Tales* are often allegorical in themselves, but contained within realistic interplay between the pilgrims, whereas *Piers the Plowman*, in its entirety an allegory, contains passages of realism, most noticeably the alehouse scene already discussed. But to describe pictures of earthy real life, which is what many drinking-house scenes ostensibly do, leads to difficulties for writers who wish to be read as serious moral artists. Such truth to nature (as they would have seen it) entails presenting the repulsive, immoral side of life as it is, with the problem that writers can be mistakenly identified with their subject matter. To obviate the possible charge, Chaucer excuses the fact that he repeats morally unworthy material – which is mainly to do with drink-related issues – by claiming that he is dutifully recording real life: if it is unseemly that is hardly his fault. His retraction at the end of *The Canterbury Tales*, presumably added late in his life and the history of the work, betrays a worry that he feels himself more culpable for base representations than the earlier material wants to admit.

Chaucer's problem has been typical wherever the unworthy drinking place has been the occasion for literature in the realistic mode. Chaucer attempts to circumvent it by turning the narrator into a kind of host who can direct the audience's reading strategy. Making our way back to The Tabard we see that the Host is also the leader of the group. He suggests that each of the twenty-nine pilgrims tell two tales on the way out, and two on the way back. The best tale-teller wins a free supper. The Host thus provides a purpose that is worldly (in contradistinction to the pilgrimage itself) and playful. He says that the tales should be entertaining as well as instructive. As the initiator, collector and judge of the tales, our Host Harry Bailly is in an analogous position to that of the author. But *The Canterbury Tales* complicates the 'author' figure by having in addition an authorial persona named 'Chaucer'. He is the opposite of Harry Bailly the good host: diffident, unsure of his ability to tell a tale, and under the power of the Host. It suggests a complicated relationship between the literature and its audience, to the extent that anything that looks like a direct moral claim arrives through a thicket of narratorial strategies. The author/narrator/host joke is enhanced by the physical similarities of the Chaucerian persona and the Host in their corpulence: 'He in the waast is shape as well as I'.[96] By inviting readers to skip the lowlier passages in *The Canterbury Tales* if they are offended by such matter, the sensitivity (ironic or otherwise) to the better sort reinforces the idea that the literature is there for the audience's pleasure. No narrator who wished his work to be taken as a serious moral tome would invite the reader to omit a passage against adultery just because it might be boring. Moral lessons are necessary, not optional extras. *Canterbury Tales*, in its complicated narrational strategy, can play the double game we saw in the Langland passage on Gluttony. It can provide both base fare and high moral literature whilst avoiding the charge of being 'lewd' itself; readers are reminded that they are the ones in control of the on/off switch. The technical difficulty of presenting a large heterogeneous cast that does not offend its audience because it includes the antics of the lower orders is thus offset.

Although we cannot be sure of dates of composition and ordering of the tales, it seems likely that Chaucer's final feelings towards the work, as evidenced in the 'Retractions' which appear to close it, were a desire to distance himself from this more playful side. The word that James Winny uses to describe Chaucer's change of heart in this and the closing 'Parson's Tale' is 'sober'.[97] The parson 'takes over the authority granted to Harry Bailly by superior right of moral leadership, recalling the pilgrims to the vital spiritual issues that have been overlooked in their delighted absorption in a game'. What begins as a sport overseen by the Host of an inn ends as a serious moral homily by an idealised cleric.[98] We have lost the conviviality of the narrative premise to a more sober purpose, going from the everyday, material world, to the abstracted spiritual-moral world.

Notes

1. William Langland, *Piers the Plowman*, in *The Vision of William Concerning Piers the Plowman in Three Parallel Texts*, vol. I, ed. Walter W. Skeat (London, Oxford University Press, 1968 [1886]), 5.383 (B-Text, and hereafter).
2. Geoffrey Chaucer, *The Canterbury Tales*, in *The Complete Works of Geoffrey Chaucer*, ed. F. N. Robinson, 2nd edition (London, Oxford University Press, 1976), I (A) 560; 'A wrangler and buffoon, he had a store / Of tavern stories, filthy in the main' – *The Canterbury Tales*, trans. into modern English by Nevill Coghill (London, Penguin, 1977).
3. E.g., Robinson's introduction, Chaucer, *Tales*, p. 2.
4. Chaucer, *Tales*, I (A) 761–5. 'Truly gentlemen, / You're very welcome and I can't think when / – Upon my word I'm telling you no lie – / I've seen a gathering here that looked so spry, / No, not this year, as in this tavern now.' Coghill, *Tales*.
5. Langland, *Piers*, Prologue, ll. 17–18.
6. *Ibid.*, 5.9–11.
7. *Ibid.*, 5.306–10.
8. Chaucer, *Tales*, I (A) 718.
9. *Ibid.*, VI (C) 323–5. '"Outcry arose among the gentlefolk. / "No, no, don't let him tell a dirty joke! / Tell something with a moral, something clear / And profitable, and we'll gladly hear."' Coghill, *Tales*.
10. Chaucer, *Tales*, Robinson's note to I (A) 560–1.
11. Langland, *Piers*, Prologue, 11. 226–9: 'and inn-keepers were bawling, "White wine! Red wine! Gascon and Spanish! Wash down your meat with the finest Rhenish."' Modern version from *Piers the Ploughman*, trans. J. F. Goodridge, revised edition (Harmondsworth, Penguin, 1966).
12. Langland, *Piers*, 5.347–51. 'Glutton had put down more than a gallon of ale, and his guts were beginning to rumble like a couple of greedy sows. Then, before you had time to say the Our Father, he had pissed a couple of quarts, and blown such a blast on the round horn of his rump, that all who heard it had to hold their noses, and wished to God he would plug it with a bunch of gorse!' Goodridge, *Piers*.
13. Langland, *Piers*, 5.366–9. 'And after all this dissipation, he fell into a stupor, and slept throughout Saturday and Sunday. Then at sunset on Sunday he woke up, and as he wiped his bleary eyes, the first words he uttered were, "Who's had the tankard?"' Goodridge, *Piers*.
14. G. R. Owst, *Literature and Pulpit in Medieval England: A Neglected Chapter in the History of English Letters and of the English People* (Oxford, Blackwell, 1966 [1933]), especially pp. 425–41 on drunkenness.
15. Judith M. Bennett, *Ale, Beer, and Brewsters in England: Women's Work in a Changing World, 1300–1600* (New York, Oxford University Press, 1996), n. 20 to ch. 7, p. 226. Ralph Hanna's contention can be found in 'Brewing Trouble: On Literature and History – and Ale-Wives', in *Bodies and Disciplines: Intersections of Literature and History in Fifteenth-Century England*, ed. Barbara Hanawalt and David Wallace (Minneapolis, 1996), pp. 1–17.
16. Bennett, *Brewsters*, pp. 5–6.
17. *Ibid.*, p. 38.
18. *Ibid.*, p. 131.

19 Hanna, 'Brewing Trouble', pp. 6–7.
20 *The Roxburghe Ballads* (London, Taylor and Co., 1871), vol. I, pp. 451–2.
21 Robert S. Kinsman (ed.) in *John Skelton: Poems* (Oxford, Clarendon Press, 1969) dates the poem as 'probably written in 1517', p. 152.
22 *Tale of Beryn* (Anon.), Chadwyck-Healey Poetry Full-Text Database (1996–98), ll. 654–5.
23 *The Roxburghe Ballads*, vol. III, pp. 481ff.
24 'The Tunnyng of Elynour Rummyng', in Kinsman, *Skelton*, pp. 53–70.
25 John Harvey, *TLS*, 26 October 1946, p. 521, quoted in *ibid.*, n. 93, p. 154.
26 Peter Clark, *The English Alehouse: A Social History 1200–1830* (Harlow, Longman, 1983), p. 131; Arthur F. Kinney, *John Skelton: Priest as Poet* (Chapel Hill, University of California Press, 1987), n. 30, p. 218.
27 Kinney, *Skelton*, p. 170.
28 'Joan's Ale is New'. The catalogue date is 1670. The first publication, as 'Jones ale is newe', is 1594 'though copies are extant only from the reprint of 1656', Roy Palmer, ed., *Everyman's Book of English Country Songs* (London, Dent, 1979), p. 194. There is a reference to the newness of Joan's ale in John Grove's [?] *Wine, Beer, Ale, and Tobacco, Contending for Superiority: A Dialogue* (London, 1658), which suggests a wide currency for the song.
29 Kinney, *Skelton*, p. 13.
30 'Tunnyng', in Kinsman, *Skelton*, l. 100. An idea not fully developed, according to Kinsman, *ibid.*, p. xiii.
31 *Ibid.*, l. 99.
32 *Ibid.*, ll. 17–21.
33 *Ibid.*, ll. 104–5.
34 *Ibid.*, ll. 140, 141, 153.
35 *Ibid.*, ll. 180–4.
36 *Ibid.*, Kinsman n. to l. 387.
37 *Ibid.*, ll. 478–9, 488–9.
38 *Ibid.*, ll. 611–12.
39 *Ibid.*, ll. 618, 620.
40 Langland, *Piers*, 5.219–21. 'Then I bought her some barley-malt, and she took to brewing beer for retail. She would mix a little good ale with a lot of small beer, and put this brew on one side for poor labourers and common folk.' Goodridge, *Piers*. John Lydgate, 'Ballad on an Ale-Seller', in *The Minor Poems of John Lydgate edited from all available mss. with an attempt to establish the Lydgate Canon*, by Henry Noble MacCraken (London, The Early English Text Society, Oxford University Press, 1920–34).
41 *The Roxburghe Ballads*, vol. IX, p. 797.
42 *Ibid.*, l. 58.
43 *Ibid.*, ll. 63–4.
44 *Ibid.*, ll. 124–5.
45 Bennett, *Brewsters*, p. 7.
46 William Shakespeare, *2 Henry IV*, ed. P. H. Davison (London, Penguin, 1977), 2.1.13–17.
47 Quoted in Robert Ashton, 'Popular Entertainment and Social Control in Later Elizabethan and Early Stuart London', *London Journal*, 9 (183), 13.
48 *The Stage Coach*, in *The Works of George Farquhar*, ed. Shirley Strumm Kenny,

vol. 1 (Oxford, Clarendon Press, 1988), 1.1.
49 John Bickerdyke, *The Curiosities of Ale and Beer: An Entertaining History* (London, Swan Sonnenschein, 1889), p. 34.
50 Lydgate, 'The ix properties of wyne', in *Minor Poems*. This is MacCracken's gloss.
51 Robert Copland, 'The Highway to the Spital-House' (1535–36), in A. V. Judges, *The Elizabethan Underworld* (London, Routledge and Kegan Paul, 1965 [1930]). Judges gives 'base, dirty fellow' for 'haskard'.
52 Bickerdyke, *Curiosities*, p. 211.
53 John Keats, *Hyperion*, Book III, ll. 114–20, in Duncan Wu (ed.), *Romanticism An Anthology* (Oxford, Blackwell, 1994).
54 Richard Ames, *A Search after Wit* (London, 1691).
55 Thomas Heywood, *A Preparative to Studie: Or, The Vertue of Sack* (London, 1641), ll. 1–8.
56 Grove, *Wine*. An earlier version, *Wine, Beer and Ale Contending for Superiority*, exists in a virtually identical form, missing only the late arrival of Tobacco.
57 No. 88, *A Selection of English Carols*, ed. Richard Leighton Greene (Oxford, Clarendon Press, 1962).
58 Greene, *Carols*, n. to No. 88, quoted by John Ray in *A Collection of English Proverbs* (Cambridge, 1678).
59 Andrew Boorde, *Regiment of Health* (London, 1542), n.p.
60 John Taylor, *Ale Alevated into the Ale-titude: Or, A Learned Oration before a Civill Assembly of ALE-Drinkers …* (London, 1651).
61 Thomas Dogget, *The Country-Wake* (London, 1696), 4.2.
62 *Shorter Oxford English Dictionary* (Oxford, Clarendon Press, 1993) (hereafter *ShOED*).
63 Thanks to Bruce Olson for bringing this to my attention. His website at www.erols.com/olsonw provides an extensive catalogue of ballads.
64 'Sir John Barleycorn', in *Ancient Ballads, and Songs of the Peasantry of England*, ed. John Henry Dixon (Wakefield, Yorkshire, EP Publishing, 1973 [London 1846]), p. 120.
65 The riddle appears in *The Exeter Book* (eleventh century), whilst the riddles themselves may have been written in the eighth century (*The Exeter Book Riddles*, trans. and introduced by Kevin Crossley-Holland (Harmondsworth, Penguin, 1979), pp. 10–12). Bickerdyke, *Curiosities*, gives the translation (pp. 34–5): 'A part of the earth is / Prepared beautifully, / With the hardest, / And with the sharpest, /And with the grimmest / Of the productions of men, / Cut and … / Turned and dried, / Bound and twisted, / Bleached and awakened, / Ornamented and poured out, / Carried afar / To the doors of the people.' The idea of the barley being produced through violent means is the same as in 'John Barleycorn', and the riddle goes on to show the effect of alcohol on those who use it.
66 *The Roxburghe Ballads*, vol. II. Variant spellings of 'barley' and 'barly' are as given here.
67 'Kill' = 'kiln'. Later 'modernising' versions substitute kiln, even though, of course, the rhyme is with 'will' (*Ibid.*, p. 372). It also diminishes the play on 'kill'.
68 The interpretation here vies and overlaps with others. Roy Palmer observes that Sir James Frazer in *The Golden Bough* took 'John Barleycorn' to be a fertility

myth which 'parallels the ancient belief in a vegetation spirit killed for the sake of the fertility of the crops'. Palmer prefers to see it simply as a personification of 'the life-cycle of the barley grain which is used for brewing beer', *Songs*, (London, Dent, 1979,) p. 116.
69 'Teen = sorrow' – *The Roxburghe Ballads*, vol. II. *ShOED* gives this definition only for Middle English, 'teen' as a verb continuing solely in dialect usage in the North and Scotland through the later period.
70 Cyril Tourneur, *The Revenger's Tragedy*, ed. R. A. Foakes (Manchester, Manchester University Press, 1990 [?1605–06]) 4.2.183–4.
71 Thomas Young, *Englands Bane: or, the Description of Drunkennesse* (London, 1617).
72 A complete catalogue of alcohol in the Old Testament can be found in J. M. O'Brien, 'Attributes of Alcohol in the Old Testament', *Drinking and Drug Practices Surveyor*, 18 (1982), 18–24.
73 Langland, *Piers*, 1.21–33. The story of Lot and his daughters is Genesis 19.30–8, revised standard edition.
74 Chaucer, 'The Pardoner's Tale', VI (C) 485–91.
75 *Ibid.*, ll. 535–6.
76 *Ibid.*, ll. 492–7.
77 *Ibid.*, ll. 456–8.
78 Chaucer, 'The Manciple's Tale', IX (H) 69–75.
79 'Pardoner's Tale', 'For dronkenesse is verray sepulture / Of mannes wit and his discrecioun', VI (C) 558-9; 'Parson's Tale', 'dronkeness, that is the horrible sepulture of mannes resoun', X (I) 821.
80 Owst, *Pulpit*, p. 427.
81 *Ibid.*, p. 428.
82 James Samuelson, *The History of Drink. A Review, Social, Scientific, and Political* (London, Trübner & Co., 1878), p. 120 and pp. 144–5.
83 Quoted in Kinney, *Skelton*, n. 35, p. 218, from Frederick W. Hackwood, *Inns, Ales, and Drinking Customs of Old England* (London, T. Fisher Unwin, 1910), pp. 56–7.
84 *La Male Regle De T. Hoccleve*, in *Selections from Hoccleve*, ed. M. C. Seymour (Oxford, Clarendon Press, 1981), pp. 12–23. Thanks to Greg Walker for his comments on this poem.
85 *Ibid.*, introductory note, p. 106.
86 R. V. French, *Nineteen Centuries of Drink in England: A History*, 2nd edition – enlarged and revised (London, National Temperance Publication Depot, n.d. [1st edition 1884]), p. 387.
87 *Ibid.*, pp. 68–9.
88 William Shakespeare, *Othello*, ed. Kenneth Muir (Penguin, London, 1996 [1968]), 2.3.71–9.
89 Albert H. Tolman's 'Drunkenness in Shakespeare's Plays' lists most of the occurrences of drunkenness along with interpretations of their significance, in his *Falstaff and other Shakespearean Topics* (New York, Macmillan, 1925), pp. 44–52.
90 In Judges, *Underworld*, p. 21.
91 *Ibid.*, p. 314.
92 Thomas Nashe, *Pierce Penniless*, in *The Unfortunate Traveller and Other Works*,

ed. J. B. Steane (Harmondsworth, Penguin, 1972), pp. 107–8. 'Martin' is a type of monkey (Steane).
93 Young, *Bane*, n.p.
94 George Gascoyne, *A Delicate Diet, for daintie mouthde droonkards. Wherein the fowle abuse of common Carowsing, and Quaffing with hartie draughtes, is honestlie admonished* (London, 1576, reprint, 1789), p. 19.
95 Thomas Heywood, *Philocothonista, or, the Drunkard, Opened, Dissected, and Anatomized* (London, 1635), pp. 1–6.
96 Chaucer, *Tales*, VII 700/B21890. James Winny notes that the Host's planetary aspect is that of the sun, an influence which, as Bartholomaeus claimed 'hath virtue of unity and accord, for he joineth, concileth and accordeth the planets in their own effects and doings. Also he accordeth together elements that be contrary', 'Chaucer's Science' in Hussey *et al.*, *An Introduction to Chaucer* (London, Cambridge University Press, 1965), p. 165.
97 James Winny: 'the final tale is not an entertaining story but an entirely sober prose sermon on the deadly sins', and *'The Parson's Tale* … was brought in to strengthen this sobered purpose', 'Chaucer Himself', in Hussey *et al.*, *Chaucer*, pp. 12 and 13.
98 'The sketch of the Parson is an ideal portrait of a good parish priest. It should not be taken to represent Wycliff or one of his followers,' Chaucer, *Tales*, p. 663.

3

The Falstaffian state

'Forasmuch as intolerable Hurts and Troubles to the Commonwealth of this Realm doth daily grow and increase through such Abuses and Disorders as are had and used in common Alehouses and other Houses called Tiplinghouses:' It is therefore enacted ... that the Justices of the Peace ... shall have full Power and Authority ... to remove, discharge, and put away common selling of Ale and Beer in the said common Alehouses and Tiplinghouses.[1]

The Boar's Head in Eastcheap is perhaps the most famous drinking den in English literature, and Falstaff is its most infamous drinker. Mainly contained within the middle two works of Shakespeare's second historical tetralogy, *Richard II* (1595), *1 Henry IV* (1597), *2 Henry IV* (1598) and *Henry V* (1599), the complex, turbulent and changing relations between state and populace at the end of the sixteenth century are played out through the fluid dynamics of a tavern set in the early 1400s. With its chaos and conviviality, and with its roots in an older, more festive England, the Boar's Head and Falstaff are both a reflection of, and a warning to, its Elizabethan audience: the tavern and its drinkers are anathema to the physical and ideological machinery of the emergent protestant nation state. A rebellious nobility and a fractious France can be cowed and bargained with, and these are negotiations which are standard political fare. But to banish Falstaff is a much more hurtful process for an English audience, because it banishes the indulgent ideal of a merrie England, ostensibly in favour of a less attractive but more stable, more efficient, more sober Commonwealth.

Shakespeare's quartet of plays arrives on the Elizabethan stage at a time when the will to create a more pliable society had been strengthening. This can be seen in the steps taken by authorities to control 'troublesome' behaviour, and these initiatives are much in evidence in the accumulation of state legislation on drinking places. What might be identified as the first attempt at state control begins somewhat casually in the eleventh year of Henry VII's reign (1496). The Act is mainly an effort to clamp down on 'Vagabonds, idle, and suspected Persons'. The clause relating to the sale of alcohol is introduced innocuously at the end of the Act, with the proclamation that 'Two Justices of Peace may reject common selling of Ale'. It has the appearance of an afterthought, but it is this slender edict which ushers in state control of alehouses, and the fact that it is incorporated into a vagrancy Act is a fair indication of how drink-related problems will be viewed in the future.

The clause is beefed up in 1552 when those who wish to run alehouses or tipling houses must obtain licences from Justices of the Peace.[2] This Act is specifically aimed at people selling ale or beer. Taverns, which sell wine rather than malt liquor, are brought under control the following year under an Act which aims 'to avoid the excessive Prices of Wine'. The Act also says who may keep wine, at what prices wine is to be sold, and how many taverns are to be licensed in any one town.[3] These laws become administratively feasible with the emergence of a certain set of attitudes in the sixteenth century, such as those Fletcher and Stevenson describe with regard to the sixteenth century and following: 'Local communities were penetrated ever more deeply by a process of administrative and cultural integration which brought into them national standards and fashions.'[4]

In this post-Reformation era the drinking place is positioned differently within culture from its previous role as represented in either Chaucer or Langland. Alehouses and taverns are inimical to the Protestant ideas of sobriety and work that are becoming increasingly entrenched and prevalent in English society as the sixteenth century wears on. The inn sometimes falls within this censure, but is more often than not, thanks to higher legal, social and economic status, a more acceptable space. The inn's importance for the wealth of the nation becomes more apparent in this period because England requires a sound infrastructure to further its mercantile interests. Consequently, the inns function as the institution which enables the roads to be travelled, whilst continuing to serve as places for merchants and traders to do business in, and continuing to replace the open-air markets which had once served this function.[5]

Although the plays in the tetralogy have a historical subject matter, I am assuming that the conception of the tavern is contemporary with Shakespeare and that there is no attempt on his part to historicise either drinking practices or drinking places[6] (apart from the fact that nobody smokes a pipe in the tavern, which would have been a common sight for Shakespeare's audience). The issues of governance and nationality as presented in the tetralogy are pertinent to the post-Reformation sixteenth century and not the end of the fourteenth and beginning of the fifteenth centuries, when the plays are set (1398–1420).[7] There was no state control of the tavern or of drinking places in general at that earlier time, although, ironically, there was an Act passed in Richard II's reign to control the price of wine, in order to stimulate the market for it, but this legislation was part of the general effort to keep the price of victuals under control. There was some legislation extant in Tudor times, mainly from the 1552 and 1553 Acts (see above), but it does not appear to be directly at issue in the *Henriad*. Rather, it is the generalised official disapproval of tavern space which permeates the play, for although drinking was perhaps the most heavily proscribed activity in the sixteenth and early seventeenth centuries, it was still the case that before the 1620s and 1630s, control of even the alehouse – the most reviled of all the drinking places – was regarded as ineffective.[8] The one topical reference in the plays with respect to drinking houses may be the association of Gadshill with highway robbery in the 1590s (a reputation it held well into the eighteenth century), since the robbers were operating from tippling houses.[9] Nevertheless, we can observe the ideological conundrum that the tavern and Falstaff represent for a more official England by analysing how the world of the tavern and the nation state are moulded through time, space and drink.

Tavern time and national time[10]

RICHARD II   I wasted time, and now doth time waste me.
For now hath time made me his numbering clock. …
My thoughts are minutes …

Richard II[11]

FALSTAFF   Now Hal, what time of day is it lad?
PRINCE HAL   Thou art so fat-witted with drinking of old sack, and unbuttoning thee after supper, and sleeping upon benches after noon, that thou hast forgotten to demand that truly which thou wouldst truly know. What a devil hast thou to do with the time of the day? Unless hours were cups of sack, and minutes capons, and clocks the tongues of bawds, and dials the signs of leaping-houses, and the blessed sun himself a fair hot wench in flame-coloured taffeta, I see no reason why thou shouldst be so superfluous to demand the time of the day.

1 Henry IV[12]

At the end of *Richard II*, the deposed King rues his misspent time as ruler. The 'concord of my state and time' are broken he says, and as a consequence his 'sighs, and tears, and groans' are measured out in 'minutes, times, and hours'.[13] Now that Bolingbroke is in the ascendancy as Henry IV, time belongs to the new king, and Richard is fit only to be 'his jack of the clock', that is, the figure that strikes the clock's quarter hours. The sense of time being valuable, at the behest of king and nation, as if the monarch 'keeps time' (in the musical figure that Richard himself uses), and the metaphorical transformation of wasted lives into the language of mechanical time, is echoed in the dispute over time when we first meet Hal and Falstaff in the sequel to *Richard II*. Falstaff asks his drinking companion what time of day it is (above). Hal berates Falstaff for asking a superfluous question, and suggests that Falstaff could only be interested in the answer if time were measured out in cups of sack and other idle pursuits. Tavern life is immediately presented as idle time, as time wasted. In fact, the tavern, thus being without time, might be said to transcend time, but timelessness in the national and religious framework it is forced to operate within translates as uselessness; it is 'superfluous'.

The 1604 Act against 'inordinate Haunting and Tipling in Inns, Alehouses' and other drinking places, although slightly later than the tetralogy, is a sign of how those in authority viewed such time-wasting. It proclaimed that drinking houses were for the 'Receit, Relief and Lodging of Wayfaring People travelling from Place to Place', and to supply victuals for those not able to do so for themselves; they were 'not meant for Entertainment and Harbouring of lewd and idle People to spend and consume their Money and their Time in lewd and drunken Manner'.[14] Entertainment, lewd behaviour and wasting of time just about sums up the Boar's Head Tavern. The Puritan Robert Younge's declaration that 'they drink that they may drive away time; for every hour seems a day and every day a month to an idle person which is not spent in a taphouse' might in addition to the Act be said to describe the phenomenology of time spent in drinking houses.[15] Of course, the enforced idleness of the unemployed labourer or artisan is not of the same quality as Falstaff's, but the evaluation of time in relation to the drinking place *would* appear to be the same.

It can also be argued, with respect to Hal's question of Falstaff 'What a devil hast thou to do with the time of the day?' that a different distinction with time is operative, and that Falstaff's time is 'night'.[16] Biblical injunctions are littered throughout the play, as Falstaff uses scripture for his own ends (just as the Devil might). Here, as elsewhere, Hal could be playing Falstaff at his own game, turning the religious tables on him with 1 Thessalonians 5.5–8 underwriting his attack: 'For you are all sons of light and sons of the day; we are not of the night or of darkness. So then let us not sleep, as others do, but let us keep awake and be sober. For those who sleep at night, and those who get drunk are drunk at night. But since we belong to the day, let us be sober, and put on the breastplate of faith and love, and for a helmet the hope of salvation.'[17] This would be especially pertinent if Hal had discovered Falstaff asleep at the beginning of the scene, as it is sometimes performed.[18] It would also fit in with Hal's famous soliloquy at the end of the same scene when he says 'herein will I imitate the sun', hiding behind 'base contagious clouds' in order to seem the brighter when he does shine. The speech ends 'I'll so offend, to make offence a skill, / Redeeming time when men think least I will.' The final lines are a direct echo of Ephesians 5.16, 'making the most of the time, because the days are evil'. But more than this, Ephesians continues, 5.17–18: 'Therefore do not be foolish, but understand what the will of the Lord is. And do not get drunk with wine, for that is debauchery; but be filled with the Spirit.' The whole scene is permeated with such biblical contrasts between the proper use of time and idle drinking.[19] That Paul's letter to the Ephesians is a subtext is made more evident in *2 Henry IV*. Prince Henry asks Bardolph's page what drinking company Falstaff keeps. The Page answers: 'Ephesians, my lord, of the old church', with 'old church' implying 'St Paul's', and thus hinting again at this particular biblical subtext.[20]

Even though Hal has scriptural support, his overall concern is to invest time with values fit for the kind of nation he wishes to forge, and he thus makes 'time' function as national time. Time spent in debauchery, in recreational drinking, has no value, and so is in opposition to national time. This contrast in notions of time is important because in the nationalisation of time by both Henrys we can see the seeds are being sown in the Tudor period for the discipline of 'industrial time' that appears in later generations. Although perhaps time for Hal and his father is conceived of mainly within a religious framework, hence the idea of redemption, we can see that this is imbricated with national time, not surprising perhaps in that the nation's destiny is often coupled with a religious trajectory. The unfolding of the nation's history predominantly concurs with divine law. If E. P. Thompson is right in saying that plebeian culture lacks 'a predictive notation of time' and 'hence experience or opportunity is grabbed as occasion arises, with little thought of the consequences' I think it then plausible to regard the tavern time as an official distortion of plebeian time.[21] Before the introduction of factory-work discipline, Nicholas Dorn argues that there were only two means open to mercantile capitalists for controlling labour: one was wage levels, the other was to create 'a longer and more disciplined working week … [which] required a dismantling of historically established leisure customs, of which drinking customs were an integral part'.[22]

Is it anachronistic to regard the Elizabethan view of time as compatible with time as understood in later, industrialised Britain? John Kerrigan argues that with the dissemination of clock time, 'the sixteenth century saw a dislocation in man's sense of himself and the world so massive that arguably nothing like it has been seen again until, in this century, man discovered that he had the power to destroy not only himself but "the great globe itself, / Yea, all which it inherit". The invention and dissemination of mechanical time in the renaissance brought about a complete reordering of sensibility.'[23] Clocks and watches only became compact and cheap in the sixteenth century, and 'Clocks appeared in homes and workshops. Labour began to be regulated by machinery – domestic affairs were organized around the dial's hand … Clock time invaded men's lives, and was, indeed, for city-dwellers like Shakespeare, the matrix of living.'[24] Further on he notes that 'the links between Protestantism and the clock, though complex and sometimes elusive, are undeniable', and that 'predestinarian Protestantism produced a picture of the world congruent with clock-making'.[25] I labour this point to show that the matrix of work patterns, time-keeping, the Protestant religion, and the growing importance of the city, as it emerges in the sixteenth century, completely informs the way Hal spends and redeems time, as opposed to the way tavern time is spent. In fact, when Hal sneers at Falstaff by suggesting his measurement of time could only be achieved by turning hours into 'cups of sack' and clocks into 'the tongues of bawds',[26] he is sneering at a debased form of older time measurement when the agricultural year was punctuated by festivities.[27]

The distortion is compounded because of the social make-up of those who frequent the tavern. Led by Falstaff, they are an odd bunch of wasters on the periphery of the criminal fraternity, and in Falstaff's case, part of the dissipated nobility. They could hardly be seen as representative of the country as a whole. The poorer orders are missing, and what has been called the 'many in the middling ranks who belonged neither wholly to the patrician culture nor wholly to the plebeian one'.[28] Therefore we can only guess at the significance of time for the majority of those in England, Scotland and Wales. What is missing from the plays is agricultural time,[29] that is, time alloyed to the requirements of farming and husbandry, task-orientated time, although this is partly offset by the representation of the community in Gloucester, which, after all, would be the majority of the nation's experience of time. The national time, as understood by Henry IV, the majority of the nobility, and Hal from beginning to end, is some higher-order time of religious-national chronology. Falstaff and his companions are the negation of this; being without useful time they are without worth. But it is the national time, here allied to the Puritan's notion of redemption, that is precisely the notion of time that emerges as the means of state control.

Hal's vocational sensibility is very close to the Puritan's (from Luther) notion of 'calling' and sense of duty. Here the overlapping with the emergent Puritan work ethic and its treatment of time is evident.[30] Time as experienced by the majority of the nation is thus doubly effaced by the tetralogy: firstly in the timelessness of Falstaff's parody of plebeian lifestyle, and secondly, less obviously, in the lack of any sense of agricultural time, its necessity and its value. Yet it is this latter time that supports the estates of the nobility fighting within and without the borders of England, Scotland and Wales. At the battle of Agincourt, Henry V makes it clear here (and elsewhere) that he regards most of his men as thieves, liars and cowards, but in fighting for the King he tells them that they may redeem their current idleness and past wastage of time – all actions stemming, symbolically at least, from tavern life.

> HENRY V We few, we happy few, we band of brothers:
> For he today that sheds his blood with me
> Shall be my brother; be he ne'er so vile,
> This day shall gentle his condition;
> And gentlemen in England now abed
> Shall think themselves accursed they were not here,
> And hold their manhoods cheap, whiles any speaks
> That fought with us upon Saint Crispin's day.[31]

Henry V's time, and those at his side, is taken up with fighting. Those who are not fighting are of two sorts: gentlemen in bed, and secondly, implicitly, those who are scoundrels, since he appears to assume that many fighting with him will be able to redeem past bad actions – 'gentle' their 'condition' as he puts it, which seeps into the phrase of 'gentlemen now abed' that follows. This is how Falstaff's actions at Shrewsbury are indeed understood by the Lord Chief Justice, although he remains somewhat sceptical and perhaps foresees a time when Falstaff will be found out: 'Your day's service at Shrewsbury hath a little gilded over your night's exploit on Gad's Hill. You may thank th'unquiet time for your quiet o'erposting that action.'[32] Henry V's conception of what constitutes the body of England, Scotland and Wales is thus, on the one hand, idle gentlemen and criminals, and on the other hand, those who are prepared to fight with him, that is, gentlemen who are not idle, and criminals who wish to atone.

An earlier battle in *Henry V* also appears to have the majority of fighting stock as cowards, thieves and liars. The Boy who is with Nym, Bardolph and Pistol, that is, Falstaff's drinking companions, as he is expected to go once more into the breach, cries: 'Would I were in an alehouse in London! I would give all my fame for a pot of ale, and safety.'[33] Pistol agrees, and it can be assumed that their preference for the alehouse over the battlefield is an attitude typical of the nation's lower orders. Higher up the social order, when Falstaff himself is charged with leading a company of men, he says: 'O, I could wish this tavern were my drum', with the suggestion of it being both his rallying call, his rallying place and his troop.[34] Here we can see how alternative time and alternative space begin to merge. When Peto arrives at the tavern in *2 Henry IV* to tell Prince Henry the news of his father and troop movements, Peto says: 'and as I came along / I met and overtook a dozen captains, / Bare-headed, sweating, knocking at the taverns, / And asking every one for Sir John Falstaff.' The sense of urgency and crisis, and no doubt the reminder that Falstaff's home is the very same tavern where Hal has just idled away his own time disguised as a Drawer, pricks Hal's conscience. Again, a sense of duty allied with a feeling that as the future King he is under the pressure to conform to the nation's time, emerges:

> PRINCE HENRY By heaven, Poins, I feel me much to blame,
> So idly to profane the precious time
> When tempest of commotion, like the south
> Borne with black vapour, doth begin to melt
> And drop upon our bare unarmèd heads.
> Give me my sword and cloak. Falstaff, good night.[35]

Prince Henry's seriousness is now complete as he forsakes Falstaff and his tavern for his 'sword and cloak', readying himself for the fighting ahead. He does not set foot in a tavern again.

Watching this space

> The Cheapside tavern, as we fancy it, is a gabled house of four storeys, having canted bay windows and richly-carved panels. There is a door at the centre, and the lintel over the door is carved with ornament resembling a grape vine. We envision a long room with two tables and many stools. There are many guests, whose wants are attended by youthful waiters. Wooden platters, knives and wooden salt-cellars are in use. The fare is pork and souse, followed by a roast capon, and ended with a pudding which is served on the reverse of the wooden platters. Some have finished the victuals and are enjoying mazers of sack, with clean pipes and Virginian tobacco as finishing luxuries.[36]

In *Richard II* the King's body and the health of nation are conflated when John of Gaunt tells Richard: 'Thy deathbed is no lesser than thy land, / Wherein thou liest in reputation sick'.[37] In the opening lines to *1 Henry IV*, 'So shaken as we are, so wan with care, / Find we a time for frighted peace to pant'[38] there is a similar conflation, since the words proclaim an assessment of the health of the nation's body and the King's two bodies: his royal personage and his physical self. Just as Falstaff appears to retain vestiges of Richard II's time-wasting, his own body and its conflation with the tavern throughout the two *Henry IV* plays continues Richard's illness. It also provides a parallel to the conflation of the King's body with the nation throughout the *Henry* plays.

In addition to this, Falstaff's tavern lifestyle runs counter to the aims of the state that Henry IV attempts to impress upon his son, Hal, who has adopted Falstaff's bad ways. That excess leads to bodily and national disorder is a point perceived by the rebel Archbishop, who realises that his faction is perceived as 'all diseased, / And with our surfeiting and wanton hours / Have brought ourselves into a burning fever, / And we must bleed for it; of which disease / Our late King Richard being infected died'.[39] His description of 'surfeiting and wanton hours' applies equally to Falstaff's regime. And so as the tetralogy proceeds, from Richard's and the state's dissipated body in *Richard II* (as suggested here by the Archbishop), via Henry IV's exhaustion, to Henry V's and the state's perfected body in the last play, from a troubled nation to national glory, it is mirrored in the rejection of Falstaff's body and all that Falstaff represents. When Hal finally takes up his kingly responsibilities, the symbolic connection between body, order and the state is once more made evident: 'Now call we our high court of parliament, / And let us choose such limbs of noble counsel / That the great body of our state may go / In equal rank with the best-governed nation'.[40] Recent revisionist work, looking for subversions of power, has sought to overturn this (somewhat old-fashioned) view of progress in the tetralogy, from a disordered nation to a successfully cohesive nation, in favour of a reading that shows the plays as consistently radical. However, as is argued here, such an interpretation appears wilful at best, since the plays clearly deal with England as an ideological construct, and *Henry V*, despite its polyvocality, projects a triumphant nationalism, achieved, perhaps, at the expense of switching generic codes from the moral contingency of 'history' to the (here) pat resolution of 'romance' when England marries France.[41]

In taking up the throne in a responsible manner, Hal casts Falstaff aside. The action is usually taken to be consistent with his responsible acceptance of monarchical duties. For the audience, rejection of Falstaff is also understood as rejection of the tavern and tavern life. In *1 Henry IV* tavern life is enjoyable. In the second part it is clearly a less engaging and desirable environment, and in *Henry V* the tavern, like Falstaff, fades to nothing. On the face of it this progress would slot neatly with the traditional interpretation which claims that Hal's education at the Boar's Head is necessary for him to become the country's true king. It prepares him for the night before the battle of Agincourt when he wanders amongst his disgruntled soldiers to gauge their morale in 4.1. No one can imagine Richard II or Hal's father having taken such an action. Thanks to tavern life, and his former enjoyment of it, Henry V is quite at ease with the whole body of the nation, and by extension one presumes, his own. No longer shaken, but definitely stirred, the country is restored to good health. All this serves to make the tavern central to the plays and to the nation, to the extent of illustrating the problem of national governance, but only as long as Falstaff is central to Hal's development. The tavern becomes unnecessary and irrelevant once it and Falstaff have served their pedagogical function.

However, if Hal's rejection of Falstaff is also a rejection of tavern life, and by extension, in this context at least, inns and alehouses both of town and country, it must then follow that he is abandoning one of the most significant parts of England's national life and its social fabric. If the casting off of Falstaff is the exclusion of tavern life from what would be desirable for the nation and the national image, it would then seem that national glory is gained at the expense of the country's favourite place and pastime. Hal is casting off the old England in favour of his own vision of a new England, one that the play appears to endorse. Andrew Hadfield states that 'The idea of a nation is predicated upon the existence of a public space – geographical and conceptual – which will always include competing voices desiring to speak for the "nation" and fashion it according to their particular designs.'[42] In effect, Hal, as Henry V, denies that space. This should hardly come as a surprise to Falstaff since Hal has already warned him that the laws will not be enforced in a manner likely to suit Falstaff and his cohorts when Hal becomes King.[43] One irony is that in suppressing this particular space and voice, *Henry V* opens the nation up to embrace the Scottish and Irish, and more pointedly, the Welsh (as represented by Fluellen) and the French (3.4 is entirely in French). He simultaneously suppresses 'Englishness' whilst broadening out England to encompass other lands.

Falstaff's threat to order is both as a threat to a notion of the King as a mortal being with mortal failings, and to the order of the nation. Falstaff is seen to represent chaos in the form of the tempting Vice figure from the Morality plays. In this sense he is the road to moral disorder. But this is to view Falstaff through the official national imperative. This latter ideology loiters in the background throughout the first three plays, when all the ideological balls are in the air, but predominates in *Henry V* when the official line holds sway. But seen from the other side, Falstaff has his own moral order, in contradistinction to the nation's, as his speech on honour shows. In contrast to the body of the nation, Falstaff's excessive body is initially unperturbed, and he is at the height of his powers for the first half of *1 Henry IV*. The usual Elizabethan conceit of disorder in the universe and disorder in bodies might be expected to work well with Falstaff, as it does with the image of civil strife and a universe out of joint in the opening of *1 Henry IV*. The battle here is between, on the one hand, order as represented by the King's body and its conflation with the state, and on the other hand, order as represented by Falstaff's body and its conflation with the tavern. Another way of looking at it would be to see the issue in terms of Keith Wrightson's concept of two orders in tension in this historical period as society bifurcates: the one, a desire to impose control from the outside, which is what Hal represents, the other to 'maintain neighbouring relationships', which is what the tavern and Falstaff represent.[44]

The Boy claims the alehouse for his natural home, but Falstaff's natural space is the tavern, not the socially lower alehouse. Even though the drinking place is not directly named, Hal's question in *2 Henry IV* about his old drinking partner, 'Doth the old boar feed in the old frank?', and Bardolph's answer 'At the old place, my lord, in Eastcheap', points to the real Boar's Head Tavern,[45] and the audience is in any case quickly made aware of Falstaff's usual abode when we first meet him and he asks Hal 'is not my Hostess of the tavern a most sweet wench?'[46] As we have seen there was a readily understood social distinction between an alehouse and a tavern, even if terminology was not always consistent.[47] However, a knight might have been supposed to drink at an inn. By choosing a tavern over an inn there is the opportunity for high to meet low in a less stratified arena than the inn would permit. At the other end of the scale, it would have been fairly implausible to have Falstaff and Hal meet in an alehouse. There is also the faintest hint of a literary joke in that the robbery Poins, Hal and Falstaff intend to carry out from their base at the Boar's Head is to rob pilgrims on the way to Canterbury,[48] as if *1 Henry IV* were setting out to ambush *The Canterbury Tales*.

We have seen how Hal works to redeem time from tavern timelessness. What is less often commented upon is the way the plays work to redeem different spaces, so that there is a play-off between tavern space and national space. Interpretative complications set in because redemption of space involves not only ordering it within its putative boundaries – hence the gardening figuration in *Richard II* – but also reconfiguring it by taking up war outside the national space, by journeying to France, and by projected crusades. In keeping with the broadening of boundaries in *Henry V* this play allows Burgundy the peacemaker to refer to France as a garden gone to ruin that can now be returned to its former glory. With respect to the notion of 'England', these displacements serve to imbue space with nationality: through extension and difference in the case of Henry's actions in France, and with spiritual sanctification in the case of the crusades.

Whilst religion can provide the moral and divine measure for time, and fix it within these parameters, space is mutable and lacks the real possibility of such religious investiture, despite Henry IV's death in a room called 'Jerusalem'. There is never any sense of the various spaces within England meshing in the same manner that Hal brings his own time into step with destiny via redemption. The notion that the King's crown can encompass both the limited physical body of a man and the national space, and the idea that the grave is also large enough to do both, exemplifies the mutability of space.[49] In this light, the tavern serves to provide the space that threatens the crown from within: it is a social space encompassed by the crown but a space which fails to be national.[50] This is unlike the threats to space from such as the Rebels, where boundaries can be drawn and names put to spaces, since the nobles' names are, in one sense, synecdoches for the land (and country); for example in *Henry V* we have Dukes and Earls of Bedford, Exeter, York, Salisbury, Westmorland and Warwick. It is apt, therefore, that the first time we see Hal and Falstaff together in *1 Henry IV* may be the Prince's chambers or a tavern, emphasising the interchangeability of the two in Hal's early days. The slippage between space and person is keenest with Gad's Hill/Gadshill, the name of the site of the robbery and the name of one of the thieves.

But what, exactly, does the tavern space represent? In the plays it mainly appears to be the site of criminal activity. From here the Gadshill robbery is planned and executed. It is the place for lewd behaviour and is the obverse of the space the national consciousness requires. In *1 Henry IV* 2.4 the antics of Falstaff and Hal are interrupted by the Watch at the door. It is the equivalent of a pub raid. Everyone hides except Hal and Peto, and it is only through Hal's intervention that the Sheriff is convinced to leave the tavern alone. It indicates that none of the tavern crowd is in a secure position, their lifestyle depends upon Hal's patronage, a quasi-state patronage.[51] However, interpretation is further complicated because of the position the tavern has within the hierarchy of drinking places, and the way the plays position the tavern's workers and frequenters.

The use of a tavern rather than an inn carries economic significance. An inn would be perceived as having a usefulness as part of the coaching transport network and as a place often frequented by merchants and traders, that is, it would not have the necessary association of a place for idling away the time. The tavern did not serve this role within the national infrastructure and national business community, at least, to nowhere near the same extent. As Peter Clark comments, inns were important before 1800 'as a commercial centre for merchants and traders, and this function expanded rapidly in the Tudor and Stuart period. Inns attracted a growing amount of business away from the old open-air markets,' and inns were important as a 'nexus of overland transport and communications. From the Tudor period inns were the main staging points for the multitude of carriers who rode the track-ways of the kingdom,' whilst the tavern was not allowed to offer accommodation.[52] In mitigation of tavern space it can be argued that 'Taverns, like inns, were places for business to be done; investments arranged, lawyers and physicians consulted,'[53] but this is clearly not the type of tavern presented in *1* and *2 Henry IV*. In any case, 'As the preserve of the upper classes, inns enjoyed relative freedom from the heavy burden of statutory controls imposed on alehouses from the sixteenth century. Ancient inns could only be prosecuted under common law, and though there was an attempt under James I to license inns, this proved abortive.'[54] A final example of the social role of the tavern is provided by the Privy Council who in 1614 'complained to the Lord Mayor of London that "there is nothing more usuall in that cittie then [than] to convert the better sort of houses into taverns to the maintenance of ryot and disorder"'.[55]

The tavern space is a parasitic alternative to the state economy, as is made evident on a couple of occasions. The first begins with Gadshill complaining about Falstaff and his thieving cronies:

> GADSHILL   And yet, zounds, I lie, for they pray continually to their saint the commonwealth, or rather not pray to her, but prey on her, for they ride up and down on her, and make her their boots.
> CHAMBERLAIN   What, the commonwealth their boots? Will she hold out water in foul way?
> GADSHILL   She will, she will, justice hath liquored her.[56]

'Boots' are 'spoils', and 'liquored her' has the meaning of 'greasing' (boots) for protection but also of making drunk. The alternative economy preys on the commonwealth to fund tavern life. In the second instance, Bardolph tells his colleagues to get masked up, ready for the robbery:

> BARDOLPH   Case ye, case ye, on with your vizards, there's money of the King's coming down the hill. 'Tis going to the King's exchequer.
> FALSTAFF   You lie, ye rogue, 'tis going to the King's tavern.[57]

Our analysis of the Boar's Head can be further refined. Even though the tavern has its place midway between the alehouse and the inn – 'a degree, or (if you will) a paire of stayres above an Alehouse, where men are drunk with more credit and apology' – it still retains a hierarchy of its own. John Earle in his *Micro-Cosmographie* (1628) noted that in the tavern 'customers are carefully segregated into rooms ranging from "the bottom of the cellar to the great chamber"', and Alison Findlay writes that 'the Boar's Head has distinct upstairs and downstairs areas and cultures to match.[58] Its rooms include the Dolphin Chamber, the Pomegranate Chamber and the Half Moon. Pistol's riotous entry into an upstairs chamber of the Boar's Head is deemed just as unsuitable for one of his station, as is his ostentatious language.'[59] Hal does not really mix – the time he spends with drawers is reported to the audience second-hand as a game in which he has quickly learnt their argot and matched them for drinking. So whilst it might provide support for the argument that Hal gets to know his country, the play does not see fit to show him so demeaned as to be on speaking terms with them and getting drunk. They are there for his amusement, 'loggerheads amongst three or fourscore hogsheads. I have sounded the very bass string of humility.'[60] He and Poins will make fun of the 'puny drawer' until Falstaff arrives. Hal's semi-serious behaviour relates to Falstaff, a member of the nobility, and when Hal is totally serious, he is in dialogue with his father. Hal's intermingling with 'a leash of drawers' is implicitly shown to be playful since when we see 'ordinary people' in their own environment and not through Hal's eyes, such as the carriers and ostler at the inn in Rochester at the beginning of *1 Henry IV*, 2.1, their life is hard and defiantly unpleasant.[61]

Hal's education in the tavern consists of mingling with the thieves, liars and cowards he appears to regard as constitutive of the nation in the Agincourt speech previously alluded to. We do not see any real connection between Hal with the lower orders or with any kind of respectable middle mass in the tavern. The tavern allows Shakespeare to sharpen the difference between Hal now and Henry V later. Compare the social make-up of the Boar's Head Tavern with the section of society in *The Merry Wives of Windsor* (?1597/?1600) where the Host is host of an inn, not a tavern, and the husbands are drawn from the middling ranks. Such an environment would not have provided the contrasts necessary for the dynamics of the three *Henry* plays. The tavern space serves Shakespeare's requirements well in the *Henry* plays, but it is a London space and a city space rather than a rural space – as is clear if compared to the Gloucestershire section of *2 Henry IV*. The point to be made here is that the tavern as a space for normal social bonding, as might be experienced by the majority of the country, is *denied* by the plays because the tavern, as portrayed here, does not provide those virtues which the nation, with nationality defined by the nobility, demands. Friendships in the tavern are shown to be fickle and treacherous, despite references to boon companionship, and Falstaff's treatment of Justice Shallow underlines the contempt for the majority of more mundane enjoyments. The main spaces for social discourse and social intercourse of both Shakespeare's and medieval times – the drinking places of alehouses, taverns and inns – are here, via the tavern, implicitly rubbished. Rejection of tavern life is rejection of this social interaction in favour of the specialised bonding Henry applauds on the battlefield, the band of brothers he finds in France.

The tetralogy's movement from Richard's poor governance, through Henry IV's troubled reign, to Henry V's glory in uniting a nation, to the concomitant detriment of tavern life, needs to be tempered with an awareness of the tavern scenes themselves. Undeniably the picture drawn of tavern life in *1 Henry IV* show a relatively carefree existence amongst thieves and pranksters, and much time and space is devoted to the tavern. In the second *Henry* play Act 2.4 would appear to parallel the same scene in the first part. This scene in the second part is the longest scene in the play. Whilst the scenes in *1 Henry IV* concentrate on companionship and wit, in the second part there is an emphasis on more realistic detail.[62] Thus the length of the scene and its commitment to portraying tavern life is significant in light of the fact that this is what Hal is about to reject. He is too good for it on social and imaginative levels; and perhaps the scene also shows how dull, mundane and repetitive tavern life can be, that perhaps you have to be drunk in order to sing its praises. In itself it does not represent the tavern as a convivial, congenial place. Instead, the play itself repositions the tavern outside of what is desirable. The tavern is no longer a tempting space that Hal must forego, as it might be interpreted in the first part; instead, in the second part, tavern life is simply not pleasurable at all. Whilst the tavern still looms large, it is not full of life. To banish this would hardly be to banish the world, as it might be in the first part. And in *Henry V* there is only one tavern scene, the short 2.3, and that only appears in order to inform the audience of Falstaff's demise.

Rather than allow tavern life to go on unmolested even in its drabness, the death of Falstaff is also the death of the tavern. What was initially a space for a putative symbolic majority to enjoy, albeit filtered through the distorting lens of official representations of taverns, is rejected by the fourth play as a space that can only live if Falstaff lives. In this sense *Henry V* itself disposes of tavern life. Nor is this done primarily on the symbolic level, as it is with Falstaff. The denial of a place for the tavern in the last play is a social act on the King's and the play's parts, a fulfilment of the state's desire to literally and metaphorically eliminate drinking spaces from the nation.[63] It is not stretching the point too far to see it as part of the general withdrawal by the nobility and gentry from an older, traditional way of life, in their attempt to assimilate the new norms of national culture in the Tudor period, as here represented by Henry V.[64] In this light, Hal's rejection of Falstaff is tantamount to saying that the English people are ungovernable and unacceptable in their present plight.

Henry V, although emptied of tavern space, remains haunted by its symbolic presence. At the simplest level the idea of the tavern reverts to a more normal role within English culture when it becomes shorthand for the disreputable in everyday joshing. Pistol, now married to Mistress Quickly, is offended at being called 'mine Host' because he has pretensions to a higher social status. His pompousness is immediately and further deflated by Falstaff's Boy's arrival and opening address to 'Mine host Pistol'. Hostess Quickly bemoans the fact that no matter if she lodged a dozen or fourteen gentlewomen, it would still be called a bawdy-house, and she continues to feature as the stock butt of innuendo and malapropisms.[65]

But at a more sophisticated level, *Henry V* reconfigures the movement from 'the tavern', Falstaff and Hal, to Henry V/*Henry V*, in terms of a young, reckless nation that has now matured. In 1.2, Henry enters into a conversation with the French Ambassador and is made aware of how the Dauphin views Henry's behaviour. The Dauphin believes that Henry wants to 'revel into dukedoms' in France, a direct consequence of the Dauphin's knowledge of Henry's former behaviour when Hal. Henry's reply is a recapitulation of his excuse that such riot had a national purpose, but adds an idea that resonates with his jaunt to France:

> KING HENRY And we understand him well,
> How he comes o'er us with our wilder days,
> Not measuring what use we made of them.
> We never valued this poor seat of England,
> And therefore, living hence, did give ourself
> To barbarous licence; as 'tis ever common
> That men are merriest when they are from home.[66]

The excuse is that the King's own youthful behaviour simply mirrored England's juvenile era. Previously the nation was little valued, and acted as if it were 'away from home', that is, without restraint or licence – 'merrie England'. Now that England has grown up, become sober, it has come home, so to speak, that is, its behaviour matches what Henry V would wish it to be. The idea that England's past was this thoughtless youthfulness is ventured once more when the Dauphin directly expresses his view that England is busied with a Whitsun morris-dance and 'idly kinged' by a 'vain, giddy, shallow, humorous youth'.[67] His impression of 'merrie England' is based upon the image of Hal and Falstaff in their former glories. The French King is more circumspect, but the point is still well made. The rehabilitation of Hal into a responsible Henry, symbolised once more by his rejection of Falstaff (and now, more clearly, a rejection of an old England, merrily drunk out of its wits), is completed in 4.7. Fluellen compares Henry to Alexander the Great. Fluellen is referring to Alexander's murder of his friend Cleitus when 'in his ales and his angers' (35–7), a story that would have been familiar to an Elizabethan audience as a typical pulpit warning against drunkenness. The tale continues:

> FLUELLEN As Alexander killed his friend Cleitus, being in his ales and
> his cups, so also Harry Monmouth, being in his right wits and his
> good judgements, turned away the fat knight with the great-belly

doublet – he was full of jests, and gipes, and knaveries, and mocks:
I have forgot his name.
GOWER   Sir John Falstaff.[68]

This spatial and historical realignment of the nation is carried out in miniature if we return to the closing scenes of *2 Henry IV*. In 5.2 the newly crowned Henry V makes his peace with the Lord Chief Justice, the symbol of the nation's law, thus accepting those laws he had previously flouted in his riots with Falstaff. In his acceptance of the Justice's proper rule, he firmly constructs the national space as a legal space, a properly constituted body, something his father could not completely do because of the dissenting actions of the rebels and his own usurpation of the crown. The following scene shows Falstaff at Shallow's, unaware of Hal's elevation. The scene emphasises that Falstaff is in the 'country' when Shallow insists that Falstaff see his pippins and his orchard. Falstaff's geographical position here in the country, beset by bumpkins, isolates him from the Court and the seat of national power. When the Court news comes via Pistol that Hal is now King, Falstaff is encouraged to believe that he will be elevated on the back of Hal's enthronement. Falstaff's self-delusion is underlined by dramatic irony for we have seen in the previous scene how Henry V admires the Lord Chief Justice's probity, yet here is Falstaff claiming that the Justice's days are numbered: 'I know the King is sick for me. Let us take any man's horses the laws of England are at my commandment. Blessed are they that have been my friends, and woe to my Lord Chief Justice!'[69] That Falstaff says this in the country, away from London and his own tavern kingdom, is a sure sign of his, and the old nation's, demise.

The dramatic trajectory continues in 5.4 when Hostess Quickly and Doll Tearsheet are arrested. This is the categorical end of Falstaff's world. But the play also uses their fate as a test case for Falstaff in the next scene. Here, Falstaff has rushed to London to see the King's coronation. Pistol tells Falstaff that Doll is in prison, and Falstaff, still under the illusion that the laws of England are now at his command, says 'I will deliver her.'[70] But all he gets from his old drinking partner is the claim that as he is 'turned away my former self; So will I those that kept me company'.[71] Falstaff may only approach the King if the King himself returns to his former ways, but 'Till then I banish thee, on pain of death, / As I have done the rest of my misleaders, / Not to come near our person by ten mile.'[72] It appears to give Falstaff some freedom, even if the banishment is one of distance within England (compare Bolingbroke's banishment *from* England). But when Henry V leaves the stage, and Falstaff is left with the Justice, the Justice throws him in the Fleet, presumably until the Coronation is over. It is the final spatial isolation, since all the major players of the Boar's Head are now in jail – Quickly, Doll and Falstaff. They have no part in Henry V's constitution of the new nation.

The casting of the tavern in the role of the state's iniquitous space is also carried out at the meta-dramatic level. In *1 Henry IV* Hal and Falstaff improvise a scene between Hal and the King, his father. The tavern space inverts normal societal relations – it substitutes in miniature the day of misrule – by allowing such role reversals. The joke hovers around the true nature of Hal's and Falstaff's relationship and the nature of Falstaff's character. Just at the point Falstaff is about to defend himself after Hal's onslaught, the tavern is raided. So Falstaff never does get to defend himself. Once cut off, Hal's distancing from him is continued because in the next scene Hal reveals his true, honourable intentions to his father, with no apparent connection to the previous scene. Hal can play other roles but Falstaff is condemned to play himself. Falstaff is rendered insignificant by this juxtaposition of scenes, and so, according to this tetralogy, is an England whose fabric was woven from alehouses, taverns and inns. The tavern space, as we have seen elsewhere, allows for some loosening of social codes, rather as the court jester is licensed to behave in a manner normally circumscribed or prohibited. In the extemporised playing of parts Hal can work out in a fluid and imaginative way his future role, a role that will be 'fixed'. Once fixed, of course, there is again no further need for the place that has provided such a platform for his reign.

Drink without a home

PRINCE JOHN   Fare you well, Falstaff. I, in my condition,
Shall better speak of you than you deserve.

Exeunt all but Falstaff

FALSTAFF   I would you had the wit; 'twere better than your dukedom. Good faith, this same young sober-blooded boy doth not love me, nor a man cannot make him laugh – but that's no marvel, he drinks no wine. There's never none of these demure boys come to any proof, for thin drink doth so over-cool their blood, and making many fish meals, that they fall into a kind of male green-sickness; and then when they marry they get wenches. They are generally fools and cowards – which some of us should be too, but for inflammation. A good sherris-sack hath a twofold operation in it. It ascends me into the brain, dries me there all the foolish and dull and crudy vapours which environ it, makes it apprehensive, quick, forgetive, full of nimble, fiery, and delectable shapes, which delivered o'er to the voice, the tongue, which is the birth, becomes excellent wit. The second property of your excellent sherris is the warming of the blood, which before, cold and settled, left the liver white and pale, which is the badge of pusillanimity and cowardice; but the sherris warms it, and makes it course from the inwards to the parts' extremes. It illumineth the face, which as a beacon, gives

> warning to all the rest of this little kingdom, man, to arm; and then the vital commoners, and inland petty spirits, muster me all to their captain, the heart, who, great and puffed up with this retinue, doth any deed of courage; and this valour comes of sherris. So that the skill in the weapon is nothing without sack, for that sets it a-work, and learning a mere hoard of gold kept by a devil, till sack commences it and sets it in act and use. Hereof comes it that Prince Harry is valiant; for the cold blood he did naturally inherit of his father he hath like lean, sterile, and bare land manured, husbanded, and tilled, with excellent endeavour of drinking good and good store of fertile sherris, that he is become very hot and valiant. If I had a thousand sons, the first human principle I would teach them should be to forswear thin potations, and to addict themselves to sack.[73]

As well as the moulding of the nation's 'time' and 'space' through manipulation of these elements in the Boar's Head, the constitution of the new nation is also played out through 'drink' and its associations. This is seen clearly in the shift between the first part of *Henry IV* and the second part. In *1 Henry IV* the attractions of tavern life are self-evident, but when Hal withdraws from Falstaff and the tavern, Falstaff is forced to stand up for himself. This is not done through the tavern itself, but by Falstaff's defence of the innate qualities of drink in his long eulogy to sack in Gaultree Forest, given in full above. There is a poignancy to Falstaff's speech in this context since it occurs outside his natural tavern habitat. To have a speech where he advocates the significant role of drink in Hal's career in the middle of a battlefield apropos of nothing in particular verges on pathos, and further distances Falstaff from the national glory that his speech here and the tavern's gradual waning in significance within the play makes possible. By taking the speech out of the tavern it is further evidence of the abandonment of the drinking place in the nation's life.

Falstaff is fully aware of the qualities that he needs to claim for a hero: passion, wit, leadership, martial skills, courage and fertility. By drawing on a catalogue of proverbial beliefs in the powers and associations of wine he can stake his claim that sack can provide all these qualities. Hal, he says, has inherited cold blood from his father when it is heat that is required. Falstaff is close to the mark here, for 'cold blood' is an accusation Henry IV makes against himself: 'My blood hath been too cold and temperate, / Unapt to stir at these indignities'.[74] Blood has further significance as 'blood line', since he feels Hal's riotous youth must be punishment for something he himself has done wrong in the past, God's revenge operating through the issue of his own blood,[75] and so again Falstaff's self-serving hymn to sack is close to a proper target. But Falstaff's soliloquy is mainly concerned with the manly qualities of drinking sack, and he claims that youngsters like Prince John are sickly because they do not drink.

Most importantly, '[Prince Harry] hath like lean, sterile, and bare land manured, husbanded, and tilled, with excellent endeavour of drinking good and good store of fertile sherris, that he is become very hot and valiant.' Thus it seems sherris is to be praised in the final analysis for giving Hal his courage. Not only that but the image used is of poor land well tended by drinking, land that would be nothing without it. Falstaff manages to make drink the source of the nation's well-being. But in the eyes of the audience Falstaff condemns himself, confirmed as he is in his own delusion that the tavern life of sack-drinking has saved the nation. What once might have passed as tavern badinage, purely and simply, in this context becomes a last desperate attempt to save the abandoned tavern space. When in *1 Henry IV* Hal needs a pistol from Falstaff, but finds that he has replaced it with a bottle of sack, he throws it at Falstaff and walks away angry.[76] That is the real attitude Hal feels towards Falstaff's drinking-cowardice, although he can later forgive Falstaff when he allows him to lie about a kill. Such generosity on Hal's part is missing in *2 Henry IV*.

But to reiterate, the fact that Falstaff praises drink rather than the tavern diminishes the tavern and the more common life we have seen. The ne'er-do-well elements fighting the good fight in *Henry V* are those we have found in the tavern, but it is precisely that lifestyle Hal, when he is King, asks them to *redeem* by fighting; in other words fighting is redemption when seen from a particular view of the nation, but a dismissal, denial and castigation of the tavern from the point of view of that portion of the nation that frequents drinking places. Thus drinking time and drinking space are here already imbued in the tetralogy with those very values which will be more readily enshrined as *not* in the national interest when it comes to legislating against them.

There is also a change in the symbolic role of drink from that of a catalyst for conviviality in *1 Henry IV* to a means of treachery in *2 Henry IV*. The irony is heightened because Falstaff's praise of sack comes immediately on the heels of the abuse of drinking customs by Prince John, who has just defeated the rebels by asking them to reconcile themselves to Henry IV and the state. He insists that they drink a pledge. Compliant and off their guard, the rebels disperse their forces, only to be arrested. It is further evidence of the rejection of an older England. Even if his audience would not all have been aware that in the annals of English history the Danes were believed to have stabbed the English while they were drinking, hence the need to 'pledge', that is, to stand guard for a friend whilst they drank, Shakespeare certainly knew the significance. In *Timon of Athens* it is alluded to when Apemantus says: 'the fellow that sits next him, now parts bread with him, pledges the breath of him in a divided draught, is the readiest man to kill him: 'thas been proved. If I were a huge man, I should fear to drink at meals, / Lest they should spy my windpipe's dangerous notes.'[77] 'Drink' is also used in a rather deceitful way in *Henry V* by the King himself. A man is under threat of execution for slandering the King whilst drunk. Henry, in what at first appears a return to his drinking roots, argues for clemency, that it was only 'excess of wine that set him on'.[78] But Scroop says that such leniency will breed more of the same, and Cambridge and Grey agree. However, the whole scene has been an exercise in teasing out the opinion of mercy held by these three, so that when Henry reveals them as traitors he can mete out the same kind of mercy they themselves would have shown to the drunken slanderer. They are sent to their deaths (what happens to the railing drunk unfortunately remains a mystery, that is, if he ever existed in the first place. Perhaps Barnardine in *Measure for Measure* signals his reappearance).

The switch in the function of alcohol between the plays is also indicative of the change in tone and dismissal of the fellowship of merrie England. The boisterous good nature of *1 Henry IV* gives way to a more sober attitude in its successor. Falstaff's appeal to drink as a provider of heat to counteract the typical Lancastrian cold blood is one of Falstaff's intuitive bullseyes in which he sees further than he knows. It is precisely when Prince Henry begins to give way to his own cold-bloodedness that Falstaff is shunned. Only cold blood, uninspired by tavern heat, can successfully take charge of the nation. It would seem that *Henry V* manages to restore, at least in part, some of the tradition of an earlier England in 3.5. The (French) Constable doubts that the English can have the constitution for battle since their climate is 'foggy, raw, and dull'.[79] This is followed by a distinction in national drinks and national valour: 'Can sodden water, / A drench for sur-reined jades, their barley broth, / Decoct their cold blood to such valiant heat? / And shall our quick blood, spirited with wine, / Seem frosty?' Thus again the national symbolism of drink comes into play. But this use of national drinking associations and national characteristics, on the back of the two *Henry IV* plays, operates in a curious way. The Constable's speech would ally Falstaff with the French, since the Constable, like Falstaff, believes wine (here the French national drink) to be a giver of heat. This is in contrast to English ale, which is consistent with a cold constitution. Henry's victory is thus a victory of ale over wine, England over France, and Lancastrian cold blood over Falstaffian sanguinity. The supposed victory of ale in this interpretation does not necessarily imply a rehabilitation of the tavern, since, as already mentioned, *Henry V* displaces the national space and removes the tavern. The oppositional codings of national drinks are united when England is reconciled to France and the latter will now have the time to attend to its vineyards.[80] But this is a new vision of England, in keeping with a more mature, sober, disciplined, less riotous outlook, rather than a desire to reclaim or incorporate the 'Falstaffian state'.

Notes

1. 'For Keepers of Alehouses and Tiplinghouses to be bound by Recognisance', 5 & 6 Edw. VI, c. 25 (1552).
2. 5 & 6 Edw. VI, c. 25.
3. 6 Edw. VI, c. 5.
4. Anthony Fletcher and John Stevenson (eds), *Order and Disorder in Early Modern England* (Cambridge, Cambridge University Press, 1985), p. 3. Also, Christopher Hill, *Reformation to Industrial Revolution: British Economy and Society 1530/1780* (London, Weidenfeld and Nicolson, 1968): 'The sixteenth century saw the integration of English towns into a single national unit, to an extent that was not paralleled on the Continent', p. 13.
5. Peter Clark, *The English Alehouse: A Social History 1200–1830* (Harlow, Longman, 1983), p. 8. In a similar vein, A. E. Richardson and H. Donaldson Eberlein note that: 'The London tavern of the third quarter of the sixteenth century, and likewise the hostelry, had gained a fuller significance', *The English Inn Past and Present: A Review of its History and Social Life* (London, Batsford, 1925), p. 101.
6. 'Shakespeare makes constant reference to the inns of the fifteenth century; he drew on the inns and inn life of his own time for details and incidents', and although Shakespeare's description of the inn yard at Rochester refers to 1402, it 'has evidently been drawn by the poet from life', Richardson and Eberlein, *Inn*, p. 75 and p. 101.
7. Shakespeare is doing what David Gervais argues was typical of the Victorians, a present England is being constructed by using another historical period, *Literary Englands: Versions of 'Englishness' in Modern Writing* (Cambridge, Cambridge University Press, 1993), p. 7.
8. Clark, *Alehouse*, p. 166.
9. 'highway robbers operating at Gadshill in north Kent during the 1590s stayed at several tippling houses in the area', *ibid.*, p. 146. There is also the more general context of the 1590s being a rather tense period, with the problem of social order predominant.
10. Nigel Wood's introduction to *Henry IV Parts One and Two* gives a good discussion of the role of 'time' in the plays (Buckingham, Open University Press, 1995, pp. 1–34); and Davison's introduction to *2 Henry IV* (London, Penguin, 1977) deals with 'time' in relation to the aged characters in that play, pp. 36–7.
11. William Shakespeare, *Richard II (King Richard the Second)*, ed. Stanley Wells (London, Penguin, 1969 [1595]), 5.5.49–51.
12. William Shakespeare, *1 Henry IV*, ed. P. H. Davison (London, Penguin, 1968 [1597]), 1.2.1–12.
13. Shakespeare, *Richard II*, 5.5.47 and 5.5.57–8.
14. 1 Jac. I, c. 9.
15. Quoted in Clark, *Alehouse*, p. 111, who also notes 'One cannot believe that more than a few of the unemployed enjoyed their enforced, penurious idleness.'
16. Shakespeare, *1 Henry IV*, 1.2.6, and Davison's note, 'Night is Falstaff's time, not day'.
17. 1 Thessalonians 5.5–8.
18. Davison's note to the setting of 1.2.

19 Hotspur's idealism parallels Hal's cynicism through the same phrase when he berates his father for the usurpation of Richard II: 'yet time serves wherein you may redeem / Your banished honours...', *1 Henry IV*, 1.3.178–9.
20 William Shakespeare, *2 Henry IV*, ed. P. H. Davidson (London, Penguin, 1977 [1598]), 2.2.141–2.
21 Thompson quoted in Fletcher and Stevenson, *Order*, p. 6.
22 Nicholas Dorn, *Alcohol, Youth and the State* (London, Croom Helm, 1983), p. 35.
23 John Kerrigan (ed.), *William Shakespeare, 'The Sonnets' and 'A Lover's Complaint'* (Harmondsworth, Penguin, 1986), p. 34. Thanks to Alison Findlay for drawing my attention to this essay. General studies on the social and cultural impact of clock time on western civilisation can be found in Carlo M. Cippola, *Clocks and Culture 1300–1700* (London, Collins, 1967) and David S. Landes, *Revolution in Time: Clocks and the Making of the Modern World* (Cambridge, Massachusetts, Harvard University Press, 1983). For 'time' in the Middle Ages see the work of Jacques Le Goff, *Time, Work and Culture in the Middle Ages* (Chicago, University of Chicago Press, 1980), and Jean Leclerq 'Experience and Interpretation of Time in the Early Middle Ages', in *Studies in Medieval Culture*, vol. 5, ed. John R. Sommerfeldt, Larry Syndergaard and E. Rozanne Elder (Western Michigan University, 1975), pp. 9–19. Nigel Thrift's '*Vivis voco*: Ringing the Changes in the Historical Geography of Time Consciousness' brings much of this material together in a useful, if densely theoretical manner, in *Spatial Formations* (London, Sage, 1996), ch. 5, pp. 169–212.
24 Kerrigan, *Sonnets*, pp. 34–5.
25 *Ibid.*, pp. 35–6. Also see Hill, *Reformation*: 'The problem was to establish a regular rhythm of labour (abolition of saints' days, emphasis on the Sabbath rest, establishment of regular meal-times). The importance of this regularity, and of saving time, seems to have been accepted by the middle class during the seventeenth century. An alarm clock appears in a poem of 1654. But the lower classes were more resistant,' p. 77.
26 Shakespeare, *1 Henry IV*, 1.2.7–8.
27 Implicitly, this would be Catholic 'time', and festivities such as Saints' Days.
28 Fletcher and Stevenson, *Order*, p. 13.
29 E. P. Thompson, 'Time, Work-Discipline and Industrial Capitalism', *Past and Present*, 35 (1967).
30 See Max Weber's *The Protestant Ethic and the Spirit of Capitalism*, Introduction by Anthony Giddens (London, George Allen and Unwin, 1976 [1930]). This notion of 'calling' has been criticised as not especially a characteristic of Protestantism, as Giddens notes in his Introduction, p. 11. However, the idea is evidently necessary for capitalism at this stage, regardless of which way round we view the causal connection between capitalism and Protestantism.
31 William Shakespeare, *Henry V*, ed. A. R. Humphries (London, Penguin, 1968 [1599]), 4.3.60–7.
32 Shakespeare, *2 Henry IV*, 1.2.150–2.
33 Shakespeare, *Henry V*, 3.2.11–12.
34 Shakespeare, *1 Henry IV*, 3.3.203, and see Davison's gloss on the various interpretations of 'drum'.
35 Shakespeare, *2 Henry IV*, 2.4.352–61.

36 Richardson and Eberlein, *Inn*, p. 11.
37 Shakespeare, *Richard II*, 2.1.95–6.
38 Shakespeare, *1 Henry IV*, 1.1.1–2.
39 Shakespeare, *2 Henry IV*, 4.1.54–8.
40 Shakespeare, *2 Henry IV*, 5.2.134–7.
41 See Peter Womack's gloss on this circular debate in response to Nigel Wood, in Wood, *Henry IV*, pp. 160–1, supplementary material to Womack's essay 'Henry IV and Epic Theatre', pp. 126–61.
42 Andrew Hadfield, *Literature, Politics and National Identity: Reformation to Renaissance* (Cambridge, Cambridge University Press, 1994), p. 3.
43 Shakespeare, *1 Henry IV*, 1.2.56–67.
44 As summarised by Fletcher and Stevenson, *Order*, p. 36.
45 Shakespeare, *2 Henry IV*, 2.2.139–41.
46 Shakespeare, *1 Henry IV*, 1.2.39–40.
47 Clark, *Alehouse*, p. 5.
48 Shakespeare, *1 Henry IV*, 1.2.124–5.
49 Hal's speech over the dead Hotspur, *ibid.*, 5.4.88–91.
50 Such an interpretation is compatible with Mark Taylor's idea that Falstaff's tavern represents a withdrawal from public space, in 'Falstaff and the Origins of Private Life', *Shakespeare Yearbook* (1992), 63–83.
51 Shakespeare, *1 Henry IV*, 2.4.474–510.
52 Clark, *Alehouse*, pp. 8, 9 and 11.
53 *Ibid.*, p. 13.
54 *Ibid.*, p. 10.
55 Robert Ashton, 'Popular Entertainment and Social Control in Later Elizabethan and Early Stuart London', *London Journal*, 9 (1983), 10.
56 Shakespeare, *1 Henry IV*, 2.1.79–84.
57 *Ibid.*, 2.2.51–5.
58 Alison Findlay, 'Theatres of Truth: Drinking and Drama in Early Modern England.' Paper delivered to English Staff Seminar, Sheffield Hallam University, 1996, p. 2, including quotation from Earle.
59 *Ibid.*
60 Shakespeare, *1 Henry IV*, 2.4.4–6.
61 *Ibid.*, 2.1, opening.
62 As Davison argues, *ibid.* Similarly, Angelo in *Measure for Measure* seeks to eliminate the stews of Vienna.
63 This may also explain why the tavern in *2 Henry IV* is more realistic, since it is about to be condemned, and why Quickly and Tearsheet have to be removed as part of this social control, since bawdiness and drinking were usually linked.
64 See Fletcher and Stevenson, *Order*, p. 4.
65 Shakespeare, *Henry V*, 2.1.
66 *Ibid.*, 1.2.267–73.
67 *Ibid.*, 2.4.25–8.
68 The comparison of Henry V to Alexander the Great is in *ibid.*, 4.7.11–49.
69 Shakespeare, *2 Henry IV*, 5.3.133–6.
70 *Ibid.*, 5.5.39.
71 *Ibid.*, 5.5.61–2.
72 *Ibid.*, 5.5.66–8.

73 *Ibid.*, 4.3.85–122.
74 Shakespeare, *1 Henry IV*, 1.3.1–2.
75 *Ibid.*, 3.2.4–11.
76 *Ibid.*, 5.3.54–5.
77 William Shakespeare, *Timon of Athens*, ed. J. C. Maxwell (Cambridge, Cambridge University Press, 1968), 1.2.45–50.
78 Shakespeare, *Henry V*, 2.2.42.
79 *Ibid.*, 3.5.15–16.
80 *Ibid.*, 5.2.41.

4

Wonderfull yeares

Amongst the inns and taverns frequented by Shakspere may be mentioned the Falcon Tavern, by the Bankside, which was the place of meeting of the mighty poets and wits of the Elizabethan age – of Shakspere, Ben Jonson, Marlowe, Massinger, Ford, Beaumont, Fletcher, Drayton, Herrick, and a host of lesser names. An assemblage, indeed, unique in any country or in any age! Here took place those 'wit combats,' of which Fuller speaks, between Shakspere and Ben Jonson, 'which two I behold like a Spanish great galleon, and an English man-of-war; Master Jonson (like the former) was built far higher in learning; solid, but slow, in his performances. Shakspere, like the English man-of-war, lesser in bulk, but lighter in sailing, could turn with all tides, tack about, and take advantage of all winds by the quickness of his wit and invention.'[1]

Minor examples elsewhere in Shakespeare illustrate the heightened importance of the control of drinking places in the late sixteenth century and early seventeenth century. *Twelfth Night* (*c*. 1600) is particularly apt because Malvolio is presented as a Puritan. Toby, Maria, Andrew and Feste are sufficiently rowdy to attract his rebuke: 'My masters, are you mad? Or what are you? Have you no wit, manners, nor honesty, but to gabble like tinkers at this time of night? Do ye make an alehouse of my lady's house, that ye squeak out your cozier's catches without any mitigation or remorse of voice? Is there no respect of place, persons, nor time in you?'[2] It is the type of complaint that is both implicit and explicit against Falstaff, who openly flaunts all received notions of what is acceptable behaviour. Famously in *Twelfth Night*, Toby goes on to respond to Malvolio's attempt to suppress their enjoyment in terms which are distinctly anti-Puritan: 'Dost thou think, because thou art virtuous, there shall be no more cakes and ale?'[3] A short while later Maria confirms that Malvolio is indeed of the Puritan caste: 'Marry, sir, sometimes he is a kind of Puritan.'[4] The play manipulates its audience into approval of the harsh treatment that Malvolio receives whilst in prison, and thus appears to side with good-natured revelry. But again, there is no simple reading of the role of drink and conviviality, as if *Twelfth Night* were a comedic antidote to the discussions of the last chapter. In place of Falstaff, merrie England is suggested by the significance of 'Twelfth Night' cake-and-ale festivities, but it does not receive any kind of untempered endorsement. Feste, asked by Olivia to describe what a drunken man is like, replies 'Like a drowned man, a fool, and a madman. One draught above heat makes him a fool, the second mads him, and a third drowns him;'[5] the sottish Toby is drawn into uttering 'I hate a drunken rogue',[6] and both Andrew and Toby are made to appear foolish in their drunkenness, much as drunkenness is shown in *The Tempest*. A joke on the drunken hypocrite is better delivered in *The Merry Wives of Windsor* when Slender proclaims: 'I'll ne'er be drunk, whilst I live, again, but in honest, civil, godly company, for this trick. If I be drunk, I'll be drunk with those that have the fear of God, and not with drunken knaves.'[7] That it takes drink to undo the stalwart Cassio in *Othello* is a sign, if taken across the range of Shakespeare's work, that drink, at its worst, is a treacherous thing. Drugged nightcaps cause Duncan's guards to fall asleep in *Macbeth*. Drink in various forms is thus also a useful device for furthering the plot.

In *Measure for Measure* (1604) 'Vienna' is a thinly veiled London at the beginning of James I's reign, with an intriguing exposition of the problem that monarch faced in his attempt to impose law and order on the stews and taverns of the capital.[8] Leinwand argues that Barnardine's refusal to be executed is where 'the higher and lower orders reach an impasse over drink, and to some extent, over sexuality. But in this instance, it is the lower orders who refuse to negotiate.'[9] This could be a comic representation of those who now reject the control-by-consent of former years in favour of control-by-imposition. What do you do when the drunken populace simply refuses to play the new game? For *The Tempest*, Leinwand argues that 'Drunkenness propels Caliban, and Stephano and Trinculo, to both insurrection and to the assertion of order' – 'The point is not that Stephano and Prospero are identical; rather the drunken butler and his foolish and deformed coconspirators at once mimic and unnerve their master',[10] but surely drunkenness and state control is nothing more than an entertaining side issue, with Stephano dreaming of a land to call his own when hopelessly intoxicated. There is no serious threat here, and no serious issue. Leinwand's 'alehouse dynamic', whereby high and low are brought together in social confrontation, I think does not stretch this far. But these cullings from Shakespeare all stand as rather perfunctory, if entertaining, examples.

The Taming of the Shrew provides more substantial matter. The play opens in an inn or tavern,[11] and its function is both structural and symbolic, as it is in the *Henry IV* and *Henry V* plays discussed in the last chapter. The hostess tries to evict Sly, a tinker, from her hostelry, but, after some raillery, he instead falls asleep. The social distinctions come into play in ways we are already familiar with: for instance, he cannot be a man of substance because he does not drink wine. But the tavern may also be working once more at the meta-dramatic level. As with 2.4 in *1 Henry IV*, the tavern allows for a play-within-a-play, although this time the audience (Sly) is physically removed from the tavern to a private house. There may have been a meta-dramatic joke with Hal's and Falstaff's play extempore, since their play was acted in a tavern, and inn courtyards were once the natural homes of plays. So their play in miniature is enacted in the older theatrical environment (or maybe even the suggestion of a debased space, since this is a tavern rather than an inn), which in the wider context has seceded its ground to a specifically built theatre. It is as if this movement between play-in-the-tavern and play-in-the-theatre replays the movement from the medieval space to a modernised space, and thus from merrie England to post-Reformation England (although the theatre, like the tavern, had its own problems with authority). The meta-dramatic joke in *The Taming of the Shrew* might also be a comment on mirrored spaces: the rougher tavern environment is deemed unsuitable for a more elevated entertainment, so Sly is removed. But the joke might also be the typical opposition of tavern/alehouse versus domestic scene beloved by ballads.[12] This is more in keeping with the play's battle-of-the-sexes theme. The hostess is 'shrewish' in her attack on Sly, and his drink-induced dream functions as an escape from her, just as the drinking place was generally understood to function as an escape from the family home. The opposition between tavern space and domestic space is even more explicit in the related (anonymous, but possibly Shakespeare's) play *The Taming of a Shrew*.[13] The frame is completed when we see Sly wake up. He believes his dream has shown him the way to tame a shrew, and so he intends to go home and do just that – the power of 'tavern' space to be imposed upon that of 'domestic' space.

The Taming of the Shrew has other features which draw upon the complex of drinking-place associations. In 'Induction 1' Sly insists to the hostess, who attempts to evict him from her establishment, that he is not a rogue because he came over with 'Richard Conqueror'. The hostess threatens to remedy the situation by calling in the law. Thus issues of legality, order and drunkenness are immediately to the fore, along with competing images of what constitutes respectable Englishness. That Sly has been rowdy is shown by his refusal to pay for the glasses. The Lord and Huntsmen arrive, automatically introducing the theme of social distinctions which we have seen before. But the play as a whole might be seen as an extended metaphor on the idea that to be drunk is to be as good as a king, and/or 'as drunk as a lord', although, more precisely, since Sly is the butt of the aristocracy, a subversion of the commonplace. In any case, Sly is carried off asleep to the Lord's abode.

He reappears in 'Induction 2'. His first words (presumably on waking) are 'For God's sake, a pot of small ale!', which, for the literary-minded, trails memories of Gluttony's first words on awaking after his mammoth sleep at Betty's alehouse in *Piers the Plowman*. They offer Sly sack, which he says he has never drunk in his life, since sack is only fit for lords. Amusingly, Sly sticks up for his position as 'tinker': 'Ask Marian Hacket, the fat alewife of Wincot, if she know me not. If she say I am not fourteen pence on the score for sheer ale, score me up for the lying'st knave in Christendom.'[14] Of course, there is a comic reversal, since previously Sly was arguing for his noble lineage, but with his sanity under threat he holds fast to the sure knowledge that he is lowly. However, they convince him that he is a lord, although he continues to ask 'once again a pot o'th' smallest ale'. He is now speaking in verse rather than prose, as if he genuinely has become, on some level, lordly. They continue the deception, say that he has slept for fifteen years, occasionally speaking some idle words. Part of this idle muttering has been against the hostess, who he has accused of deceitful practices, another reference in our literary history to cheating alewives.

The play that is acted out for Sly has a number of interesting parallels with the material in the Inductions, although how deliberate or casual they may be is open to debate. In the opening scene, Lucentio has come to Padua seeking an education. He asks his man Tranio his opinion of this plan. Tranio's response is that he should not let such studies be at the expense of pleasure (that Aristotle should not oust Ovid) – 'No profit grows where is no pleasure ta'en'.[15] This is an obvious irony, since we have just seen the pitfalls of 'pleasure' in the fate of Sly. Other parallels emerge as the play unfolds, the most commanding of which is the idea that Petruccio is Sly's alter ego. Given the frame's return in *A Shrew*, it has been deemed most plausible that Shakespeare's play likewise had a frame return. If Sly is thus apprised of how to treat a shrew, the frame itself makes Petruccio the imagined version of Sly. But the parallels occur in many other instances. In 3.2 Petruccio is about to marry Kate, but turns up in shoddy clothes, with a direct echo of Sly's own transformation (in the opposite social direction) from tinker to lord. In 3.3 we learn of Petruccio's behaviour at his marriage to Kate. Petruccio has hit the priest, sworn at him, drunk off some wine and thrown the sops in the sexton's face, all evidence of alehouse behaviour. And since the Hostess in the Induction may be described as shrewish, she compares directly with Kate.

In *The Taming of a Shrew* (1594) it is a (male) Tapster who evicts Sly, rather than a hostess, so a conflict between the sexes is not so quickly signalled. But the main difference in comparison between the two versions that have come down to us is that the anonymous play has more of the meta-dramatic.[16] Through Sly's interruptions of the play-within-a-play the audience can enjoy jokes at Sly's expense. At line 47 he asks 'Is there not a fool in the play?' to which the Lord says, 'Yes, my lord'. Stephen Roy Miller glosses the Lord's confirmation as a reference by him to Sanders, who is about to play the fool. However, this might also refer to Sly, since if delivered correctly 'Yes, my Lord' might easily imply Sly himself, operating at the meta-dramatic level. This would then set up a running joke, as in Sly 'Interlude 1' (end of scene 3), where Sly's fascination with the fool continues and the Lord can easily make 'fool' work on the two levels:

SLY Sim, when will the fool come again?
LORD He'll come again, my lord, anon.
SLY Gi's some more drink here. Souns, where's the tapster?[17]

Sly's request for 'more drink' is the fool's immediate 'coming again'. The next 'interlude' is along similar lines – 'Look Sim, the fool is come again now!' which can refer both to Sanders' arrival and Sly's interruption.[18]

The language and sub-plot of *The Taming of a Shrew* may be simplified in comparison to Shakespeare's play,[19] but Sly's frame-breaking creates a continuous, foregrounded meta-dramatic interest that, by comparison, is diminished in *The Shrew*. (The meta-dramatic nature of *A Shrew* is most obvious when it is named as the play to be performed for Sly's benefit,[20] so that the play the audience watches is in fact a play within the play.) In the third frame-breaking interlude Sly objects to a proposed imprisonment for no apparent reason, showing to his audience (us) that his grasp of drama is tenuous throughout. His own disreputable behaviour is again put in relief because once he knows that the couple have escaped prison by running away, he calls for more drink.[21] However, somewhat curiously, he falls asleep, yet the play goes on. Again this is a meta-dramatic moment, since the play, ostensibly performed to fool Sly, continues without him as the audience. The Duke's opening words at this juncture, 'Ah treacherous boy', could have a double reference, taking the audience from Sly's sleeping treachery to the Duke's son. But at this point what is the purpose of the performance if Sly is asleep? It perhaps focuses attention on Sly's significant relationship to the play he is (not) watching. The fourth interlude shows that the Lord recognises Sly's inattention (although we do not know if he has only just realised this or has been aware throughout the scene) and Sly is carried back to the alehouse.[22] The meta-drama becomes even more interesting now since the play enacted within the Lord's private house is at this point twice removed from its putative audience: not only is Sly sleeping through the play, he is not even in its vicinity. When he reappears in his own dress, he is awakened by the Tapster. His first words are familiar, although transformed into the more noble vinous context: 'Sim, gi's some more wine. What's all the players gone? / Am not I a lord?'[23] The meta-frame jokes on the idea that all the real actors have gone, leaving only the Tapster and Sly. The idea that a play is some equivalent to a drunken imagining is completed (compare Hal and Falstaff's play extempore). That the Tapster offers to walk home with Sly and 'hear the rest that thou hast dreamt tonight' is a comic idea, since we are in danger of hearing or witnessing the whole performance again.[24]

Yet despite these other manifestations, Falstaff and the Boar's Head Tavern remain Shakespeare's most concerted and vivid representation of the English drinking place and the place of drink within English culture. It juggles diverse contexts and voices, and it might seem that with such a broad canvas he captures the English drinking place and its cultural cachet fairly comprehensively. Other dramatic representations are cameos in comparison. In John Marston's *The Dutch Courtesan* (1605) Mulligrub is greeted as the stock, cheating landlord: 'Nay, comfort, my good host Shark, my good Mulligrub',[25] and supplemented with 'most hardly-honest Mulligrub' and 'my most sharking Mulligrub'. On the other hand, we have the description of the idyllic Bell Inn at Waltham in Beaumont and Fletcher's *The Knight of the Burning Pestle* (1607). The food is plentiful, prepared by the host's own lady; the chamberlain prepares beds with 'snowy sheets'; the tapster fills the pots without the aid of froth; and the hostler is honest.[26] But this knight, this English Don Quixote, mistakes the inn for a castle, a motif we shall return to in later chapters. Philip Massinger's *A New Way to Pay Old Debts* (1625), like *The Dutch Courtesan*, opens with abuse directed at the keeper of a drinking establishment, Tapwell. But Tapwell's replies to the dissolute 'gentleman' are in language less polite. The play warrants mention because in Sir Giles Overreach – 'a cruel extortioner' – is a portrayal of the real-life abuser of the monopoly on drinking-house licences. Sir Giles Mompesson was granted the patent to license inns in 1618. Until then inns could only be dealt with by the law for inconvenience. But Mompesson was entitled to half the money for each licence issued, and within four years he had given out twelve hundred. He was impeached and banished in 1621, with 'much rejoicing' in the House of Lords, who 'resolved that the 26 March should be a sermon day for ever throughout England in appreciation of the punishment meted out by the King to the patentee'.[27]

Into the ordinary

> this *London* hath within the memory of man lost much of hir pristine lustre, and renowne, by being pestered and filled with many great and crying sinnes, which were first hatched, and are ever since fostered and maintained in Play-houses, Ale-houses Bawdy-houses, dicing-houses otherwise stiled Ordinaries.[28]

Some of the most interesting material is to be found in those writers whose credentials are usually taken to be a few degrees lower than those of Shakespeare and Jonson, but in *The Pub in Literature* receive more credit, some simply for their subject matter, others for both subject matter and literary sparkle. Their milieu is given in the description of A. V. Judges' *The Elizabethan Underworld* – 'A Collection of Tudor and early Stuart tracts and ballads telling of the lives and misdoings of vagabonds, thieves, rogues and cozeners, and giving some account of the operation of the criminal law' – and much of the best work is to be found in this book. It begins with Robert Copland's 'The Highway to the Spital-House' (1535–36). The 'spital' is the hospital where many people 'of very poor estate' turn up for shelter and respite. Copland is eager to know on what grounds some are taken and some rejected. The Porter maintains that only the truly needy are admitted. The Porter is asked to describe all the types of people that come to him. Amongst them are:

> Rufflers and masterless men that cannot work,
>   And sleepeth by day, and walketh in the dark,
> And with delicates gladly doth feed,
>   Swearing and cracking – an easy life to lead!-
> With common women daily for to haunt,
>   Making revel, and drink adieu taunt,
> Saying, 'Make we merry as long as we can,
>   And drink apace; the Devil pay the maltman!
> Wine was not made for every haskard,
>   But beer and ale for every dastard.'
> And when their money is gone and spent,
>   Then this way is most convenient.
>
> Taverners that keep bawdry and polling,
>   Marring wine with brewing and rolling;
> Innholders that lodge whores and thieves,
>   Seldom their getting anyway proves,
> So by reason their gains be geason,
>   This way they run many a season.
>
> Bakers and brewers, that with musty grain
>   Serve their customers, must take it again,
> And many times have they no utterance,
>   For their weights and measures is of no substance
> And lose both their credence and good,
>   Come this way by all likelihood
> For they do infect what should be man's food.[29]

The complaint by officialdom is similar to those we have already observed – the common herd waste time and money drinking, here with little distinction between male and female revelry. What is perhaps new is the context of 'provision' for these despised orders. Although there had always been wariness of the 'sturdy beggar', the person who would rather claim alms than work, the problem is now recognisable as of sizeable proportion within a city. We are starting to move to the urban environment and associated difficulties. It is not so much the moral failing of the disreputable masses that is at issue, that they are not attending church or that by frequenting the 'devil's church' they reveal themselves as godless, but that they are a secular, social problem.

If we return directly to the tavern, then we see yet another new manifestation in the sixteenth century, already glimpsed above – that the drinking place is a site for innocent gallants (gulls, coneys) who provide rich pickings for their corrupted social equals or for rogues (cozeners) of lesser social status. The opening salvo is fired by Thomas Harman's *A Caveat for*

Common Cursitors, Vulgarly called Vagabonds (1566), a manual on the tricks of the trade which set the trend for such literature up until the Civil War. Although this work is confined to the lower orders, it nevertheless proved the standard for other warnings.

In the chapter 'A Rogue' it is the alehouse which provides the dangerous ground for these beggars. Two tricksters find themselves drinking at an alehouse with a parson. When the parson has left, they pass themselves off as brothers and the long lost nephews of the parson of the parish, who is also their godfather, and con the hostess into giving them information about his house and other details. They go there and lament pitiably outside the house. Finally he opens the window to give them alms. They grab his hand and force him to give them all the money. After he insists it is all he has: '"Well," quoth they, "Master Parson, if you have no more, upon this condition we will take off the lock, that you will drink twelve pence for our sakes to-morrow at the ale-house where we found you, and thank the good wife for the good cheer she made us."' He promises faithfully he will do so. He goes there the next day, and the hostess bids him drink. She advises him not to tell the story of how they gained entrance, otherwise he will be the laughing stock of the village. Even though a guide against beggars, there is something good-natured in their final demand that he return to the alehouse to drink some more, a repayment for the alewife's unwitting kindness. Her advice to keep the story quiet is also of a piece, hinting at a close community bound by such codes and the power of narrative to shame.

Dekker, from whose 'plays and pamphlets may be learnt more about contemporary life in London than any other of the Elizabethan men of letters' according to Judges, had great success with *The Bellman of London* (1608). It provoked counterblasts from an author, S. R., within the same year, including the charge that Dekker had done nothing more than plagiarise Harman's *Caveat* from forty years previous, a charge which had some basis, though not enough to detract from *The Bellman*'s originality elsewhere. He is dubbed 'the true heir of Apollo'[30] by another writer of the period for this work. In the follow-up volume, *Lantern and Candlelight or the Bellman's Second Walk* (1608), a work also devised to bring to light all the iniquities of present-day London, a messenger is sent forth from hell to the capital to find out suitable customers.[31] He is told:

> Haunt taverns, there thou shalt find prodigals. Pay thy twopence to a player; in his gallery mayest thou sit by a harlot. At ordinaries mayest thou dine with silken fools. When the day steals out of the world, thou shalt meet rich drunkards under welted gowns search for threescore in the hundred. Hug those golden villains, they shine bright, and will make a good show in Hell. Shriek with a cricket in the brewhouse, and watch how they conjure there.[32]

There is a clear overlap with taverns we have already seen in that they are the site of lewdness and prodigality, but the idea of 'rich drunkards' haunting the taverns is a sign of things to come rather than of things past. Falstaff is dissolute nobility, but here we see that catch-all title of 'gentleman' coming into play, men who ranged from sons of aristocrats living off future entitlements, real and imagined, or present allowances that would not support the highest of lives, or the sons of wealthy middling classes with nothing but appearances to sustain them and be sustained. Such is the substance of Dekker's next chapter, 'Gull-Groping', which begins with a section on 'How gentlemen are cheated at ordinaries', and here Dekker is describing a social set that we shall see haunting the drinking place well into the eighteenth century. It provides new comic and moral material for chroniclers of taverns and inns.

Introduced by the comedian Richard Tarleton in 1560,[33] the 'ordinary' in its most common usage (as described here by Dekker) was a type of open buffet where the customer could eat as much as he wanted for a fixed price.[34] A room in an inn or tavern might therefore be the ordinary, that is, it would serve this type of meal. The attraction was its cheapness. Hence came the gull-groper, that is, the rogue who will catch the 'gull', the young, innocent gallant, newly arrived in town. The gull-groper, who is a somewhat older gallant living off his wits, 'comes to an ordinary to save charges of housekeeping, and will eat for his two shillings more meat than will serve three of the guard at dinner, yet swears he comes thither only for the company, and to converse with travellers'.[35] The trick is to lend money to the gallant who is luckless at dice, later reclaiming the money at an extortionate rate. The gull-groper thus beggars the younger gallants so that he can maintain his own fashionable lifestyle: 'And thus are young heirs cozened out of their acres, before they well know where they lie.'[36]

The cozening signifies more than just a disreputable trick practised on a few luckless innocents looking for excitement. The state of the nation was a theme that Dekker always had before him, and this behaviour threatens its health, as he puts rather obviously: 'Vices in a common-wealth are as diseases in a body; if quickly they be not cured, they suddenly kill. They are Weedes in the fayrest Garden, if eare they take roote, you pull them not up, they spoyle the wholesome Hearbes and Flowers, and turne the Ground into a Wildernesse.'[37] Whilst the gallants are those most directly involved, others might be drawn in as well. In *The Dead Tearme* (1608) Dekker imagines a dialogue between the cities of Westminster and London – the nation's centre on which all rests – in which they point up each other's sins and bemoan their own ills. Much of the imagery plays on the importance of the sitting of court sessions (the terms), hence the 'dead term' can be something like 'fasting' for Westminster, whereas term times are more akin to continual feasting. The Steeple of St Paul endorses the prevailing views: 'What whispering is there in Terme times, how by some slight to cheat the poore country Clients of his full purse that is stucke under his girdle? What plots are layd to furnish young gallants with readie money (which is shared afterwards at a Tavern) therby to disfurnish him of his patrimony?'[38]

In *The Guls Horne-booke* (1609)[39] Dekker once more, with his brand of mock-seriousness, appears to associate the future of the nation with the plight of gulls as it opens with a dedication 'To all Guls in generall, wealth and Liberty'. For which patrons could it be better to dedicate the book than to those whose 'hands are ever open, your purses never shut'? He has devised a horn-book (a child's primer) because: 'I know that most of you (O admirable *Guls*!) can neither write nor reade.' Dekker proceeds to instruct the Gallant in the art of dressing and swaggering. The Gull is even told how to warm himself by the fire in the morning, 'by sitting in that hot-house of the chimney, thou feelest the fat dew of thy body (like basting) run trickling down thy sides: for by that meanes thou maist lawfully boast, that thou livest by the sweat of thy browes'.[40] And of course, no guide would be complete without instruction on how to make the most of the ordinary and the tavern. Of the former, Dekker advises: 'First, having diligently enquired out an Ordinary of the largest reckoning, whither most of your Courtly Gallants do resort, let it be your use to repair thither some halfe houre after eleven; for then you shall find most of your fashion-mongers planted in the roome waiting for meate.'[41] Then the Gull must know how to make his entrance: 'Being arrived in the roome, salute not any but those of your acquaintance: walke up and downe by the rest as scornfully and as carelesly as a Gentleman-Usher', and what conversation to employ: 'If you be a Courtier, discourse of the obtaining of Suits: of your mistresses favours, etc.'[42] The Gallant should smoke ostentatiously, and when the 'Knight is upon his stewed mutton' he tells the Gull that he should be 'in the bosome of your goose'. During dinner the gull may 'aske for a close-toole' (commode), remembering to take a friend along for company 'as you sit in that withdrawing-chamber'. On returning to the food, remember 'to ask what Pamphlets or poems a man might think fittest to wipe his taile with'.[43] Fine advice.

William Fennor's *The Counter's Commonwealth or A Voyage Made to an Infernal Island* (1617) also describes the fashionable times, but from his place within the Counter, that is, the debtor's prison. Whereas Dekker offers his work up 'to the nation', Fennor more circumspectly offers it up to those who, like himself, are most likely to make their way straight from the ordinary to gaol. Gallants are the main focus, but Fennor shows them drawn from a number of different sources: 'To all cashiered captains, or other inferior officers, heedless and headless young gentleman, especially elder brothers, forsaken serving-men, roaring boys, broken citizens, country clients, or any other of what art of fashion soever that shall by chance, rather mischance, be unresistably encountered, and so become tenants against their will, within the territories of this ensuing commonwealth, greeting and meeting – rather at an ordinary than here.'[44] It is aimed at 'young heirs', to keep them out of the gins of others who were like themselves but are now in reduced circumstances and forced to prey on their own. With tracts like these reflecting upon as well as creating an image of London (and therefore the nation) as one of a Sodom and Gomorrah, with its future inheritors in hock, no wonder there was a flurry of legislative activity during the early years of James I to put down all manner of drinking places, from tippling-houses to stews.

'Then *Bacchus* drinkes not in gilt-bowles, but sculls'

We might return to Dekker via a return to *The Taming of the Shrew*. At first glance it is no more than a standard remark when the Lord sees Sly asleep and says 'What's here? One dead, or drunk?' Just as the symptoms of madness and drunkenness were accounted indistinguishable on occasion, so the sleep that followed drunkenness could easily be reckoned as death. Again, when the Lord continues 'O monstrous beast! How like a swine he lies. / Grim death, how foul and loathsome is thine image. / Sirs, I will practise on this drunken man' it might seem that we have no more than another common image, that men who are drunk take on the appearance of bestiality, and 'swine' suggests one of the categories of animal-states associated with drunkenness (as well as a humour category – 'melancholy'). But the second part, 'Grim death', is a different figure, out of proportion to common sentiment that drunkenness disfigures, as if it is the Lord's personal reaction to mortality. The threat to 'practise' on the man might therefore be a punishment both for Sly's drunkenness and for his role as a *memento mori*.

What we might have is a casual return to the connection between drunkenness, death and plague first witnessed in Chaucer's 'The Pardoner's Tale'. Admittedly, the evidence is slight, but the Lord's disproportionate horror at the vision of death Sly represents appears to resurface at the end of *A Shrew*. When Sly asks 'Am not I a lord?' the Tapster replies 'A lord with a murrain!' (that is, a lord with the plague). Is there something about the Lord himself which is 'plaguey'? With the frequent plagues in London and the country as a whole, it would have been natural to fear the plague, but it might also seem that somehow the Lord himself is afflicted. How else could making Sly think himself a Lord be a punishment rather than a pleasant, drunken sojourn, unless the Lord himself were under sufferance?

In Dekker's *The Wonderfull yeare 1603. Wherein is shewed the picture of London, lying sicke of the Plague*,[45] the interlinking of drink, plague, money and death recurs in different guises. The broader context once again is the fate of the nation. In that year the people mourned the death of Elizabeth, celebrated James I's enthronement, the union, and then, to cap it all, another visit from the plague. The combination of elements furnishes Dekker's particular vision of England and its people under stress as they try to come to terms with 'that strange out-landish word *Change*'.[46] It is filtered through

Dekker's mordant wit; in his dedication he says it is his desire to make the recipient laugh: 'because mirth is both *Phisicall*, and wholesome against the *Plague*: with which sicknes (to tell truth) this booke is (though not sorely) yet somewhat infected'.⁴⁷ *The Wonderfull yeare* begins by ushering in Spring, and paints an idyllic vision of England, in town and country: 'But O the short-livde Felicitie of man! O world of what slight and thin stuffe is thy happinesse!'⁴⁸ proclaims Dekker with some relish. He lists the events that make it a year full of wonder:

> As first, to begin with the Quéene's death, then the Kingdomes falling into an Ague upon that. Next, followes the curing of that feaver by the holesome receipt of a proclaymed King. That wonder begat more, for in an houre, two mightie Nations were made one: wilde *Ireland* became tame on the sudden, and some English great ones that before séemed tame, on the sudden turned wilde … And last of all (if that wonder be the last and shut up the yeare) a most dreadfull plague.⁴⁹

After he has described the plague in general terms, he turns to more concrete cases. He tells of the Dutchman who tried to escape the plague by returning to the Low Countries. When he realises that he has been followed there by Death, he drinks off some healths and returns 'to try the strength of English Béere: his old *Randevous* mad men was the place of méeting, where he was no sooner arrived, but the Plagye had him by the backe' and he is forced to return to Bedlam.⁵⁰ Dekker links the allure of English beer with madness and the plague in what makes for a new set of associations. We have seen drink combined with either of the two separately, but here all three are flung together in surreal association.

In a more extended tale Dekker relates a story of a group of people fleeing London, amongst which is a Citizen. When the group sees that their companion has got the plague they leave him with some alacrity, also leaving him to wonder on the fickle nature of friendship. The Citizen returns to an inn where they have previously been. Even then they had been forced 'to stand and drinke some thirtie foote from the doore', a sure sign that English social codes are cracking. But now the house is hastily shut up and the inn, that bastion of English sociability and communality, is the nation's disgrace. If Creighton is right in his assertion that after the Reformation the behaviour of humanity towards plague victims was cast into a testing Christian environment, whereas previously it had been one of accepted indifference,⁵¹ the role of inns and other hostelries would have been paramount as sites of viewing the strength, or otherwise, of Christian virtue:

> mine Hoste and Hostesse ran over one another into the backe-side, the maydes into the Orchard, quivering and quaking, and ready to hang themselves on the innocent Plumb-treés (for hanging to them would not be so sore a death, as the Plague, and to die maides too! O horrible!) As for the Tapster, he fled into the Cellar, rapping out five or six plaine

Country oathes, that hée would drowne himselfe in a most villanous Stand of Ale, if the sicke Londoner stoode at the doore any longer … The dolefull catastrophe of all is, a bed could not be had for all *Babilon*: not a cup of drinke, no, nor cold water be gotten, though it had bin for *Alexander* the great: [if] a draught of *Aqua vitæ* might have saved his soule, the towne denyed to do God that good service.[52]

The suggestion is also that London is infecting the rest of the country as the plague carries with it associations of corruption. Eventually another Londoner turns up to bury his fellow inhabitant, although the only place allowed is in a field, only to die of the plague himself.[53]

The next tale connects drunkenness and the plague in a manner suggestive of one of Dekker's 'merry jests'. A sexton has left a grave open, when at night a drunkard emerges from an alehouse and falls into the pit. Believing himself to have made his way home, he thinks his companions are simply asleep. The sexton returns in the morning, reckoning up how much money he is making: 'for Sextons now had better doings than either Tavernes or bawdy-houses'. Seeing some bones and a skull roundabout he throws them into 'this Coffer of wormes'. One of the skulls wakes up the sleeper, who lets out an oath. The sexton hears the goblin's voice and runs away, chased by the drunk. 'But it appeares the Sexton had the lighter foote, for he ran so faste, that hée ranne out of his wittes, which being left behinde him, he had like to have dyed presently after. / A meryer bargaine than the poore Sextons did a Tincker méete withall in a Countrey Towne; through which a Citizen of *London* being driven.'[54] The Citizen stops at a country alehouse. After the Host has attended to his needs, the guest is left to himself. He drinks a toast to his sick friend in the city, only to keel over himself and die. When the Host returns and sees the man laid out he thinks it evidence that Londoners can't take their ale. Eventually he realises that he is dead of the plague. When the Towne finds out, they see no alternative but to set fire to the alehouse. The Host pleads, but they fear he too now has the plague. The townsfolk decide that the best course of action is to offer forty shillings for the person who will bury the dead man, but no one is willing to do it: 'they loved money well, [but] mary the plague hanging over any mans head that should meddle with it in that sort, they all vowde to dye beggers before it should be Chronicled they kild themselves for forty shillings'. A tinker arrives and he is invited to view the body. The Host offers him a crown if he will bury it, but the tinker insists on payment of ten shillings, which of course the Host is pleased to oblige him with, since he will have saved them thirty shillings. The town pays the tinker, who first fortifies himself with a drink before heaving the body away into a field. He rifles the pockets before he buries him, finds seven pounds there, so on his way back through the town he cries out to see if they have any more Londoners to bury. 'You sée therefore how dreadfull a fellow Death is, making fooles even of wisemen, and cowards of the most valiant.' Dekker proceeds with his moral, that Death removes men's 'power to looke higher than their owne roofes'.⁵⁵ The failure of the country's social centres, inns and alehouses, to provide some form of succour in England's hour of need, is here used by Dekker as a potent symbol of just how 'wonderful' the year is.

End of the season

> You are welcome, welcome all, to the New Inn;
> Though the old house, we hope our cheer will win
> Your acceptation.
>
> Ben Jonson, *The New Inn*

Dekker stands as the poet of his beloved and behated London, and as such represents the prejudices of the city, its self-belief that it is the mother of the nation, that its corruptions, its mores and its wealth affect the whole country. But such a view also ties in with the gradual move from an idea of England as a land of estates, of which the nobles in *1* and *2 Henry IV* and *Henry V* are the inheritors and guardians, to a country with an urban seat of power and its uneasy mix of court and city. The move is also one away from a year based on the seasons to one moving to the rhythms of London – hence Dekker's metaphorical manipulation of law-court sessions in *The Dead Terme* becomes the most appropriate representation of movement from times of plenty to times of scarcity, rather than the agricultural year of sowing and reaping. The death-knell of 'John Barleycorn' – in the sense that people might feel close to the production and consumption of ale and beer – is therefore being tolled. A weariness with the old seasonal frame of mind occurs in Thomas Nashe's *Summer's Last Will* (1592). Will Summers asks – 'What have we to doe with scales, and hower-glasses, except we were Bakers, or Clock-keepers?', which, like the Hal/Falstaff interchange, is redolent of nostalgia for an older, timeless England.

Nashe's play is basically a dialogue between seasons and festivals like harvest and Christmas. Will finds that most of the seasons and festivals are 'a miserable bunch'. As a response he praises indifference to time-keeping in favour of drinking with good fellows. It is only when Bacchus appears that things are brought to life. However, as the play wears on, Will finds that Bacchus urges him to drink too much and he eventually becomes disgusted with the god of drink. Even so, Bacchus manages to dub him a knight, Sir Robert Tosspot, before leaving. Thus the love-hate relationship with drinking and conviviality that is a feature of 'John Barleycorn' is here played out through the country's rituals of seasons and festivals. When Bacchus is gone, Will complains: 'What a beastly thing is it, to bottle up ale in a mans belly, when a man must set his guts on a gallon pot last, only to purchase the alehouse title of a *boone companion*?' When Christmas arrives it might seem that a better version of Bacchus has been found, since Christmas is hailed as the god of hospitality. However, Christmas is as miserable as the rest (except Bacchus, of course). For if he is the god of hospitality, he moans that: 'So will he never be of good husbandry. I may say to you, there is many an old god, that is now growne out of fashion. So is the god of hospitality.' Summer – 'What reason canst thou give he should be left?' Christmas – 'No other reason, but that Gluttony is a sinne, & too many dunghils are infectious.'[56]

If *Summer's Last Will* is a sign of the agricultural world of England giving way to the urban, Jonson's *The New Inn*[57] (1629) is likewise the sign of the end of an old order – the Elizabethan ideal of England based upon estates and their families.[58] The play was disliked at its first performance and has hardly played since, but in our history it takes on a significant role. Jonson uses the inn's space in a number of interesting ways. It plays at a metadramatic level with the idea of theatrical space, social space and existential space; it functions as social commentary; it works away at characterisation via humours and the heart; and it stands as a symbol of an England gone and an England to come. The play is set entirely within an inn, the Light Heart.

The plot of *The New Inn* is an instructive narrative in itself, as a sign of both what has been lost and of what horrors are augured for England. Lord Frampul (for no discernible reason – a point I shall return to) has forsaken his wife and two daughters to run the Light Heart at Barnet, incognito. When his wife, Lady Frampul, discovers that he has disappeared, she reasons that he must have abandoned her because she could not produce a male heir. She herself vows not to return until he is recovered, and likewise goes missing. The first daughter is already lost – believed abducted – and thus the sole heir is the second daughter, Frances. Frances assumes the mantle of Lady Frampul, and with her elevation comes the desire to be 'mistress' of many minions, to which end she really needs a husband. Daringly, accompanied only by her chambermaid Pru, she lodges at the inn and provides a time of revelry for all her friends. The action centres on the melancholic Lovel, wasting away at the Light Heart. His life is transformed when Frances's entourage materialise at the inn and he falls in love with the Lady. The courtship is enacted through the setting up of a Parliament of Love, where Lovel has two separate hours in which to plead his cause to Frances. He is meant to use each hour – one after dinner, and one after supper – to discourse on love. This world turned upside down is presided over by Pru, who is made Sovereign of Sports for the day.

We have already seen, in *1 Henry IV* and *The Taming of the/a Shrew* how situating action in a hostelry allows for a day of misrule, how the temporary suspension of accepted social codes enables otherwise difficult transgressions to take place in order that harmony may be restored and respected. In *The New Inn* Frances is able to act out her desires under such licence, openly 'forward' in a manner which her normal situation as Lady of an estate would not permit. Pru warns her lady that their adventure will look odd in society's eyes. Frances asks why:

PRU   A lady of your rank and quality,
        To come to a public inn, so many men,
        Young lords, and others i' your company,
        And not a woman but myself, a chambermaid!
FRANCES   Thou doubtst to be overlaid, Pru? Fear it not,
        I'll bear my part, and share with thee i' the venture.
PRU   O but the censure, madam, is the main:
        What will they say of you or judge of me,
        To be translated thus 'bove all the bound
        Of fitness or decorum?[59]

Unlike Mistress Quickly and other stock females in drinking establishments, Frances is in charge of her own sexuality, demonstrated through her use of double entendres. Women in drinking places are usually the butt of their own words, unaware of the sexual nature of their own language, there for the amusement of the audience. But Frances's deliberate joke on 'overlaid' – meaning both to have too much work and to have sexual intercourse – shows her power under licence. Pru, at this point already sovereign, is the voice of 'fitness and decorum', Frances's social conscience now that Frances is licensed to act without those restrictions. Hence Frances can make a bawdy joke and promise adventure in keeping with this tone. 'I'll bear my part' would also be heard by an audience as 'bare my part', further indication of the licensed freedom Frances enjoys.

As well as gender codes, and in keeping with how the drinking space functions, social hierarchies are also turned upside down. Lovel indicates to the audience how great Lord Frampul's fall from grace is when he suggests the Lord 'should / Have made another choice than of a place / So sordid as the keeping of an inn' where 'Rogue, bawd, and cheater, call you by the surnames'.[60] Although the Host defends his own character as an honest one, and the inn as a space where he might 'imagine all the world's a play', these are no answers to the charge that he is in extremely reduced social circumstances. When at the end of the play the drunken one-eyed Irish nurse is revealed to be none other than his wife Lady Frampul, the fall from grace is complete. But the actual social system that is reinstated by the play is quite complex, and achieved at some cost.

'Chivalry' as a social standard is mocked throughout. The host will not send his adopted son Frank (who eventually turns out to be his other daughter, Laetitia) to receive such a knight's education, since now mounting steeds has become nothing more than mounting chambermaids, and leaping over vaulting-horses nothing more than going to the vaulting-house (the brothel). In addition, the knight, Sir Glorious Tipto, who neglects to do his duty and wait on Frances, prefers to drink with the lower social orders, much like Falstaff, and creates downstairs with the ne'er-do-wells an inverted militia. The lower orders themselves in the guise of Fly (an original bar-fly), Pierce, Jordan, Jug, Peck, Bat Burst and Hodge Huffle are given generous tranches of stage time in which to utter drunken twaddle, but this only serves to keep them in their place rather than allow for any mixing of the social orders. The desirable social ground is occupied by the abstract ideal of the estate, represented by Frances: 'This lady, being a brave, bountiful lady, and enjoying this free and plentiful estate',[61] allied to noble sentiment, represented by Lovel's long speech on 'valour', which Frances asks for a disquisition upon instead of 'love'.[62] The comedy is apparently set in motion because Frances's character, to continue the quotation: 'hath an ambitious disposition to be esteemed the mistress of many servants, but loves none'.[63] The only bar therefore to the ideal estate is that Frances's heart needs to be won, and from this the comedy proceeds. That 'love' is replaced with, and preceded by, 'valour', in order to create the perfect union, is a sign that the social ground is properly prepared for a dignified restoration of an England of estates.

Yet taken in the context of our literary history, the play fails to restore the estate and in its stead substitutes the drinking place.[64] There is no proper motivation for Lord Frampul abandoning Lady Frampul, and in this might be the play's refusal to acknowledge the greater historical forces which are bringing down the old estates and old England. The belief on Lady Frampul's part that her husband's desertion is down to her inability to produce a proper heir hints at the problems of hereditary success, but this is not carried through the drama. Lord Frampul names himself 'Goodstock' for his role of host of an inn, once more hinting at the problem of England's true lineage. The joke is that 'good stock' is no longer properly able to maintain an estate, but only an inn. The slippage from 'estate' to 'inn' is given when Lovel asks 'How long have you, if your dull guest may ask it, / drove this quick trade, of keeping the Light Heart, / Your mansion, palace here, or hostelry?' His reply is: 'Troth, I was born to somewhat, sir, above it.'[65] Although the swerve of comedy appears to make all well, and Jonson pointedly refuses to usher in the lower orders at the end – the playwright 'could have haled in / The drunkards and the noises of the inn / In his last act ... / But better 'twas that they should sleep or spew / Than in the scene to offend or him or you'[66] – the fact is that the estate has indeed been moved to an inn. This motif will be repeated with variations in later works in the following centuries, where most usually an inn is mistaken for a house, mansion or castle, a sign of preoccupation with respectable and desirable social orders moving ever downwards.

This preoccupation is carried out at the meta-dramatic level. The play opens with the Host's entrance. He complains to Ferret, Lovel's servant, that he will not let Lovel's melancholy ruin his inn. The Host says: 'And if his worship think here to be melancholy / In spite of me or my wit, he is deceived; / I will maintain the rebus 'gainst all humours / And all complexions i' the body of man – / That's my word – or i' the isle of Britain!'[67] In other words, he will maintain his inn's significance as a place of harmony in the face of all woes to the contrary. Thus his ideal condition is set in opposition to Lovel's attack. The Host also conflates the idea of body and the idea of the nation, as we have seen so often before. But again, the opposition serves to highlight that all is not well in the realm, that Goodstock has to struggle to maintain a 'light heart' against all attempts to turn his world to the contrary. The Light Heart is not just the name of his inn, it is the symbol of a harmonious, merry England, of a particular world view. So this battle is fought out at the level of comic structure.

The meta-drama of inn as theatre, already signalled when the Host tells Lovel that his inn is 'Where I imagine all the world's a play' places both the Host and Lovel in the position of audience at the beginning, forming opposite poles of an audience at a play – melancholic and jovial.[68] When Lady Frampul arrives, the Host comes in and announces to Lovel: 'My guest, my guest, be jovial, I beseech thee. / I have fresh golden guests, guests o' the game, / Three coachfull.' In effect 'the world' (of England's estates) comes in to test out whose view of England is right. When the Host and Lovel discuss the break up of the Frampuls, the Host is reduced himself to saying 'A strange division of family', as if the causes of this fracturing of the social order are inexplicable (and once again emphasising that, within the play, the break-up of the ideal estate – represented by Lord Frampul's abandonment – is without adequate motivation or explanation).

The play is consistent with its representation that normal laws of inheritance have gone awry, since not only is 'the family' dispersed, but Frances, a woman, now 'enjoys the land' 'And takes all lordly ways how to consume it / As nobly as she can: if clothes and feasting / And the authorised means of riot will do it.' It suggests she is acting like a young gallant, taking upon herself the modish way of using the estate that, as we saw in Dekker and others, was a most worrying symptom for those intent on diagnosing England. Here England is both losing its base of patrinomy and is becoming feminised. The trick is to awaken the 'proper' inheritors to their duty. This is ostensibly done when Lovel is won over by Frances. He waxes lyrical on love being life itself, and says: 'I was the laziest creature, / The most unprofitable sign of nothing,' and when his discourse on 'valour' replaces the one to be given on 'love' the movement back to a properly constituted estate, 'sign', is complete. The importance of 'sign' resonates with the play's opening explanation and intention to defend the inn's rebus – a feather over a heart. The inn's name works as both a heart that refuses serious love or amours, and also love placed in a 'light', that is comic, environment. When Lovel has finished his eulogy to love, the Host deflates his rhetoric with a simple: 'But is your name Love-ill, sir, or Love-well?' – as if Lovel has now gone too far in interpretation. But Lovel does not know himself, only enough to say: 'But it is love hath been / The hereditary passion of our house'. By a chain of association, the inheritance of 'love' is firmly underpinned by a more socially acceptable virtue – 'valour' – since Frances asks for a discourse on the latter in place of the former. The inn functions as the social and dramatic arena for effecting an 'awakening' to current national ills, an attempt to allow for a transition from a body with a heavy heart to one with a light heart. When the Host refers to his own son, he says: 'But the Light Heart, / It is his father's, and it may be his'. Inheritance of estate and inheritance of a world view are at stake. Unlike Shakespeare's tetralogy, however, the resolution is compromised by the space itself. The players may seem to leave the inn at the end of *The New Inn*, but the audience can only remain, with Fly, to be the inheritor of this symbolic version of the new England. *The New Inn* is the new England that the play fights against.

Notes

1 John Bickerdyke, *The Curiosities of Ale and Beer: An Entertaining History* (London, Swan Sonnenschein, 1889), p. 205.
2 William Shakespeare, *Twelfth Night*, ed. Herschel Baker (New York, Signet, 1965 [c. 1600]), 2.3.78–93.
3 Ibid., 2.3.114–15.
4 Ibid., 2.3.140.
5 Ibid., 1.5.130–2.
6 Ibid., 5.1.201.
7 William Shakespeare, *The Merry Wives of Windsor*, in *The Complete Oxford Shakespeare*, ed. Stanley Wells *et al.* (London, Guild Publishing, in association with Oxford University Press, 1987 [?1597/?1600]), 1.1.165–8.
8 Ch. 4, 'London', of Leah Marcus's *Puzzling Shakespeare: Local Reading and its Discontents* (Berkeley, California, University of California Press, 1988), gives a detailed reading of the historical context for the play. Given its subject matter, the play deserves much fuller treatment than can be offered here.
9 Theodore B. Leinwand, 'Spongy Plebs, Mighty Lords, and the Dynamics of the Alehouse', *Journal of Medieval and Renaissance Studies*, 19:2 (1989), 179.
10 Ibid., p. 183.
11 That it is an inn, or at least a tavern, rather than an alehouse is suggested by a couple of features: the 'hostess' and the fact that the Lords turn up here. Also, Sly has broken 'glasses', which might signify a higher-class establishment, since glasses were only just beginning to appear as drinking vessels and would presumably have been costly. The problem is that why should a tinker, whose natural habitat would be an alehouse, be at an inn/tavern in the first place? The most probable explanation is that he is a chancer there, because as he protests later on, his normal haunt is Marian Hackett's alehouse, where he has run up a considerable debt.
12 Stanley Wells suggests a particular ballad for the theme of shrew wooed by fortune hunter, 'A merry jest of a shrewd and curst wife lapped in morel's skin for her good behaviour', *c.* 1550, introduction to *The Taming of the Shrew*, in *The Complete Oxford Shakespeare*, ed. Stanley Wells *et al.* (London, Guild Publishing in association with Oxford University Press, 1987), p. 481.
13 See Stephen Roy Miller's introduction to *The Taming of a Shrew: The 1594 Quarto* (Cambridge, Cambridge University Press, 1998), for a full discussion of

the relationship between the two plays.
14 Shakespeare, *The Taming of the Shrew*, Induction 2, 20–3.
15 *Ibid.*, 1.1.25–39.
16 Shakespeare's version might also have been littered with such interruptions. One survives at the end of 1.1, where mention is made of Sly's falling asleep, as he does in *A Shrew*, but thereafter the play continues uninterrupted.
17 *A Shrew*, 3.309–11.
18 *Ibid.*, end of Scene 11, beginning Scene 12.
19 The usual view, according to Miller, *ibid*.
20 *Ibid.*, l.61.
21 *Ibid.*, 13.52–3.
22 *Ibid.*, end of Scene 13.
23 *Ibid.*, 15.8–9.
24 *Ibid.*, 15.21–2.
25 John Marston, *The Dutch Courtesan*, ed. M. L. Wine (London, Edward Arnold, 1965), 1.1.1; 1.1.3; 1.1.39.
26 Francis Beaumont and John Fletcher, *The Knight of the Burning Pestle*, in *Six Plays by Contemporaries of Shakespeare*, ed. C. B. Wheeler (London, Oxford University Press, 1964), 2.6.37–52.
27 H. A. Monckton, *A History of the English Public House* (London, Bodley Head, 1969), pp. 40–1.
28 Richard Rawlidge, *A Monster late found out and discovered ...* ([London] 1606).
29 A. V. Judges, *The Elizabethan Underworld* (London, Routledge and Kegan Paul, 1965 [1930]), pp. 15–16. Judges gloss on 'haskard' is 'base, dirty fellow' and 'geason' is 'barren, unproductive'.
30 William Fennor, *The Counter's Commonwealth*, in *Ibid.*, p. 439.
31 Jonson's play, *The Devil is an Ass*, has a similar idea. The Devil (Pugg) visits London, but is outwitted by tricksters who are even more cunning than hell can offer.
32 Judges, *Underworld*, p. 323.
33 Thomas Burke, *The English Inn* (London, Longmans, Green and Co., 193), p. 135.
34 The term 'ordinary' has not survived in popular consciousness in the way that inns, taverns and alehouses have, although there are instances of its continued usage in the twentieth century. John Fothergill, a famous 'innkeeper' in the 1920s, held a Market Day Ordinary at his Spreadeagle, Thame (*An Innkeeper's Diary*, London, Faber, 1987 [1931]), p. 21, to keep the local farmers happy whilst he attempted to gain a more exclusive clientele (it didn't work).
35 Judges, *Underworld*, p. 326.
36 *Ibid.*, p. 327.
37 Thomas Dekker, *The Dead Tearme. Or Westminsters Complaint for long Vacations and short Termes*, [1608], in *The Non-Dramatic Works of Thomas Dekker*, vol. 4, ed. Alexander B. Grosart (London, 1884–85), p. 52.
38 *Ibid.*, p. 50.
39 Thomas Dekker, *The Guls Horne-booke*, [1609], in *The Non-Dramatic Works of Thomas Dekker*, vol. 2.
40 *Ibid.*, p. 223.
41 *Ibid.*, p. 237.

42 *Ibid.*, pp. 238 and 239.
43 *Ibid.*, pp. 242–3.
44 Judges, *Underworld*, p. 425.
45 *The Non-Dramatic Works of Thomas Dekker*, vol. 1.
46 *Ibid.*, p. 87.
47 *Ibid.*, p. 76.
48 *Ibid.*, p. 85.
49 *Ibid.*, pp. 95–6.
50 *Ibid.*, pp. 121–2.
51 'Difficult points of casuistry arose out of that steady perception of an indisputable rule. Could flight from a plague-stricken place be reconciled with duty to one's neighbour? How ought a Christian man to demean himself in the plague?' Charles Creighton, *A History of Epidemics in Britain from A. D. 664 to the Extinction of Plague* (London, Cambridge University Press, 1891), p. 310.
52 *The Non-Dramatic Works of Thomas Dekker*, vol. 1, pp. 123–4.
53 *Ibid.*, pp. 124–5.
54 *Ibid.*, pp. 135–7.
55 *Ibid.*, pp. 137–45.
56 Thomas Nashe, *A Pleasant Comedie, called Summers Last Will and* Testament (London, 1600 [1592]), n.p.
57 Ben Jonson, *The New Inn*, ed. Michael Hattaway (Manchester, Manchester University Press, 1984).
58 According to Michael Hattaway's introduction, Jonson is nostalgic for the lost Elizabethan England, and mourns the break-up of the estate household as the centre of English life, epitomised by Jonson in his poem 'To Penshurst'.
59 Jonson, *Inn*, 2.1.46–55.
60 *Ibid.*, 1.3.110–12 and 116.
61 *Ibid.*, The Argument, ll. 24–5.
62 *Ibid.*, 4.4.24ff.
63 *Ibid.*, The Argument, ll. 25–6.
64 There is a similar figure in Massinger's *A New Way to Pay Old Debts*, where it is Wellborn, the dissolute son of a gentleman, who has squandered his father's wealth, and the man who was once a servant on Wellborn's father's land is now, as proprietor of the tavern where Wellborn has spent all his money, Wellborn's creditor.
65 Jonson, *Inn*, 1.3.93–6.
66 *Ibid.*, Epilogue, ll. 13–18.
67 *Ibid.*, 1.1.7–11.
68 The audience is alerted to the meta-dramatic in other ways. Lord Frampul apparently became a puppet master when he left his estate, before taking up the inn, and offers to provide entertainment for Lovel by manipulating his guests. There is a meta-dramatic joke when Frances says that Pru's suit can be given to the players.

   PRU   That were illiberal, madam, and mere sordid
               In me, to let a suit of yours come there.
       FRANCES   – Tut, all are players and but serve the scene, Pru. (2.137–9)

5

Pepys pissed

The Civil War and its aftermath, the Restoration, appear to have encouraged a link between imbibing and politics. Possibly the production of stereotypes in the forms of 'Cavaliers' and 'Roundheads' readily lent itself to the easy targets beloved of song-writers and pamphleteers.[1] The Cavaliers were characterised as great drinkers, and so drinking itself became a political act.[2] *The Roxburghe Ballads* prints a whole range of drinking songs with a political point, and such songs lasted well into the eighteenth century, when the polarisation had transformed into 'Whigs' and 'Tories'.[3] The combination of drink, literature and politics found its natural home in hostelries and in the bosom of a social institution supposedly invented by Sir Walter Raleigh during Elizabeth's reign, the club, which truly started to come into its own in this period. Similarly, the drinking of toasts, which was supposedly introduced by 'soldiers serving in the Dutch revolt in Elizabeth's reign',[4] became a national pastime and the excuse for marathon drinking sessions, for politicians and plebs alike. The literary productions that promoted this were ballads and drinking songs, popular entertainment across the social spectrum. An example which Ebsworth, one of the editors of *The Roxburghe Ballads*, dates somewhere between 1642-52, shows how the old antagonisms between malt liquor and fruit of the grape, and between alehouse and tavern, are now commandeered to political ends:

> Away with Beer, and such like geer,
>   That makes our spirits muddy,
>   For Wine compleat will do the feat,
> That we all notes can study.
>   ...
> And also we that do agree,
>   As one, for boon good fellows,
> We'l sing and laugh and stoutly quaff,
>   And quite renounce the Alehouse;
>
> For Ale and Beer are now both dear,
>   The price is rais'd in either,

> Then let us all, both great and small,
>   To th' Tavern walk together:⁵

Cavalier drinking songs often took a swipe at 'the Brewer' Cromwell because of his mother's connections with brewing. Other songs might name him 'the Brewer of Huntingdon' or 'Purge-Pryde the Drayman', or even 'a *Cooper* with a red nose'.⁶ The dismissal in this song of both alehouse and beer is also a class act, repeated in the song 'Canary's Coronation' (?1657),⁷ where ale and beer are the tipple of the 'popular' (populace, plebs), and wine belongs to the Royalists. It begins: 'From Hopps and Grains let us purge our braines; / They do smell of Anarchie', whereas on the Royalist side, in distinction, stand the 'Wine-bred Witts'. A little later than above, with the monarchy restored, is this typical Royalist drinking song:

> Come, boyes, fill us a bumper,
>   we'l make the nation roare;
> She's grown sick of a Rumper
>   that sticks on the old score.
> Pox on Phanaticks, rout 'um,
>   they thirst for our blood;
> We'll taxes raise without 'um,
>   and drink for the nation's good.
>
> *Fill the pottles and gallons,*
>   *and bring the hogshead in;*
> *We'l begin with a tallen,*
>   *a brimmer to the King.*⁸

The targets, injunctions and epithets are standard. The call to be merry, to make 'the nation roar', is a *de facto* rebuttal of the Puritan attitudes of sobriety we saw in *Twelfth Night*, and to the more recent attempts at repression of customary revelling, with all of its social, political and religious associations – a maypole was erected in the Strand and there was Morris dancing to celebrate the return of the monarchy.⁹ Drinking is also good for the nation's health since the more that is drunk the more money is raised in taxes. The Puritans are fanatics, and their politics is reduced to the farce of the Rump Parliament. The chorus is the usual call for drink and a toast to the king.

The songs could get nastily personal, and those directed at Anthony Ashley Cooper, 1st Earl of Shaftesbury, form a sub-genre of their own. In his lifetime he served with both the Parliamentarians and the Royalists, becoming Chancellor of the Exchequer and then Lord Chancellor under Charles II, only to be dismissed by him after a year. He was a patron of Titus Oates, and when the Popish Plot was discovered as an invention he was tried for treason. In the literary canon he finds an unwanted place in Dryden's verse satire *Absalom and Achitophel* (1681) as the 'false Achitophel'. More interestingly for us, Shaftesbury had had an operation for what we now know to have been a hydatid cyst of the liver. A tube was inserted during the operation to drain the abscess, and the decision was made by Shaftesbury himself to leave it in.[10] K. H. D. Haley, a biographer of the Earl, writes: 'for the rest of his life he was unique amongst men in possessing the famous tube which led later Tory pamphleteers to christen him "Tapski" as though he were a barrel of beer with a tap – perhaps in combination with other jibes about a Cooper'.[11] This makes the literature sound reasonably amiable, but in fact it was fairly malicious. 'A Litany from Geneva' begins: 'From the *Tap* in the guts of the Honourable Stump, / From which runs Rebellion, that stinks like the Rump, / On purpose to leaven the Factious Lump; *Libera nos, Domine!*'[12] The liturgical form is a reminder of the mass-mocking Goliardic tradition. That rebellion could pour out from his side aligns the mob with liquor (an association that becomes more common in the eighteenth and nineteenth centuries), and 'the Rump' reminds us of his connection with the Parliamentarians. After his trial appeared: 'Did you not hear of a Peer that was tried? / *With a fa, la, la, la, la.* / That looks like a cask with a tap in his side; / *With a fa, la, la, la, la.*' And at his death, the majority of literature was derogatory. *Last Will and Testament of Anthony, King of Poland* begins: 'My tap is run; then Baxter tell me why / Should not the good, the great Potapskie die?'[13]

Yet despite the heated rhetoric of the partisan's drinking song, it was perhaps the return to unfettered enjoyment that dominated the political posturing. A 'play-song' such as 'Content's a Treasure; Or, The Jovial Loyalist' has a few digs at the political scene and gives due acknowledgment to the Crown, as might be expected, yet inevitably ends with three cheers for hedonism:

> We have the world at will, Boys, there's nothing we can lack,
> Since our Cups with Nectar flow, tis [the] Nectar we call Sack:
>   *And so merry we will be, etc.*
>
> There's none so happy live as we, on us delights do showre,
> We live from hate and envy free, more safe than those in power:
>   *And so merry we will be, will be, will be, will be,*
>   *And so merry we will be.*[14]

The call to convivial arms against the memory of Puritan dominance leads neatly in to our main subject.

Pepys

Strange to see how easily my mind doth revert to its former practice of loving plays and wine, having given myself a liberty to them both these two days; but this night I have again bound myself to Christmas next, in which I desire God to bless me and preserve me, for under God I find it to be the best course that ever I could take to bring myself to mind my business.

30 September 1662

The combination of England, literature and drinking places emerges in a new conjunction when we reach that unique literary document, Pepys's diaries (1660–69), and in this section I shall attempt to describe the environment and mind-set that brings these elements together. Of special interest to us is that the diaries record Pepys's ongoing struggle to curb his passions for drinking and the theatre so that he can attend more to making his way in the world. His inner war on both plays and ales is no coincidence – they had been two of the main bugbears of Puritanism for about a hundred years[15] and Pepys himself had been brought up a Puritan.[16] What is perhaps most readily called the Protestant work ethic shines through Pepys's continuous attempts to forswear drink and theatre. As well as his own upbringing, it can also be seen as a direct consequence of the more general sober ideology we have already observed emerging in the sixteenth century. The widespread dissemination of such attitudes throughout England is noted in another diary from the same period, kept by someone living at the other end of the country from Pepys – Ashton-in-Makerfield in Lancashire – and at the other end of social expectations, if not the other end of the social scale – a shop-keeper. An entry in Roger Lowe's diary for 4 February 1663 reads: 'Roger Naylor and Richard Twisse came, and would have me to goe with them to Alehouse. I went, and very mery we ware. I must not spend a 1d., but yet I did.'[17] Just like Pepys, the social world pulls Lowe into the drinking place and competes with his wish to be at work and save/accumulate money. Like Pepys, Roger Lowe's religious spirit is troubled every now and then, and Lowe not infrequently kneels down no matter where he is and prays. But such pangs of conscience sit alongside an enjoyment of the sociable that can be at odds with the serious outlook.

Roger Lowe lived far from London and what passed for the centre of the nation and national endeavour. Another aspect of the fascination that Pepys's diaries hold is that he is witness to 'national' events. In an entry which to us looks to all intents and purposes like a curious lack of self-recognition – yet another feature of the diaries' interest – we find a juxtaposition of Pepys's own life with that of the monarchy: 'I find myself lately too much given to seeing of plays and expense and pleasure, which makes me forget my business, which I must labour to amend', yet (and?) in the same entry he is censuring the Court for the vices we see Pepys himself guilty of: 'at Court things are in very ill condition, there being so much emulacion, poverty, and the vices of swearing, drinking and whoring, that I never know what will be the end of it but confusion'.[18] As we shall see, Pepys himself is given to drinking and lewd behaviour (and he is also accused of swearing; see below, 27 September 1665).

Pepys's diaries abound with inns, taverns, alehouses, ordinaries and coffee-houses. Like many people of that period, he begins his morning with a draught of ale or beer and drinks sporadically throughout the rest of the day, ending it not unfrequently with an evening drinking session. He uses all categories of drinking establishments – from the grandest inns to the most disreputable blind alehouses – and for all purposes – refreshment, relaxation, entertainment, contemplation, clubbing, sodality, trysts. He also makes no class distinction between ale, beer and wine, even though we find in other literature (as above) these symbolic markers are very much in vogue. After the turmoil of the English Civil War, the disjunctive mix of freedom to make merry and concern about the consequences of free living are visible in Pepys. The Puritans had done their best to stamp out merrie England, although both Puritans and Royalists were guilty of introducing an excise on drink to fund their share of the war. Both parties promised that it would be removed at the war's cessation, yet it remained in place until 1757.[19]

Much of what Pepys records about his drinking places is incidental to other concerns, such as his job, his accumulation of money, his conscience and his amours. As a consequence he does not view drinking places as 'objects'. His one comment of any substantial reflection is about the convenience of ordinaries, where, unlike those commentators in the last chapter, he finds them an excellent idea: 'and among other things, talking of the way of ordinaries, that it is very convenient because a man knows what he hath to pay, one did wish that among many bad, we could learn two good things of France – which were that we would not think it below the gentleman or person of honour at a taverne to bargain for his meat before he eates it'.[20] (The other good thing to be learnt from France is always to insist on references when taking on a servant.) He was not so keen on ordinaries on 25 April 1661 however: 'At noon Mr. Moore and I went to an ordinary at the King's-head in Tower-street and there had a dirty dinner.'

The rest of this chapter follows him through the swinging 1660s via chronologically ordered diary entries. As such it begins as the diary of a talented, underemployed, ambitious young man of twenty-six years. I have given the records in this way in the hope that the daily materiality of social drinking which weaves in and out of the diaries is preserved in its immediacy. To this end I have mostly avoided reference to general biographical information which would force the diaries into the larger narrative of Pepys's life beyond 1669, the date the diaries end. It also helps maintain the sense of the diaries as an autonomous piece of literature, which, one might argue, is the spirit in which they were written: when Pepys finishes the private diaries he acknowledges that by using other people to write his journal in longhand he will be constrained to airing only what it is fit for them and the world to know. The record of the diurnal drinking routine and associated activities which I have tried to distil here would have no doubt been mundane for contemporaries of Pepys, but is acutely fascinating for the glimpses it affords us. As Pepys makes his way through career, conscience and domestic life, we can see the impact of drinking places on the man's existence and write a new narrative.

1660[21]

9 February 1660

'Went to bed with my head not well, by my too much drinking today. An I had a boyle under my chin which troubled me cruelly.' I open with this entry as a taste of the world of Pepys. Much of the diaries is taken up with charting his body's well-being, and his reference to a boil on his chin is just a small instance of this preoccupation.[22] On the other hand, throughout the diaries he gives thanks to good health through celebration each year of the successful removal of his kidney stone on 26 March 1658.[23] His struggle to control his alcohol drinking is somewhere along this continuum of bodily concern, but takes on an extra dimension in that he feels drinking prevents social progress in terms of career – hence an ailing body is a constant reminder of lack of investment in his getting of wealth and promotion, whilst good health is a spur to a more sober lifestyle. But of course Pepys, like Roger Lowe, is in a double bind – to get on in the world he must keep himself in the thick of social and commercial intercourse, and this involves a great amount of convivial drinking.

12 February 1660

It is the Lord's day, and Pepys is searching with Mr Kirton's apprentice for a tavern that is open. They are shut by law during hours of divine service, although the fact that they are trying to find one open suggests not all followed suit (see next entry). Pepys appears to have no particular opinion about this law, even though it is an obvious inconvenience to him, or what the significance in religious terms of his attempts to side step it might be.

26 February 1660

A Sunday a fortnight later, yet we find Pepys drinking without any apparent difficulty. He is in Cambridge, waiting with an acquaintance in the Rose tavern for Mr Pechell who has gone to church, 'where we sat and drank till sermon done; and then Mr. Pechell came to us and we three sat drinking the King's and his whole family's health till it begin to be dark'. What might seem to us a delightful irony – Pepys is waiting in the tavern for a drinking partner to return from church – goes unnoticed. Pepys stresses his loyalty to the King throughout the diaries, and here we can see that it is typically done through drinking healths, an act that had obvious importance as a political act, as already seen above. On 1 and 2 May later this year he tells of people going down on their knees to drink the King's health.[24]

This particular Sunday drinking session ends, but Pepys returns later the same day with his father and some others, without revealing to them that he has already been there. Pepys does not explain why he fails to admit this. However, he does tell us that he treats them to 'a quart or two of wine', and when he goes to his cousin's for supper, he has two bottles of wine brought over from the same tavern. This was a common practice, as was sending wine as a gift – Pepys had received a dozen bottles of sack from his Lord Montagu on 2 January this year. Pepys notes that: 'I had not the wit to let them know at table that it was I that paid for them, and so I lost my thanks for them', a typical Pepys entry, showing his preoccupation with gaining the good opinion of others, which we usually see in a context concerning his own social and career advancement.

2 July 1660

A small note for this day shows how invitations to the tavern were usually handled, but on this occasion are not, and Pepys is peeved: 'Met with Purser Washington, with whom and a lady, a friend of his, I dined at the Bell Taverne in King's-street; but the rogue had no more manners than to invite me thither and to let me pay my club.' On the 26th of this same month he goes to 'Woods at the Pell-mell (our old house for clubbing)' which Robert Latham and William Mathews (editors) state was where Pepys and other 'young government clerks' met during Cromwell's time. The very act of 'clubbing' and going to inns and taverns must have had the taint of politics for Pepys.

9 August 1660

This day, at The Leg, King Street, is one of the few times he appears in a tavern with his wife Elizabeth. As to women in general being found at inns, taverns and alehouses, where they are mentioned Pepys does not note the occurrences down as in any way unusual. An entry for 4 October 1665 states: 'Thence to the King's-head to dinner, where we three [Mr Andrews, Mr Gawden], and Creed and my wife and her woman, dined mighty merry – and sat long talking; and so in the afternoon broke up.' However, respectability is still to be guaranteed by male guardianship – Pepys does not record an instance of women alone; and women serving in these places are invariably prey to sexual comment, as an entry on 21 March 1663 reveals: 'Here [Westminster Hall] I met with Chetwind, Parry, and several others, and went to a little house behind the Lords' house to drink some Wormewood ale, which doubtless was a bawdy house – the mistress of the house having that look and dress.' A few years later, Pepys goes to a tavern, simply 'to get a sight of the pretty mistress of the house', but finds she scolds too much and thinks that she is probably an 'ill-natured devil' so that he makes no effort to speak to her.

17 August 1660

Pepys has been drinking at the Half Moon Tavern in the Strand. 'This night I saw Mr. Creed show many the strangest evasions to shift off his drink that ever I saw in my life.' The editors explain the significance of this. 'It was often customary for each member of a drinking party in turn to propose and pay for a toast: to "shift it off" was to miss one's turn.' Mr Creed (aptly enough) is a Puritan, and the editor also indicates that Creed may have refused the toasts 'on principle'. Like many of his time, Pepys believes Puritans to be out-and-out hypocrites, and he often rejoices when he finds Creed acting against avowed principles, as on 12 May in the following year when he finds Creed going to a drinking house on a Sunday, whereas previously he would rather have hanged himself than done this. On 11 October in this year, Pepys is drinking healths with Creed and another Puritan, Mr Blackburne, at the Rhenish winehouse, and he notes that the latter took part in the toasting, which he had formerly refused to do, further grist to the anti-Puritan mill. Yet it appears that Pepys may have changed his views towards the Puritans towards the end of the diaries, perhaps a sign that he himself is finally utterly disgusted with the tenor of the times as set by the merry monarch. He sees a puppet version of Jonson's *Bartholomew Fayre* on 4 September 1668, and comments: 'an excellent play; the more I see it, the more I love the wit of it; only, the business of abusing the puritans begins to grow stale, and of no use, they being the people that at last will be found the wisest'. Since one of the play's main thrusts is an intense dislike of Puritans, for Pepys to enjoy it and yet find this aspect of it out of step with the contemporary scene (or at least, Pepys's understanding of it), this later diary entry reveals his mixed feelings towards Puritan ideology tending towards one of greater sympathy. (In addition, 'Bartholomew Fair' itself had been extended to two weeks with the Restoration in place, in a determined effort to reintroduce merrie England, and Jonson's play had since been performed as an adjunct to this political posturing.)[25] By the end of the diary period it is as if Pepys has come to a more comfortable accommodation with his Puritan self and his drinking, theatre-going and extramarital sexual activities. But this is to leap ahead.

22 September 1660

This entry provides an example of just how badly Pepys could be affected by drinking: 'To Westminster to my Lord's; and there in the house of office vomited up all my breakfast, my stomach being ill all this day by reason of the last night's debauch.' It is also an example of how his drinking habits could not help but permeate his working life – not just in the social transactions conducted in taverns (see next entry), but in his bodily health. He is in an even worse state the morning of 24 April the following year, when he wakes to find himself 'wet with my spewing. Thus did the day end, with joy everywhere' – a reference to the previous night's celebrations of Coronation Day. Pepys certainly drank hard in the name of the King, but with a suppressed admiration for Cromwell in his youth, it may be a case of Pepys covering his back.

14 November 1660

'So home to dinner; and after that to the office till late at night; and so Sir W. Pen, the Comptroller and I to the Dolphin, where we found Sir W. Batten (who is seldom a night from hence); and there we did drink a great Quantity of Sack. And did tell many merry stories, and in good humours we were all. So home to bed.' As may have already been surmised from the opening of this chapter, Falstaff's favourite tipple is still going strong. Pepys also shows us here his love of tavern life, which makes his attempts to deny himself – as with his attempts to avoid the theatre – a sign of the battle he is fighting with himself to forge his character in the sober ideal.

2 December 1660

An instance of Saturday Night/Sunday Morning as Pepys has yet another hangover: 'My head not very well and my body out of order by last night's drinking – which is my great folly.' It reminds us (and himself) that his battle with drink is at this stage a fairly unequal one.

1661

2 April 1661

As if it is some revelation, Pepys notes how men who are normally 'wise', 'do now in their drink betwitt and reproach one another with their former conditions and their actions as to public concernments, till I was shamed to see it'. The implication is that Pepys himself is above such low behaviour, that he can hold his drink and is not given to exposing the former faults of public servants.

3 April 1661

Pepys suffers the following morning with another hangover. But Pepys discovers yet again something new about the properties of alcohol. Pen gets him to 'drink two good draughts of sack today, to cure me of last night's disease – which I thought strange, but I think find it true'. For a man who drinks so much, sees and hears so much, it is a surprise for the reader that Pepys is unaware of the well-known remedy, 'hair-of-the-dog'. Earlier in the year, 25 February, he had been advised by a doctor that his worsening memory was down to his drinking, as if this too were an unknown idea to him.

31 December 1661

A sad day: 'I have newly taken a solemne oath about abstaining from plays and wine, which I am resolved to keep according to the letter of the oath, which I keepe by me.' The oaths that Pepys takes to leave off drinking usually refer only to wine, regarded no doubt as 'strong liquor', whereas ale and beer could be classed more in the way of refreshment, and Pepys continues to drink these latter beverages.

1662

26 January 1662

Pepys gives himself a moral boost for his oath-taking, as the benefits begin to materialise: 'But thanks be to God, since my leaving drinking of wine, I do find myself much better and to mind my business better and to spend less money, and less time lost in idle company.' It is almost as if Pepys were familiar with early Stuart legislation against idle tippling and haunting of alehouses and taverns, for having forsworn such behaviour his business and economy begin to thrive. However, a month later, 17 February, he finds he has had to drink 'wine upon necessity, being ill for want of it. And I find reason to fear that by my too sudden leaving off wine, I do contract many evils upon myself.' Pepys is drawing upon the common knowledge that an abrupt cessation of alcohol intake is dangerous, and hence gives a perfect cameo of the self-serving nature of the drinker's thinking. But in June he is patting himself on the back once more for going a whole dinner without drinking a drop of wine, and in August he reads over his vows and is pleased to find that he is a changed man. Such self-congratulation may however have been because there was light at the end of the tunnel, for not so far away was …

29 September 1662 (Michaelmas day)

'This day my oaths for drinking of wine and going to plays are out, and so I do resolve to take a liberty today and then to fall to them again.' The boom-bust nature of Pepys's plan appears to be the only way to cope with the contradictions of his own predilections to drink and theatre, against his ambitious career and monetary aspirations, and against his Puritan self.[26] The following day he notes how easily he returned to his drinking and theatre-going, but this only strengthens his resolve 'to bring myself to mind my business'. His vows are perhaps best understood as strict guidelines which every now and then are broken. On 10 November 1662, he drinks a pint of wine without any reference to temperance, although he abstains from drinking it a couple of days later.

1663

5 January 1663

The same attitude surfaces here. Pepys drinks a lot of wine, and says he will forswear it in a day or two. But the intricacies of Pepys's thought processes are observable for the entry the next day: 'And I do find my mind so apt to run to its old wont of pleasures, that it is high time to betake myself to my late vows.' Pepys's 'self', the narrating 'I', is a separate entity from Pepys's 'mind'. The mind has a will of its own which the self must battle with in order to construct the ideal Pepys: a sober, hard-working, thrifty individual who will gain his just rewards in social status and wealth. This is another interest of the diaries, the manner in which it shows a Pepys under construction.

Even though Pepys renews his vows on 18 January, on 25 January he is on his way home when he meets Sir W. Batten, turns back to a coffee-house 'and there drunk more, till I was almost sick'. The irony of this is that he has just bought a self-help pamphlet, Audley's *Way to be Rich*, and the editors wryly quote from this: 'Cf. Audley's warning …. "Drink not the third glass."' Pepys however appears to forego the wine, although he can still drink 'fine Lambeth ale', and is occasionally reminded of the dangers of drink in social life. On 27 April Pepys hears a story of a Captain Browne killed by a drunken servant, and his own servant, Susan, is sneaking out two or three times a day to the alehouse (24 May).

19 July 1663

Pepys reads over his vows, 'and encreased them by a vow against all strong drink till November next, of any sort or Quantity', but as mentioned above, this does not include beer or ale. Beer was preferable to water for Pepys, if the entry on 6 August shows a general tendency: 'I drank no wine, but sent for some water, the beer not being good.' It was also preferable to small beer: 'And by my drinking of small-beer and not eating, I am so mightily troubled with wind that I know not what to do almost' (19 August). From here on, Pepys mainly remains true to his vows, often reading them to himself. On occasion it is nothing less than torture not to drink: 'By and by up to dinner with my Lord Mayor and the Aldermen; and a very great dinner and most excellent venison, but it almost made me sick by not daring to drink wine' (2 September 1663). As late as 20 February 1666 he notes that his drinking of wine at a christening that day was perhaps his first glass in two years. In fact, in 1663 it is his infidelity with one Mrs Lane that now begins to be more troublesome than the drinking, and he even takes an oath for this, limiting his time with her to fifteen minutes (5 April 1664). But drinking places continue to play a big part in his life and we learn of other aspects of everyday living. He goes to the New Exchange Tavern for the first time on 17 November only to find an old schoolfriend is master of it. It seems a perfectly respectable position to hold. And we find Pepys acting as an arbiter in a dispute between two parties at a tavern on 2 December.

1664

6 June 1664

We meet William Prynne at a dinner Pepys attends. Prynne was a Puritan and author of *Healthe's Sicknesse* ... (1628), an anti-drink tract. Pepys notes how Prynne refused all healths, including the King's, and remained seated 'with his hat on all the while, but nobody took notice of it at all'. Except Pepys, who appears slightly obsessed with the behaviour of Puritans, who are both too close for comfort as role models and yet too soberly dogmatic to imitate or join.

15 August 1664

Pepys goes to the Trumpett, where he meets Mrs Lane. 'I had my pleasure of her.' Pepys's concern with taking of strong liquor and going to the theatre give way to concerns over his sexual activities. As with drink, the narrating 'I' is at odds with the Pepys who/which desires dalliance, or, put another way, Pepys is split between his merrie England self and his Puritan self. The drinking place now becomes a new kind of space for him, since his amours are limited to either a house or a tavern. The domestic space becomes less used as the diary proceeds, although Pepys makes no comment on this. References to difficulties in finding somewhere to be together are casual in the sense that Pepys does not make an issue of them, but they do structure his amorous behaviour.

3 November 1664

'At noon to the Change; and thence by appointment was met with Bagwells wife, and she followed me into Moorefields and then into a drinking-house – and all alone eat and drank together. I did caress her; but though I did make some offer, did not receive any compliance from her in what was bad, but very modestly she denied me; which I was glad to see and shall value her the better for it – and I hope never tempt her to any evil more.' The split between the controlling Pepys and the controlled Pepys is very much in evidence. There is a difference however in that Pepys is both tempter and tempted, whereas, with respect to drink and theatre-going, he can only be in the position of a person tempted. The construction of the ideal Pepys now involves casting out another facet of the narrated figure – Pepys as 'evil-doer', thereby putting a new factor into his sense of self. Yet there is no sense throughout this year that he makes any concerted effort, as he has done with forswearing drink, to seriously curb his inclinations. He moves from one woman to the next, one minute with Mrs Lane and the next flirting with a prostitute (23 July 1664). A modern reader cannot but help expect some mental anguish over his unfaithfulness as a husband, yet he does not see it in these terms. Mrs Pepys is not mentioned. Unlike drinking and theatre-going, which are injurious to his health and his attention to business, he gives no particular reasons for wishing to stop his flirtations. Some of the entries, as above, are in the shorthand he uses throughout the diaries, but increasingly he further codes his records by using some pigeon-European language of his own invention, a mixture of French and Spanish. Given that some of the material that is not coded in this way is equally damning – that is, if his main worry is having the diary read by others – one hypothesis must be that this language is a way of avoiding direct psychological confrontation with his actions.[27]

For instance, on 15 November he meets up with Mrs Bagwell who 'with much ado fallowed me through Moor-fields to a blind alehouse, and there I did caress her and eat and drank'. He eventually gets what he wants: 'by degrees I did arrive at what I would'. In the context of other diary entries it is clear that 'what I would' is some kind of sexual event, although the entry is evasive in that what he 'arrives at' is not specified. A blind alehouse would be a dark, out-of-the-way drinking place, but any activity would still be public. It is unlikely (though not impossible) that there would have been a separate room where they could go privately for sexual intercourse, as they might in a tavern or an inn. The diary entries in this period reveal his struggle with his conscience over sexual matters, his use of an invented, personal language, and the problems of finding suitable drinking spaces for sexual activity. The latter is evident in the next couple of entries.

Pepys pissed

15 December 1664

'and I thence to Moorefields, and there up and down to several houses to drink, to look for a place pour rancontrer la femme de que je sais quoy against next Monday, but could meet none'. Pepys is basically cruising the alehouses looking for women. Four days later he is using alehouses again, but this time he is with Mrs Bagwell. He believes that she does not want to do too much because they (he) cannot find a decent place for their tryst. But the next day, 20 December, he manages something at her house. Pepys's inability to find a suitable drinking place hints at more than simply a lack – Pepys, one can only presume, with his wide knowledge of drinking places, would surely have known places where he could easily have booked private rooms. Perhaps he is too guilty to plan anything in advance, or is never in a position to do so. The latter seems unlikely, however, as the next entry shows.

1665

2 January 1665

Pepys plans another liaison, this time with Jane Welch, at an alehouse the following Sunday, but the alehouse is shut (by law) when the time comes around, and Jane is nowhere to be seen.

24 July, 1665

Pepys, amidst his own misdemeanours, notes that the general talk is of the looseness of the Court. Yet we have another irony when a couple of months later, 27 September, Pepys complains that he is being bad-mouthed. Creed has told him that people say Pepys has 'come to be a great swearer and drinker', to which Pepys comments: 'though I know the contrary; but Lord, to see how my late little drinking of wine is taken notice of by envious men to my disadvantage'. The dangers of the drinking environment become all too clear to Pepys, who is thus now associated with the vices we have seen from the beginning are taken to be integral to drinking places. But the entries around this time do show Pepys frequenting taverns much more often, and a couple of entries give a negative gloss on drinking. He notes the necessity of using 'drink and bribe' to make someone friendly to a cause (10 October) and he makes an oath (yet another) that he will drink no more wine until he has finished paying all his accounts.

24 September 1665

An odd entry. Pepys goes to a blind alehouse to buy 20–25lb of cloves from some 'wretched seamen'. They offer him what they think is 20lb, but Pepys discovers them to weigh 25lb. 'But it would never have been allowed by my conscience to have wronged the poor wretches, who told us how dangerously they had got some and dearly paid for the rest of these goods.' It is evidence, however, of a generous nature amongst so much in the diary that makes him out to be rather petty and mean-spirited.

1666

2 September 1666

Pepys views the great fire of London from an alehouse.

What are we to make of this? Why an alehouse? Why not an inn or tavern? Did it offer the only decent view? And why not just watch it, without drinking? Does Pepys view the fire as entertainment? We cannot answer these questions. Historians have focused on his description of the conflagration, not on where it was described from. It is only because of Pepys's desire for precision that the alehouse is mentioned at all, otherwise it has the invisibility of these places taken for granted. On a lesser scale, Goldsmith was to observe the burning down of his theatre whilst sinking a pint. There is something of the nature of resigned frivolity in these actions.

10 October 1666

We have the complete set of contradictions on this day. He hears a sermon, goes off to the Swan, and then kisses 'la fille' (Sarah Udal). He then travels to Islington with a few people 'where I find mine Host dead. Here eat and drank, and merry; and so home and to the office a while.' It is virtually impossible to interpret the sequence. The charm of the diaries is that they often simply record without comment. His mixture of religious observation and taverns we have seen before. What is new is the abrupt movement from finding the host dead to making merry, which reads like a comic juxtaposition. Pepys has a few asides on the life of the host, but appears to have no emotional view of their particular lot. If anything, he has a slightly derogatory attitude, which is perhaps evinced in two entries later that year for December. On the 3rd we get 'Thence at noon home, and there find Kate Joyce, who dined with me. Her husband and she are weary of their new life of being an Inn Keeper, and will leave it, and would fain get some office; but I know none the fool is fit for.' The harsh commentary appears to have affected the editors who note: 'Anthony Joyce was now an inn-keeper in Clerkenwell. He had suffered in the Fire from the loss of several of the houses he owned. He committed suicide in January 1668.' Pepys must have known Anthony Joyce's difficult circumstances. Three days after this entry,

6 December, Pepys records that Will Joyce, a tallow-chandler, mocks his brother's inn-keeping business, as if the neutrality of the entry is authority for his own opinion. On 24 February 1667, Pepys records the death of the mistress of The Bear Tavern, and is somewhat affected by her departure, as she had often tried to kill herself. But Pepys is also drawn to comment on how profitable or otherwise inn-keeping can be. On 30 January 1668, he notes that 'a little Ordinary in Hercules-Pillars-Ally, the Crowne, (a poor sorry place)' brings in six hundred pounds a year, 'which is very strange'. Pepys obviously thinks that this is a reasonably substantial salary, but his attitude shows that he also feels that keeping a drinking place is not quite socially acceptable. Although we cannot tell from the diaries, it might be that Pepys himself had in mind that he would one day inherit an alehouse. The editors' note to 10 October 1667, states: 'By Robert Pepys's will, ownership of the alehouse kept in Brampton by Mrs Gorham was to pass to Pepys's father at her death, and to Pepys after his father's death.' Unfortunately, we hear no more of this alehouse.[28]

1667

2 January 1667

'So down to the Hall and to the Rose tavern, while Doll Lane came to me and we did biber a good deal de vino, et jo did give ella 12 solidos para comprar ella some gans for a new ano's gift. I did tocar et no mas su cosa, but in fit time and place jo creo que je pouvais faire whatever I would con ella' (which I roughly translate as 'we drank a lot of wine, and I gave her 12 shillings [?] to buy some things for a new year's gift. I touched her "thing" but did nothing else, although at another time and place I believe I could do whatever I want with her.') Pepys is still up to his old tricks, using the tavern as the site for his affairs. Again (although we get no explanation) he is stymied by not finding privacy.

26 March, 1667

In an ironic gender twist, Pepys finds that he is forced to drink wine because whenever he is in women's company he is expected to drink their health.

The remainder of the entries for this year are rather cursory with respect to drinking places, and illustrate that we have by now built up a reasonable picture of their use and social integration. There is a brawl in his street at the Three Tuns Tavern door in which one brother kills another. The event does not seem to bother Pepys over much because the next day, 10 May, he dines at the very same place and then goes to church to see the corpse! Pepys casually comments that in fact the brother meant to kill the coachman, who did not please him, but the brother stepped in and was killed instead. On Sunday of that week, 12 May, Pepys goes to an ordinary kept by a periwig maker in an ugly street in Covent Garden, where he has a good meal. On 15 May Sir J. Mennes has to rush into The Devil Tavern 'to shit', the effect on his belly of drinking some whey. On 21 May there is discussion of Sir W. Penn's rise and the significance of him drinking to the King, then turning Roundhead. The 'coffee-house' talk throughout the year comes to be a nostalgic indulgence of how wonderful things were in Cromwell's time (e.g. 12 July and 9 August), and how 'the King and Court were never in the world so bad as they are now for gaming, swearing, whoring, and drinking, and the most abominable vices that ever were in the world – so that all must come to nought'. This is remarkably similar to the complaint against Pepys. To his credit there is no evidence of gloating, and no doubt with the Court going to rack and ruin and the Dutch apparently poised to invade England (manned by disgruntled English sailors) Pepys must feel insecure. Of passing interest is the story the editors tell about the hostelry Pepys stays at in Bishop's Stortford, The Reindeer Inn. Elizabeth Aynsworth, banished from Cambridge by the university authorities, ended up there, and did very well. On one occasion she served the proctor who had sent her away.[29] So it is still possible for women to do well out of the drinking place.

1668–69

We have already seen a number of entries for this year – his visit to the Crowne ordinary at Hercules-Pillars-Ally (see entry 10 October 1666) and his visit to The Ship Tavern to see the 'pretty mistress of the house' (see entry 9 August 1660). Pepys does not refer much to his struggle with drinking and the theatre any more. What dominates in this chapter's narrative is the way his sexual desire and the drinking place intersect, and how these are configured by his attempts to be a more sober-minded individual.

9 February 1668

This is a Sunday filled with business, sexual combat and release. Pepys's own mind now appears to have become hypocritical in the manner he has previously castigated Puritans for. When he says: 'Up, and at my chamber all the morning and the office, doing business and also reading a little of *L'escolle des Filles*, which is a mighty lewd book, but yet not amiss for a sober man once to read over to inform himself in the villainy of the world' we have a clear indication of how the morally upstanding claim the right to 'enjoy' what pleasures they would deny others. The same entry shows that later on that day Pepys masturbates. So, whilst professing his increased sobriety he is able to continue fulfilling his desires. See next entry.

18 February 1668

Yesterday Pepys was in the Swan kissing the maid Sarah. Today he goes to The Dog Tavern where he meets Doll Lane (Mrs Martin), 'and she tells me she is my valentine; and there I did tocar sa cosa and might have done whatever else yo voudrais, but there was nothing but only chairs in the room and so we were unable para hazer algo'. This hints at the fact that Pepys has been in this situation before, entertaining privately, and that there is (usually) furniture appropriate for his wishes which is here absent. Curiously, Pepys appears to make no attempt to change the arrangements, for a month later, 18 March, he again meets Doll Lane at The Dog Tavern, 'and there yo did hazer what I did desire with her and did it backward, not having convenience to do it the other way'. Presumably Pepys and Doll are prevented from a more congenial position yet again by a lack of appropriate furniture. However, Pepys may have warmed to this position because a few days later, 21 March, he goes to see Doll Lane at her house, where, we might presume, there is furniture enough for any position they wish. 'Here yo did hazar la cosa with Mrs Martin backward.' The constraints of tavern space upon sexual activity may have thus encouraged Pepys and Doll to become more sexually adventurous. At this late stage in the diaries tavern and domestic space, in this context at least, are interchangeable places. The tavern truly is a home from home.

19 March 1668

We have already seen Pepys's attitude to women who run taverns and inns. His immersion in a culture where the mistresses of drinking houses are judged upon looks and sexual availability becomes his own problem when his cousin Kate Joyce takes over the inn after her husband's suicide in January of this year. He thinks that she will ruin herself by marrying. 'I do fear that this keeping of an Inne may spoil her, being a young and pretty comely woman and thought to be left well.' He repeats his worry on 22 March, where he hopes that she will marry well in order to get rid of the inn, 'for the trade will not agree with a young widow that is a little handsome; at least, ordinary people think her so'.

1669

This is the last year of diary entries. The usual reason given for Pepys giving up his daily records is that his eyes were failing and that he put this down to his diary-keeping and having to strain his eyes at work. However, given the nature of this chapter's narrative it may be worth considering that Pepys entertained another notion. As early as 25 April 1662 Pepys recorded 'I was much troubled in my eyes, by reason of the healths I have this day been forced to drink.' Did Pepys give up diary writing because of his drinking? The most reasonable explanation was that alcohol exacerbated the problem rather than caused it. Ollard notes the early blame Pepys gives to drinking, and the corresponding subsidence of sore eyes with his greater sobriety, but indicates that Pepys's later understanding is to blame the 'long hours of close work, much of it by candlelight',[30] and such a view cannot really be disputed. However, only a couple of months before Pepys signs off, he writes for 28 March 1669: 'and so, that being done and my journall writ, my eyes being very bad and every day worse and worse, I home. But I find it most certain that strang [sic] drinks do make my eyes sore, as they have done heretofore always, when I was in the country, when my eyes were at the best – there strang beere would make my eyes sore.' It is plausible that Pepys held both views – candlelight and alcohol – and that the threat of blindness, along with the curtailment of his beloved journal, was some kind of moral judgement for his enjoyment of strong drinks.

Notes

1 See David Underdown, *Revel, Riot, and Rebellion: Popular Politics and Culture in England 1603-1660* (Oxford, Clarendon Press, 1985), pp. 140–3 and pp. 217–18, for a discussion of stereotyping.
2 'But as the 1650s wore on, the exiled Charles II became an evocative symbol for a whole constellation of political, social, and cultural aspirations. It is entirely appropriate that many of the reported expressions of popular royalism should have occurred when tongues had been loosened in taverns. Two days before Christmas 1656 William Higgory led the singing in the Black Boy at Ashcott: "Let us drink, let us sing / Here's a health to our King, / And 'twill never be well / Till we have one again."' *Ibid.*, p. 270.
3 *Ibid.*, p. 289.
4 Editors' note in *The Diary of Samuel Pepys*, ed. Robert Latham and William Matthews, 11 vols (London, G. Bell and Sons/Bell and Hyman, 1970–83), for 6 June 1664, from H. Peacham, *Compleat Gentleman*, 1634, reprint 1906.
5 'Sack for my Money; or / A Description of the operation / Of Sack that is still'd in the Spanish Nation', in *The Roxburghe Ballads* (Hertford, Stephen Austin and Sons, 1883–99), vol. VI, p. 318.
6 Note to 'Sack for my Money', *ibid.*
7 *The Roxburghe Ballads*, vol. IX, additional material, p. xcv.
8 *The Roxburghe Ballads* (London, Taylor and Co., 1871), vol. III, p. 630.
9 Leah S. Marcus, 'Pastimes with a Court', in Thomas Healy, ed., *Andrew Marvell* (Harlow, Addison Wesley Longman, 1998), p. 94.
10 Ebsworth calls it 'a silver tube with valves', 'The Wine-Cooper's Delight', in *The Roxburghe Ballads* (Hertford, Stephen Austin and Sons, 1883–99), vol. IV, n. 2, p. 54.
11 K. H. D. Haley, *The First Earl of Shaftesbury* (Oxford, Clarendon Press, 1968),

p. 205. For details of the operation, see pp. 202–5.
12 'A Litany from Geneva', in *The Roxburghe Ballads*, vol. V, p. 196.
13 Haley, *Shaftesbury*, pp. 684, 735.
14 *The Roxburghe Ballads*, vol. V, pp. 161–4, p. 164.
15 See Underdown, *Revel*, especially pp. 50–2.
16 For the full picture of Pepys see Richard Ollard's *Pepys: A Biography* (London, Hodder and Stoughton, 1974).
17 *The Diary of Roger Lowe of Ashton-in-Makerfield, Lancashire, 1663–74*, ed. William L. Sachse, Foreword by Wallace Notestein, n.d., Preface dated 1938.
18 Pepys, *Diary*, 31 August 1661.
19 Lord Askwith, *British Taverns: Their History and Laws* (London, Routledge, 1928), p. 12. Parliament imposed duty on beer in 1643, and on hops in 1645; Charles levied the same duties on beer in 1645 – H. A. Monckton, *A History of English Ale and Beer* (London, Bodley Head, 1966), p. 116.
20 Pepys, *Diary*, 10 May 1663.
21 I have followed the editors' notation for starting the year at the 1st of January, but it should be noted that for Pepys the New Year would have been on 25 March, as it remained until 1752. References to 'next entry' etc. refer to those cited in this chapter.
22 Francis Barker in *The Tremulous Private Body: Essays on Subjection* (London, Methuen, 1984) discusses the role of 'the body' in Pepys's diaries using the work of Derrida, Lacan and Freud, amongst others.
23 For more details of the lithotomy see Ollard, *Pepys*, pp. 42–3. As with the operation on the Earl of Shaftesbury, the chief danger with surgery in a world with no knowledge of sepsis was infection.
24 The editors' note to 26 May 1661 states: 'Puritans objected to kneeling at the receipt of communion', so it may have been a further instance of anti-Puritan sentiment, Pepys, *Diary*.
25 Marcus, 'Pastimes', p. 94.
26 Ollard quotes J. R. Tanner's assessment of Pepys's strategy for dealing with excessive drinking. Tanner says that Pepys used 'the ingenious idea of enlisting a lesser vice to destroy a greater. Pepys was careful about money and he attached money penalties to the breaches of his vow, thus fining himself into sobriety', Ollard, *Pepys*, p. 88.
27 Ollard has a similar conclusion. If Elizabeth had overcome the obstacles of the locked volumes and the shorthand in which they were written, the 'absurd macaronic jumble of languages … would hardly have deceived' her. 'The only gaze from which he was disguising them was his own,' Ollard, *Pepys*, p. 97.
28 According to Ollard, Pepys inherited the Brampton estate in 1661 when his uncle Robert died. There is no mention of the alehouse, however. Ollard, *Pepys*, p. 91.
29 Note to entry 7 October 1667, Pepys, *Diary*.
30 Ollard, *Pepys*, p. 188.

6

'Jovial, brutal, vulgar, graphic Ned Ward'[1]

> Why should a Poet, if he brews,
> Become a Scandal to his Muse?
> And e'ery Blockhead think his Brains
> Run only upon Hops and Grains?[2]

'I have no apology to offer for Ned Ward', begins Howard William Troyer's biography of the Grub Street hack (1667–1731), and it is true that few critics have felt able to justify serious discussion of Ward as a writer of literature. He first gained public attention with *A Trip to Jamaica* (1698), and had other notable successes over the next thirty-odd years, but his outpourings were always to remain in the category of the 'sub-literary'. His fans have ever been on the back foot, aware that the scurrilous, scatological, populist poetry and prose was, and probably always will be, an affront to decent taste (whatever that is), both literary and social. Even in the twentieth century, two editions of *The London Spy* (1698–1700), his most famous production, were bowdlerised because of its gross nature.[3] In 1712 Ward added to his occupation of writer that of landlord. Troyer believes that the move would make sense, for even though Ward 'was at the height of his success as a journalist', the pressures of having to pander to a volatile public taste meant that success might only ever be temporary, as might the political patronage that he also partly depended upon. In addition, 'the popular writer was distinctly without status in society'.[4] His first step on a more promising social ladder was thus inaugurated when he took on an alehouse. His verse advertisement for it reminded potential customers of his literary bent and sense of English heritage: 'There, on that ancient venerable Ground, / Where Shakespear in Heroick Buskins trod, / Within a Good Old Fabrick, may be found / Celestial Liquors fit to charm a God. / Rich Nectar, Royal Punch, and Home-Brew's Ale, / Such as our Father's drank in Times of Yore, / When Beer, Fat Bacon, and salubrious Cale, / Were Food and Physick for the Rich and Poor.'[5] A short time after he moved on to running The Bacchus, a tavern and therefore socially superior to the alehouse, a point he insisted upon in his spat with Alexander Pope (see below).

In the subtitle to one of his works, *The Hudibrastick Brewer: Or, a Preposterous Union Between Malt and Meter* (1714), published a couple of years after he took the alehouse, we get an idea of how Ward viewed himself: a jobbing writer with no pretensions to greatness, yet with a flair for his newly twinned vocations of landlord and writer, which in the narrative of *The Pub in Literature* makes him something of a hero. Evidence that Ward did care for his own work is given in both *Durgen, or a Plain Satyr upon a Pompous Satyrist* (1728) and *Apollo's Maggot in His Cups* (1729), where he takes umbrage at Alexander Pope's denunciation of him in the original version of *The Dunciad* (1728) and in the *Dunciad Variorum* (1729).[6] Ward's analogy between writing and prostitution elsewhere also shows that he was not wont to inflate the profession, as well as showing that he was fully aware of the exigencies of his precarious self-employment, although there is still a certain Wardian zest to the justification: 'The condition of an author is much like that of a strumpet … and if the reason be required why we betake ourselves to so scandalous a profession as whoring or pamphleteering, the same excusive answer will serve us both, viz. That the unhappy circumstances of a narrow fortune hath forced us to do that for our subsistence which we are much ashamed of.'[7]

The London Spy

Ward's greatest achievement is *The London Spy*, which came out in eighteen monthly parts between November 1698 and May 1700. It provides a mainly caustic and humorous view of the smells, sounds and sights of London, and it offers some of the best tavern scenes in literary history. Paul Hyland identifies Ward's general success in the *Spy* as a mixture of having 'pioneered the exploration, representation and study of the life and character of the city as a literary science' and the fact that 'we have come so readily to regard his writings as essentially a faithful record'.[8] Like much of Ward's writing, it was an attempt to create something that would sell well. Although the marketplace is usually derided as a device more prone to produce inferior artistic goods than work of great artistic merit, an argument can be made out that the constant pressure to find new formats has provided literature, especially the novel, with a necessary laboratory for experiment.[9] It also makes for works that are *sui generis*, a hotch-potch of generic transgressions and incorporations. *The London Spy* is also an early example of a literary enterprise with a journalistic base. According to Philip Pinkus in *Grub St. Stripped Bare*, Ward and Tom Brown, another Grub Street hack, were 'forerunners of a tradition of low-style realism which includes Defoe and Dickens',[10] and in Ward's use of a journal-keeping narrating I and eye (notwithstanding its inconsistent application), he provides the type of narrative voice that filtered through to later, more 'respectable' literary productions. These factors are also part of *The London Spy*'s achievement.

Ward himself is in a tradition of the 'sub-literary' that goes back to those writers we saw in 'The Wonderfull Yeares' – Nashe and Dekker.[11] His claim in the dedicatory section of *The London Spy* that his purpose is 'to scourge vice and villainy'[12] takes us directly back to Harman's *A Caveat for Common Cursitors* (1566), and in the best of this tradition the material has its salacious cake and eats it. Like Nashe's *Pierce Penniless* (1592) and Dekker's *The Seven Deadly Sins* (1606) the heart of the nation, London, is anatomised from the point of view of a denizen, but unlike them, Ward does not allegorise it via the deadly sins, which may help bring it even 'closer' to its people, since the pretence of moral justification for its publication is overtly threadbare. His eye for the choicest imagery and an ear for the choicest language are his strength, and can also be claimed as part of this tradition. Ward's originality is that he appears to his readers to be more immediate in his representation of the city, a genuine participant in the low-life scenes he describes rather than an outside observer. The continuous journalistic reporting, with a sense of real time passing, at least in the first few issues, helps give the monthly instalments a novelistic quality. The method also means that any Pepysian critical, clarifying eye is absent, replaced by a different kind of curiosity and wonder, one that attempts to recreate scenes and sensations for the reader's enjoyment, to take part in them; the epithet for Ward's work of 'graphic' is thoroughly deserved.

The first issue begins with the well-worn conceit that the narrator[13] is newly arrived from the country. He says he has had enough of studying 'dreaming prophets, fabulous poets and old doting philosophers' and has 'one by one' got rid of them, 'with a fig for St Augustine and his doctrines, a fart for Virgil and his elegance, and a turd for Descartes and his philosophy'. He is equally scathing of his education in disputation 'which had raised me to the excellence of being half fool and half madman in studying the weighty difference betwixt upside-down and topsy-turvy'.[14] This dismissal of the paraphernalia of an educated gentleman is Ward's two-fingered gesture to polite culture, and typical of the Grub Street writers. They had a smattering, and sometimes much more, of this kind of education, but decided to turn their backs upon it.[15] Indeed, Ward's own knowledge of the great thinkers – superficial or otherwise – is arrayed in his poem *The Tippling Philosophers*, which catalogues the drinking habits of a large number of ancient thinkers.

It is also typical of Ward that the characterisation of the narrator is what we would consider inconsistent. The narrator's formative background has no bearing on what follows, but is there simply to provide an excuse for presenting an innocent eye with which to view the capital's iniquities, although it does give some explanation for the fact that we have a more literate guide than might otherwise be expected: 'Having thus broke loose from the scholar's gaol, my study, and utterly abandoned the conversation of all my old calf-skin companions, I found an itching inclination to visit London.' There is an inference to be drawn that previous guides to the city have been book-bound, literary fictions rather than the real article, and here Ward is breaking out of received understanding to describe London at first hand, as it really is. He makes the recording of London almost a duty, for in order to keep his friends happy he says he will keep a journal whereby the innocent may profit by reflecting upon his 'observation and intelligence' rather than having to learn the hard way 'by practice or experience'.[16] Once there, Ward immediately meets an old friend who lives in London and can be his guide, and after the usual pleasantries they decide to dine at a tavern nearby. So far, nothing out of the ordinary, so to speak.[17]

'As soon as we came near the bar, a thing started up, all ribbons, lace and feathers, and made such a noise with her bell and her tongue that had half a dozen paper-mills been at work within three yards of her, they'd have signified no more to her clamorous voice than so many lutes to a drum, or ladies' farts to a peal of ordnance.' The impressment of hyperbole, the coarse language and the delayed cognition of events conjoin to render this initial experience of the tavern as a vivid, hyper-real, even surreal scene that draws the audience in, rather than reifying it – provided that readers are prepared to accept Ward on his own terms. It continues to exclude any readers who demand literary refinement, both in subject matter and in style. The analogies for the woman's bustle and voice are imaginative, humorous and bizarre, trademark Ward.

He and his schoolfellow are conducted upstairs to a room where his guide's companions are. The acquaintances perform 'wriggling fits' which the narrator finally understands to be an attempt to show 'one another how many sorts of apes' gestures and fops' cringes had been invented since the French dancing-masters undertook to teach our English gentry to make scaramouches of themselves, and how to entertain their poor friends and pacify their needy creditors with compliments and congees'.[18] We are in the world of gallants at the ordinary, updated since we saw them a century ago. They proceed to devour the feast and drink toasts – to the Queen, the Church Established and to the toaster – and fall into nonsensical tavern talk, which annoys the narrator. Ward's facility with metaphoric extravagance remains conspicuous. Of their swearing he comments: 'Oaths were as plenty as weeds in an almshouse garden, and in triumph flew about from one to t'other like squibs and crackers in Cheapside, when the cuckolds-all-in-a-row march in splendour through the City.'[19] On taking his leave, Ward is told by the 'noisy flatterers' that he does not have to pay his share, and once clear of them he asks his friend what sort of people they are. This is an excuse for the drawing of a number of character sketches. These sparks turn out to be a counterfeiter, a fortune-seeker, a treacherous highwayman, a pimp and gambler. His friend is a physician to the rich. They next go to a coffee-house, another excuse for making fun of the sparks, but there is also a member of the Royal Society present, and Ward believes the place could be either 'Quack's Hall, or the parlour of some eminent mountebank'.[20] It is Ward's first day in London and so far he has seen a tavern and a coffee-house. For the evening's entertainment, rather than branch out, it is back to a tavern. It should be noted that Ward mainly describes taverns in *The London Spy*, which fall somewhere between reputable inns and disreputable alehouses. It may be that he (more strictly speaking, his narrative persona, but it may also indicate Ward's preference and social ambition) wishes to be regarded as belonging to the middling classes, too respectable to drink in an alehouse but not aiming so high as the aristocratic. His friend, already identified as a surgeon to those suffering from venereal diseases – prostitutes and the better off – is perhaps the best indication of the social caste to which the narrator adheres. His friend is a self-confessed libertine[21] who maintains himself in this semi-respectable manner, and it is noticeable throughout the *Spy* that money is never presented as an obstacle either to the narrator or his friend.

Once in the tavern Ward describes the easy glide into merriment, free from the foppishness of the first tavern: 'when a glass or two round had given fresh motion to our drowsy spirits, we abandoned all those careful thoughts which make man's life uneasy. Wit begot wit, and wine a thirsty appetite to each succeeding glass. Then open were our hearts, and unconfined our fancies.'[22] The evening is rounded off with songs and catches, and a 'A Song against Music' begets 'A song by a Musician against Poetry'. Ward inserts both of these, and it is a feature of *The London Spy* that Ward is quite happy to insert such doggerel. In fact, the impression given is that he finds it easier to write verse than prose, possibly because in his use of the former he has no narrative to engineer, and it is certainly the case that in general the more demanding prose is better than his verse. However, there is some narrative justification for the conceit at this point in that he claims everyone is so inspired they can 'scarce speak without rhyme and measure, and everyone, like a country fellow at a football meeting, was for showing what he could do, or telling what he had done'.[23] Implicit is the idea that wine inspires wit and poetry, and this is an intermittent theme of the *Spy*.

Ward suddenly tells us that there are some young ladies there. As we have seen before, the representation of women in the drinking-space environment is a complex one. Sometimes they are present without warranting comment – especially in the lower-order environments. Sometimes their presence in the alehouse, tavern or inn is not given out as unusual, although it might still provide a pretext for contrasting the vices and virtues of men and women. And thirdly their presence might be observed purely in sexual terms. Their visit to a drinking place does not in itself signify to others that they are sexually loose. The significance of women in a drinking place is therefore one dependent upon a large number of contextual factors. In this instance, the women are 'equal but different' members of the party – they are simply 'there', and Ward only notices them in order to provide a springboard for some of his generalisations about them, a digression he is prone to in later issues. One of the women feels slighted by a poet who has not thought her worthy of his muse. He replies with: 'Madam, how great and good your virtues are, / I can't well tell, or truly do I care', and continues in this vein.[24] She responds herself in verse with dignity and wit, which, when she has finished gives Ward leave to praise and patronise women in equal measure.

Someone next offers a poem which has supposedly been written by an inhabitant of Bedlam. What Ward says of it after is perhaps another insight into how his own work is viewed. 'This frantic piece of bombast pleased wonderfully. No profane jest to an atheist, or bawdy story to an old bachelor, could have been more acceptable. One commended the loftiness of the fancy; another the aptness of the language; a third, the smoothness of the verse; so that the madman had like to have run away with the bays from us all had not one in the company been author in print to the great applause of the whole nation.'[25] There is a market-sense of literature here, that literature must work for its audience. We also have here a configuration of the elements of literature, drinking space and a national dimension that we have noted before. There is the belief that this writing is as good as any other, yet national taste elevates a different literature. There is a meta-fictional element in that the commentary is of course a commentary by Ward upon work by Ward. What counts for good literature is placed within the context of inspiration, but is undermined by the idea that these are drunken sots rather than genuine poets. It is further undermined by its appearance within this particular tavern space, an inapt space for the lofty sentiment and elevated form (compare with The Crown below), an undermining which may have been doubled when we think that the publication itself would most likely have been found within the tavern, sold and read out there.

By now 'the nimble spirits of the reviving juice had rather overpowered than enlivened the noblest of our faculties' and reason has been ousted from its throne. It is ten o'clock and, once they have paid their 'clubs', time to ramble and seek out 'the dark intrigues of the Town', the 'staggering bravadoes and strolling strumpets'.[26] On this cliff-hanger does the first part of *The London Spy* end.

The next instalment informs the reader that the hour is not ten but the more modest one of nine – when Bow Bell rings out the time and all the apprentices know they can pack up work – in theory at least. Ward renders the confusion of noise, sights and smells with his usual liveliness. In his depiction of the latter we get: 'We had not walked the usual distance between a church and an alehouse, when some odoriferous civet-box perfumed the air and saluted our nostrils with so refreshing a nosegay that I thought the whole city (Edinburgh-like) had been overflowed with an inundation of sir-reverence.'[27] The connection between alehouse and church is not unusual, and the ratio between the two in any given place was often a cause of concern for the authorities and moral guardians. It was a ready marker for mapping a town or city and judging its moral worth. Ward takes it as read that the distance between the two is minimal, and that there is a necessary connection, as if the Lord's church presupposes the Devil's chapel. However, Ward is also mapping the space in his own manner, with the emphasis as ever on lower body functions – the prevalence of faeces ('sir-reverence') overwhelms everything. It is a way of placing both church and alehouse on the same level, but also a way of suggesting that London itself is overwhelmed by filth, literally and metaphorically. Once again Ward continues to use delayed cognition to represent the city, for the smell is then apparently explained by the arrival of 'a deadmonger's wagon laden with a stinking corpse (by reason of long keeping)', another detail that creates London as a physical, diseased body. But Ward has to be undeceived of this apperception, for it is no other than a vehicle for carrying muck by those who have realised too late that excrement cannot be turned into gunpowder after all.[28]

Next port of call this evening is a coffee-house which his friend the doctor is familiar with, because some of his clients work there. Like the alehouse later, Ward describes a hidden London full of dark passages and surreal topography: 'we blundered through the long dark entry of an ancient fabric, groping our way like subterranean labourers in the caverns of a coal-pit, till we found the stairs, which were raised as perpendicular as a tiler's ladder'.[29] The landlady's coffee-room they enter is full of incongruous elements: 'a large old Bible open, with her spectacles upon one of St Paul's epistles; next to it was a quartern pot, two or three stone bottles, a roll of plaster, and a pipe of tobacco, with a handful of fire in a rusty grate, a pint coffee-pot before it, and a green earthen chamber-pot in the chimney-corner'. A crowning touch is 'an abstract of the Acts of Parliament against drinking, swearing, and all manner of profaneness', for we soon learn, via the shaking of the room from above and the subsequent appearance of 'a couple of airy youths' from the room upstairs, that this is a brothel.[30] The youths leave and the prostitutes appear, and after some flirting the doctor asks for payment from one of them for the last treatment she received from him. She berates and silences him. Ward and his friend depart, leaving a newly arrived aged man to his sado-masochistic whipping treat. In need of repose as well as further entertainment, they head for 'the dark house at Billingsgate', a drinking place (boozing-ken) popular with sailors.

On their rambles they are stopped by a constable who seeks to arrest them on the merest whim. The narrator's friend calls himself 'a surgeon' when asked his profession, to which the constable retorts: 'and why not a chirurgeon, I pray, sir? I could find in my heart to send you to the Compter for presuming to corrupt the King's English before me, his representative'.[31] The two words were interchangeable.[32] Of course Ward's whole literary enterprise is a type of corruption of the King's English and a threat to authority, just as their mere presence before the constable appears to be suspect in the state's eyes. But, as with the lack of any real distinction between those poets who are lauded by the nation and those who recite their wares in a tavern, there is a sense that one word or one type of literature may be as good as the next, that the differentiation between official language and literature and that which is not authorised is arbitrary. The two escape his clutches on this occasion when they claim that they are 'sober, civil persons' – although the constable suggests they may only be asserting this to cover their drunkenness. It seems, however, that this is the image that is required by authority. In any case, they are alerted to the fact that 'one word of contradiction would have cost us a night's lodging in the Compter, for he makes no more of committing a man than a tavern-drawer does of kissing the cook'.[33] Their tavern-crawl is a challenge to the state.

They reach their destination, finding 'the entrance of that nocturnal theatre in whose delightful scenes we proposed to terminate the night's felicity. At last we stumbled upon the threshold of a gloomy cavern where, at a distance, we saw lights burning like candles in a haunted cave where ghosts and goblins keep their midnight revels.'[34] Ward does not just foreground the nature of these drinking spaces as living theatre, and as magical, transformative spaces, but he is also showing that those who use them share in this sense. In this instance what they first appear to have stumbled into is something akin to Elynour Rummyng's alehouse, here called a 'smoky boozing-ken', for it is full of women, 'a tattered assembly of fat motherly flat-caps' drinking warm ale and brandy. Ward's descriptive powers are reminiscent of Skelton's:

> every one as slender in the waist as a Dutch skipper in the buttocks, and looked together like a litter of squab elephants. Their noses were as sharp as the gnomon of a dial, and looked as blue as if they had been frost-nipped. Their cheeks were as plump as an infant's buttocks, but adorned with as many crimson carnosities as the face of a nobleman's butler who has lived forty years in the family, and plainly proved by the depth of their colour that brandy is a nobler dye than claret. Their tongues were as loud as the Temple horn.[35]

When one of them overhears Ward's friend allude to them as 'whores' he gets an earful, and the two of them slink off into another room, where there are watermen playing dice. It materialises that this place serves a number of functions, for in come a couple who pretend to wait for the next boat to Gravesend. When they are told that the boat will not leave till four o'clock in the morning they ask if they might not have a bed until then. '"Yes, yes, sir, if you please," replied the pious beldam, "God forbid else! We have several couple above in bed, that wait for the tide as well as you, sir."' A couple of sailors arrive and entertain the crowd by hoisting a fiddler on to a hook by his breeches. He is so scared that he fouls himself, 'begging with humble submission to be set safe upon terra firma, all the time dripping his guts upon the hearth like a roasting woodcock'.[36] Eventually he wriggles free and falls into his own mess. The night continues until they are worn out and go to bed (the boozing-ken also serving as a doss house), in preparation for the delights of the next day when they will do the London sights. So ends Issue II.

Issue III opens with them waking up, washing and dressing. By now *The London Spy* has picked up a narrative pace and whetted the reader's appetite for more adventures, for more insights into the city of London, whilst having enough concrete description to create a realistic environment. The details of preparation, and particularly the room they wake to find themselves in, is presented through Ward's hyperbolic lens, but nevertheless imbues the activities with the kind of 'low-life realism' Pinkus avows:

> Its walls were adorned with as many unsavoury finger-dabs as an Inns of Court bog-house. The ceiling was beautified like a soldier's garret, or a Compter chamber, with smutty names and bawdy shadows sketched by unskilful hands with candle-flame and charcoal. The bed, 'tis true, was feathers, but most of them large enough to make pens or tooth-pickers. And an earthen chamber-pot, as big as a three-gallon stein, glazed o'er with green, looked as fine as any Temple mug, or country pudding-pan.[37]

Custom House, Monument and Gresham College are duly visited. As Hyland observes, it is only in this third issue that 'official' London is seen. Up until this point the visits have been to 'the ordinary junctions of popular society where each sixpenny issue of the *Spy* would have been sold, perused, and read aloud along with other newspapers and journals'.[38] When he visits Bedlam (which the narrator mischievously guesses to be the Lord Mayor's palace before he is told otherwise[39]) – he finds a madman with a drinker's nose, and suggests he send to the man in the moon for some more bottles of claret (the joke relies on the then commonplace that 'the man-in-the-moon drinks claret'[40]).

At the beginning of IV, and after these and some other sights they are in need of some refreshment. Their choice is a Quaker tavern, where the Quakers are now allowed to drink as well as any 'Protestant priest, or a Latitudinarian fuddle-cap'.[41] The Quakers were heartily despised at this time, and Ward duly targets them as objects of hypocrisy. The place is as silent as a funeral, and the Quakers are drinking only half pints. 'We, like true Protestant topers, scorning the hypocrisy of tippling by half-pints, as if we drank rather to wash away our sins than our sorrows, appeared barefaced, called for a quart at once, and soon discovered our religion by our drinking.' Thus the religious/political symbolism of drinking emerges in the unlikeliest of places. Ward notes that the Quakers' method of slyly drinking as much as they wish is to first remove their hat and ask their companion how much they think it cost. 'But before thou tellest me, let me drink, and I hope thou understandest my meaning.'[42] A little tipsy, Ward and his surgeon friend begin to sing a song on the natural relationship between wine and religion, and are evicted for being too unruly.

They repair to The Angel in Fenchurch Street, where some of his friends' companions are drinking. Things are going well, with merry songs and catches, when the tavern is raided by a 'carrionly cony-fumble' and 'his crazy crew of cornigerous halberdiers, who looked together like Judas and his complices, or a parcel of Tom turd-men with their long poles coming to gauge a vault'. As with the previous meeting with a constable, the 'surgeon'/'chirurgeon' episode, Ward cannot refrain from disgraceful punning. There it was 'coniwable', with a play on 'coney'. It means dupe (as in 'coney-catching'), but also whore. Hyland's glossary notes a sexual pun if pronounced 'cunny'. Here, 'fumble' is from 'fumbler', 'a sexually impotent man',[43] and so the combination of 'cone' and 'fumble' is an apt punning conjunction.

The constable complains: '"Look you, d'ye see me, gentlemen? 'Tis an unseasonable time of night for people to be tippling. Every honest man ought to have been in bed an hour or two ago." "That's true," said I, "for nobody ought to be up so late, but constables and their watches."' It is the first instance of repartee on Ward's own part, for which they are committed to the Compter (prison). Once inside Ward presents it as a microcosm of the outside world already seen, full of injustice for those on the margins, and with a cruel sense of humour: once again we see someone humiliated through excreta.[44]

With the Compter we have our complete round of generic low-life spaces: taverns, coffee-houses-cum-brothels, boozing-kens-cum-doss houses, and prison. Other spaces are for the tourists or business men: the Exchange, Bedlam and the Custom House; or particular sites, the New Exchange or Bartholomew Fair. However, even in prison there is a drinking place, and in the morning they go to this cellar. He falls into talking with a woman who is there because she refused to sleep with a creditor. Here, as on occasion in other parts of *The London Spy*, Ward appears to show genuine compassion for those who are punished for no other crime than poverty: 'For people that are poor to pay such unreasonable extortion as cent per cent, it's a scandal to the laws and a shame to Christianity that such indigent wretches should be so heavily oppressed, contrary to all charity and justice, to satisfy the unreasonable interest, or else the unmerciful revenge, of such unconscionable misers.'[45] His description of this 'subterranean boozing-ken' is as fulsome as many of his other pictures, but he manages to give this one a biblical quality, as if by being there they are progeny of the Fall: 'Like undutiful children, we trod and spat upon the bare sin of our first parent, Earth, for 'twas floored like a barn, though it stunk like a stable, for everybody pissed as they sat, without the use of a chamber-pot.'[46] The charges are laid against them – late drinking, refusing to go home – but worst of all Ward is accused of 'aggravating words', another reminder of the power of (his) aberrant language. With a sense of poetic justice, Ward claims he was out on the King's business as a gauger (Excise officer) and is released. There is nothing for it but to celebrate their freedom by taking a glass of wine at The Rose Tavern in the Poultry.

The strain of continuing the semblance of a narrative purpose starts to become apparent. Once the pretence of the innocent abroad has been dispatched, and the novelty of seeing London through fresh eyes has worn off, *The London Spy* has to crank up each new scene. Part V takes us to St Paul's and St Paul's Churchyard. We see a few more types – again, interesting enough in themselves, but evidence of the lack of narrative urgency in Ward's 'rambles' – and after a tiring day's sightseeing we repair to another tavern, The Crown, where Ward represents the tavern space in a new light. His sympathies for the monarchy are evident, for he believes any hostelry with such a sign should have a decent cellar: 'We were near the sign of Honour's fountain, the Crown, the representation of which royal diadem I thought no vintner would presume to distinguish his house by, unless he had wine in his cellar fit to bless the lips of princes.' It casually reminds us that the symbolic importance of these places and names are woven into the fabric of everyday life. The idea that this place bears some relation to the source of England's well-being is continued, because Ward proceeds to measure the place against some ideal of a royal space, albeit shot through with drink. Their arrival in this representative of the monarchy is greeted as it should be, 'where the jolly master, like a true kinsman of the Bacchanalian family, met us in the entry with a manly respect and bid us welcome'. The language continues to suggest the reverence due to the monarchical space. They ask to go upstairs, always a sign of social status, and they are shown to 'a large stately room'.[47] The sense of being inside the equivalent of a royal residence is continued when Ward discerns 'the master-strokes of the famed Fuller's pencil',[48] an artist renowned for his decorations of taverns (and, incidentally, for his drunkenness). The majestic scenery revives their senses, just as good art should (so the implication is). It is 'noble entertainment'. In respect of such scenes, they request claret fit for such heroes as are drawn in the decorations: 'He accordingly gave directions to his drawer, who returned with a quart of such inspiring juice that we thought ourselves translated into one of the houses of the Heavens, and were there drinking immortal nectar, amongst gods and goddesses.' Perhaps with the desire to display his own aesthetic worth and sense of judgement, Ward configures drink, art, nobility, inspiration and the (monarchic) state into one glorious tavern space. As a token of thanks – for the fact that The Crown has met all his aspirations as to what a heavenly tavern should be – he scribbles some lines, as if only poetry can rise to the occasion.

They have to leave and as soon as they step not ten strides from the door they are faced with a London (the nation) that reveals itself still to be ever the dangerous place the *Spy* has already shown us. There are some 'tun-bellied mortals' with 'bulldog countenances and preposterous bodies' who are waiting to press people into the army. The juxtaposition, with some irony, is that the royal motif, the ideal space and haven they have just departed, is a tavern only. The world of actual authority is much harsher, a point emphasised when in the next issue he visits Bridewell and sees people incarcerated unjustly and receiving cruel punishment. But the disparity between the current parlous political state and times when the country was blessed by a proper monarch is proposed by Ward throughout. In Issue VIII, at the sight of King Charles II's effigy in Westminster Abbey, he says that 'as much as he excelled his predecessors in mercy, wisdom and liberality, so does his effigy exceed the rest in liveliness, proportion and magnificence',[49] and in IX a statue of Charles I reminds him of that king's 'righteous life, unjust sufferings and unparalleled martyrdom', and crowns it with more verse: 'Thus the mad crowd, who could not ills foresee / Of just restraint endeavouring to be free, / Took off thy head, because themselves would headless be.'[50]

After Bridewell, in a coffee-house, he sees an advert in the *Flying Post* for 'my Dame Butterfield's invitation to her Essex calf and bacon'. This event is to take place at Mob's Hole, in Wanstead parish, Essex, that is, outside the city of London – about seven miles from Mile End, according to the distance he complains of walking. Ward obviously has some concern that he is selling his literary goods under false pretence: 'I am sensible it is something of a digression, or rather a deviation from the title, but though the feast was in the country, yet the guests were Londoners, and therefore what we shall observe among 'em may be reasonably admitted.'[51] He conjures up a vision of a carnival exodus from London to the country: 'Horses, coaches, carts, wagons and tumbrels filled the roads, as if the whole town had been going to encamp; all occupied by men, women and children, rich, poor, gentle and simple, having all travelling conveniences suitable to their quality.'[52] The complete social mix is evidence that the spaces within London itself are more clearly demarcated: different taverns and coffee-houses attract differentiated social groups. The public 'house' at Mob's Hole takes on the quality of a social melting pot, where all are welcome regardless of gender or social class. But it is not to the narrator's liking. The place is surrounded by 'the mobility' (the 'mob') and it is all he and his friend can do to find a quiet spot in the garret – Ward is upstairs once again. He reminds the reader of the vastness of the social scale represented: 'the parade where ragtag and bobtail were promiscuously jumbled amongst City quality from beau to booby, and the merchant's lady to the thumb-ringed ale-wife'.[53]

They take a stroll amongst 'the buzzing multitude' when a coach with 'four merry dames' arrives. Ward enters into some banter with them. They ask him the time. He says he has no watch. Another suggests that it is not working and that he is ashamed to show it. Ward then starts up a chain of innuendo, although it is not clear whether the women participate in the ribaldry or are unwilling dupes. '"Indeed, madam, if it be, I can see nothing in your ladyship's face that will wind it up again." "Why, sir," says the third, "can faces be used to wind up watches?" "Yes, madam," answered I, "such a one as I carry about me, which is made without wheels and will give such a lady as you are a better time of day, when it's standing, than other watches do when they are moving."' The conversation continues along these lines, but Ward fears he will be 'out-talked' by them – either they are too easy targets or they are better at innuendo – makes his excuses and leaves. The narrator's persona is not always in evidence, and when it disappears the reader is left with a flatter, more neutral tone. Here, however, there is something of the manner of a wit who is prepared to concede failure at certain junctures, and it is touches like this which help make the narrator more of an engaging 'character'. A controlling conscience that experiences, rather one that merely observes or is ostensibly moralistic, is part of the attraction of the *Spy*.[54]

When he moves into the kitchen the sight of the calf is not appetising, for what meat there remains is burnt. He eats nothing and, ever in search of entertainment, finds 'a poor fiddler scraping over the tune of "Now Ponder Well You Parents Dear", and a parcel of country people dancing and crying to't'. The guise of the narrator as the innocent come to the city is well and truly lost with his criticism of these simple folk enjoying third-rate music and dancing. They are so moved by the sorrowful song that 'their dancing seemed rather a religious worship than a merry recreation'.[55] If the *Spy* has shown up the dark side of the capital, it has also shown a distaste for country life, both in the narrator's original abandonment of it, and here when the city comes to lap the country's pleasures up for its own amusement, only to despise the unsophisticated nature of their attractions. It also helps maintain the sense that London is the nation's vanguard in all things.

But of course Ward is also unsparing when he returns to the capital. They enter another coffee-house in Issue IX: 'We squeezed through the fluttering assembly of snuffing peripatetics till we got to the end of the room, where, at a small table, we sat down, and observed that though there was abundance of guests, there was very little to do, for it was as great a rarity to hear anybody call for a dish of Politician's porridge, or any other liquor, as it is to hear a sponger in a company ask what's to pay, or a beau call for a pipe of tobacco.'[56] Like taverns, the coffee-house space cannot be solely classified in terms of use or clientele – we have already seen that the coffee-house, like the tavern, could be used as a brothel (see above, Issue II). The fact that although the number of coffee-houses rapidly increased until there were at least 500 in London at the beginning of the eighteenth century, the number of taverns did not decrease,[57] and both here and in Pepys's diaries we can see that the same people moved freely between both. It has been argued that the emergence of coffee-houses some time in the 1650s sowed the seeds for a new kind of space for public debate. They were readily used for gathering of intelligence, newspapers were freely available and they were a favourite resort for politicians. This particular coffee-house that Ward is describing is 'Man's', the most famous at that end of town. His description of it overlaps with the received image we have of the coffee-house in general. 'Politician's porridge' is an epithet for coffee, and some lines Ward scribbles upon the coffee-house suggest that the place is frequented by such state hangers-on, spies and courtiers eager for news. It is also partly filled with the kind of beaux and fops Ward so readily dismissed in the first tavern. In Man's, Ward and his friend alienate the gallants by smoking, in opposition to the snuff that the gallants take. A dumb idiot appears outside and mimics the gallants' gestures – 'the strut, the toss of the wig, the carriage of the hat, the snuff-box, the fingering of the foretop, the hanging of the sword'.[58] What the coffee-house has, in spite of all these comic antics, is the sobriety and seriousness that those who have argued for its importance as a public forum require. What it clearly lacks, in Ward's eyes, is the excitement and conviviality that a tavern provides. (The one coffee-house in the *Spy* that does receive his unqualified approval is the Little Devil coffee-house in XIV, but this is because of its excellent punch.)[59] His dislike of the function of coffee-houses as a meeting place for political discussion is signalled at his arrival, for he surmises that the apartments at the end of the main room were where 'the beau-politicians retired upon extraordinary occasions to talk nonsense by themselves about state affairs, that they might not be laughed at'.[60] His indifference to politics here, coupled with his praise of Charles I and II (as described above), show us that Ward's ideological sympathies are matters of faith rather than thought, but also suggest the level of political-(non)engagement at street level.

When the narrator and friend emerge from the coffee-house, his friend asks him to note 'two great taverns on the other side the way'. They are ordinaries where 'many fools' estates have been squandered away'.[61] Evidently nothing has changed since the 'wonderfull yeares'. On to Charing Cross, Covent Garden market and Turkish Baths (Hummums). He returns to another coffee-house in X, the Wits', and uses it as an excuse to discourse on the nature of a modern critic. But the strain on the *Spy*'s narrative *raison d'être* shows once more when for no reason whatsoever Ward inserts 'A Letter from a Lawyer in Town to a New-Married Officer in the Country' in verse. The instalment picks up again when they visit Bartholomew Fair, which Ward stretches across two issues. An alehouse provides the setting for two hard-up servants, but even this compares favourably with the visit to a coffee-house next in Aldersgate Street 'where doctors of the body, who study Machiavelli much more than Hippocrates, metamorphose themselves into State politicians, and the slippery tongues of thoughtless mechanics undertake to expound the mysteries of Scripture'[62] and they end up arguing with some men who nostalgically remember the good old days of Cromwell.[63]

The next time we get to the tavern is in pursuit of the roasting of a 'magnificent piece of beef' of some four hundred and fifteen pounds.[64] When they get there Ward comments that the tavern 'abounded in those delights that were in other taverns very difficult to be found'. When they finally squeeze their way into the kitchen past the throng, there are a group of 'jack-winders' considering how to spit such a huge, recalcitrant beast, and their machinations are described as 'heathen priests going to kill the sacrifice'.[65] The beef, when it arrives, is 'rich, fat, young, well-fed, delicious meat',[66] and they write a verse thank you on the wall and leave for a coffee-house.

Ward's distaste for the coffee-house space, as opposed to the tavern space, is again evident, this time through religious associations: 'Considering coffee to be a liquor that sits most easy upon wine, we thought it the best way to check the aspiring fumes of the most Christian juice by an antichristian dose of Muhammadan loblolly.' He also makes the usual snide comment that coffee-houses are the seat of unsubstantiated gossip for 'credulous noddles'.[67] Amidst the silence, a 'jolly red-faced old toper' gives a speech on the state of the capital and the nation to the effect that proper order has been restored, in the form of the Established Church, now that Dissenters and their compatriots have been duly ousted. It is Ward at his knee-jerk political enthusiasms again. Praise is given to the present Lord Mayor, and this sets the scene for Ward's observation of the Lord Mayor's Show.

Once again Ward appears as a highly interested 'spy' who is also an onlooker. Some people fill a leather apron with excreta, prick the apron with holes and then wave it above the crowd. He calls these 'the ingenious rabble',[68] 'the mob' and the 'plebeian gentry'.[69] His zest for scatology would identify him with the people described, whereas his objectification of the people into these epithets suggests a wished-for distance. These may or may not be the same people he meets with in the taverns and coffee-houses, but in those spaces he is more likely to be at one with them; there is more a sense of camaraderie with fellow drinkers. Out in the open, here, at the feast at Mob's Hole, at Bartholomew Fair, the mob are to be derided and described as different from himself. Some of the complexity of attitudes is neatly framed in the verse with which Ward ends this Issue XII: 'The bully cits marched after in a throng, / Huzza'd by the mob, as drummed and piped along, / Whilst wise spectators did their pomp disdain, / And with contempt behold the draggling train.'[70] But all together it can be seen that the narrator's own position as a 'wise spectator' is hardly unassailable.

Wandering about Tower Hill he is astonished to be able to walk 'by forty or fifty houses and not see an alehouse, which was a greater sign of a sober neighbourhood than I had observed before, since I came to London'.[71] However, his friend draws attention to a tavern called the Green Monster which has ruined most of its owners, the sole purpose of which appears to provide a jest on the fate of a jiltish wife who is herself jilted by a vintner. She ends up with a draper, which Ward thinks wise, for when the draper is tired of her he cannot 'without dishonour to the linen-draper's trade, leave her without a smock to her back'.[72] Such an insertion is a prelude to an admittance that the *Spy* is once again rudderless, sailing about 'till mere accident and our own motion, without shaping course' brings them to a tabernacle.

The narrator discovers that the preacher has a chin 'as long as the handle of [a] pickaxe' and a whiney voice. It is none other than the disgraced Titus Oates, preaching in Wapping.

The aimless sailing continues in XIV until they find an alehouse. Ward describes the landlady in unflattering terms of corpulence and a fiery-red face,[73] who nevertheless regards his friend as 'noble Captain', which distinguishes him from the other sailors in the Wapping hostelry. Ward and friend watch as she berates a 'poor dejected water-rat' having a smoke. His idleness takes away her living and is no way to get further employment. But she nevertheless takes pity on him and gives him sixpence to seek out a job.[74] Again, Ward uses this drinking-house setting to show some compassion for certain social groups, here it is 'salt-water kind of vagabonds'. This is immediately followed by the entry of a sailor who has just been paid and wants to 'swim and toss in an ocean of good liquor'.[75] Of course, the alehouse turns into a trap to take all Jack's nine months' pay, although there is a less sympathetic tone at this observation and more the note of harsh, resigned fate.

From thence to a place that is half tavern, half music-hall. They are shown round and admire the public music room and other rooms for entertaining.[76] The kitchen is likewise regally fitted. Having given us the praiseworthy aspects of the establishment, Ward renders another surreal drinking-house scene. They are taken by the landlord downstairs 'to a subterranean sanctuary, where his [the landlord's] friends may be protected from the insolence of the churchwardens, who every Sunday, like good Christians, break the Sabbath themselves, to have the lechery of punishing others for the same fault'. Rather than describe any of its customers, he describes the wall panels, the main purpose of which is to show women as devilish and lewd: one panel shows 'a parcel of drunken women tormenting the Devil, some plucking him by the nose like St Dunstan, some spewing upon His Worship, others endeavouring to piss his eyes out, and many other suchlike whimsies'. Another panel shows women fighting to gather the fruit of a banana tree for lascivious ends. On leaving the place Ward says the house 'may very justly be styled, by such who love good wine and a pleasant room to sit in, the "Paradise of Wapping"'. Within a single hostelry Ward creates an absurdist heaven and hell through the decor. The music room is beautifully decorated, but appears to have originally been designed for religious purposes; the entertainment rooms are painted with humorous panels; the kitchen – the most expensive room – is fitted out lavishly enough to dress dinner for a prince; and the lowest room is a haven for Sabbath-breakers who are to be surrounded by blasphemous and lewd pictures. However, the noticeable lack of custom in the 'Paradise of Wapping' is perhaps the biggest comment on the heavenly space, functionally and symbolically barren. Without hustle and bustle it is no real tavern.

It must have seemed to Ward that the *Spy* had reached the end of its saleable attractiveness for in XV he likens its fading charm to 'a fair Town Miss, of a twelvemonths' standing, when she has surfeited the appetites of those debauchees who are always ranging after novelty' and so changes her look. The *Spy* attempts to transform itself by treating 'more upon men and manners, opening the frauds and deceits practicable in many trades', recording conversations, characters of trades, 'and remarks upon all occurrences worth notice'. He describes victuallers, how they become haughty after humble beginnings, astrologers and wise-women, constables and informers. In XVI his guide abandons him, and when he lists all the sites so far visited he purveys the sense that London has been exhausted: 'the tombs at Westminster, the lions in the Tower, the rogues in Newgate, the mad people in Bedlam, and the merchants upon the 'Change'. Thus left alone, as if he were 'a man-hater that loved no company', he immediately goes to a tavern, as if the *Spy* were about to redo London through the eyes of an experienced but friendless outsider, since a tavern is where the narrator began in Issue I.[77] He amuses himself by listening to the conversation of the sailors there until he is befriended by an old man, who rails against his lot in life. To a coffee-house and then a private house – the only one we see in the *Spy* – where, once drunk, the entertainment is a Quaker and a parson arguing with each other. The conceit of not having his friend with him all the time allows for the narrator to arrange to meet him in various places, and so in Issue XVII they meet at The Dolphin in Lombard Street, and after eating start to swear against money, only to be given a warning against such talk by another customer. The *Spy* peters out into a description of a christening, Dryden's funeral, and a dispute between two astrologers in the last issue, XVIII.

It is a limping end to the *Spy*, which has given its audience such an entertaining view of London at the very end of the seventeenth century. The tavern space is clearly Ward's preferred habitat, the coffee-shop only coming close when it can provide the same kind of inebriety and conviviality. The conceit of the 'spy' as guide to the city begs the question of patronage. Ward is a naturalised Londoner, spying on Londoners, for the amusement of Londoners. Although the overlap with journalism is evident, a journalism that simply reported events – as with the Lord Mayor's Show and Dryden's funeral – was not the strength of the *Spy*. If it had been, it could have gone on indefinitely. Nor was the isolated description of men and manners, as Ward overtly turns to in the later issues, its predominant attraction. Simple descriptions of the main tourist sites was likewise not sufficient. Where the *Spy* succeeds is in its rendering of all these features through the Wardian eye, by turns gross, witty, compassionate, surreal and revealing. But when the narrative premise rambles on too long, he begins to separate out the constituent factors, trying out character descriptions, discoveries of trade secrets, current events, and the whole is somewhat lesser than the sum of the parts.

A guide to good fellows

Although *The London Spy* is the beginning and end for most references to Ward, his other work is also of interest for *The Pub in Literature* for he found a number of other angles for the alehouses and taverns of early eighteenth-century London, works in which they are the main subject. A tavern is the setting for a 'moral' tale in *The Rise and Fall of Madam Coming-Sir: Or, An Unfortunate Slip from the Tavern-Bar, Into the Surgeon's Powdering-Tub* (1703),[78] where a country girl goes from high to low after she takes up work in the tavern. It details the usual country–city distinction: within a week or so she has learned to divest herself of innocent ways and look the part of a Lazy Gentlewoman in order to take her place 'working' in the bar. The story draws upon the common cheating practices that we have seen in alewife literature: she learns about inflated reckonings and how to flirt with men so that they spend more. Although she is courted for her beauty no man will offer marriage: 'every Body talk'd to me of *Love*, but no body of *Matrimony*; so that I found they all wanted me for a *Mistress*, but none car'd to take me for a *Wife*'.[79] In miniature it foreshadows Defoe's *Roxana* and *Moll Flanders*, with its perfunctory tone and depiction of a predatory environment in which women are hard-pressed to survive. A young officer persuades her to meet in his lodging at St James's 'where I suffer'd that to be spoiled in one Minute, which had been Eighteen Years in Nursing to a Perfection'.[80] He is posted abroad and so she is abandoned, managing to get just thirty guineas out of him before he leaves. She agrees to become a prostitute for a woman for a year in return for being looked after during her unwanted pregnancy. Her clients become of lesser and lesser status until she gets venereal diseases and is kicked out. The inexorable trajectory of her downfall is a consequence of the tavern environment, and one that we will see in later narratives.[81]

The Rambling Fuddle-Caps: Or, A Tavern-Struggle For a Kiss (1709)[82] likewise has a tavern as its central locus, where a rake spends his time attempting to kiss Nell, who defends herself in body and word. The father turns up, gives his son some good advice, only to receive the reply: 'But what need you Cobble so loud at a Body, / A Tavern sometimes is as good as a Study: / I've heard you oft say so, That Conversing and Drinking, / Must quicken our Brains more than Reading and Thinking'.[83] But in a work which has only the minimal narrative structure it simply ends up with father and son drinking together and burying their differences.

More substantial is *The History of the London Clubs* (1709), which was in its seventh edition by 1756. Ward is in typically irreverent form in the Epistle Dedicatory, offered up 'To that luciferous and sublime Lunatic, the Emperor of the Moon', and in the Preface, where, unlike Fielding's opening comments to *Tom Jones* a few decades later, Ward refuses to give a Bill of Fare in case it palls the reader's appetite. After the preliminaries, Ward soon gets into the heart of the matter:

> Though the Promotion of Trade, and the Benefits that arise from Conversation, are the specious Pretences that every Tippling-Club, or Society are apt to assign as a reasonable Plea for their unprofitable Meetings; yet most considerate Men have found by Experience, that the general End thereof, is a promiscuous Encouragement of Vice, Faction, and Folly, at the unnecessary Expence of that Time and Money, which might be better employed in their own Business, or spent with much more Comfort in their several Families.[84]

As we have already seen, clubs became a major feature of London life in the seventeenth century and this has continued until the present day. Their venues were originally taverns and alehouses (although in later centuries, when clubs were bigger and wished to be more exclusive, they used private buildings, one of the factors which led to the demise of 'tavern life'[85]). They would usually meet once a week and members would pay a fixed amount which would go towards drink. Each club would draw up a list of rules and aims. Ward typically punctures the whole idea and observes that such 'Suck-bottle assemblies' are nothing more than an excuse for boozing, and draws on the familiar idea that these places are the antithesis of a sober work ethic. He is scathing of the idea that the laws of the Society can really 'preserve Peace, Unity, and Sobriety' and that the penalty for breach of these codes, fining, simply provides more money with which to get drunk at the quarterly festival. His target is the notion that order can be maintained simply by 'a few insignificant orders'.[86] The humour probably betrays Ward's Tory sympathies, in that clubs with their regulations are no substitute for rule by deference to tradition. He pours further scorn on this idea that clubs are in a position to legislate against tippling anarchy by suggesting prudent men might just as well meet at a bawdy-house and expect that 'a table of Laws against Fornication and Adultery' could 'fortify weak Nature against the Temptations of the Petticoat'. The fact that these clubs make up their own rules and then enforce them is further nonsense, for 'a Man may as reasonably propose to secure himself a Peace, by haunting a Bear-Garden on the Public Days of their confus'd Revels, as to wisely govern himself within the Bounds of sobriety, by making himself a Member of a Tavern-Convention, or what is more scandalous, though less expensive, an Ale-house Club'.[87] It is no doubt further evidence of Ward's political sympathies and growing antipathy for the party politics that had emerged at the end of the seventeenth century, for all this leads to is corrupt statesmen, intrigues and factionalism.[88]

Of course, the purpose of this history is to expose 'the Vanity of those whimsical Clubs' and prove that 'Birds of a Feather will flock together',[89] the usual instance of salacious cake and eating thereof, for the whole exercise is a pretext for vulgar, diverting entertainment. Ward mixes in the more recognisable clubs, such as The Kit-Kat, with fantastical ones, thus giving that same mix of satirical bullseyes and distasteful misses we saw in *The London*

Spy. Of the fantastical groups, Ward excels himself with The Farting Club (meeting at a public-house at Cripplegate parish) and The No-Nose Club.[90] The latter meets at The Dog Tavern, Drury Lane, a gathering of 'that abundance of both Sexes [who] sacrificed their Noses to the God Priapus'. They have been brought together for someone else's amusement (the reader's presumably) and are annoyed, but when the drink starts to flow, those desires that caused them to lose their noses in the first place are rekindled. The titles of some of the other clubs give a fair indication of the remaining matter: The Man-Killing Club, The Surly Club – 'chiefly composed of Master Carmen, Lightermen, old *Billingsgate* Porters, and rusty tun-belly'd Badge Watermen', The Club of Ugly-Faces, etc. But as with *The London Spy*, Ward stretches an idea further than it can profitably go. Nevertheless, this work is a kind of amusing category-error classification of contemporary social groups, conveniently divided up into diverse tavern and alehouse spaces.

Much of Ward's other work is concerned with drink and taverns, although a discussion of them would, unfortunately, offer no further insights than those already afforded. *The Compleat Vintner: Or, the Delights of the Bottle* is a hymn to Bacchus and its inspirational powers: 'Yet first, my Muse shall let you see / What Vintners are, or ought to be, / Those Demy Gods, from whose rich Cellars / Arise, Popes, Addisons, and Knellers, / And ev'ry Worthy that can claim / A place in the Records of Fame; / For all that's excellent or fine, / Derive their Origin from Wine'.[91] The second part of the poem is a complaint against the kind of customers who plague the honest vintner: Stingy Wranglers; Dinner Spungers; Jill Tiplers; Beef Beggars; Cook Teasers; Pan Soppers; Plate Twirlers; Table Whitlers; Drawer Biters; Spoon Pinchers; and other Tavern Tormenters. Ward was well placed to draw these character sketches. In Dialogue XVIII of *Nuptial Dialogues and Debates* (1723) 'Between a teazing Husband, and his vexatious tipling Wife' Ward gives equal weight to both sides of the fractious arguments. In one of quite a few witty retorts from the wife she warns: 'Use me not thus, you contradicting Fool; I'll drink the more, the more you ridicule.'[92] But all of this literature is firmly in the tradition of what we have already seen, and this is perhaps the limit of Ward's achievement. The tavern space had significance in other ways in the opening decades of the eighteenth century, as we shall see in the next chapter.

Notes

1 Description by George Augustus Sala, quoted in Howard William Troyer, *Ned Ward of Grubstreet: A Study of Sub-Literary London in the Eighteenth Century* (Cambridge, Massachusetts, Harvard University Press, 1946), p. 8. I have used Troyer's 'Bibliography of the Writings of Edward Ward' (Appendix A) from this

book for first dates of publication.
2 Ned Ward, *The Hudibrastick Brewer: Or, a Preposterous Union Between Malt and Meter* (1714), Chadwyck-Healey English Poetry Full-Text Database (1992), ll. 128–31.
3 Ned Ward, *The London Spy*, ed. Paul Hyland (East Lansing, Colleagues Press, 1993), Introduction, p. xi.
4 Troyer, *Ward*, pp. 169–71.
5 Quoted in *ibid.*, pp. 169–70.
6 Pope first grouped Ward with the hacks in *Peri Bathous, or the Art of Sinking in Poetry* (1718). According to Troyer, *Ward*, it was the continuous reference to Ward as an alehouse-keeper in the *Dunciad Variorum* (1729) that annoyed Ward the most, rather than as a writer whose place was amongst the lowest of poets – p. 201. (See Troyer, pp. 198–202, for a full account of the attacks and counter-attacks.) Pope was a poet whom Ward greatly admired, but his attacks offended him into arguing that there were two Popes – a true poet and a little man: 'Epigram [In one prolifick Age, two Popes appear'd]' – 'One dy'd possess'd of universal Praise, / But the rude Dunciad blasted t'other's Baies' (ll. 7–8).
7 Quoted in Ward, *Spy*, p. xix.
8 *Ibid.*, Introduction, p. xviii.
9 See J. Paul Hunter's *Before Novels: The Cultural Contexts of Eighteenth-Century English Fiction* (London, Norton, 1990), for a discussion of the novel's predecessors.
10 Philip Pinkus, *Grub St. Stripped Bare* (London, Constable, 1968), p. 159.
11 There are others of course, most notably Greene.
12 Ward, *Spy*, p. 9.
13 I shall use 'Ward' and 'narrator' as interchangeable, since this is the intended persona. At one point he refrains from giving a description of some Plantation traders because he has already done so in his *Trip to Jamaica*, Ward, *Spy*, p. 61, obviously advancing the narrator as 'Ned Ward'.
14 *Ibid.*, p. 11.
15 'Many of these Grub Street hacks were just as learned, intelligent and witty as the best of their present-day counterparts, but with fewer inhibitions,' Pinkus, *Grub St.*, p. 14.
16 Ward, *Spy*, p. 11. The importance of London for the nation at this time is that, according to Peter Earle, 'it was the only real city in England, and … totally dominated English urban culture and indeed invented it', *The Making of the English Middle Class: Business, Society and Family Life in London, 1660-1730* (London, Methuen, 1989), p. xi.
17 Ward, *Spy*, Introduction, p. xiii.
18 *Ibid.*, p. 13.
19 *Ibid.*, pp. 13–14.
20 *Ibid.*, p. 18.
21 *Ibid.*, p. 162.
22 *Ibid.*, p. 22.
23 *Ibid.*, p. 24.
24 *Ibid*.
25 *Ibid.*, p. 27.
26 *Ibid.*, p. 27 and p. 28.

27 *Ibid.*, p. 29. Civet-box = dung-cart.
28 *Ibid.*, pp. 29–30.
29 *Ibid.*, p. 30.
30 *Ibid.*, p. 31.
31 *Ibid.*, p. 38.
32 That is, as far as I can ascertain. In any event, the constable is using the quibble as a specious reason for wielding his authority.
33 *Ibid.*, p. 39.
34 *Ibid*.
35 *Ibid.*, p. 40.
36 *Ibid.*, p. 42.
37 *Ibid.*, p. 45.
38 *Ibid.*, Introduction, p. xiv.
39 *Ibid.*, p. 54.
40 Its currency was probably due to the popularity of the stage-song 'The Man in the Moon Drinks Claret' or to the song 'Mad Tom of Bedlam; Or, The Man in the Moon drinks Clarret, / With Powder-beef, Turnip and Carret', the latter popular in the theatres until about the 1840s, according to William Chappell, *The Roxburghe Ballads*, vol. II (Hertford, Stephen Austin and Sons, 1874), p. 259. I have not been able to discover the origins of the phrase, although it perhaps had something to do with the aggressively Royalist 'newsbook' *The Man in the Moon*, first published 16 April 1649: Lois Potter, *Secret Rites and Secret Writing: Royalist Literature 1641–1660* (Cambridge, Cambridge University Press, 1989), pp. 15–16, 18. As previously noted, Royalists were associated with wine-drinking so this at least would make sense.
41 Ward, *Spy*, p. 63.
42 *Ibid.*, p. 64.
43 *Ibid.*, Hyland's glossary.
44 *Ibid.*, p. 69.
45 *Ibid.*, p. 72. He also appears genuinely compassionate when he observes the treatment of women at Bridewell in Issue VI, pp. 110–12.
46 *Ibid.*, p. 73.
47 *Ibid.*, p. 91.
48 *Ibid.*, pp. 91–2.
49 *Ibid.*, p. 142.
50 *Ibid.*, pp. 160–1.
51 *Ibid.*, p. 112.
52 *Ibid.*, p. 113.
53 *Ibid.*, p. 114.
54 As Paul Hyland notes in his Introduction to *The London Spy*.
55 *Ibid.*, p. 116.
56 *Ibid.*, p. 154.
57 *The Diary of Samuel Pepys*, ed. Robert Latham and William Matthews, 11 vols (London, G. Bell and Sons/Bell and Hyman, 1970–83), vol. X, Companion, 'Coffee-Houses', p. 71.
58 Ward, *Spy*, p. 156.
59 *Ibid.*, p. 255.
60 *Ibid.*, p. 155.

61 *Ibid.*, p. 158.
62 *Ibid.*, p. 209.
63 The argument is evidently still going strong – compare the same 'coffee-house talk' discussed in the chapter on Pepys and the entry for 26 March 1667.
64 *Ibid.*, p. 212.
65 *Ibid.*, p. 213.
66 *Ibid.*, p. 218.
67 *Ibid.*, p. 219.
68 *Ibid.*, p. 223.
69 *Ibid.*, p. 224.
70 *Ibid.*, p. 225.
71 *Ibid.*, p. 241.
72 *Ibid.*, p. 242.
73 *Ibid.*, p. 246.
74 *Ibid.*, p. 247.
75 *Ibid.*, p. 248.
76 *Ibid.*, p. 250.
77 *Ibid.*, p. 281.
78 Ned Ward, *The Rise and Fall of Madam Coming-Sir: Or, An Unfortunate Slip from the Tavern-Bar, Into the Surgeon's Powdering-Tub* (Stamford, Lincolnshire, 1720 [1703]).
79 *Ibid.*, p. 7.
80 *Ibid.*, p. 23.
81 For example, Patrick Hamilton's 'A Glass of Port'. See ch. 11 below.
82 Ned Ward, *The Rambling Fuddle-Caps: Or, A Tavern-Struggle For a Kiss* (London, 1709).
83 *Ibid.*, p. 12.
84 Ned Ward, *A Compleat and Humorous Account of all the Remarkable Clubs and Societies in the Cities of London and Westminster* (London, J. Wren, 1756 [1709]), p. 1.
85 Thomas Burke, *The English Inn* (London, Longmans, Green and Co., 1931), pp. 136–7.
86 Ward, *Clubs*, p. 2.
87 *Ibid.*, p. 3.
88 *Ibid.*, p. 4.
89 *Ibid.*, p. 6.
90 *Ibid.*, p. 24. Sufferers of syphilis would often lose their noses.
91 Ned Ward, *The Compleat Vintner: Or, the Delights of the Bottle* (1720), Chadwyck-Healey English Poetry Full-Text Database (1992), ll. 360–7.
92 Ned Ward, *Nuptial Dialogues and Debates* (1723), Dialogue XVIII, 'Between a teazing Husband, and his vexatious tipling Wife', Chadwyck-Healey English Poetry Full-Text Database (1992), ll. 106–7.

7

Scene, *An Inn*? And horrible gin

A chapter on Pepys and a chapter on Ned Ward have invariably placed the centre of national life in London, and in *The Pub in Literature* that has meant city taverns and alehouses. Since London set the pace and fashions for the rest of the country this might appear only natural, especially when social status was so dependent upon Court patronage. But the capital has its own dynamic, paradoxically central to providing the lead in nationhood yet unique and therefore atypical for the country as a whole. The shape and idea of England have a different perspective from the provinces and the countryside, the sense of how England is being transformed is different, even if the administrative coherence spreading out from London since Tudor and Stuart times has created some homogenisation of the idea of 'England'. Space is valued in a different way.

One of the most noticeable changes in England at this time is the decline of the country estate and manorial territory and a consequent shift in sensibility. During the eighteenth century, country inns, with the opening up of a better road infrastructure and better transport – sprung coaches – are a sign of a burgeoning economy. But reliance upon inns, rather than the hospitality of manorial estates, is a sign of a changing England, moving from customary obligations to those based on cash and contract, a process begun by the Tudors and their eschewal of local feudalistic power bases.[1] In London an inn is at the apex of the drinking-establishment hierarchy. In the country, it can symbolise the descent of the manor estate. When no one can tell the difference between one or the other, as in *She Stoops to Conquer* (1773), a major perception of olde England is well and truly gone. But this is to view it from on high. The contrast between inn and manor house in the eighteenth century also signals the advance of the former at the expense of the latter: 'In a sense the Hanoverian inn was a kind of epitome of Hanoverian society: a society in which the leisure classes particularly were more numerous, more cultivated and more wealthy than ever before.'[2] It reflects social decline for one group – the (rural) gentry – and social advancement (or expansion) for another – the middling classes (or 'pseudo-gentry', or 'urban gentry').

William Shenstone's mid-eighteenth-century lines 'Written at an Inn at Henley' offer a host of positive features for the 'humble inn': it is free from the 'flattery, cards, and dice, and din' found in 'mansions higher'; it is free from fashionable pretentiousness – 'pomp' and 'plate'; and it offers what cannot be bought at Court – freedom itself. The country inn therefore retains what is natural in opposition to artificial (implicitly, London) and so feeds into the idea that will become more widespread in the nineteenth century, that the inn is symbolic of England's heritage. In the last verse the poem makes valuable what had already become a common associated metaphor, that the inn is a 'staging post' on life's journey; Dryden's lines 'The world's an inn, and death the journey's end', for example.[3] There is a certain neutral fatalism to this (and see Marvell's 'Upon Appleton House' below), a way of seeing the world in a resigned, philosophical manner. But Shenstone ignores the after-life in favour of the inn that is here-and-now, a structure that cannot be gainsaid: 'Who'er has travelled life's dull round, / Where'er his stages may have been, / May sigh to think he still has found / The warmest welcome at an inn.'

Contemporary with this phase is the rise of gin-drinking in England at the beginning of the eighteenth century, particularly from the 1720s onwards. The name derived from 'geneva' from the French for 'juniper', the berries of which flavour the liquor. The taste was 'sweet', unlike the 'dry' gin more familiar to later audiences. It had been popularised during William and Mary's reign (1689–94/1702) and Anne's reign (1702–14), and legislation had encouraged its production and consumption, originally to reduce the excess of corn produced by good harvests in the 1690s.[4] Writing in 1713 Defoe argued that the distillation of corn was essential 'to support the Landed Interest',[5] but a few years later gin became the bane of the nation.[6] Its popularity with the lower orders and the ensuing drunkenness meant that it soon became a marker for class distinctions. *The Tavern Scuffle* (1725), a work in 'dialogue' form and reminiscent of 'Ale, Wine, and Beer together by the Ears' (see above) personifies the new drink through 'Scorch-Gut' the distiller, whereas beer and ale are 'Swell-Gut' the brewer. The subtitle calls gin 'The Reigning Liquor now in Vogue among the common People', thus firmly placing it in its lower social degree. Although in the actual dialogue there is little to choose between the two forms of drink, the subtitle claims that the 'hot dispute' between the two shows gin to have 'ill-effects' on the body, and a later (1726) publication of *The Tavern Scuffle* includes a damning report on gin shops by Middlesex JPs after the dialogue. According to the report, gin 'never fails to produce an invincible Aversion to Work and Labour'.[7] The drink may be different, but the class concerns are the same.

The first government attempt to produce legislation that would curb its excesses came in 1729, making the drink more expensive, but this was resisted by farmers and distillers and the Act was reformed in 1733. The Act remained ineffective and public campaigns against gin, which had begun in the 1720s, led to the Gin Act of 1736.[8] But in a capital city where it was reckoned one in six houses sold gin,[9] and a hundred thousand drank it, such legislation was not popular, and there were riots. In any case the Act was ignored, and anti-gin agitation continued, of which Hogarth's prints *Gin Lane* and *Beer Street* (1751) are the most famous examples. Henry Fielding, in his capacity as magistrate, entered the anti-gin fray with *An Enquiry into the … Late Increase of Robbers* (1751), where the blame fell squarely on this new kind of drunkenness. Distinctions between wine-drinkers and ale- and beer-drinkers continued, but now gin took the place of out-and-out pariah. To live in 'Beer Street' was to live in a jovial, convivial, flourishing environment. To live in 'Gin Lane' was to live amid poverty, vice and disease. Arguments as to why the problem of excessive gin-drinking subsided centre on two aspects: poor harvests in the 1750s naturally inflated the cost of gin, no longer making it a cheap alternative to beer,[10] and in 1751 the sale of spirits was confined to public houses alone.[11]

Literary productions in the eighteenth century – other than broadsides perhaps – are curiously negligent when it comes to reflecting the gin problem. Ned Ward does not turn to it in his writings, ever remaining the superior tavern-keeper in his own eyes and an alehouse-keeper in Pope's. Although a couple of the prostitutes in *The Beggar's Opera* (1728) are accused of drinking gin,[12] its low lifes still remain within the literary codings of the tavern space – the highwayman Macheath, like Falstaff, is disreputable but admirable. The type of drunkenness consequent upon spirit drinking – in itself relatively new in England – and the class significance of gin-drinking mean that, just as with blind alehouses, some things are perhaps simply too low to be presented to a middling-class audience. We can have inns and taverns, but the dram shop and gin shop are outside acceptable literary limits. In fact even the alehouse had achieved a level of acceptance. According to Peter Clark, it had become more respectable thanks to pressure from customers for an improved environment and the higher social ambitions of alehouse-keepers.[13] In addition, England's increasing prosperity saw that 'The economic world of the alehouse was converging with that of the inn.'[14] The gin shop and the dram shop now begin to occupy that low symbolic position previously held by the alehouse.[15]

As to literary production, it still remained the case that virtually everything was published and acted in London. Restoration drama's representation of witty, sophisticated, immoral London society was giving way to sentimental comedy at the turn of the century, and Farquhar was the playwright who helped usher in the change. But drink continued to loom large in both forms and might not only be a topic of conversation but actually impinge upon a performance. At Henry Higden's play, *The Wary Widow, or Sir Noisy Parrot* of 1693, the audience had to be 'dismissed at the end of the third act, the author having contrived so much drinking of punch in the play, that the actors all got drunk, and were unable to finish'.[16] The Prologue to

Farquhar's first play, *Love and a Bottle*, 1698 (probably[17]) is given by a servant holding a bottle of wine.

The title of Farquhar's play also heralds a new theme – the more realistic portrayal of drink in marital relationships. The connections between wine and women had, until this period, always taken on a stereotypical bent, operating in praise of both. Shakespeare's Porter in *Macbeth* is one of the few occasions when some semblance of actuality is enlisted: drink promotes the desire but takes away the performance. Popular literature on the other hand had always shown drunken husbands and sober wives (and vice versa) and the poverty or cuckoldry that might ensue, or the scheming, flirtatious alewife, but the representations rarely went further than this. But now there appears to be an either/or situation, not so much 'love and a bottle' but 'love *or* a bottle'; in literary terms, as Anya Taylor in *Bacchus in Romantic England* heads one of her chapters, 'Bacchus contra Venus'. It can be seen as having a frivolous start in the Restoration. In the first scene of William Wycherley's *The Country Wife* (1675), part of the sparkish banter between Horner, Harcourt and Dorilant turns on the choice between wine and women. Horner concludes: 'Wine gives you joy; love, grief and tortures, besides the surgeon. Wine makes us witty; love, only sots. Wine makes us sleep; love breaks it.'[18] Rochester's struggle between the two is evident in a letter where he classes himself a drunken lover and 'errant fumbler'.[19] But in his poetry he could also argue that it was better to drink than to desire women: 'Let us (since Witt instructs us how) / Raise pleasure to the topp, / If Rivall Bottle you'll allow, / I'll suffer Rivall Fopp.'[20]

The point of view of the wife married to the drunken sot also begins to take on a more pointed, less codified, aspect. The coping strategies for an unfortunate but indissoluble bond appear more heartfelt than the usual literary conventions had previously allowed. In *The Beaux' Stratagem* (1706/07), discussed in more detail below, Mrs Sullen complains about her husband:

> O Sister, Sister! if ever you marry, beware of a sullen, silent Sot, one that's always musing, but never thinks: – There's some Diversion in a talking Blockhead; and since a Woman must wear Chains, I wou'd have the Pleasure of hearing 'em rattle a little. – Now you shall see, but take this by the way; – He came home this Morning at his usual Hour of Four, waken'd me out of a sweet Dream of something else, by tumbling over the Tea-table, which be broke all to pieces, after his Man and he had rowl'd about the Room like sick Passengers, in a Storm, he comes flounce into Bed, dead as a Salmon into a Fishmonger's Basket; his Feet cold as ice, his Breath hot as a Furnace, and his Hands and his Face as greasy as his Flanel Night-cap. – Oh Matrimony! – He tosses up the Clothes with a barbarous swing over his Shoulders, disorders the whole Oeconomy of my Bed, leaves me half naked, and my whole Night's Comfort is the tuneable Serenade of that wakeful Nightingale, his Nose. – O the

Pleasure of counting the melancholly Clock by a snoring Husband! – But now, Sister, you shall see how handsomely, being a well-bred Man, he will beg my Pardon.[21]

But of course the options available to women are extremely limited, especially so in literature once the promiscuity endorsed by the Restoration ethos has faded. Mrs Sullen cannot simply fraternise with another man for diverting amusement. A poem by Anne Finch (Countess of Winchilsea) in the latter half of the seventeenth century, 'The Prevalence of Custom', foretells a similar scenario to that suffered by Mrs Sullen: 'A Female, to a Drunkard marry'd, / When all her other Arts miscarry'd / Had yet one Stratagem to prove him, / And from good Fellowship remove him.' Her plan is to make him think he is in hell when he wakes from a drunken slumber. She tells him he has been 'Convey'd, last Night, from noisie Tavern, / To fill this thy still, and dreary Cavern'. She tells him it is her job to find out what he would like to eat, and then give him less. But her husband is unmoveable in his dissipation and simply asks for something to drink. 'A *Bumper* fetch: Quoth she, a *Halter*, / Since nothing less thy Tone can alter, / Or break this Habit thou'st been getting, / To keep thy Throat in constant wetting.'[22] It is indeed rare to see any drunken sots reformed in the literature of the period.

'Sir, I take this for an extraordinary Inn'
Susanna Centlivre, *The Man's Bewitch'd*[23]

The idea that estate houses were functioning as inns rather than fulfilling their medieval role of centres for customary hospitality – the social and economic focus for the surrounding area the estate would have encompassed – is made explicit in Andrew Marvell's poem 'Upon Appelton House: To My Lord Fairfax' (?1654) – 'The house was built upon the place / Only as for a mark of grace; / And for an inn to entertain / Its Lord a while, but not remain.'[24] One element of this sentiment is that the house is not socially centred but rather a convenient lodging to pass, and the conceit works both to describe man's life on earth and the changing function of the estate house.[25] Coupled with this shift was the problem of what to do with male offspring when the law of primogeniture predominated. Increasing numbers of gentlemen were either given an education and then apprenticed so that they could find their own living, or simply hung around waiting to inherit. The prevalence of highwaymen in the eighteenth century has partly been put down to 'gentlemen' down on their luck. We have already seen the predatory nature of gallants in London.

Farquhar's *The Stage-Coach* (1704[26]), if a lightweight farce, nevertheless alerts us to the convergence of a number of these elements. A stagecoach arrives at an inn and immediately the house is aroused into action – as if inns only 'come alive' with the input of city folk. Fetch, one of the traveller's servants, shouts for attention, and complains that service is poorer than that of famous London taverns, whilst at the same time apprising the audience of his rakish lifestyle: 'No attendance in these Country-Inns; – This is worse than the *Rose-Tavern* after Play, the *Sun-Tavern* after Change, or the *Devil-Tavern* after Church.' So whilst the scene ('An Inn') is in the country, as usual the anchor-point is the capital and doings in the country are always under judgement of the implied centre. The farce depends upon a love triangle, and the inn is incidental in any real dramatic sense, except of course it allows for the acceptable loosening of moral codes before proper order can be restored, a thematic patterning that we have seen before and will see again. The town–country or city–country distinctions are thus easily filtered through the country inn.

The Stage-Coach formed in part a blueprint for Farquhar's more substantial *The Beaux' Stratagem* (8 March 1706/07). Like the earlier play, it too begins in an inn (here it is set in Lichfield), and begins with the arrival of a stagecoach. The complaint about slow service is the same, and the introduction of Cherry, the landlord Bonniface's daughter, mirrors the role of the Barmaid Dolly in *The Stage-Coach*. London is immediately established as the economic and fashionable centre when Cherry ignores the Warrington coach in favour of the newly arrived London coach and its socially elevating livery. The plot revolves around the scheme of two 'gentlemen', Aimwell and Archer, to find themselves a fortune. They roam the country taking it in turns to play Lord and servant. After Lichfield they intend to go to Nottingham, Lincoln and Norwich,[27] and so for such a stratagem the inn would thus of course be their natural habitat – a place that throughout the eighteenth century existed for those without any reputable fixed abode.

Their citified duplicity is matched against that of Bonniface's inn/country deceptions (the play was so popular that 'Bonniface' would soon become the generic name for innkeepers everywhere). When he talks up his ale in the opening scene, Aimwell and Archer give as good as they get and take the upper hand with deflatory repartee. The descent of the country house is perhaps alluded to when amongst Archer's life-dictums is 'I love a fine House, but let another keep it; and just so I love a fine Woman.'[28] The inn space allows these irresponsible squibs to shoot forth, but of course we know the London roguishness will be redeemed, and of course we know the inn is a halfway space at best before this social order is restored, at base nothing more than a stepping-stone for a social class in difficulty. That difficulty is the one already described, the consequence of primogeniture, for Archer declares to Cherry that though born a gentleman, he 'went to *London* a younger Brother' where he fell into bad company. The inn itself could not represent the requisite social order, for not only is Bonniface the deceiving landlord, he is in league with a 'gang', the highwaymen Gibbet, Hounslow and Bagshot. As Bonniface says when he thinks that Aimwell and Archer are themselves highwaymen and he considers giving them up to the authorities: 'I don't think it lawful to harbour any Rogues but my own.'[29] Clearly, Bonniface cannot change his social status or moral substance, and nor can the inn. The moral movement in the play is firmly with Archer and Aimwell, and the inn functions to help them along but itself remains untouched as a symbol of backwoods England, a place of cunning ancillary to England's centre in the south-east.

Customary England is personified by Lady Bountiful – 'An old civil Country Gentlewoman, that cures all her Neighbours of all Distempers' as the Dramatis Personae describes her – and it is her house which is set up in structural opposition to the inn. The scenes alternate between her house and the inn as Archer and Aimwell work to climb the social ladder from 'inn' to 'estate'. Everything that is good about England is presented through her olde world patronage and the house that embodies it. Her weakness is that she is 'foolishly fond of her son *Sullen*', and it is he, 'a Man of a great Estate' and 'A Country Blockhead',[30] who represents the dead end of olde England. He may also be a blockhead because he descends from a weaker social line – he is Lady Bountiful's son by her first husband, only a squire, whereas her daughter, the much more refined Dorinda, is the offspring of her second husband, a 'knight', Sir Charles. However, country life is also under the cosh, and this through the complaints of Mrs Sullen, a London lady recently married to the country blockhead. She is given leave to mock the dullness of 'country pleasures', where she characterises 'rural Accomplishments' as 'drinking of fat Ale, playing at Whisk, and smoking Tobacco with my Husband; or of spreading of Plaisters, brewing of Diet-drinks, and stilling Rosemary-Water with the good old Gentlewoman, my Mother-in-Law'[31] – the latter all a swipe at Lady Bountiful. A subtext of drink symbolism reinforces the lack of dynamism in the country compared to London: Bonniface's ale has made him fat and contributed to the death of his wife, whilst the running joke of Lady Bountiful's home-made soft drinks signifies the tameness of country life. Her home-brewed ale is drunk by the servants (Scrub entertains Archer in the cellar), not a drink for the higher orders. Over and beyond this the dramatic structure serves to reinstate the idea that 'gentleman' is an 'intrinsic' quality and that the good-natured rakes Aimwell and Archer serve England's preferred future gene pool well enough. In doing so, *The Beaux' Stratagem* nods nostalgically towards olde England but accepts and advances the supposed new order – a countryside beholden to city mores. In fact, the category of 'gentleman' was as much a dead end, but this social caste as presented in the play would reflect back a congenial picture to a certain section of the audience. When Aimwell finds out that he is in fact entitled to call himself Lord Aimwell, rather than simply use his elder brother's title fraudulently, we know that the proper version of England has been restored and England is once more stable. The initial trajectory of the play appears to be one that would support an England that relied on its wits to make money, men who would do well regardless of luck or government, men who have 'Heads to get Money, and Hearts to spend it'.³² But the discovery at the close of the play that he is a Lord, rather than someone who has simply made good, places rentier culture once more above mercantile capitalism. This too can be related back to the status of the inn, for Bonniface's hostelry is on Sullen's land, and he thus pays quarterly rent. The inn's role as a nodal point in England's improving infrastructure, crucial for the mobility of commerce, is thus ignored in favour of 'land'. The real problem – primogeniture within attachment to an outmoded feudalism – can be safely ignored.

The inn, in *The Beaux' Stratagem* intimately tied up with the lower orders, is seen to encroach upon England's legitimated national space when Bonniface and the highwaymen plan to break into Lady Bountiful's house. What is kept in place at the play's end is a sense of England that rests upon 'gentlemen', 'estates', and a fashionable centre in London. The play manages to reconcile London and country in the name of England, whilst the lower orders, as represented by the inn, remain its servants. But England is thus, in many ways, nowhere, since the outmoded feudal system has been reduced to the landowner Sullen and his life spent in the public house on his own land. This conclusion is evident when Sir Charles Freeman (Mrs Sullen's brother) arrives at the inn from London to find Sullen still carousing whilst his wife is left alone in bed at home.³³ Aimwell's ascendancy to the gentleman's rightful place is an inheritance of something profoundly messy in its ideological import, an olde England that retains all the best values but which at the same time is seen to be at an end. At the beginning of the eighteenth century, the literary inn is a threat to 'England', a sign of the descent of estate and the threat from the lower orders, hence the constant to-ing and fro-ing between inn and estate house mirrors the slippage between England past and England to come. The play manages to keep them apart, but at some cost to the dramatic conclusion. The *deus ex machina* is the death of Aimwell's elder brother so that Aimwell can inherit the estate. The unbounded joy of all at these circumstances rather than grief at the loss of the brother, someone who was regarded as honourable and worthy, is difficult to swallow, although, if played in a certain way, no doubt offers its own comic possibilities:

> SIR CHARLES   My dear Lord *Aimwell*, I wish you Joy.
> AIMWELL   Of what?
> SIR CHARLES   Of your Honour and Estate: Your Brother died the Day before I left *London*.³⁴

The idea of 'inn' as threat because somehow it is the obverse side of the English-house coin is also evident in a play contemporary with Farquhar's, Mrs [Susanna] Centlivre's *The Man's Bewitch'd* (1709). A guardian, Sir David, jealously protects his young female protégée Laura against her new lover Faithful. When they are discovered together (3.2) Faithful, who has supposedly been carried to an inn after an accident, pretends that this house is itself the inn, and that Sir David is a landlord and Laura is a serving wench. He thus treats Sir David with disdain, garnering humour from the juxtaposition of landlord of a house and landlord of an inn.

> FAITHFUL (*to the Servants*) Ay Scoundrels, where are you? Ye Dogs, what is / the reason we can have no Attendance? /
> (*Strikes one of them.*)
> Fetch us a Bottle of Claret, Sirrah, and bring us word what / we can have to Eat—
> SIR DAVID Bring a Bottle of Claret! bring a Halter— / What do you strike my Servants for? ha, Sir.
> FAITHFUL Your Servants, Sir! They are my Servants, as long / as I pay for what I call for—Ho! I find you are / the Landlord of this well-govern'd Inn—Make your / People more tractable, de you hear, Sir? Or / I shall not only / beat them, but you too—Death ye Villains, why don't / you stir?[35]

The conceit, like the fluctuation between inn and estate house in *The Beaux' Stratagem*, can only work if there is some measure of common ground between the two spaces. The evidence once again is that there is some convergence between the two as England slips (or rises, depending upon your point of view) from landed gentry to commercial enterprise. It is not until later in the century the inn will become the symbolic shorthand with which we are more familiar, and itself come to represent olde 'England', and even then it is not uncontested. Only in the nineteenth century would it be undisputedly a nostalgic construction of a golden age.

Seventy years on from Farquhar and Centlivre, Oliver Goldsmith's *She Stoops to Conquer* (1773) certainly owes a debt to Farquhar's play, and perhaps also to Centlivre's.[36] The characters Hastings and Marlow take the place of Archer and Aimwell. The problem is not so much the seeking of fortune but Marlow's shyness in the presence of 'ladies'. He has no such timidity with barmaids and so the play's love interest is moved along when he takes a daughter of the house for such a servant and is consequently uninhibited in her presence. The 'looseness' of the drinking-place environment thus allows Marlow to overcome his difficulty.

The play does two things to lend some plausibility to the conceit that a house can be mistaken for an inn. The first scene specifies 'A Chamber in an old-fashioned House', and the dialogue between Mr and Mrs Hardcastle lets the audience know that we are in the backwoods English countryside (once again). Like Mrs Sullen in *The Beaux' Stratagem*, Mrs Hardcastle complains to her husband that she never gets to see any town excitement (London), and that 'Here we live in an old rumbling mansion, that looks for all the world like an inn, but that we never see company.'[37] The second contribution to plausibility follows in the next scene when Marlow and Hastings turn up lost at the Three Pigeons alehouse. The customers persuade the two gentlemen that they will not find their way to the Hardcastle house that night, but might be put up at the Buck's Head inn not too far away. The 'inn' is, of course, Hardcastle's rambling mansion, and so the scene is set for comedy when Marlow and Hastings treat Hardcastle as if he were a landlord: they demand drinks and a bill of fare, and expect goodfellow conversation. The construction of house-as-inn is enhanced when just before the arrival of Marlow and Hastings, Hardcastle is seen instructing his rather dim servants in the art of serving guests.

The feeling that olde England has gone is made explicit in the Three Pigeons alehouse when one of the Fellows remembers Tony's father as 'the finest gentleman I ever set my eyes on. For winding the streight horn, or beating a thicket for a hare, or a wench, he never had his fellow. It was a saying in the place, that he kept the best horses, dogs, and girls in the whole county.' Tony Lumpkin promises to live up to such high standards of rude health, a sure sign that these are not qualities revered by the play. The demise of a slightly different version of olde England is also made explicit when the two gentlemen comment on their lodgings when they first arrive. Hastings: 'Upon my word, a very well-looking house, antique, but creditable.' Marlow: 'The usual fate of a large mansion. Having first ruined the master by good housekeeping, it at last comes to levy contributions as an inn.' *She Stoops to Conquer* represents a shift in sensibility from the literature at the beginning of the century since the decline of customary England is now only occasion for a passing comment, it is not integrated into the dramatic structure. The confusion of house/inn in Goldsmith's play is not intended to hide a problem of what to do with offspring who are not first-born, because Marlow and Hastings are not the fortune hunters that we saw in Aimwell and Archer, they are simply gentlemen, one of whom is rather shy. In the alehouse they are socially and geographically misplaced, there is no sense in which this is what they have been reduced to and must rise from.

The element of 'inherited wealth' is carried by Tony Lumpkin, Mrs Hardcastle's son by her first husband. As his name suggests, he is the fly in the social ointment. He has an inheritance of £1500 per year to live off and spends it all down the Three Pigeons. The hierarchy of drinking places remains similar to former representations. The scene in the alehouse is described as 'Several shabby fellows, with Punch and Tobacco' and Marlow and Hastings are relieved that there is no room for them to stay in the alehouse. In opposition is Hastings' praise (above) on first seeing what he believes to be an inn. The comedy throughout depends upon these social distinctions – between inn and country mansion at the Hardcastle's, and between alehouse and inn at the Three Pigeons. When Mrs Hardcastle discovers her son is going out for his usual drink she tries to restrain him.

    TONY   I can't stay, I tell you. The Three Pigeons expects me down every moment. There's some fun going forward.

> HARDCASTLE   Ay; the ale-house, the old place: I thought so.
> MRS HARDCASTLE   A low, paltry set of fellows.
> TONY   Not so low neither. There's Dick Muggins the exciseman, Jack Slang the horse doctor, Little Aminadab that grinds the music box, and Tom Twist that spins the pewter platter.[38]

The alehouse banter provides low comedy; that in the Hardcastle mansion is slightly more refined. However, once we return to the mansion the alehouse is forgotten and the play remains within the family home; there is no need to alternate between the two as we saw in *The Beaux' Stratagem*. Drinking-place associations do continue in that Miss Hardcastle keeps up the pretence of being a barmaid in order that Marlow is brought out of himself. The notion of gentlemanly 'intrinsic quality' is upheld when Miss Hardcastle admires Marlow's scrupulousness in marrying only those of the proper social caste, that is, not a barmaid, and admires him for bowing to social opinion and his father's authority. It is also upheld because Mrs Hardcastle admits to failure in making Tony 'genteel'; his only interest remains in the fortune. Thus class remains a mixture of inner worth and money. The play shows that no one who is comfortable with low alehouse company could possibly be 'genteel'. There is a slight redemption of Lumpkin right at the end of the play when he renounces any claim on Miss Neville, but by this time his association with the alehouse has faded considerably. On the other hand, there is a certain dramatic acceptability in the social proximity of inn and mansion. The fact that Hardcastle can be mistaken for a landlord without real detriment to his character, and the fact that his daughter is able self-consciously to stoop to the role of Cherry in *The Beaux' Stratagem* in order to conquer her man without taint, shows this.[39] It is interesting that Goldsmith uses the drinking-house environment rather than drink itself to provide the 'lowering' of social constraint. There might even be a wistfulness in that when Marlow flirts with Kate, believing her to be a barmaid, the dialogue is free from romantic conventionality. After all, it is not just Marlow who is allowed conversational licence as a consequence.

> MARLOW   One may call in this house, I find, to very little purpose. Suppose I should call for a taste, just by way of trial, of the nectar of your lips; perhaps I might be disappointed in that too.
> MISS HARDCASTLE   Nectar! Nectar! that's a liquor there's no call for in these parts. French, I suppose. We keep no wines here, Sir.
> MARLOW   Of true English growth, I assure you.
> MISS HARDCASTLE   Then it's odd I should not know it. We brew all sorts of wines in this house, and I have lived here these eighteen years.

Marlow and Kate are returned to their elevated social positions at the play's end. It is Tony Lumpkin who is left outside this social gene pool, a single man free to indulge his alehouse sympathies and to emulate his boorish country-squire father.

'A tavern near Newgate'

The Beggar's Opera (1728) was the most popular dramatic production of the eighteenth century. Its villain 'Macheath' became a byword for the swaggering, philandering highwayman. His natural habitat, until he makes the short journey to Newgate prison, is the tavern. The predominant moral point is made by Jemmy Twitcher, a pickpocket, and one of the many criminals who crowd the drama. He wonders (2.1): 'Why are the laws levelled at us? Are we more dishonest than the rest of mankind? What we win, gentlemen, is our own by the law of arms, and the right of conquest.' The same point could perhaps be made against those plays which allow rakes to get the girl and her fortune – fraudulent behaviour is socially sanctioned with a happy ending because the class these 'gentlemen' belong to is ultimately respectable. Any dishonesty by those lower than a gentleman cannot be redeemed. It is an early example of 'white-collar crime', and there is a certain amount of complicity on the part of those narrative structures which give this escape route. Gay's work provides a completely different world view. He sees all thieving as the same, regardless of social caste.

Those in authority are represented by Peachum the thief-taker, helped by his common-law wife, and Lockit, the Newgate jailer who is in league with Peachum. They are unpleasant characters who exploit the criminals for their own gain. So when the burlesque moves from Peachum's house in Act 1, to the tavern and then jail in Act 2, the juxtaposition of spaces underlines the moral proximity of the social spheres. The separation of worlds has no moral authorisation, only the arbitrary power of rich over poor. It also leads to different attitudes. Peachum and Lockit are in a position to accumulate wealth because they can envisage long lives. Macheath's gang, ever aware that their lives are precarious, can only live for the present moment; execution, as Matt of the Mint acknowledges, is 'what we must all come to'.[40] Hence Act 2's opening Air is a drinking song, followed by one in praise of the easy money to be made by holding up carriages, and then other tunes praising a life of hedonism, of wine, women and song, for example in 'Youth's the season made for joys' with the pertinent lines 'Let us drink and sport today, / Ours is not tomorrow.' Even though *The Beggar's Opera* was popular, and Macheath an anti-heroic role model, its overriding sentiment is harsh. The tavern, initially presented as offering some kind of sodality for the highwaymen, pickpockets and prostitutes, soon turns out to be a treacherous environment, for the women give Macheath up to Peachum. The view is broadened out to one of general misanthropy when Lockit, intent on revenge against Peachum, uses the idea that humans are different from other animals because of their sociability in order to trap him: 'Of all animals of prey, man is the only sociable one. Every one of us preys upon his neighbour.'[41] Lockit's plan is to get Peachum drunk, and so the treacherousness of tavern conviviality is mirrored in the deceit of social drinking in general. Gay even takes the trouble to make the social distinction clear by prefacing the scene in which Peachum and Lockit appear (3.5) with the simple header 'A table with wine, brandy, pipes and tobacco' to signify a different level of goodfellowship in terms of its more refined accompaniments, yet still a social situation comparable with the criminals in their own drinking lairs. The same exploitation of sociability is in evidence when Lucy wants to murder Polly, her rival for Macheath. She proposes a 'glass of cordial' (that is, 'strong-waters'/gin) 'in the way of friendship', with the intention of poisoning her with rats-bane.[42] Ironically, Polly believes that Lucy wants her to drink in order that she will become tipsy and reveal some secrets, and so echoes the actual plan of Lockit's described above.

The importance of drink is crowned when, about to die, Macheath, amidst dancing prisoners, gives a medley of tunes, mainly on the theme of liquor: 'Of all the friends in time of grief, / When threat'ning death looks grimmer, / Not one so sure can bring relief, / As this best friend, a brimmer,' and to the tune of 'Joy to great Caesar' 'A man can die / Much bolder with brandy. / (*Pours out a bumper of brandy.*)'[43] Gay, however, forces a happy ending without care for even a semblance of dramatic logic. Macheath is reprieved. Done in the name of poetical justice, the play's observation that given the similarity 'of manners in high and low life, that it is difficult to determine whether (in the fashionable vices) the fine gentlemen imitate the gentlemen of the road, or the gentlemen of the road the fine gentlemen',[44] the irony is complete. In reality, those criminals who are protected by position, authority and class, deserve the same end as Macheath, but since this is a (burlesque of) light opera that same end is transformed into a ridiculously happy one.

Fielding

> Being very full of Adventures, which succeeded each other at the Inn
> Henry Fielding, *Joseph Andrews*

By turning to Henry Fielding, we can take a step back and view the broader eighteenth-century picture in relation to drinking places, England and literary history. A man famous in his own lifetime as a dramatist and novelist, as well as for his work as a justice of the peace in his later years, he saw a good spectrum of the life of contemporary England. His novel *Tom Jones* (1749) remains one of the greatest comic works within the literary canon, and perhaps more than any other writer from the eighteenth century he is responsible for the general impressions later generations have held of the drinking places from that era. The inn at Upton-on-Severn in *Tom Jones*, teeming with social improprieties, hypocrisies and aspirations, is the inn that most readily encapsulates the activities of an energetic England in rude irreverent health.

In social history Fielding's work as a JP for Westminster and Middlesex is seen as laying the foundations of Scotland Yard and the modern police force. Like many educated men of his time, his interests were far-ranging, and the social, religious, literary and economic spheres were taken to be intrinsically interconnected. His world view was conservative in that he believed in a 'static, hierarchical society'[45] and his ideal for the nation was that of something akin to the customary England of yore, with the lower orders happy giving due deference to their betters, and the higher orders conducting themselves fairly and responsibly with respect to their social inferiors. In addition, the well-being of the nation depended upon the good health of the 'mechanic' part, that is, those who worked with their hands. The upper classes might be dissolute, but they were irrelevant (except that they set a bad example). When it came to a properly working nation, and one that could defend itself in times of war, a fit, fully employed work-force was required, with a large pool of labour available to keep wage prices down. By taking on board these views about England at the mid-point of the eighteenth century, as expressed in his non-fictional work, it is possible to position his use of drinking places in *Tom Jones* and *Joseph Andrews* (1742) within his self-consciously 'English' context.

Fielding's sense of 'nation' was underpinned by his beliefs in the 'constitution'. He took 'constitution' in a broad sense to include 'the original and fundamental Law of the Kingdom, from whence all Powers are derived, and by which they are circumscribed; all legislative and executive Authority; all those municipal Provisions which are commonly called *The Laws*; and, *lastly*, the Customs, Manners, and Habits of the People'.[46] On the one hand Fielding offers a fixed idea of England, founded on ancient and original law(s) and authorised by them. This is England's bedrock, fleshed out by the legislature and the society so governed. In *An Enquiry* Fielding shows a clear admiration for Anglo-Saxon society and 'the Constitutions of *Alfred*'.[47] His general belief in the superiority of the English constitution (a widespread belief), evident in the *Enquiry*, is also observable in *A Charge Delivered to the Grand Jury* (1749 – the year of *Tom Jones*). This was an address given to the Grand Jury before it was sworn in, an opportunity to remind them of their duties and the sphere within which they operated: 'The Institution of Juries, Gentlemen, is a Privilege which distinguishes the Liberty of *Englishmen* from those of other Nations.'[48] On the other hand, Fielding's view of the constitution was also a dynamic one that saw it as 'changing and variable'. All of which bears witness to the grand national picture within which Fielding is operating.

Before moving on to a full discussion of the novels, it is worth noting Fielding's attitude to drink and drunkenness as shown in *A Charge* and *An Enquiry*. Zirker observes that in *A Charge* Fielding cites the usual litany of contemporary crimes – 'blasphemy, misprisions, "Riots, Routs, and unlawful Assemblies", gambling, bawdy-houses, libels', but, surprisingly, he ignores 'the evils of gin-drinking and drunkenness'.[49] The inconsistency is all the more surprising since in *An Enquiry* he regards drunkenness as 'the Parent of all others',[50] poised to 'infallibly destroy a great Part of the inferiour People'[51] and sees gin-drinking as the sole cause of a majority of the cases brought to his attention.[52] If allowed to continue it will diminish the ability of the English to produce a convincing armed body of men, since they will have been conceived in gin, and nourished by it 'both in the Womb and at the Breast'.[53] The large discrepancy between the concern shown here for the new problem of gin-drinking and his omission of it in *A Charge* is blatant in Fielding's rhetorical question in *An Enquiry*: 'In solemn Truth, there is nothing of more serious Consideration, nor which more loudly calls for a Remedy, than the Evil now complained against. For what can be more worthy the Care of the Legislature, than to preserve the Morals, the Innocence, the Health, Strength and Lives of a great Part (I will repeat, the most useful Part) of the People?'[54] There is no easy answer as to why the gin problem should be at the root of most crime in the one piece, and omitted in the other.

It might be possible to speculate, however, that the inconsistency rests on Fielding's endeavour to find a correct attitude to drunkenness. Hogarth's *Beer Street* and *Gin Lane* show two different kinds of drunkenness, one conducive to a prosperous nation, and one productive of poverty, crime and damaged offspring. No one would deny that drinking ale or beer would get you drunk, just as gin might, so it was necessary in some way to mobilise all the old objections to alcohol in order to demonise gin without demonising what might be regarded as part of the 'customs, manners and habits of the people', the perfectly respectable drinking of beer and ale. Speculation aside, Fielding has his own problem, at the philosophical level, with understanding 'drunkenness' and how it should be dealt with by the legislature.

He was clearly taken with a story told by Aristotle to illustrate how the law should view drunkenness, for the same example appears in both *An Enquiry* and *Tom Jones*. According to Aristotle, in the time of Pittacus, if a drunken man were to strike someone, this should be more harshly treated than if the aggressor had been sober. The reasoning is that 'the Utility of the Public' is the first consideration, and 'drunken men are more apt to strike', therefore in general terms presenting a greater danger to the public.[55]

When Fielding uses the story in *Tom Jones*, it is because the eponymous hero himself gets drunk. Blifil, the villain of the piece, uses the occasion to represent Tom as being indifferent to his benefactor Squire Allworthy's illness. Tom is consequently ejected from the house and the adventures of the novel truly begin. It is another instance in which narrative is progressed when alcohol provides a rupture in the accepted order of things. Tom's drunkenness is a half-acceptable transgression which ushers in the more morally 'loose' environment of the 'road' and its numerous equally loose drinking places. Drunkenness here, unlike its representation in *An Enquiry*, is *not* the parent of all other crimes. After all, Blifil's actions in his vendetta against Tom are executed when sober. Blifil claims that Tom became drunk when he heard that Allworthy was about to die, when the truth is that Tom gets drunk celebrating the news that Allworthy is set to recover. It is at this point that the example given by Aristotle of Pittacus is wheeled in: 'to say the truth, in a court of justice, drunkenness must not be an excuse, yet in a court of conscience it is greatly so; and therefore Aristotle, who commends the laws of Pittacus, by which drunken men received double punishment for their crimes, allows there is more of policy than justice in that law. Now, if there are any transgressions pardonable from drunkenness, they are certainly such as Mr Jones was at present guilty of.'[56] This is clearly not the drunkenness or condemnation of drunkenness apparent in *An Enquiry*. To be sure, this is a comic novel, and any realism is 'selective'.[57] But Fielding took his prose art seriously, as the comments in *Joseph Andrews* make clear. Human nature is on display, and that is the same whether from ancient Greece or contemporary England.[58]

What we have is a Fielding looking both backwards and forwards in time. His pragmatic, reactionary persona in *An Enquiry* looks to make a more efficient judicial and police system. That is the future. His more congenial narrator's persona, inviting us to skip passages if we find them boring, inviting us to regard Allworthy and his generous paternalism as the social and moral centre of England, is a vision of olde England in which the narrator, and perhaps Fielding himself, can indulge a court of conscience rather than one of policy. It is this latter version which has survived in literary history, for the inns of *Tom Jones*, whilst not always the most pleasant places if viewed with a cynical eye, are the inns compatible with Fielding's literary persona and an acceptable literary heritage. Given the influence of Fielding's novels, it is not surprising then that in the nineteenth century the inn becomes the nostalgic symbol of England's golden age, for the novels themselves, although helping to inaugurate a new literary form, were a fair distance away from the England Fielding was prepared to uncover to a different audience in his judicial role.

The narratives of both *Joseph Andrews* and *Tom Jones* are fairly similar. The protagonists are unjustly forced out of the place where they live and then have to fend for themselves in the world at large: Joseph defends his 'honour' against the advances of his mistress so much that she evicts him; and Tom is believed to have behaved immorally against his master and is likewise evicted. Joseph's love is Fanny, Tom's is Sophia; Joseph's road-companion is Parson Adams, Tom's is Partridge. The form for both novels is essentially 'picaresque', that is, they chronicle episodically the adventures of a rogue-hero. The plot is therefore mainly a device for enabling the heroes to get into a variety of entertaining scrapes, the necessity for which is not an issue. The picaresque form sees both Joseph and Tom take in many inns and other hostelries.

A feature of Fielding's style in *Joseph Andrews* and *Tom Jones* is the role of the intrusive narrator – an avuncular commentator, a character in his own right separate from the action he describes. It is a characteristic that helps define (and which Fielding helped create) a certain type of novel – one with a 'realism' that is self-consciously playful and constructed, but realism nevertheless because, in Fielding's view, he is presenting an accurate picture of an unvarying 'human nature'. This is in contradistinction to the type of novel which prefers to make the 'realism' seem natural, and therefore works towards deflecting the reader away from thinking that what is 'real' has been contrived by an author, so that the 'novelistic' aspect is negligible or denied. This type of novel does not self-consciously present itself as a 'novel' but works to create the illusion that it is reporting back from 'real life', that it is not a novel at all, or at least, that there is no artifice involved. This type of novel is exemplified by Samuel Richardson's *Pamela* (1740–41). Written in epistolary and journal form, it helped add the dimension of 'psychological realism' to the type of realistic prose fiction engendered earlier on in the century. About a female servant who is under sexual threat from her master, the work was intended as a moral guide to young girls. Its mode is overtly didactic and moralistic. The Preface is supposedly written by the Editor of the Letters, and gives the impression that the letters are real. In writing *Joseph Andrews* and *Tom Jones* Fielding was writing against Richardson's type of novel. The work of both novelists is seen as seminal in the development of the novel genre, and these two views about the nature of the novel have dominated much of its subsequent history. Allied with Fielding's previous background as a dramatist, this debate about the form of the novel provides the context for discussing Fielding's two comic novels.

In helping to mark out the fictional territory he thought proper, Fielding offers a set of images clustered around the drinking place in both *Joseph Andrews* and *Tom Jones*. It is evidence, if nothing else, of the pervasiveness of these social centres in the world view of certain eighteenth-century mindsets. As suggested above, a feature of Fielding's style is to have a narrator who 'interrupts' the flow of story to comment on the narrative, its construction and anything else that may happen to come into purview. This itself requires comment from the narrator in *Joseph Andrews*, when he argues for the uses of such a method. At the start of Book 2, Chapter 1, 'Of Division in Authors', the first use stated is that 'those little spaces between our chapters may be looked upon as an inn or resting-place, where he [the reader] may stop and take a glass, or any other refreshment, as it pleases him. Nay, our fine readers will, perhaps, be scarce able to travel farther than through one of them in a day.'[59] A second use is that he likens the 'contents prefixed to every chapter' (a glossary of the chapter's contents is provided at the head of each) to inn signs, 'informing the reader what entertainment he is to expect', leaving the reader to choose whether this chapter is worthwhile or whether he should move on to the next. Although Fielding also provides two other images for such chapters – as a kind of padding material, as a butcher who carves meat – it is this more extensive use of the inn metaphor that holds sway.

This digression regarding the architecture of a novel might be regarded as relatively inconsequential as a general statement of artistic intention. However, it gains much greater importance in *Tom Jones* when he chooses to frame the whole novel with an associated image. 'The Introduction to the Work' is termed a 'Bill of Fare to the Feast' as Fielding whets our appetite for the book that is to follow. Here is the extended metaphor that opens the novel.

> An author ought to consider himself, not as a gentleman who gives a private or eleemosynary treat, but rather as one who keeps a public ordinary, at which all persons are welcome for their money. In the former case, it is well known, that the entertainer provides what fare he pleases; and tho' this should be very indifferent, and utterly disagreeable to the taste of his company, they must not find any fault; nay, on the contrary, good-breeding forces them outwardly to approve and to commend whatever is set before them. Now the contrary of this happens to the master of an ordinary. Men who pay for what they eat, will insist on gratifying their palates, however nice and even whimsical these may prove; and if every thing is not agreeable to their taste, will challenge a right to censure, to abuse, and to d—m their dinner without controul.
>
> To prevent therefore giving offence to their customers by any such disappointment, it hath been usual, with the honest and well-meaning host, to provide a bill of fare, which all persons may peruse at their first entrance into the house.[60]

Why should Fielding set the tone for *Tom Jones* by considering the authorial role as that of an 'honest' victualler, as he goes on to state?[61] And does it not demean the status of the work to compare its architecture as somehow comparable to the offerings of an ordinary, rather than an inn? We have already seen the relatively low social esteem in which such places were held.

It is clearly operating as a counter-example to Richardson's type of novel. In opposition to the idea that the work is moral, a piece of charity ('eleemosynary') designed for the good of its audience (as was *Pamela*), the authorial persona of *Tom Jones* has no authority other than that of 'mine Host'. In doing this Fielding sets up a different relationship with the reader from that of Richardson. Although the premise of 'author-as-host' was not new, in the context of the relatively new literary form of the novel, its meaning is significant. In defining the parameters of 'the novel' Fielding chooses to focus upon the type of contract set up between the reader and the author, and finds the best image that of 'the ordinary', a hostelry with a fixed-price menu. This might have been a dangerous thing to do, given that the novel had a reputation as a 'low' genre, but it is further evidence that Fielding is operating within the realm of the court of conscience – where all are welcome and empowered – rather than that of policy. There is also a sense of fair-play, since the presentation of the reckoning in places where the prices were not fixed was a source of eternal friction between landlords/landladies and their guests (and something Fielding himself recorded in *Journal of a Voyage to Lisbon*; see below). Here Fielding appears to follow Pepys's line on the essential good sense of having ordinaries.

In opposition to *Pamela*, by using the image of an ordinary it also automatically presents a social space that is far removed from Richardson's novel. Although, not surprisingly, the movement of Fielding's two novels and Richardson's is the same – towards the conclusion of respectable marriage – the movement through space is different. Richardson's is possibly the more daring since he shows that the domestic space is inherently dangerous, for Pamela is threatened within Mr B's house, on his estate. There is no escape for Pamela. But in *Tom Jones*, where Allworthy, as his name implies, is the anchor of common sense and moral rectitude, Tom is cast out under a grave error. The estate space itself remains the 'proper' one, the one that best represents a virtuous England. 'The road' and its numerous resting places are not 'ideal'. The inns and the road are England in chaos, the site of sexual improprieties and highwaymen, the comic representation of the same ungoverned England as seen in *A Charge* and *An Enquiry*, at the conceptual level.

The novel moves from Allworthy's and Western's country estates – representing the good and bad of the squirearchy, but nevertheless underpinned by 'traditional' England – to the open road with its dangerous flux of English types and social codes; and then on to London – a corrupt centre. Once on the road Tom has to deal with a complicated set of social encounters. He is first persuaded by a Quaker to stay at a public house – but gets on the wrong side of the Quaker, because he is unwittingly cast in the role of a worthless man who is attractive to daughters. Tom's social descent is confirmed by the landlord when he learns that Tom is a bastard and consequently worries about being robbed by him. At the same inn soldiers arrive, get drunk, and argue about the bill. With their entrance it also becomes clear that the novel is set in the time of the Jacobite rebellion (1745). The 'road' and its main resting place 'the inn' are thus dangerous in a variety of ways not available on Squire Allworthy's estate. Although it is this estate which has mistakenly shunned Tom, this space can be redeemed. As usual, the drinking-house space remains unstable, reflecting 'real' concerns: rebellion, social snobbery and caste, down to the very basics of shelter (inns are routinely resorted to when the weather turns bad), food and drink. It is the eighteenth-century version of 'man' stripped of his social gloss, yet rather than revert to some 'heart-of-darkness' primitive, native state, the reversion is to a reliance on basic human sympathy – the kindness of strangers.

The inns help Fielding create a patchwork of English types. At the first inn the landlord and landlady refuse to give due to their own social class, desiring only those of a higher station. But at the next inn, The Bell at Gloucester, referring to an actual place for which Fielding had high regard, everything is as it should be, and the narrator recommends it to the reader. The constant movement between inns and their respective social codes demonstrates a range of social levels available in contemporary England. Ironically, it is also the case that when the inn is congenial, there is no adventure. After The Bell, having rescued one Mrs Waters from the man Northerton, he arrives with the lady at another inn which deems itself 'respectable'. The landlady tries to get rid of the unsuitable couple but her attitude changes when she discovers that Mrs Waters is a lady. The inn plays host to bedroom farce – a Captain Fitzpatrick discovers Tom in bed with someone he initially thinks is his wife (it is Mrs Waters). Unbeknown to Tom, Sophia and her maid Honour turn up at the same inn. Thus the generic inn space allows for something that could not possibly occur in Tom's and Sophia's normal 'respectable' social environment, for Tom is sexually engaged with a woman other than Sophia, under the same roof as Sophia. The inn is the place of licence, an alternative to the strict social spaces of fixed lodgings – Squire Allworthy's for Tom, Squire Western's for Sophia. The only other place where this can happen, again fulfilling its generic symbolic role, is London, for when Tom is there he is again involved in sexual misdemeanours. In this way it can be argued that the country inn and London function within the narrative in a similar way. With the large range of inn-types present in *Tom Jones*, the inn is symbolically fluid, a consequence perhaps of the length of the novel, but also of the transitional importance of the inn in the eighteenth century. It is possible for Fielding to find both an ideal domestic space, symbolic of all that is right about traditional England – Allworthy's estate; and an ideal (yet 'real') public space – The Bell at Gloucester;[62] and it is possible to find the obverse of both – Squire Western's overbearing, tyrannical estate, and the inns that have cowardly, deceitful, snobbish landlords.

This returns us to the broader picture of the two faces Fielding set to the world, his court of conscience and his court of policy. In deciding to treat the gin-soaked, crime-ridden nation in his addresses to the establishment, Fielding gave a picture of England gone wrong. In *An Enquiry* he is quite certain why the English have become an ungovernable people. The main problem is that the lower orders, thanks to the general wealth created by trade, have now ascended to a power they never had before, whilst that of the state has not grown apace: 'the Power of the Commonalty hath received an immense Addition; and that the Civil Power having not increased, but decreased, in the same Proportion, is not able to govern them'.[63] Whilst Fielding can laud the benefits of trade, at the same time he fears 'every riotous independent Butcher or Baker, with two or three thousand Pounds in his Pocket,' who can laugh at the 'power' of the J.P.[64] These are the causes of crime: the type of drunkenness caused by 'spirituous liquors', the lack of respect for authority, and an ineffective judicial system and policing. Yet in *Tom Jones*, after being accosted by a highwayman that he overpowers, good-natured Tom pardons his assailant. The narrator addresses his audience: 'Our readers will probably be divided in their opinions concerning this action; some may applaud it perhaps as an act of extraordinary humanity, while those of a more saturnine temper will consider it as a want of regard to that justice which every man owes his country.'[65] The novel's deference to the wisdom contained within the parable of the good Samaritan perhaps demonstrates that it is inclined to an England of conscience and humanity. In a digression on drunkenness in *Tom Jones*, the narrator offers a tempered version of Albion's children: 'And yet as no nation produces so many drunken quarrels, especially among the lower people, as England; (for, indeed, with them, to drink and to fight together, are almost synonymous terms) I would not, methinks, have it thence concluded, that the English are the worst-natured people alive.'[66]

At the end of his life, in order to improve his failing health, Fielding decided to set sail for Lisbon. The period is recorded in the *Journal of a Voyage to Lisbon* and it is here that we finally see Fielding encounter England as any English gentleman in the mid-eighteenth century might. In his description of the time he spends at an inn in Ryde (then just a village on the Isle of Wight), waiting for the right wind to come along so that the boat can sail, we have a description of a hostelry that rivals anything in the novels. Although his powers of observation may have been honed in literature and the law, his experience is presented at a much more immediate and personal level – 'forced' as he is 'to travel about the world in the form of a passenger'.[67]

The *Journal* is a mixed bag of diary entries and general musings. It shows his continued and compelling interest in the constitution of the nation, with sundry digressions on the economy and the English people. At the start of the *Journal* he relates how he was asked to help curb a recent spate of robberies and murders, at some cost to his health. Thus there is an implicit, inverse relation between Fielding's own failing health and the improved health of the nation, and Fielding goes on to discourse about the sacrificial nature of public duties. It is also noteworthy that Fielding defends this work by resort to Richardson's dictum that literature should instruct as well as entertain; Fielding argues that this is especially so in such a contrivance as the *Journal*, which is fact, not fiction. But this defence is not confined to non-fictional works, for in his dedication to Ralph Allen at the opening to his last novel, *Amelia* (1751), he declares that 'The following book is sincerely designed to promote the cause of virtue, and to expose some of the most glaring evils'.[68] His sense of literature as a moral and social tool was greater than ever and much closer to Richardson's than his earlier productions.

Fielding's time spent at Mrs Humphrys' inn at Ryde, representing nearly a quarter of the *Journal*, becomes emblematic of the state of the nation, and should perhaps be as well known as any of his 'fictional' inns. He had begun the journey on Wednesday, 26 June 1754, allowing himself about three weeks to get to Lisbon. But after three weeks, due to unfavourable wind conditions, he is no further than the Isle of Wight. He goes ashore, sending provisions (beans and bacon) from the ship ahead to 'a house, which seemed to bid the fairest for hospitality of any in Ryde'.[69] However, despite strict instructions to have the food dressed for eating at four o'clock, they find the food on the table in exactly the same state in which it had been sent forward. The landlady justifies herself by saying she did not want the food over-done or cold on their arrival, which, according to the good lady, would be 'worse than waiting a few minutes for our dinner'. Fielding takes this as an occasion for general, ironic comment: 'But tradesmen, inn-keepers, and servants never care to indulge us in matters contrary to our true interest, which they always know better than ourselves, nor can any bribes corrupt them to go out of their way, whilst they are consulting our good in our own despight.' In fact, Mrs Humphrys had immediately set about washing the house in preparation to receive gentility on learning that she was to entertain, rather than preparing the food – more concerned with her own vanity than the hunger of her guests, as Fielding sees it.[70]

The venison is brought into the room where he is seated, and one side, 'and that a very bloody one, was laid on the brick floor', because the table is not big enough. Mrs Humphrys returns, is upset by Fielding's behaviour, and storms out of the room complaining that she 'ever took the trouble to wash the house, and "If this was gentility, much good may it do such gentlefolks, for her part she had no notion of it!"' At which point Fielding becomes aware that the room he is in is damp. His wife,[71] acting admirably, discovers a room 'which had escaped the mop', purely because Mrs Humphrys thought 'it could not possibly be visited by gentlefolks. This was a dry, warm, oaken floored barn, lined on both sides with wheaten straw, and opening at one end into a green field, and a beautiful prospect. Here, without hesitation, she [Fielding's wife] ordered the cloth to be laid, and came hastily to snatch me from worse perils by water than the common dangers of the sea.' Of course, Mrs Humphrys is outraged: 'it was the first time, she believed, that quality had ever preferred a barn to a house'.[72] But Fielding's implied sentiment is clear: simple rural pleasures are best, pretensions to higher social decorum by the lower classes are to be avoided.

'At length we were seated in one of the most pleasant spots, I believe, in the kingdom, and were regaled with our beans and bacon, in which there was nothing deficient but the quantity.'[73] The catalogue of errors continues, but in the passage here, and later, Fielding often takes time out to compare his predicament to the nation as a whole. This might be the pleasantest spot, but he has to fight hard (through his wife) for decent accommodation just to eat the food. When they ask if there is a butcher in the village to make up the deficiency in quantity, they are answered that yes, of course there is, but he is not selling meat at present because it is the time for pease and beans.

Fielding accidentally discovers that there is a fishmonger nearby, after which piece of good fortune 'we completed the best, the pleasantest, and the merriest meal, with more appetite, more real, solid luxury, and more festivity, than was ever seen in an entertainment at White's'.[74]

In one journal entry, having run out of things to say for that day, Fielding turns to a description of his landlady, who would seem to fit into the tradition of the ugly alewife: Mrs Humphrys 'was a short, squat woman; her head was closely joined to her shoulders, where it was fixed somewhat awry; every feature of her countenance was sharp and pointed; her face was furrowed with the small-pox; and her complexion, which seemed to be able to turn milk to curds, not a little resembled in colour such milk as had already undergone that operation'.[75] Although both approaching their grand climacteric, Mrs Humphrys and her husband have nothing to show for their endeavours (he is a hard-working farmer) but the signs of want and antiquity.

Fielding turns the inn into the image of a troubled national space by comparing it with a lady's house discovered not far away from Mrs Humphrys' lodgings. The lady is 'not only extremely polite in her behaviour to strangers of her own rank, but so extremely good and charitable to all her poor neighbours, who stand in need of her assistance, that she hath the universal love and praises of all who live near her'.[76] He later compares her garden to 'an earthly paradise'.[77] She is the Lady Bountiful of the area, an exemplar for Fielding of what should pertain in England. The village itself also gets the idyllic treatment: 'The fertility of the place is apparent from its extraordinary verdure, and it is so shaded with large and flourishing elms, that its narrow lanes are a natural grove or walk, which in the regularity of its plantation vies with the power of art, and in its wanton exuberancy greatly exceeds it'.[78] Allied to this is Fielding's description of the battleships harboured there where he evinces admiration for a necessary evil. Fielding's inn, or Mrs Humphrys' inn, represents the material reality of England gone (or going) wrong. She overcharges him in the final reckoning, and it is the inclusion of 'candles' in the bill that makes Fielding lose his temper. Her unwarranted inflation is of a piece with the watermen, who, according to Fielding, can make enough money out of two to three hours rowing to fund their drinking for the rest of the week. This causes him to wish once more for the golden age of olde England, already implicit in the contrast he has drawn between his treatment at the inn and that of the generous lady. But Fielding's actual idea of the past is a timely reminder of just what that particular hierarchical society demanded, for Fielding believes that the vagrancy acts, now fallen into disuse, should be enforced. Vagrancy acts compelled people to work 'for the usual and accustomed wages', at levels set by the local justices.[79] Cast adrift in England, on an island which is a microcosm of England, waiting to quit its shores, Fielding offers a vision of how to put in place a system that would ensure a return to the better past. Whilst his fictional inns are the place of bucolic humour, and are the ones that have remained in literary history and popular consciousness, his last, troubled inn, in a *Journal* that is touted as instructive literature, is the inn that has been erased from such cultural memory.

Notes

1. Bruce King, *Seventeenth-Century English Literature* (Houndmills, Basingstoke, Macmillan, 1992), p. 2.
2. Alan Everitt, ed., *Perspectives in English Urban History* (London, Macmillan, 1973), Introduction, p. 7.
3. Quoted in Frederick W. Hackwood, *Inns, Ales, and Drinking Customs of Old England* (London, T. Fisher Unwin, 1910), p. 180.
4. Andrew Barr, *Drink: An Informal Social History* (Bantam, London, 1995), p. 189.
5. Quoted in John Gay, *The Beggar's Opera*, ed. Bryan Loughrey and T. O. Treadwell (Harmondsworth, Penguin, 1986), Introduction, p. 14, n. 12.
6. Although 'As early as 1695 Charles Davenant warned of the dangers of brandy and spirits to the poor and recommended that they be taxed so that "it may be worth no Man's while to take it, but for Medicine"', from Davenant's *An Essay upon Ways and Means of Supplying the War*, quoted in Malvin R. Zirker's (ed.) Introduction to Henry Fielding's *An Enquiry into the Causes of the Late Increase of Robbers and Related Writings* (Oxford, Clarendon Press, 1988), p. 88, n. 5.
7. *The Tavern Scuffle* (1725) (anon.) with 'The Report of the Committee appointed to Enquire out the Number of Publick Shops that sell Geneva in the Out-Parishes of London. To his Majesty's Justices of the Peace for the County of Middlesex, in their General Quarter Sessions assembled' (London, 1726). Report quotation, p. 37.
8. Barr, *Drink*, p. 189.
9. H. A. Monckton, *A History of the English Public House* (London, Bodley Head, 1969), p. 64. Dorothy M. George, *London Life in the Eighteenth Century* (Harmondsworth, Penguin (Peregrine), 1966 [1925]), speculates that in St Giles, the area depicted in Hogarth's *Gin Lane*, it was one in four, p. 54.
10. Barr, *Drink*, p. 192.
11. 'The Act of 1751 really did reduce the excesses of spirit-drinking. It was a turning-point in the social history of London and was so considered when this time was still within living memory,' George, *London*, p. 49.
12. Gay, *Beggar's*, 2.4. Macheath advises Betty Doxy to drink 'good wholesome beer' rather than strong waters (gin), and Jenny Diver, when accused of drinking gin, says that 'Wine is strong enough for me.' In 3.6 Peachum and Lockit entertain Mrs Diana Trapes and Peachum greets her with: 'One may know by your kiss, that your gin is excellent.'
13. Peter Clark, *The English Alehouse: A Social History 1200–1830* (Harlow, Longman, 1983), chs 9 and 10.
14. Clark, *Alehouse*, p. 231.
15. Ibid., p. 239.
16. R. V. French, *Nineteen Centuries of Drink in England: A History*, 2nd edition –

enlarged and revised (London, National Temperance Publication Depot, n.d. [1st edition 1884]), p. 243, quoting from a note by Derrick.
17 Shirley Strum Kenny, ed., *The Works of George Farquhar*, 2 vols (Oxford, Clarendon Press, 1988), Introduction to *Love and a Bottle*, p. 10.
18 William Wycherley, *The Country Wife*, 1.1, in *Restoration Plays*, ed. Robert G. Lawrence (London, Dent, 1985).
19 Anya Taylor, *Bacchus in Romantic England: Writers and Drink, 1780–1830* (Houndmills, Basingstoke, Macmillan, 1999), p. 192.
20 John Wilmot (Earl of Rochester), 'How happy Cloris (were they free)', in *Love Poems* (Cambridge, Chadwyck-Healey Poetry Full-Text Database 1996–98).
21 George Farquhar, The *Beaux Strategem*, 2.2.56–74, in Kenny, ed., *Farquhar*.
22 Anne Finch [Countess of Winchilsea], *Miscellany Poems, on Several Occasions* (London, 1713), 'Prevalence', pp. 22–4.
23 Susanna Centlivre, *The Man's Bewitch'd; or The Devil to do About Her* (Cambridge, Chadwyck-Healey English Prose Drama Full-Text Database, 1996 [1709]), 3.1.500.
24 Andrew Marvell, 'Upon Appleton House: To My Lord Fairfax', in Alastair Fowler, *The Country House Poem: A Cabinet of Seventeenth-Century Estate Poems and Related Items* (Edinburgh, Edinburgh University Press, 1994), ll. 69–72.
25 It had previously been a nunnery and so the meaning also has a religious aspect to it.
26 According to Kenny, it was probably written sometime between 1700 and 1701. The first publication is in Dublin, 1704, and the first London edition is 1705; Kenny, Introduction to *The Stage Coach*, in Kenny, ed., *Farquhar*, vol. 1, pp. 317–42. The plays are hereafter referred to individually.
27 Farquhar, *Beaux'*, 1.241–3.
28 *Ibid.*, 1.230–1.
29 *Ibid.*, 1.307–8.
30 *Ibid.*, 1.88–9, and description in Dramatis Personae.
31 *Ibid.*, 2.1.32–6.
32 *Ibid.*, 1.166.
33 *Ibid.*, 5.1.
34 *Ibid.*, 5.5.101–4.
35 Centlivre, *Bewitch'd*, no lineation.
36 At one point in the play Kate Hardcastle asks her maid, 'Don't you think I look something like Cherry in the Beaux' Stratagem?', Act 3. The influence of Centlivre's play was first suggested by Mark Schorer in 1933; anecdotal evidence suggests that Goldsmith got the idea for the inn/house substitution from an early experience in his own life: *Collected Works of Oliver Goldsmith*, 5 vols, (Oxford, Clarendon Press, 1966), vol. V, p. 123, n. 1. *Don Quixote* may yet lie behind both when early in his adventures the hero mistakes an inn for a castle (Miguel de Cervantes, *Don Quixote* (Harmondsworth, Penguin, 1986 [1605]), p. 37.
37 Oliver Goldsmith, *She Stoops to Conquer*, Act 1. Goldsmith's sympathies probably lie with Mr Hardcastle. In the essay 'Happiness, In a great Measure, Dependant on Constitution' Goldsmith had expressed his preference for simple country life over sophisticated city life – rustic mirth over 'refinements on

happiness'. *The Bee*, No. III, Saturday 13 October 1759, Goldsmith, *Collected Works*, vol. I, pp. 384–5.
38 Goldsmith, *Stoops*, Act 1.
39 *Ibid.*, Act 3. To convince her own maid that she can act the part she tries barmaid argot: 'Did your honour call? – Attend the Lion there. – Pipes and tobacco for the Angel. The Lamb has been outrageous this half hour.'
40 Gay, *Beggar's*, 3.14.
41 *Ibid.*, 3.2.
42 *Ibid.*, 3.8ff.
43 *Ibid.*, 3.13. It may also be an ironical take on Gay's own first literary production of note, the poem 'Wine' (1708) which extolled the virtues of the 'celestial liquor' in a traditional manner. The change from youthful exuberance to middle-aged bitterness on Gay's part can be read in a comparison between the two.
44 *Ibid.*, 3.16.
45 Zirker, Introduction, in Fielding, *Enquiry*, p. lxiv, quoting from Fielding's *Social Pamphlets*.
46 Fielding, *Enquiry*, Preface, p. 65.
47 *Ibid.*, p. 72.
48 *Ibid.*, p. 3.
49 *Ibid.*, p. xxix.
50 *Ibid.*, p. 85.
51 *Ibid.*, p. 88.
52 *Ibid.*, p. 90.
53 *Ibid.*
54 *Ibid.*
55 *Ibid.*, p. 85.
56 Henry Fielding, *Tom Jones* (London, Penguin, 1985), p. 207.
57 R. P. C. Mutter, Introduction to *ibid.*, p. xviii.
58 Henry Fielding, *Joseph Andrews* (London, Penguin, 1977), p. 185.
59 *Ibid.*, p. 99.
60 Fielding, *Jones*, p. 23.
61 *Ibid.*
62 Similarly, in *Joseph Andrews*, Joseph puts up at the sign of the lion, with its landlord Timotheus, which also (probably) refers to a real inn, the Red Lion at Egham, Surrey, run by Timothy Harris, also mentioned in *Tom Jones*, Book 8, Chapter 8; – n. to p. 67, Fielding, *Andrews*, with information taken from Brissenden.
63 Fielding, *Enquiry*, p. 73.
64 *Ibid.*, p. 72.
65 Fielding, *Jones*, p. 561.
66 *Ibid.*, p. 203.
67 Henry Fielding, *Journal of a Voyage to Lisbon* (London, Chiswick Press, 1892 [1755]), p. 128.
68 Henry Fielding, *Amelia*, ed. A. R. Humphreys, 2 vols (London, Dent, 1968 [1755]), p. 3.
69 Fielding, *Journal*, p. 97.
70 *Ibid.*, pp. 98–9.
71 His second wife, Mary Daniel, his first wife's maid.

72 *Ibid.*, pp. 99–102.
73 *Ibid.*, pp. 101–2.
74 *Ibid.*, p. 105. White's was a famous coffee-house.
75 *Ibid.*, p. 116.
76 *Ibid.*, p. 129.
77 *Ibid.*, p. 143.
78 *Ibid.*, p. 141.
79 *Ibid.*, p. 125.

8

Where did the Romantics drink?

Age, care, wisdom, reflection, begone – I give you to the winds. Let's have t'other bottle: here's to the memory of Shakespear, Falstaff, and all the merry men of East-cheap.
Such were the reflections that naturally arose while I sat at the Boar's-head tavern, still kept at East-cheap.

Oliver Goldsmith[1]

But what have we not omitted also! No less an illustrious head than the Boar's, in Eastcheap, – the Boar's-head Tavern, the scene of Falstaff's revels. But who knows not Eastcheap and the Boar's-head? Have we not all been there time out of mind? And is it not a more real as well as notorious thing to us than the London tavern, or the Crown and Anchor, or the Hummums, or White's, or What's-his-name's, or any other of your contemporary and fleeting taps?

Leigh Hunt[2]

A thought suddenly struck me: 'I will make a pilgrimage to Eastcheap,' said I, closing the book, 'and see if the old Boar's Head Tavern still exists.'

Washington Irving[3]

Praising Fielding's description of The Lion at Upton, Hackwood says: 'no better conception of the daily routine of a country inn at that period can be obtained elsewhere, either in the domain of fiction or in the serious pages of history'.[4] Yet for all Fielding's centrality to impressions of the eighteenth-century inn, it should be noted that he does not 'describe' an inn in terms of its architecture – if we have particular visions of galleried inn courtyards filled with the excitement of coaches arriving and departing in our mind's eye they are from other sources. The relationship between the inns of fiction and the inns of England is further complicated by the patina of cultural memory and the manner in which 'real' drinking places might already be 'literary' (see Introduction). When Boswell enters a London tavern with 'two very pretty little girls' on 19 May, 1763, *The Beggar's Opera* comes to his mind, he thinks himself Captain Macheath and sings 'Youth's the Season' when he surveys his seraglio. But for many writers intent on conjuring up olde England it was back to Falstaff and the Boar's Head. Even for Boswell's tavern jaunt the Bard remains the touchstone, for Boswell reminds himself a couple of times that the place is called 'The Shakespeare's Head', as if his whole experience takes place within the dramatist's imagination.

The quotations at the head of this chapter span George III's reign – Goldsmith is writing in 1760 and Washington Irving in 1820. In these pieces, the sense of England present and England past is contrasted through the Boar's Head. Further, for both Hunt and Irving (or Irving's persona, Geoffrey Crayon) the revels of Falstaff are more real and important than any historical record or socially current drinking place. It is an indication that this idea of England is now time out of mind, as arguably it had not been up to the beginning of the eighteenth century. Goldsmith's 'reverie' is an opportunity to compare England's current fortune with its former life; Hunt conjures up a literary golden age; and Irving plays the admiring American outsider, looking for 'England' in the dramatic tavern. Only the latter's Geoffrey Crayon, Gent., is prepared to offer the reality of the situation rather than submit to nostalgia, perhaps because by then the Boar's Head had in reality finally disappeared: 'I sought in vain for the ancient abode of Dame Quickly. The only relic of it is a boar's head, carved in relief in stone, which formerly served as the sign, but at present is built into the parting line of two houses, which stand on the site of the renowned old tavern.'[5] In the conclusion to Goldsmith's 'reverie' Goldsmith berates the landlord (transformed into Mrs Quickly in his semi-conscious musings) for using the occasion to do nothing more than simply describe the tenor of the times, noting banally 'that whenever taverns flourish most, the times are then most extravagant and luxurious'. Goldsmith complains that such a discourse is tedious; he wants to hear stories only.[6] The 'tavern' always emerges as Falstaffian, 'revelry' is always a reprise of Elizabethan life. The demise of the actual Boar's Head ends any tangible connection between the possibility of England and the reality of England, and ends the possibility of substituting Shakespeare's England for contemporary England.

I have so far in the book relied heavily on the triumvirate of alehouse, tavern and inn for much of the discussion on the appearance of drinking houses in literature. They have a long heritage, successors to distinctions made between the three types of house offering beverages in Anglo-Saxon times (see Introduction). In this chapter we will see that the trio can still operate in like terms for this period, a period whose 1830 endpoint marks both the nominal end of Romanticism, and, with the arrival of the Beer Act that year, the nominal end of the alehouse. Clark's history of *The English Alehouse* terminates here for the reason that the alehouse is no longer recognisable, and this should alert us to the fact that the distinctions between the three are shading into a relatively new formation. Even if the dram (spirits) shop had taken over the position of the lowest place in some schema, the three remained in a similar relative position to each other, and as we have also seen, the dram shop rarely made its way into the literature studied here. The term 'alehouse', although still in use, gave way to 'public house', whose own golden age is usually placed in the Victorian period. Even in *Tom Jones*, Fielding deliberately slides between calling the same hostelry both an alehouse and an inn. Being a well-informed magistrate, his joke is perhaps an insider's, knowing that an inn may legally be called an alehouse if it 'descends' into the behaviour of an alehouse.

The shifting nature of the terms can be observed in different works of single authors, sometimes using the fixed social significances of hostelries, sometimes finding no use for such distinctions. In Goldsmith's *She Stoops to Conquer* the metonymic and symbolic baggage of an alehouse is fully exploited as a means of setting up character, theme and environment. But in his *The Vicar of Wakefield* (1766), although there is a reference to sermons the Reverend Primrose may have given against alehouses before he is forced to leave his parish, the remainder of the novel is littered with incidental visits to alehouses and inns, and the nomenclature would appear to indicate very little, for 'a little ale-house' becomes an 'inn' without embarrassment in the space of a page.[7] However, towards the end of the novel, all references are to 'inns', as if the Vicar's emergence from prison warrants consistent use of the higher place.

We should remain circumspect on all fronts. Hackwood argues that towards the end of the eighteenth century fast mail coaches were making inns more elitist.[8] The sense of impending elitism may even be the case at a slightly earlier date, for one of the chapters in *Tom Jones* ends with: 'nor did the landlady condescend to wish him a good journey: for this was, it seems, an inn frequented by people of fashion; and I know not whence it is, but all those who get their livelihood by people of fashion, contract as much insolence to the rest of mankind, as if they really belonged to that rank themselves'.[9] And whilst Goldsmith can use the alehouse in *She Stoops to Conquer* as the site of indolent inheritors in the shape of Tony Lumpkin, in his poem *The Deserted Village* (1770), although not named as 'an alehouse', the decaying hostelry there becomes the place where all the best, simple values of the English countryside once resided. That it is an alehouse is suggested by the reference to 'nut-brown draughts' and 'ale' as the drinks taken. Goldsmith can do this since the village alehouse and village inn are interchangeable as symbols of an England being lost (or already lost), whereas the town/city alehouse and inn remain distinct in terms of their respective functions as sites of idle resort and provision of lodgings.[10] In *The Deserted Village*'s idealised hostelry, workers from all walks of life at one time met and drank away their worries: 'Thither no more the peasant shall repair / To sweet oblivion of his daily care; / No more the farmer's news, the barber's tale, / No more the wood-man's ballad shall prevail; / No more the smith his dusky brow shall clear, / Relax his ponderous strength, and lean to hear'.[11] Of course, the different types of hostelry signal different Englands. The Falstaffian, Boar's Head version is the golden age of Elizabethan England, conflated by later generations with the victories of Henry V and Elizabeth's triumphs, intermingling the merrie England of Shakespeare with an older rural idyll. *The Deserted Village*, an alternative eighteenth-century vision, is a belated elegy attacking enclosure. It prefers 'nature' over 'artifice', happier with an older England that did less trade and enjoyed the simple pleasures of the countryside. Both hanker after an idealised past of the all-inclusive, organic community.

Part of the same complex of issues is evident in Cowper's poem *The Task* (1785). Its style is one of conversational grandeur as it discourses associatively on the state of the nation. 'The task' of the title is never explained, but inductively and accumulatively it emerges as some idea of Christian duty to maintain 'virtue' in the face of modern pressures. Its main target is luxury, a theme that ran throughout the eighteenth century. When Fielding in *An Enquiry* complains about the ill-consequences of the lower classes having too much money, he is using an argument against 'luxury'. In this sense luxury is whatever is accrued or available over and above what is deemed appropriate or necessary. Hence, given his belief in a 'static hierarchical society', for the lower orders to have more money than necessary for their station in life is to indulge in luxury in the same manner that the idle rich do. His ambivalence towards flourishing trade is a consequence of this – it makes for a healthy nation in terms of wealth, but the creation of wealth can also lead to the enervation that comes with luxury. Unlike Fielding, Goldsmith had no such ambivalence about the ill-effects of an expanding Empire. In *The Deserted Village* he waxes: 'A time there was, ere England's griefs began, / When every rood of ground maintained its man; / For him light labour spread her wholesome store, / Just gave what life required, but gave no more. / His best companions, innocence and health; / And his best riches, ignorance of wealth.'[12]

As with Goldsmith both in *She Stoops to Conquer* and *The Deserted Village*, Cowper uses the alehouse to his own literary and ideological ends. *The Task* is divided into six books, beginning with 'The Sofa'. For a short while it takes the reader on an epic serio-comic journey through the cultural significance of this item of furniture, a sign of 'luxury'. It has evolved from the plain, simple (and hence virtuous) 'joint-stool' upon which King Alfred must have sat. Thus the opening fulfils its epic function of providing a history of the nation. It is the object from which Cowper can proceed to give an appraisal of the present 'state-of-the-nation', taking into his purview any number of items: 'profusion' – an adjunct of luxury; the cowardice of the clergy in tackling the ills of society; the praise of nature over artifice and country over city (London). The delineations are not always as sharp as perhaps these oppositions suggest, and Cowper has been seen as much as describing a country idyll as providing an analysis of its harsh reality.[13] It is true that Cowper depicts the poverty of the cottager, as well as the lives of 'scroungers, topers, subversives and burglars',[14] but the cottager represents the virtues of honest and plain living, whereas the latter are the equivalent of sturdy beggars and the indolent lower classes.

It is in Book 4, 'The Winter-Evening', where Cowper declaims against public houses. The section subtly sets up an opposition between 'inn' and 'alehouse', 'sobriety' and 'sottishness', in the opening lines. It begins with a description of the narrator waiting at home for the post to arrive with all the news of a world struggling for stability. The post is dropped at the 'destin'd inn', and the 'inn' is carefully submerged within the idyllic domestic scene; sobriety is introduced as a leitmotif: 'Now stir the fire, and close the shutters fast, / Let fall the curtains, wheel the sofa round, / And, while the bubbling and loud-hissing urn / Throws up a steamy column, and the cups, / That cheer but not inebriate, wait on each, / So let us welcome peaceful ev'ning in.'[15]

He immediately contrasts his perfect retreat with the crowd of the world at large and after a while wanders into the following theme: 'Time, as he passes us, has a dove's wing, / Unsoil'd, and swift, and of a silken sound; / But the world's time is time in masquerade!'[16] He argues against the idle time of the fashionable, inventing as they do 'tricks' 'To fill the void of an unfurnish'd brain, / To palliate dulness, and give time a shove'.[17] His own time he puts to good use. There are echoes of the idle time/useful time divide we have seen before. The difference is that, unlike Hal's sense of time redeemed for a nation, the poet's time is private. This associates with Book 2 of *The Task*, entitled 'The Time-Piece', where the object of the title is a symbol of discipline.

From line 466 onwards Cowper begins a diatribe against the alehouse:

> Pass where we may, through city or through town,
> Village, or hamlet of this merry land
> Though lean and beggar'd, ev'ry twentieth pace
> Conducts the unguarded nose to such a whiff
> Of stale debauch forth-issuing from the styes
> That law has licens'd, as makes temperance reel.
> There sit involv'd and lost in curling clouds
> Of Indian fume, and guzzling deep, the boor,
> The lacquey and the groom.

The power of Cowper's poetic antagonism towards the alehouse is amongst the most vehement literature in this tradition and would not have looked out of place in later Tudor literature. The rhetorical sentiment would become familiar fare in the next century. It is clear that this is not just any alehouse, this is the nation at large. The sensual disgust is palpable, the anger that this is approved by the state is its political point, and its class-economics is transparent. The latter is expanded upon a few lines later: 'Smith, cobbler, joiner, he that plies the shears, / And he that kneads the dough; all loud alike, / All learned, and all drunk.'[18] The collection of working types takes us back to Chaucer and Langland. More immediately, it is a mirror image of Goldsmith's hostelry, but here used as national dystopia rather than an idealisation of community. It also reinforces Cowper's desire for the 'private world' over a shared world. His central placing of the domestic sphere as the seat of all that is good foreshadows the more virulent temperance campaigning in the next century which privileged domestic space (home) over communal space (public house).

Like Fielding and many others before him, there is an in-built despair and fear that the mechanic part of the nation is engaged in time-wasting conviviality. Cowper's particular twist is that he regards them as intellectually very capable: 'Behold the schools in which plebeian minds, / Once simple, are initiated in arts / Which some may practise with politer grace, / But none with readier skill!'[19] With this Cowper appears to initiate an additional class fear that the lower classes are sophisticates rather than unthinking simpletons. In other words, they are not just wasting away their 'work' time; on the one hand they are squandering their intellectual capabilities in the time-worn tradition of the idle poor, and on the other have become more frightening because they are now the educated lower classes. At the back of this are no doubt the first stirrings of a perception that the working classes are becoming self-aware (Priestman sees the description as indicating a working-men's political club[20]), and partly a literalisation of the notion of 'drinking schools', a concept that also has a literary history.

In an image cluster similar to that of Falstaff's speech in praise of sack (*2 Henry IV*) Cowper marries the idea of alcoholic drink with fertilisation of the land, although here he takes the opposite view. Unlike the 'filth' (manure) the peasant legitimately uses to feed 'his hungry acres', 'Th' excise is fatten'd with the rich result / Of all this riot'.[21] With the word 'riot' is trailed in once more fears of lower classes and mob action. When Cowper leaves off his jeremiad, he immediately turns to a golden era for comfort: 'Would I had fall'n upon those happier days / That poets celebrate, Those golden times, / And those Arcadian scenes that Maro sings'.[22] He realises that such times never existed, but he argues that at least there was a time when it was possible to envision such scenes. It is an interesting manipulation of the symbolic function of the 'golden age', where England's current disgrace is now measured against times when there was not such 'drinking', rather than the usual nostalgia for the revels of olde England. His earlier, ironic mention of 'this merry land' has already set up these lines, as if there is not now, nor has ever been, a 'merrie England', since such a phrase could only signify a 'debauched' land.

The state is complicit with the people in its degradation: 'And ten thousand casks / For ever dribbling out their base contents, / Touch'd by the Midas finger of the state, / Bleed gold for Ministers to sport away. / Drink and be mad then. 'Tis your country bids.'[23] It should be remembered that the British government's dependency on 'indirect taxes' was heavy. In the 1730s a quarter of the national revenue was raised from excise on the drink trade;[24] income tax is not introduced until 1798, at five pence in the pound, and does not gather in a sizeable sum until the First World War, at thirty pence in the pound.[25] Cowper was right to point out that an unhealthy nation was, indeed, a wealthy one. Part of 'the task' then, as we have seen throughout, was to engender a 'proper' constitution in all senses. And if anything symbolised the improper composition of the body politic and the physical body, it was the alehouse.

Unhealthy, class-ridden, Romantic England

> Banish money — Banish sofas — Banish Wine — Banish Music; but right Jack Health, honest Jack Health, true Jack Health — Banish health and banish all the world.
>
> John Keats[26]

> On December 28th the immortal dinner came off in my painting-room…
>
> Benjamin Haydon[27]

> When a man in easy circumstances gets drunk at a public-house and staggers along the streets; here he is seen by every body, and is inconsiderately taken as a fair example of his class; and thus, through the occasional drunkard, or the drunken vagabond, the whole body are stigmatized and condemned as drunkards when in fact the number of those which are really drunkards is, when compared with the whole body, a very small number.
>
> Francis Place[28]

Cowper's argument that the state is complicit in the country's degradation, that its coffers depend upon a drunken nation, had some justification. The more the nation was inebriated, the wealthier it became. *The Task*'s indictment of ministers may also refer to the fact that government members were themselves part of the general sottishness, for stories of drunken ministers were not uncommon. A letter written in 1787 complains of the habits of the top statesmen, although it should also be noted that here they are redeemed by another characteristic of the eighteenth century, great wit, traditionally inspired by wine: 'Men of all ages drink abominably. Fox drinks what I should call a great deal, though he is not reckoned to do so by his superiors, Sheridan excessively; and Grey more than any of them; but it is in a much more gentlemanly way than our Scotch drunkards, and is always accompanied with lively, clever conversation of subjects of importance. Pitt, I am told, drinks as much as any one.'[29] The story is also told that Fox was sometimes taken straight from the tavern at night to the Commons when there was an emergency, 'in such a condition that he required a long application of wet towels to his head before he was able to go to his place and speak'.[30] Another anecdote from the period relates to Henry Mackenzie, author of *The Man of Feeling* (1771). Having held out as long as he could at a drinks party, he finally fell under the table along with the rest of the crew. He soon found a boy's hands at his throat. He had been assigned the duty 'when the guests were becoming helpless, to untie the cravate in fear of apoplexy or suffocation'.[31]

There was kudos attached to being a hard drinker, the 'three-bottle-a-day man' was to be respected.[32] Undoubtedly still a moral failing, a sin that one knowingly committed rather than something one was unhealthily addicted to, drunkenness did however come more under the medical and sociological microscope towards the end of the eighteenth century. Until then 'Drunkenness was considered a normal and satisfactory condition as much by Defoe or Sir Robert Walpole as it was later by Johnson or Wilkes.'[33] Defoe had written in 1702, 'an honest drunken fellow is a character in a man's praise'[34] and fifty years later Johnson claimed that a man was never happy 'but when he is drunk'.[35]

When we view the later part of the eighteenth century and the first decades of the nineteenth in more detail, we find that the literature of the period has very little to offer us in terms of substantial representations of drinking places. The dates incorporate, in literary-historical terms, the Romantic period, usually put somewhere between 1780 and 1830, but the Romantics in particular are parsimonious when it comes to giving us either boozing kens or magnificent inns. Not that they didn't drink. Some, like Lamb, were known to be habitual drunkards, and Coleridge, Byron and Keats were not slow to praise 'wine' and the effects of intoxication. But when references to hostelries occasionally occur, as the quotation from Hunt at the head of this chapter illustrates well, the preference is for thinking of them in purely literary terms. The contemporary genius for these writers, Wordsworth, became a water-drinker. The one reference to his own drinking remains wrapped up in the anxiety of poetic influence. In *The Prelude*, when he describes his taking of rooms at Cambridge, he becomes drunk in the apartments that Milton once had.[36] It would not be possible for Wordsworth (in Wordsworth's eyes) to have shown greater disrespect for the 'temperate bard', drunk then as never before or since. However, Wordsworth did provide us with one of the few Romantic conjurings of a drinking house, in his little-regarded (then and now) *The Waggoner*, discussed below.

Yet the taverns, alehouses and inns of England certainly continued to house the English literati as we move from the mid-eighteenth century through to 1830: Boswell, Johnson, Goldsmith, Lamb, Coleridge, Keats, Byron … But as the century wears on, unless Shakespearean in some way, drinking houses become increasingly invisible to literature. Even when we come upon representations outside the Romantic canon, we find a continued anxiety that inns and alehouses are not fit material for serious literature. The 'Boar's Head' has cachet because it is old, fictional and Shakespearean – it is safe from all charges of 'low life'. The 'Salutation and Cat', the tavern on Newgate that haunts Lamb's early letters to Coleridge as the symbol of their carefree, intimate, golden past (well, December 1794 into January 1795 to be precise), cannot be found in their literature, except for an oblique reference in Lamb's plangent 'The Old Familiar Faces': 'I have been laughing, I have been carousing, / Drinking late, sitting late, with my bosom cronies— / All, all are gone, the old familiar faces.'[37]

Anya Taylor's *Bacchus in Romantic England: Writers and Drink, 1780–1830* covers the relationship between the Romantic writers and the drinking environment for these years. It incorporates material on drinking from writing other than 'literature' to show that there was a general concern in that era for all things drink-related. The emphasis, as suggested by the use of 'Bacchus', is on the 'literary' notion of drink, and so the material is seen in relation to this tradition. Taylor can frequently show how the celebration of drink was at odds with the more tawdry reality of the lives of the writers, and the book treats the more hardened drinkers (Lamb, Coleridge, Hartley Coleridge, Burns) very much as 'alcoholics', as 'cases'.

Part of Taylor's argument is that drink was often the fault-line for examining a (the 'Romantic') divided self, and that particularly in a work like Lamb's *Confessions of a Drunkard*, where there is a complex form of 'denial' in play, we can see such Romantic concerns manifest. But apart from a page on the cultural place of taverns in Britain,[38] the role of drinking houses is not a specific concern of Taylor's. To summarise the Romantic attitude to drink, I think it fair to say that 'Bacchus' did indeed inform the more literary productions of those writers recognised as 'Romantic', but there was little connection made between drink as it appeared in literature under the guise of Bacchus and the reality of drinking with which they were so familiar. It sometimes feels that they were so steeped in literary tradition that even recognising their own drinking habits was impossible except through the intoxication of literature.

For example, Keats is obsessed with 'the juice of the grape', and by concentrating on the drink of literary gods this subject matter of his poetry is easily abstracted into an asocial lyricism. We do not learn of the places he visited with the Piccadilly Club, a group he fell in with early in his life. Reference to his new-found, short-lived lifestyle is couched in a manner reminiscent of Hal and his leash of drawers; Keats talks of learning the language of goodfellows, that 'dyin' scarlet' is 'drinking deep'.[39] He would have been remiss if he had not paid his due to his literary forebears, and sure enough he provides lines on the Mermaid Tavern where he imagines the literary topers drinking in Mermaid heaven.

As to Coleridge, Taylor has encouraged critics to look at his drinking songs, an area of writing that she regards as overlooked. One song proceeds:'Ye drinkers of Stingo and Nappy so free / Are the gods on Olympus so happy as we?' – 'Why, then we ad[?] the Gods are equally blest, / And Olympus an Ale-house as good as the best'.[40] In play is the drinking song's celebration of the good life, but to move on to the 'drinking place', we can see that the conceit works by choosing the highest classical (literary) place and the lowest contemporary (real) place so that the humour emerges from the juxtaposition of opposites. An inn would not do because, as consistently noted, in the drinking-place hierarchy it is at the top. Yet, despite Coleridge's penchant for drinking songs, he had a strong sense of hierarchies of genre and would surely have regarded his drinking songs as something less than 'serious Literature'.[41]

The middle-class outlook of many of the Romantics clearly affects their treatment of drink and drinkers. The lower classes take their social drinking in public, the middling and upper classes in private. The middling classes drink wine, the lower classes ale, beer and gin. A dinner party – no matter how much drinking might be involved – will always have the polish of gentility and the mask of privacy to excuse it. This is the case with what has come down to us as the 'immortal dinner party' of 1817. The painter Benjamin Haydon hosted the occasion, and it is from the description in his *Autobiography* that we are granted a glimpse of the lives of the poets and artists of the day in relaxed (that is, drunken) mood.

> On December 28th the immortal dinner came off in my painting-room, with Jerusalem towering up behind us as a background. Wordsworth was in fine cue, and we had a glorious set-to—on Homer, Shakespeare, Milton and Virgil. Lamb got exceedingly merry and exquisitely witty; and his fun in the midst of Wordsworth's solemn intonations of oratory was like the sarcasm and wit of the fool in the intervals of Lear's passion.[42]

All the elements are here – the greatest poet of his day in the company of the greatest poets of the past; the sense of irreverence; the immersion into a Shakespearean scene; the religious backdrop – as if this were the new Jerusalem; the production of wit from wine; the glow of genius. Things fall apart when a civil servant appears, who (unknown to Wordsworth) happens to be his London boss, since Wordsworth had taken a part-time post to supplement his earnings back home in the Lakes. In an attempt to impress the hallowed gathering the comptroller asks the Lakeland bard whether he regards Milton as a genius. Getting no response, he asks if he regards Newton as a genius. The continued questioning simply compounds the social awkwardness and the look on Wordsworth's face is something akin to 'who is this man?'

> Lamb got up, and taking a candle, said: 'Sir, will you allow me to look at your phrenological development?' He then turned his back on the poor man, and at every question of the comptroller he chaunted: 'Diddle diddle dumpling, my son John / Went to bed with his breeches on.'

Keats and Haydon have to cart Lamb off into another room where all three fall into uncontrollable laughter.[43] 'It was a night worthy of the Elizabethan age', Haydon declares.[44] Again, the revelry is in terms of Shakespeare, but this is the private replication of the past, a middle-class exercise in nostalgia.

The acknowledgement that there is a class division of pleasures is always bubbling under the surface. One piece that offers some measure of the gap between the private Romantic world and the world at large is De Quincey's *Confessions of an English Opium-Eater* (1821).[45] After his description of absconding from school to wander about North Wales and London, and after near-starvation, he throws himself on Lord D—. De Quincey then presents the reader with the following:

> I had, however, unfortunately at all times a craving for wine: I explained my situation, therefore, to lord D—, and gave him a short account of my late sufferings, at which he expressed great compassion, and called for wine. This gave me a momentary relief and pleasure; and on all occasions when I had an opportunity, I never failed to drink wine – which I worshipped then as I have since worshipped opium. I am convinced, however, that this indulgence in wine contributed to strengthen my malady.[46]

The import is clear – De Quincey was so addicted to wine that he would take it rather than food even if starving, and even in the knowledge that it contributed to ill-health. This also prepares the ground for an understanding of the strength of his opium addiction. Why wine? He does not say, and the reader is left to conjecture that there was something intrinsic that was addictive. That a man should crave wine when in the throes of hunger must be a sign of the genteel addict; Lord D— would surely not have respected a craving for ale.

When De Quincey does turn to opium, he distinguishes between this and wine by saying that opium does not 'intoxicate'. He argues to the effect that opium is celestial whilst wine is bestial, to the extent that his first druggist is given the appearance of an angel descended from heaven.[47] He then goes on to affirm that he would regulate his intake to a Saturday night, to align himself with the lower classes, not out of sympathy for their misfortunes, but so that he can empathise with their pleasures. 'Now Saturday night is the season for the chief, regular, and periodic return of rest to the poor' – 'On this account I feel always, on a Saturday night, as though I also were released from some yoke of labour, had some wages to receive, and some luxury of repose to enjoy.' However, such avowed 'empathy' through tying his own pleasure-taking to the weekly routine of the labouring classes reads more like a vicarious and voyeuristic thrill. Because he is most intrigued by the effects of opium in the production of dreams, his half-immersion into the sights and sounds of the markets and theatres on wage-day is the rendering of the poor into a dream state. He does not 'enjoy' the same pleasures; he views them through the opiate filter.

The distance between himself (and, I am suggesting, his literary class) and the lower classes is confirmed when he confesses that 'in candour, I will admit that markets and theatres are not the appropriate haunts of the opium-eater, when in the divinest state incident to his enjoyment. In that state, crowds become an oppression to him; music even, too sensual and gross. He naturally seeks solitude and silence.'[48] The illusion of empathy is over. What is really sought is that private space for contemplation of 'human nature'. The lives of the poor are an interesting detour but succour is always to be found out of the public sphere – either at immortal dinner parties or in the solitude of an opium haze.

The drinking places of the poor often appear as generic in a middle-class context. One of the distinguishing features of the Boar's Head, of Pepys's haunts, of Ned Ward's establishments, of the Three Pigeons alehouse, is that there is a particularity granted. It is not that the Romantics did not have their specific drinking resorts. Wordsworth would go to The George at Keswick with Shelley and Coleridge. Visitors to Wordsworth, such as Scott, might be found taking refuge from his poor hospitality in the nearby Swan at Grasmere[49] (still extant, and in which the visitor will find that 'Wordsworth's Chair' now has its due place and plaque). But somehow, inns, taverns and alehouses just never took serious hold of the English Romantic poetic imagination. The two instances that can be teased out are, as already hinted, Lamb's 'Salutation and Cat' in his letters, and 'The Cherry Tree' in Wordsworth's *The Waggoner*.

In Edwin Marrs' 1975 collection of *The Letters of Charles and Mary Anne Lamb*, the first missive is to Coleridge, 27 May 1796, and it inauspiciously introduces us to the 'Salutation's' ghostly presence: 'Dear C— / make yourself perfectly easy about May. I paid his bill, when I sent your clothes. I was flush of money, & am so still to all the purposes of a single life, so give yourself no further concern about it. The money would be superfluous to me, if I had it.' May was the landlord of the Salutation and Cat and had probably 'retained Coleridge's belongings as surety against a bill Coleridge left unpaid when he left the inn, in January 1795 for The Angel, in St. Martin's le Grand, Newgate Street'.[50] Lamb was known for his generosity of spirit, and this is further confirmed in the next letter recorded in Marrs' collection (30 May 1796) when Lamb asks a single favour of Coleridge – that he not mention the money he has been loaned. Reading this in the light of his references that follow, perhaps Lamb wanted his memories of their evenings there free from the taint of materialism.

Another letter to Coleridge, 14 June that year, records: 'I have been drinking egg-hot and smoking Oronooko (associated circumstances, which ever forcibly recall to my mind our evenings and nights at the Salutation); my eyes and brain are heavy and asleep, but my heart is awake', and the letter goes on to quote some lines on the nature of friendship past. The tavern is already associated with better times in Lamb's maudlin prose, for which he excuses himself by saying that he is a little bit drunk: 'I am writing at random, and half-tipsy, what you may not *equally* understand, as you will be sober when you read it; but *my* sober and *my* half-tipsy hours you are alike a sharer in. Good night.' There is an anxiety to forge a bond based upon goodfellowship, and he creates a virtual reality through his own altered state. The same letter, but composed a couple of days later, has lines that portray a growing ennui and regret at Coleridge's married state: 'I am heartily sick of the every-day scenes of life. I shall half wish you unmarried (don't show this to Mrs. C.) for one evening only, to have the pleasure of smoking with you, and drinking egg-hot in some little smoky room in a pot-house, for I know not yet how I shall like you in a decent room, and looking quite happy.' It is a continuation of the desire for male camaraderie, slightly seedy surroundings, all politely corralled. The cosy drinking place – as it had so often been for generations of English – is gradually becoming *the* personal symbol of something irrevocably past for Lamb.

The letter he sends Coleridge on 1 December 1796, has an even greater note of desperation. A reference to an obscure sonnet in a review reminds him of the time Coleridge wrote sonnets on Bowles, Priestly and Burke 'in that nice little smoky room at the Salutation, which is even now continually presenting itself to my recollection, with all its associated train of pipes, tobacco, Egghot, welch Rabbits, metaphysics & **Poetry**—. Are [sic] we *never* to meet again?' It is as if he is calling to his mind the Salutation as a substitute for a concatenation of elements that he is unable to reproduce, as well as a defence for the worry that he might not see Coleridge again. It is as if his memory of the Salutation and Cat simply *is* his relationship with Coleridge.

The fact that such tenderness for a tavern/inn never finds its way into literature may be down once more to literary decorum and snobbery. Lamb's class distaste for certain aspects of tavern life remain when confronted with the possibility of it in poetry. He writes to Coleridge incredulous that Coleridge will transform Joan of Arc 'into a pot girl' and in another letter on the same subject, worried about a 'certain faulty disproportion in the matter and the *style*' – 'After all this cometh Joan, a *publican's* daughter, sitting on an ale-house *bench*, and marking the *swingings* of the *signboard*, finding a poor man, his wife and six children, starved to death with cold.'[51] The old antagonisms to the drinking house remain, shown by the contrast between his despair at the use of the figure of a 'pot girl' in literature and his glorification of the Salutation in his letters. There is no connection to be made. He continues to write letters bemoaning the loss of 'Salutation scenery', where the fading amounts to 'a sort of sacrilege in my letting such ideas slip out of my mind & memory'.[52] The Salutation and Cat has become an ideal to worship, safe in the privacy of a (projected) shared past.

So it is with some irony that we must turn to the abstemious Wordsworth for a representation of a 'Romantic' drinking house. I should note, before moving on to *The Waggoner*, that I must forbear discussing one of the most endearing pictures of anything approaching a recognisable description of a tavern, inn or alehouse in Romantic literature. This is Burns's 'Tam O'Shanter', where Tam, the 'blethering, blustering, drunken blellum' is ensconced 'fast by an ingle', drinking the 'nappy' and 'O'er a' the ills o'life victorious'.[53] For all Burns's acknowledged greatness by his Romantic heirs, the homely picture of Tam's 'local' is no doubt only acceptable to the period because embedded within the fashionable ballad form and written by a (as Wordsworth characterised him) plough-boy naif. It did not inspire others to follow, and the fact that drink was deemed to have killed Burns could not have helped.[54]

Tam's refuge before he plunges into the wild night is described in Burns's characteristically fresh manner. *The Waggoner* comes with Wordsworth's characteristically involuted literary and autobiographical style. The story is of Benjamin, the worker of the title, who loses his job because of a fondness for social drinking. The poem was originally written in 1805 (although some elements might date from 1801[55]), but perhaps because it was based on personal circumstances Wordsworth did not feel able to publish it until about ten years later, a feature he works into the poem's conclusion. It has never been a highly thought-of work, no doubt because it lacks any striking poetics, is condescending to its hero and has a mediocre narrative. If it is meant to be a light-hearted piece, it never quite strikes the right note, perhaps because Wordsworth cannot bring himself to see the subject matter in a purely comic light: the waggoner himself is a typical Wordsworthian rustic, full of simple good nature, deserving of empathy, yet the only reward he gets is the loss of livelihood and the distinction of being in a Wordsworth poem, not all grounds for humour.

Part of the failure could be due to the poem's psychological uncertainty. Wordsworth was a water drinker surrounded by addicts (De Quincey, Coleridge) – it was either one extreme or the other. The poem is never quite sure what attitude to adopt to someone who has not got Wordsworth's own power of denial yet is not an addict, and this may be partially due to the uncertain social status of people on the edge of habitual drinking. The blame for Benjamin's downfall therefore has no proper target, and the poem wavers between a number of objects potentially culpable for his demise: Benjamin's own weakness; a working out of the Fates; the revenge of nature; a heartless economic system; the poet's/muse's manipulation. In fact, viewed in this manner, it has many similarities with Hardy's *Mayor of Casterbridge* (discussed in Chapter 10). Although there is not the psychological complexity of *Casterbridge*'s Henchard, Wordsworth nevertheless does attempt to draw out the mind of a character struggling with a weakness. The poem has many interesting features that have perhaps been overlooked because of the satire it provoked at the time and the general uncertainty of its theme and tone.

The poem begins by setting the scene – the end of a scorching June day, and the picture is one of nature – birds, glow-worms, stars, clouds, mountains. A slight note of unease is introduced when the wind comes 'a haunting and a panting, / Like the stifling of disease'[56] but this is not developed and gives way to the introduction of Benjamin the Waggoner 'Who long hath trod this toilsome way, / Companion of the night and day',[57] his place within the eternal cycle of nature assured. His own intimacy with nature is described when we learn that he does not use the whip on the horses he commands, and they in turn are 'pleased to win / the praises of mild Benjamin'.[58] And so the backdrop of unchanging countryside, nature and man is evoked. The story's interest then materialises, when, in the space of a few lines, Wordsworth introduces a number of themes.

> Heaven shield him from mishap and snare!
> But why so early with this prayer?
> Is it for threatenings in the sky?
> Or for some other danger nigh?
> No; none is near him yet, though he
> Be one of much infirmity;
> For at the bottom of the brow,
> Where once the *Dove* and *Olive*-bough
> Offered a greeting of good ale
> To all who entered Grasmere Vale;
> And called on him who must depart
> To leave it with a jovial heart;
> There, where the *Dove* and *Olive*-bough
> Once hung, a Poet harbours now,
> A simple water-drinking Bard;
> Why need our Hero then (though frail
> His best resolves) be on his guard?[59]

The narrative promise of 'mishap and snare', and the introduction of heaven and prayer, suggest some kind of moral-religious framework. Then the verse appears to follow through its own question of where the danger to Benjamin could possibly lie. Is it from thunderous nature? 'No' is the immediate answer, but then the poem draws the reader into a world of ambiguity, for although disclaiming the sky or anything else as dangerous, this is only as 'yet'. In other words, these might or might not be the mishap and snare that lie in waiting. It then proceeds as if giving the proper explanation – 'For at the bottom of the brow' – and goes on to describe the drinking place that used to be there, the Dove and Olive. The 'for' is highly ambiguous, since following on from the two previous 'for's – 'for threatenings' and 'for some other danger', 'for at the bottom' would seem to implicate the Dove in Benjamin's worries.

'At the bottom of the brow' is where Wordsworth begins to weave himself into Benjamin's narrative. The Dove and Olive is where the waggoner used to drink, but the poet now 'harbours' there. Wordsworth places himself alongside Benjamin at the same time as he distances himself from him. The Dove is the poet's place, not the waggoner's. The distance is reinforced by the poet's claim to be a water-drinker, as opposed to an ale-drinker. And in calling himself 'a simple water-drinking Bard' Wordsworth calls to mind his poetic forefather Milton, whom he was to refer to as the 'temperate bard' in *The Prelude* (see above). In doing so Wordsworth sets up a series of implied oppositions: the house of poetry against the drinking place; the Puritan ethos against an older festival culture. But the poem plays a double game, both using and dissolving the oppositions. The Puritan aspect is enforced when the house looks 'cold' to Benjamin, and whilst Wordsworth claims that the folk within are 'honest', nevertheless Benjamin is left doubting 'Whether they be alive or dead!' Given that the main drive of the story is how Benjamin loses his job through alehouse drinking, this is another example in our history of how sobriety and endeavour are set out as those human attributes which will ultimately be rewarded. But Wordsworth's positive contrasting of the more alive waggoner with the 'cold' 'water-drinking' poet is evidence of a balancing act throughout the poem, of a wish to give due weight both to Benjamin's weakness and Benjamin's heroic qualities. Although the poet has ousted the drinkers from the house, what has replaced them is by no means unequivocally endorsed.

Benjamin walks proudly by, knowing that within a mile he will face the test of a real hostelry, The Swan at Grasmere, which the poem foresees to be tempting in its offer of friendly voices and brightness on a dark night. He passes by, proud of his strength, and now the poem moves into Benjamin's mind. With The Swan conquered, 'the evil One is left behind',[60] a formulation which suggests once more the vaguely wider religious world the poem operates within. This is especially good news since he 'trespassed lately worse than ever'.[61] The lines continue inside the good man's head: 'Yes, let my master fume and fret, / Here am I — with my horses yet.'[62] The poem thus sets up the master–servant relationship under which Benjamin is suffering, hinting that there is something that corrupts 'good' nature – that is, the bond Benjamin shares with both the horses and the landscape. The refusal to name the Master (he was one Mr Jackson, known to Wordsworth at least when he rented out Greta Hall in Keswick to Coleridge and later De Quincey[63]) helps to take the story into this more exemplary realm. If Benjamin were his own master, perhaps, there would be no problem. In the context of the poem as a whole, 'master' may also be read as more generally whoever 'controls' Benjamin's life, those unseen forces already mentioned, such as the Fates, nature, and the poet himself who manipulates his story. The 'master' might also be Benjamin's 'personality', since he casts out the 'master' here when he is with his horses – a sign that he is properly engaged, as opposed to being in the alehouse or tavern.

After Benjamin has congratulated himself on his self-control, the poem switches to third person once more and introduces the sequence of events which lead to his downfall: the weather takes a turn for the worse, in a manner which has something of pathetic fallacy about it – the storm has struggled inwardly to be free, 'busily employed as he', and once again there is a discordant note in nature – the air is as 'still as death',[64] in an echo of the stifling of the wind/disease earlier on. The whole scenery becomes like 'one dismal room',[65] an implicit contrast with the sociable rooms available in The Swan. Preternatural forces continue to be at work as the poem describes 'A burning of portentous red' above Helm-crag, where Benjamin espies the astrologer Sidrophel before the increasing darkness obscures all.

The next unfortunate event is that he gives shelter to a sailor, the sailor's wife and her child. The comment on the weather by the sailor again suggests that the Fates and/or nature are conspiring against Benjamin: 'Rough doings these! as God's my judge, / The sky owes somebody a grudge!'[66] The sailor follows Benjamin with his own ass. By now it is twelve o'clock, and as they pass under the gaze of Helvellyn they hear the noise of a fiddle coming from the Cherry Tree, which causes Benjamin to remember that this is 'Merry-night', that is, the night of the week when many come for the social occasion. 'His heart with sudden joy is filled, — / His ears are by the music thrilled',[67] he feels that he has earned this pleasure, and his fate is sealed when the sailor offers to treat him. In the footsteps of Burns's 'Tam O'Shanter', Wordsworth creates an attractive picture of the interior, a description that makes it understandable to the hardest-hearted reader why the waggoner, spurred on by the sailor, would enter: '"Blithe souls and lightsome hearts have we, / Feasting at the *Cherry Tree*!" / This was the outside proclamation, / This was the inside salutation; / What bustling—jostling—high and low! / A universal overflow! / What tankards foaming from the tap! / What store of cakes in every lap! / What thumping—stumping—overhead!'[68] The rosy picture continues for a few lines before Wordsworth puts it back into the psychological-moral framework, challenging the reader to condemn Benjamin, and more than this, challenging the reader to condemn what can only appear as the worthy qualities in the Cherry Tree. It is third person, but is perhaps working more as free indirect discourse: 'What greater good can heart desire? / 'Twere worth a wise man's while to try / The utmost anger of the sky: / To seek for thoughts of a gloomy cast, / If such the bright amends at last. / Now should you say I judge amiss, / *The Cherry Tree* shows proof of this; / For soon of all the happy there, / Our Travellers are the happiest pair; / All care with Benjamin is gone— / A Cæsar past the Rubicon!'[69] For all its bright and breezy imagery, its upbeat measures and easy rhythm, the poem is cleverly ensnaring the reader into the enjoyment of the Cherry Tree whilst showing how the wider concerns of Benjamin are cast to one side. The naturally happy-go-lucky sailor adds to the feeling that there is nothing wrong with irresponsibility. The 'maleness' of all this is signalled when passing reference is made to the wife and baby sleeping snugly in the waggon.

The poem then goes into surreal mode as the sailor wheels out (a model of) the ship he sailed on when he served Nelson. He tells his battle-stories to the enraptured crowd, and all of a sudden the poem has introduced the greatness of the nation amidst the revelry: '"A bowl, a bowl of double measure," / Cries Benjamin, "a draught of length, / To Nelson, England's pride and treasure, / Her bulwark and her tower of strength!"' There is perhaps at least a comic inflection in the idea of the ship in the middle of the Cherry Tree, and that in the middle of nowhere in the early hours of the morning, amongst carefree drinkers, England's greatness is being toasted. The sailor re-yokes the ship to the ass and continues on his way. The second canto ends after two hours' 'hearty stay'.

The reason for the introduction of the sailor's ship into the narrative is not clear, but the poem does then link both Benjamin and the sailor as two heroes, as if both in their way represent the pride of England. Again, perhaps, the poem is unsure of what it hopes to achieve, for it evokes empathy for the pair, yet within the confines of a story which ultimately describes personal weakness. Given the amount of literature we have already seen which shows the intimate relationship between 'drink' and 'nation' it could be argued that somewhere along the line Wordsworth is positing an idea that if such scenes as those at the Cherry Tree are to become frequent, England might be in trouble. But this is perhaps to read too much into it.

The scene switches to Benjamin's horses once more, who know that even if Benjamin is tipsy, he will still be a perfect guide. Benjamin compares his own waggon to the sailor's ship, and states that he 'steers' it through all kinds of weather just as the sailor has done with his charge, suggesting again that the two men are representative of England's best. Bathos is once more the order of the day, however, when the tar admits that Benjamin is no doubt right, but rather than the vagaries of the weather what he would most like to be saved from is the screeching of the owl.

In the last canto Wordsworth turns to the Muse, who refuses to chart the rest of their night. Instead she follows her own way. Wordsworth appears to sublimate the poetic persona into a creature that he has no control over, as if, as Benjamin's comeuppance comes ever nearer, he wants to disclaim any responsibility. To this end it is the Muse who now controls the story, and instead of continuing Benjamin's narrative directly, she flies over the land, giving a bird's-eye description of Skiddaw, Blencathara and the surroundings, intermingled with a local story. When she does return to Benjamin the note becomes sombre, and now it is nature that is censorious: 'As if the warbler lost in light / Reproved his soarings of the night'.[70] The horses are also aware of Benjamin's misdeeds and would like to protect him, so they work harder to get the waggon home in good time. But: 'who can hide, / When the malicious Fates are bent / On working out an ill intent?'[71] Again we see that Wordsworth has varied the poem's controlling agent, vacillating between nature, the Muse and the Fates. The Master has set forth from Keswick, guessing that something may be wrong. When he sees that his mastiff has been kicked by the ass, it is the final straw and Benjamin loses his job. Noticeably, this is not described in any detail but merely reprised, as if the poet fights shy of the climax.

But perhaps this is because Benjamin is not the only subject of the poem. Wordsworth turns to the poem's history and the process of its composition: 'A record which I dared to frame, / Though timid scruples checked me long'.[72] He moves on to describe his own relationship with the waggoner, his importance to their lives, and the images he has left on the poet's mind. One in particular has the appearance of a projection onto the landscape of the moral territory Wordsworth is skirting. He talks of the valley through which Benjamin went: 'While yet the valley is arrayed, / On this side with a sober shade; / On that is prodigally bright— / Crag, lawn, and wood — with rosy light. / —But most of all, thou lordly Wain!'[73] Benjamin has been both sober and prodigal, and the poem has itself negotiated a path through the two, showing the allure of bright lights (as the various hostelries were often characterised) against the gloom of nature and the cold of the poet's abode. Yet just as Wordsworth the poet has 'erased' the drinking place by turning the Dove and Olive-bough into his home, so Benjamin is finally overlaid with the poet's sober and sobering narrative. The poet remains uncertain to the end: 'Then most of all, then far the most, / Do I regret what we have lost; / Am grieved for that unhappy sin / Which robbed us of good Benjamin;— / And of his stately Charge, which none / Could keep alive when He was gone!'[74] The reader to this point, although aware that there might be something 'wrong' with Benjamin's actions, would hardly conclude that he had committed a 'sin'. The construction makes the sin the agent operating upon Benjamin, so that, in keeping with the poem as a whole, Benjamin is absolved from blame. The poem's ambiguities remain, and we are left wondering precisely the nature of the 'sin' and its cause. The confused nature of the narrative can perhaps be put down to its subject matter – a good man brought down by social drinking. Because the Romantics (apart from Burns) had little regard for the drinking place as a subject worthy of literature, this rare attempt to incorporate it indicates the problems it was likely to cause.

Crabbe

We have seen that the belief that serious literature demanded lofty subject matter has often meant that representations of low life have been either eschewed or used for other reasons, such as for comic effect or moral tub-thumping. 'Low life' does not necessarily mean all of the lower orders. It is usually synonymous with the morally disreputable. Shepherds and rustics are theoretically of the lower orders in the social hierarchy, but in literary terms their status is ameliorated through the use of 'pastoral'. Coleridge's analysis of Wordsworth's Preface to the *Lyrical Ballads* in *Biographia Literaria* is in this vein, within the wider context of what is proper for the language of poetry (literature). He notes that Wordsworth intends to use 'the ordinary language of men in real life' but that actually Wordsworth does not do this. Wordsworth uses the language of rustics and clowns ('Michael', 'The Idiot Boy'). In other words, it is not 'realistic', as (Coleridge argues) Wordsworth pretends. In fact, Coleridge criticises Wordsworth's failure in 'The Idiot Boy' to remove those instances of 'the real' which are distasteful, that is, not poetic (or 'Literature'). To emphasise his point Coleridge argues that actual low life, as it might appear in Manchester or Liverpool, would not be a worthy topic for literature. By taking Coleridge's criticisms of Wordsworth I think we can see why there are so few attempts to represent the drinking place – 'low life' remains outside the remit of proper literature (for Coleridge) and is not achievable when attempted (by Wordsworth).

This helps put Crabbe's work into context. One of his earliest productions, and his first poem to be published separately, was 'Inebriety' (1775). As the editors to *The Complete Poetical Works* note, there were precedents for such a topic in John Gay's 'Wine' and the drinking scene in James Thomson's *Seasons*. It uses heroic couplets to give a lively rendering of the nation state of drunkenness: 'See Inebriety! her wand she waves, / And lo! her pale, and lo! her purple slaves; / Sots in embroidery, and sots in crape, / Of every order, station, rank, and shape'.[75] The subject matter in parts one and two is typical, with much time spent on drink as the social leveller: 'the proud, the mean, the selfish, and the great, / Swell the dull throng, and stagger into state';[76] drunkenness the usurper of reason: 'Without a pilot, who attempts to steer, / Has small discretion or has little care / That pilot Reason, in the erring Soul, / Is lost, is blinded in the steaming Bowl';[77] and an excursion into the usual social distinctions between different beverages: 'Lo! the poor Toper whose untutor'd sense, / Sees bliss in ale, and can with wine dispense; / Whose head proud fancy never taught to steer, / Beyond the muddy extacies of Beer.'[78] It is possible to speculate that although throughout the course of our history drunkenness has often been cast as common to all classes, those who write still feel the necessity to reintroduce the class distinctions in some other way for fear of lumping themselves and their own caste with those of the lower orders. Crabbe's manoeuvre is to enlist the trope of 'muddy ... Beer', that is, a lower-class drink that is both literally unclear and metaphorically signifies a cloudy (lesser) intellect, as opposed to the more refined wine of educated taste. Another way of both noting the levelling ability of alcohol whilst maintaining class distinction is to say that 'drunken Coblers are as proud as Kings', rather than vice versa.

The novelty of Crabbe's piece of accomplished juvenilia is the third section. Here he suggests that in order to curb inebriety, women themselves should take up drinking and drunkenness. Men would then see how they themselves looked in their vice and folly: 'For this Muse, now calls the Fair to rise, / To shew our failings, and to make us wise'.[79] When Crabbe later became a reverend, he tried to suppress the poem. The editors argue that this was not so much the problem of the subject matter of 'drunkenness' but this final section which had been aimed at women, for it would have been regarded as coarse. Yet it may also have been the subject matter that Crabbe was nervous about, for in his most famous poem, *The Borough*, discussed in greater detail below, he would show a marked sensitivity to public opinion on the subject of drinking houses.

The Village (1783), again in heroic couplets, established Crabbe's career as a poet, showing the miseries of rural life. In this poem, an idyllic Sabbath is cut short by the intoxicated labourers.[80] In the Preface to *Poems, 1807* he describes the most substantial work in the collection, *The Parish Register*, as 'an endeavour once more to describe Village-Manners, not by adopting the notion of pastoral simplicity or assuming ideas of rustic barbarity, but by more natural views of the peasantry, considered as a mixed body of persons sober or profligate, and from hence, in a great measure, contented or miserable'.[81] It can be seen that although he is attempting a more socially balanced view of village life, people cannot but help fall into one of two categories, sots or temperate types. Its moral framework is religious-economic, arguing for 'frugality' and 'industry' amidst poverty. We can see the argument is shifting from that of, say, Fielding in the eighteenth century, where the peasantry and lower classes were expected to accept their place in the paternalist social hierarchy. The reliance on responsible landowners has disappeared and villagers are now expected to look out for themselves, living carefully to make the most of what they have. This is the kind of environment that will be proffered in various guises throughout the nineteenth century as the move from country to town and city accelerates.

Crabbe's main work, and for which he is now most remembered, is *The Borough*, published in 1810. A series of twenty-four 'Letters' describes the inhabitants, life and culture of a borough. It comes with a long preface in which Crabbe defends his poem, as if to forestall criticism. The reception of the Preface and poem gives a good indication of the literary environment within which all writers of this period, with pretensions to quality literature, were operating. He was praised for his satire, pathos, descriptive powers, delineation of characters, narratives and pithy style, but mixed in with this there was a considerable body of criticism aimed at his choice of subject matter. Crabbe had always offered up 'annals of the village poor'[82] but with *The Borough* it was felt that there was no engendering of sympathy in the reader at their condition, only disgust. Another criticism was that Crabbe's work, in its 'realistic pictures of "low life"' and 'dry representations of the world as it is' was not poetry because it lacked imagination.[83] Put together, these two criticisms are of the type we have seen in the past when the lower classes have been the subject of the realistic pole of literature. To incorporate them into serious literature and treat them seriously is a breach of literary taste.

Crabbe's extensive Preface, with its apologetic tone, was no doubt written in full knowledge that this was the literary criterion of the time. For example, he notes in his second Letter that 'Nothing, I trust … will seem to any invidious or offensive.'[84] But of all the defences, the oddest is surely that of Letter XI, 'Inns': 'If the Letter which treats of Inns should be found to contain nothing interesting or uncommon; if it describe things which we behold every day, and some which we do not wish to behold at any time; let it be considered that this Letter is one of the shortest, and that from a poem whose subject was a Borough, populous and wealthy, these places of public accommodation could not, without some impropriety, be excluded.'[85] The defence appears to be twofold: that in the interest of fidelity to the poem's remit, realistically to describe a borough, it is necessary to incorporate 'inns'. However, if that will not wash, the reader should not worry because it is the shortest. The ubiquity and necessity of 'inns', and perhaps we might extend this to taverns, alehouses and public houses, makes them uninteresting; the stereotypical perception of them as harbouring unpalatable sights and elements makes them undesirable subject matter for literature. In this Preface is our explanation of why representations are so relatively sparse in literature of the period. Couple this with an antagonism to what appears as unmediated realistic recording of 'life as it is', and the explanation is complete.

However, the pictures of drinking houses throughout the Borough are hardly disreputable or disgusting. He occasionally gives quite a pleasing picture. In Letter I where Crabbe's 'neutral' narrator gives a 'general description' of the affluent port, the poor dredger finds entertainment in rooms 'Where, in on the Table Pipes and Papers lie, / The steaming Bowl or foaming Tankard by' and is not begrudged these comforts.[86] However, Letter XI itself begins by arguing that the inn is a difficult subject for poetry, to which end he invokes the muse to help him. It is perhaps a sign of just how awkward a subject the drinking place continued to be for literature (poetry was still regarded as the highest form). As a header to the Letter he has a poem which is presented as his own. However, some of the sentiments appear to originate (unacknowledged) in Johnson, as recorded by Boswell in his *Life of Johnson*. Crabbe, in the voice of the landlord, declares: 'And the louder you call, and the longer you stay, / The more I am happy to serve and obey', compared to Johnson's 'You are sure you are welcome: and the more noise you make, the more trouble you give, the more good things you call for, the welcomer you are.'[87] It is a strange kind of authorisation for the Letter, as if he wants Johnson to vouchsafe his project, yet remains too squeamish to drag him into the disreputable world of 'inns' by quoting Johnson directly.

Crabbe chooses to deal with the places hierarchically, from the most socially respectable downwards, as if the concerns of the Preface about propriety of subject matter are transferred to the inns themselves. After invoking the muse to help him with this poor subject, he uses the inn signs as a way in to picture the places they advertise, playing with their symbolic accuracy. He begins with The Lion, where all the top people resort, with its kingly, awe-inspiring visage, but in which sign its customers see only a 'Pledge of Welcome and Delight': 'to him the noblest Guest the Town detains / Flies for Repast, and in his Court remains'.[88] From there he wanders to the Bear and Crown, which is also worthy, and then to The Caroline, which has seen better days. It is a good description of a once grand inn in decline: 'At length a ruin'd Stable holds your Steed, / While you through large and dirty Rooms proceed, / Spacious and cold; a proof they once had been / In honour, — now magnificently mean'.[89] After the 'Third in our Borough's list' are more inferior houses – places for those who cannot afford the more salubrious hostelries but are too proud to go to the 'low': the Full orb ('The Sun'), 'half the lunar Face' ('Half-Moon'), the Black Boy, Angel, Fountain, Vine, White/Black Horse, Silver Swan and Swan: 'All these a decent Entertainment give, / And by their Comforts comfortably live.'[90] He gives a more detailed description of one of these, 'The Boar', before moving on: 'Next are a lower kind, yet not so low / But they, among them, their Distinctions know'. These are the Chequer, Pye, Duke William, Dog, after which the Sailors have their own: Three Jolly Sailors, Anchor.

Thus far the descriptive movement has been relatively straightforward – from the social pinnacle of The Lion, down the hierarchy, ending up with those places of a lower kind, themselves with social gradations. The move to those places frequented by sailors is odd, since it is a category change (occupation rather than social class) although there is a suggestion that a social hierarchy is maintained within the particular establishments. What is most curious about Letter XI is the way it ends, with an inn called the Green Man. One of the curiosities is that it is not a description but a story of its landlord, James.

'*James* in an evil Hour went forth to woo / Young *Juliet Hart*' and for a brief period the couple act out the romance in their own unchaste manner: 'So in few Months the generous Lass was seen / I' the way that the *Capulets* had been.'[91] Having got his lover pregnant he runs away, but 'haunted both by Love and Law' he returns. The scene changes to the home of the abandoned woman and her father. 'With foulest Names his Daughter he revil'd, / And look'd a very *Herod* at the Child'.[92] She gives as good as she gets, reminding him of 'when his *Joe* was born'. James enters. It proceeds as a standard confrontation with the girl's mother cursing James, until the mother strays into an area too close to home: '"But 'tis most base, 'tis Perjury and Theft, / When a lost Girl is like a Widow left; / The Rogue who ruins" — here the Father found / His Spouse was treading on forbidden Ground.'[93] The vignette's narrative continues its intriguing twist when the father now steps in to provide an obscure argument for James to consider: in his own youth he was forced to choose between two lasses. Because of law's strictures he could only marry one, although he contrived to live with both, and then married the other when the first died. Compared to this complicated affair of the heart, the choice before James is easy, he says. Here the lass steps in to plead her own cause and restore sense to the situation. She has not merited his desertion through any untoward behaviour or entrapment on her part. Her only thought is of their boy. Won round, James promises to wed.

It is structurally interesting because after ordering the poem via the social hierarchy of inns it ends with a specific tale of how the landlord came to manage a particular inn. The digressive nature could be said to be of a piece with *The Borough* as a whole, with no attempt to make connections at a strictly formal level. Of course, all the material comes under the heading of 'inns', but the tale of James is not the same as the descriptions. However, the swerve to tale-telling coincides with other features related to the interconnection of literature and inns.

As already stated, the Preface to *The Borough* defends Crabbe's decision to include 'Inns', despite the fact that they have neither novelty nor propriety. The opening, unsigned verses, partly derived from Johnson, praise inns, but the poem proper begins by reiterating its apprehension that 'inns' are not suitable subject matter: '*Inns* are this Subject – 'tis an ill-drawn Lot'. But the muses have deigned to ennoble such humble subjects as '*Belinda*'s Lock' so 'Come, lend thy cheerful Light, and give to please, / These Seats of Revelry, these Scenes of Ease; / Who sings of Inns much danger has to dread, / And needs Assistance from the Fountain-head.'[94] There seems to be a genuine fondness for inns amidst the fear of literary transgression. The tale at the end could be an attempt at a structural level to redeem the transgression by focusing not on the inns themselves but on the people involved. Just as James repairs a potentially disreputable life, the poem is repaired by the structural transformation. The social propriety of inns is translated into the propriety of social behaviour, since Juliet's parents' stories all close with socially sanctioned behaviour after misbehaviour. Rather than leave the Letter's subject matter as the disreputable inn, therefore, it ends with a tale of social rectitude after possible transgressions.

Crabbe uses the phrase 'Love and Law' with respect to James's decision to return. This is perhaps what governs the whole Letter. Despite Crabbe's claim in the Preface that he is somewhat forced to include these places because he must describe the Borough in its entirety, the lines (above) show some enjoyment of the hostelries, and the descriptions are in the main favourable – there is nothing that might be construed as 'low life', in the sense of disreputable. This is Crabbe's affection. The 'law' can be seen as the constraints placed upon the poem by literary precedent – the invocation of the muse, the recognition of proper subject matter and, in the Preface, the context of literary criticism and theory. In the Preface he redeems the subject matter through appeals to the poem's remit and, weakly, its short length. In the poem itself he redeems it by literary strategies. The page of versified Johnson softens the reader to being predisposed towards inns. The use of muses elevates the topic, and his reference to Pope's *Rape of the Lock* is some kind of precedent for treating lowly subject matter in (mock)-epic manner. Further, the opening lines refer to the writing of this letter as his 'present Task', and towards the end Juliet tells James that his 'Task' with respect to his actions is easier than her own. Given the continued influence of Cowper's poem over this generation of poets, this represents a further appeal to literary precedent to support the structure of the Letter (and perhaps the poem as a whole) – its 'digressiveness', a conversational rambling rather than a tight adherence to an 'argument' or 'theme'.

The final element in the making good of potentially unworthy material is in the role of the narrative voice. With the invocation of the muses at the start the poem is on solid literary ground, and the voice is, if down-to-earth, still within the received poetic realm. It is essentially a poetic voice, and this is maintained as far as the tale of James and the Green Man. But in the tale not only does the material shift from the general to the specific, the narrative voice changes from the impersonal poetic to that of personal remembrance. The movement from poetic law to personal interest is how he opens his account at the last hostelry: 'But the *Green-Man* shall I pass by unsung, / Which mine own *James* upon his Sign-post hung?' The Green Man is not just the figure beloved of myth, it is also the sign of James, for he once wore the green livery of his squire – the poet. Thus there is some personal involvement on the poet's part with the Green Man's landlord. The tale comes full circle when after we have been told of the intention to marry, the poem ends: '*James* at my Door then made his parting Bow, / Took the *Green-Man*, and is a Master now.'

What does this movement signify? It is further validation of 'inns' within the context of an antagonistic tradition. It does this through the poet's own stamp of approval, and by the simple method of creating some kind of empathy for the people involved. There is also a suggestion of social mobility rather than static hierarchy, of the possibility of respectability held out to those (inns, people, poets) who risk falling outside the acceptable social sphere. Crabbe's Letter on 'Inns' shows us perhaps the possibilities of representations of inns and taverns within the confines of literary respectability, although even here such subject matter can be seen as fraught with the possibility of indecency. It is in the next chapter that we find a champion of the drinking place, drinkers and drinking.

Notes

1   Oliver Goldsmith, 'A Reverie at the *Boar's-head-tavern* in *Eastcheap*' (1760), in *Collected Works of Oliver Goldsmith*, ed. Arthur Friedman, 5 vols (Oxford,

Clarendon Press, 1966), pp. 97–112, p. 98.
2. Leigh Hunt, 'Pleasant Memories Connected with Various Parts of the Metropolis', in *Essays of Leigh Hunt*, Arthur Symons, ed. (London, Walter Scott, 1887).
3. Washington Irving, 'The Boar's Head Tavern, Eastcheap', in *The Sketch-Book of Geoffrey Crayon, Gent.* (1820) (London, Cassell, n.d.), p. 115.
4. Frederick W. Hackwood, *Inns, Ales, and Drinking Customs of Old England* (London, T. Fisher Unwin, 1910), p. 272.
5. Irving, 'Boar's Head', p. 116.
6. Goldsmith, 'Reverie', p. 111.
7. Oliver Goldsmith, *The Vicar of Wakefield*, in *Works*, vol. IV, pp. 94–5.
8. Hackwood, *Inns*, p. 239.
9. Henry Fielding, *Tom Jones* (London, Penguin, 1985 [1749]), p. 348.
10. Goldsmith in fact published an essay which in part railed against alehouses in his ill-fated journal *The Bee*: No. 5, 'Upon Political Frugality', 3 November 1759. It was mainly adapted from a French encyclopaedia entry (according to the editor of *Works*) so how much of it represents Goldsmith's own attitudes is difficult to tell.
11. Oliver Goldsmith, *The Deserted Village*, in *Works*, vol. IV, ll. 241–6.
12. *Ibid.*, ll. 57–62.
13. See Martin Priestman, *Cowper's Task: Structure and Influence* (Cambridge, Cambridge University Press, 1983). The first chapter notes how the poem 'may be offered as an example of a view of country life that is refreshingly "anti-pastoral" and realistic' (p. 2) and the influence of the 'idyllic' mode (pp. 6ff.). See also Vincent Newey's *Cowper's Poetry: A Critical Study and Reassessment* (Liverpool, Liverpool University Press, 1982), particularly for the chapter on 'Nature'.
14. Priestman, *Cowper's*, p. 2.
15. William Cowper, *The Task and Other Poems*, ed. James Sambrook (London, Longman, 1994), 4.36–41.
16. *Ibid.*, ll. 211–13.
17. *Ibid.*, ll. 208–10.
18. *Ibid.*, ll. 476–8.
19. *Ibid.*, ll. 492–5.
20. Priestman, *Cowper's*, p. 120.
21. Cowper, *Task*, ll. 502–5.
22. *Ibid.*, ll. 513–15.
23. *Ibid.*, ll. 505–9.
24. Peter Clark, *The English Alehouse: A Social History 1200-1830* (Harlow, Longman, 1983), p. 185; Christopher Hill, *Reformation to Industrial Revolution: British Economy and Society 1530/1780* (London, Weidenfeld and Nicholson, 1968), p. 180.
25. Andrew Barr, *Drink. An Informal Social History* (Bantam, London, 1995), p. 193.
26. John Keats, letter 5 January 1818, in *Letters of John Keats to his Family and Friends*, ed. Sidney Colvin (London, Macmillan, 1925).
27. Benjamin Robert Haydon, *The Autobiography and Memoirs of Benjamin Robert Haydon (1786–1846)*, edited from his Journals by Tom Taylor, (London, Peter Davies, 1926), p. 269.

28 Francis Place, *Improvement of the Working People: Drunkenness – Education* (London, 1834), p. 21.
29 Sir Gilbert Elliot to his wife, quoted in André L. Simon, *Bottlescrew Days. Wine Drinking in England During the Eighteenth Century* (London, Duckworth, 1926), pp. 45–6.
30 *Ibid.*, p. 49.
31 *Ibid.*, p. 46.
32 R. V. French, *Nineteen Centuries of Drink in England: A History*, 2nd edition – enlarged and revised, (London, National Temperance Publication Depot, n.d. [1st edition 1884]), quoting from *Reminiscences of Captain Gronow*: 'A three-bottle man was not an unusual guest at a fashionable table; and the night was invariably spent in drinking bad port wine to an enormous extent,' pp. 323–4. Thomas Trotter in *An Essay Medical, Philosophical, and Chemical on Drunkenness and its Effects on the Human Body* (1804), ed. Roy Porter (London, Routledge, 1988), notes how a famous general is renowned for being a 'three-bottle man', p. 160 – probably Wellington.
33 George Rudé, *Hanoverian London 1714–1808* (London, Secker & Warburg, 1971), p. 70.
34 Quoted in M. Dorothy George, *London Life in the Eighteenth Century* (Harmondsworth, Penguin (Peregrine), 1966 [1925]), p. 50.
35 Quoted in French, *Drink*, p. 303. French wishes it were a slip of the tongue!
36 William Wordsworth, *The Prelude*, in *Romanticism An Anthology*, ed. Duncan Wu (Oxford, Blackwell, 1994), III.294–328.
37 Charles Lamb, 'The Old Familiar Faces', in letter to Marmaduke Thompson, January 1798, in *The Letters of Charles and Mary Anne Lamb*, ed. Edwin Marrs, Jr., 3 vols (Ithaca, Cornell University Press, 1975), I, ll. 8–10.
38 Anya Taylor, *Bacchus in Romantic England: Writers and Drink, 1780–1830* (Houndmills, Basingstoke, Macmillan, 1999), pp. 94–5.
39 Keats, *Letters*, 5 January 1818.
40 Taylor, *Bacchus*, p. 96.
41 See below for a discussion of his theory of art; for a complete discussion of Coleridge and drink see ch. 4 of Taylor, *Bacchus*, 'Coleridge and Alcohol: Songs and Centrifuges'.
42 Haydon, *Autobiography*, p. 269.
43 *Ibid.*, p. 270.
44 *Ibid.*, p. 271.
45 Thomas de Quincey, *Confessions of an English Opium-Eater* (Oxford, Oxford University Press, 1998 [1821]).
46 *Ibid.*, p. 32.
47 *Ibid.*, principally pp. 38–42.
48 *Ibid.*, p. 48.
49 Denzil Batchelor, *The English Inn* (London, Batsford, 1964), p. 18.
50 Information given by Marrs, ed., *Letters*, note to 'May', p. 5.
51 Lamb in Marrs, ed., *Letters*, 16 January 1797, and 13 February 1797.
52 *Ibid.*, 29 June 1797.
53 Robert Burns, *Poems and Songs* (Edinburgh, Gordon Wright Publishing, 1978).
54 I cannot, unfortunately, discuss 'Tam O'Shanter' because of its Scottish pedigree.
55 Note in Dorothy Wordsworth's *Grasmere Journal*, in *Journals of Dorothy*

Wordsworth, vol. 1, ed. E. de Selincourt (London, Macmillan, 1941).
56 William Wordsworth, *The Waggoner*, from *The Poetical Works* (1849–50), (Chadwyck-Healey Full-Text Poetry Database, 1996–99 [1805]), I.18–19.
57 *Ibid.*, I.23–4.
58 *Ibid.*, I.39–45.
59 *Ibid.*, I.46–62.
60 *Ibid.*, I.115.
61 *Ibid.*, I.112.
62 *Ibid.*, I.116–17.
63 Note to a letter from Mr Jackson in D. Wordsworth, *Journals*, p. 45.
64 Wordsworth, *Waggoner*, I.146ff.
65 *Ibid.*, I.164.
66 *Ibid.*, I.249–50.
67 *Ibid.*, II.33–4.
68 *Ibid.*, II.52–60.
69 *Ibid.*, II.71–80.
70 *Ibid.*, IV.79–80.
71 *Ibid.*, IV.116–18.
72 *Ibid.*, IV.200–1.
73 *Ibid.*, IV.240–4.
74 *Ibid.*, IV.264–9.
75 George Crabbe, *The Complete Poetical Works*, Norma Dalrymple-Champneys and Arthur Pollard, 3 vols, (Oxford, Clarendon Press, 1988), vol.1, I.108–11.
76 *Ibid.*, I.116–17.
77 *Ibid.*, II.13–16.
78 *Ibid.*, I.132–5.
79 *Ibid.*, III.194–5.
80 *Ibid.*, *The Village*, II. 63–70.
81 *Ibid.*, p. 207.
82 Crabbe's characterisation of *The Parish Register*.
83 Commentary in *Works*, p. 714.
84 *Ibid.*, p. 346.
85 *Ibid.*, pp. 350–1.
86 Crabbe, *The Borough*, in *Works*, Letter I.61–8.
87 *Ibid.*, ll. 7–8 of the introductory verse to Letter XI, 'Inns'. The Johnson entry is Thursday, 21 March 1776, *The Life of Johnson*, 3rd edition, R. W. Chapman, corrected by J. D. Fleeman (London, Oxford University Press), 1970, p. 697.
88 The Lion is treated at Crabbe, *Works*, XI.27–52.
89 *Ibid.*, XI.89–92.
90 *Ibid.*, XI.163–4.
91 *Ibid.*, XI.235–6, 245–6.
92 *Ibid.*, XI.261–2.
93 *Ibid.*, XI.275–8.
94 *Ibid.*, XI.15–18.

9

Dickens

The Angel, The Bell, the Belle Savage, the Black Boy, the Black Lion, the Blue Boar, the Blue Dragon, the Blue Lion, The Boot, The Bull Inn, The Bush Tavern, The Crown, the Devil's Punch Bowl, the Five Sisters, The George, the George and New Inn, the George and Vulture, The Golden Inn, the Great White Horse, the Half Moon and Seven Stars, the Half-way House, the Hop Pole, the King's Head, the Jolly Sandboys, the Jolly Tapley, the Leather Bottle, the Magpie and Stump, the Marquis of Granby, The Maypole, the Old Royal Hotel, The Peacock, the Princess's Arms, the Railway Arms, the Saracen's Head, the Six Jolly Fellowship Porters, The Spaniards, the Three Cripples, the Three Jolly Bargemen, the Three Magpies, the Towns Arms Inn, the Valiant Soldier, the White Hart Inn, the White Hart Hotel, the Whitehorse Cellar, The Wilderness …

No writer has given us such a variety of hostelries and in such a variety of circumstances as Dickens. He offers the grandest and the meanest, the newest and the most antique, richly furnished and barely furnished, the labyrinthine and the functional, isolated country inns and low-life urban resorts. Sometimes they are incidental to the plot, merely stopping-off points on a staggered journey, at other times they say something about a character, about contemporary social mores or about social change. Sometimes they are places of the imagination made real, with roaring fires, good ale, comfortable landladies and pleasant companions. At other times the customers are sadly disappointed, are happy to make their excuses and leave. On occasion the narratives take their very structure from drinking places, from a diversionary tale within a tale – The Bagman's Story in *Pickwick Papers* for example – to the architecture of a whole novel, *Barnaby Rudge*.

The ghost of England past

> In the Borough, especially, there still remain some half dozen old inns, which have preserved their external features unchanged, and which have escaped alike the rage for public improvement, and the encroachments

of private speculation. Great, rambling, queer, old places they are, with galleries, and passages, and staircases, wide enough and antiquated enough to furnish materials for a hundred ghost stories, supposing we should ever be reduced to the lamentable necessity of inventing any…
Pickwick Papers[1]

If the Romantic period offered us meagre fare, the work of Dickens alone in the following decades more than makes up for it. No doubt this was helped by the emergence of the novel as the dominant literary form, where low life had more often than not felt at home (from Defoe onwards), and this coupled with social realism as the dominant mode meant that it was only natural to witness the importance the drinking place played in national life at all levels, although drinking places, particular drinks and drunkenness, have no set symbolic meaning for Dickens. They are pliant materials that serve different functions according to the dictates of different novels. However, in observing these elements, Dickens incorporates different period sensibilities: eighteenth-century 'conviviality', the 'intoxication' of the Romantic period and the more socially responsible outlook of his own era, although evidently it is with mixed feelings. In the epigram above there is a sense that something quaint has been lost in the modern environment, fuelled as it is by entrepreneurial activity and civic improvement. The inns being talked of in this instance are specifically once great coaching inns 'when coaches performed their journeys in a graver and more solemn manner than they do in these times',[2] but apart from the lack of gravitas the book does not show that coaching inns had disappeared (for example, the Whitehorse Cellar is prominent). That would come a decade or two later, with the arrival of the train, although in recording the upheaval caused by railroad-building in *Dombey and Son*, the neighbourhood itself is unclear what the future holds: 'A bran-new Tavern, redolent of fresh mortar and size, and fronting nothing at all, had taken for its sign the Railway Arms.'[3]

Dickens clearly relished describing hostelries. In numerous instances he will begin with the sign, extravagantly exploding its possibilities, sometimes just for the fun of it, sometimes to lead the reader to an understanding of a particular character, occasionally to comment upon art and sometimes to unravel a culture. The sign of the Blue Lion at Muggleton in his first novel, *Pickwick Papers* (1836–37), whose large catalogue of hostelries is a virtual blueprint for their appearance in the rest of his novels, is described thus: 'There was an open square for the market-place; and in the centre of it, a large inn with a sign-post in front, displaying an object very common in art, but rarely met with in nature – to wit, a blue lion, with three bow legs in the air, balancing himself on the extreme point of the centre claw of his fourth foot.'[4] He was not the first to remark upon these incongruities. John Taylor 'the Water Poet' had two hundred years earlier produced a whole series of epigrams on inn signs, playing on the relationship between representation, function and the object referred to. For instance: (Dragon) 'These Dragons onely bite and sting all such / As doe immod'rately haunt them too much: / But those that use them well, from them shall finde / Joy to the Heart, and comfort to the Minde.' Addison in *The Spectator*, 2 April 1710, complains: 'There is nothing like sound literature and good sense to be met with in those objects that are everywhere thrusting themselves out to the eye and endeavouring to become visible. Our streets are filled with *blue boars*, *black swans*, and *red lions*.'[5] But Dickens has no real complaint. The preposterous nature of the sign is perfect for the novel, a Fieldingesque romp with older characters, and of a piece with Pickwick's knight-errantry in the 'modern' world.

Dickens may have been taken with the absurdity of blue animals. The sign of The Blue Dragon (near Salisbury) in *Martin Chuzzlewit* (1843–44) gets extensive treatment. It hangs 'rearing, in a state of monstrous imbecility, on his hind legs', reminiscent of the blue lion perhaps, but the description is used to introduce notions of civility and greed, for the weather-beaten sign is polite and welcoming, completely unlike those dragons from the past that feasted upon a maiden a day. The novel follows the responses of a group of people who might benefit from the elderly Martin Chuzzlewit's fortune – particularly the grasping and pompous Pecksniff. Dickens uses the sign to initiate the thematic interest, expanding upon the symbolic nature of an everyday, yet fantastic object as a means to universalise this specific story of selfish human nature. But if ultimately the description of the sign goes nowhere in particular, ending on a simple note that the sign had probably never witnessed anything akin to the events described by the novel, it resonates with some of the material that has come before. When John Westlock tells Tom Pinch how Pecksniff has 'scraped and clawed into his pouch' all of Tom's grandmother's savings,[6] we have something of the character of the dragon suggested. And before that, in a chapter entitled 'An Evening Wind', when the novel accumulates its narrative interest, the narrator describes how the alehouse sign is buffeted by a wind that affects everything in the village, so that 'the Blue Dragon was more rampant than usual ever afterwards, and indeed, before Christmas, reared clean out of his crazy frame'.[7] The sign is a sign of things changing irrevocably, and the dragon is aligned with Chuzzlewit ironically as a 'courteous animal'.

In *Barnaby Rudge* Joe Willet stops off at the Black Lion as he escapes from his tyrannical father. The Lion receives him cordially, and here the joke is that the sign, the hostelry, and the landlord blend into one another: 'This Lion or landlord, – for he was called both man and beast, by reason of his having instructed the artist who painted his sign, to convey into the features of the lordly brute whose effigy it bore.'[8] It describes the landlord as a naturally quick-witted man made slow by swigging too many 'copious draughts' and then eases itself back into the sign by making it likewise drowsy, thereby completely intermeshing the two. Yet, for the most part, Dickens is playing games with the humble sign. For all its plausible familiarity, 'The Blue Dragon' would be an extremely rare sign (if it existed at all – hence, perhaps, a double bluff is involved in bemoaning its fantastic nature[9]). He would no doubt have been aware that the history of England can be read through inn signboards, that a Blue Boar and a Red Lion were heraldic signs, so his refusal to acknowledge these meanings, or to invent signs with no heraldic meaning, intentionally takes the pictures at face value for his own ends.[10] The one crucial instance when he allows historic significance for a sign is when he places 'The Maypole', with its pre-puritan festive associations, at the heart of the historical novel *Barnaby Rudge*.

Once inside a Dickensian drinking-place, when the architecture and ambience are given full treatment, the descriptions often move simultaneously in different artistic directions: the aesthetic, the realistic, the fantastic, the historic and the social. For the perfect inn the following self-conscious example must suffice: 'The candles were brought, the fire was stirred up, and a fresh log of wood thrown on. In ten minutes' time, a waiter was laying the cloth for dinner, the curtains were drawn, the fire was blazing brightly, and everything looked (as everything always does, in all decent English inns) as if the travellers had been expected, and their comforts prepared, for days beforehand.'[11] The basic ingredients for the perfect English inn never vary: a good fire, good food and good accommodation.

What makes for a good drinking place by way of architecture is less clearcut. The older places are usually 'sprawling', with no rhyme or reason to their layout. Again, this is both a sign of the past in its acceptable, 'quaint' form, and the past as a stultifying, 'unreasonable' presence. A drunken architect may have been responsible for the following unnamed place:

> It had more corners in it than the brain of an obstinate man; was full of mad closets, into which nothing could be put that was not specially invented and made for that purpose; had mysterious shelvings and bulkheads, and indications of staircases in the ceiling; and was elaborately provided with a bell that rung in the room itself, about two feet from the handle, and had no connexion whatever with any other part of the establishment.[12]

There is a certain irony in that this is the first establishment Martin Chuzzlewit the younger and his aide Mark Tapley enter on their return from America, a minor example perhaps of the best and worst of England. There is also an irony in highlighting the role of the architect in creating this shambolic edifice, since Pecksniff is himself something of a sham architect, having stolen his idea from Martin Chuzzlewit junior for a building Chuzzlewit and Tapley soon discover is now being erected nearby. In *Pickwick Papers* the Great White Horse is described as having a labyrinthine layout and poor accommodation. It is an old inn, therefore, that is not living up to the standards set by the English imagination. Of course, it is a moot point how much these inns and alehouses are fictional creations. Dickens was very familiar with the hostelries of the day, both within London and without, and many of those referred to are actual places. It is an exercise perhaps for another book to tick off his fictional hostelries against what is known of their 'sources',[13] but it is noticeable that the contrast between ideal and reality is a feature of *Pickwick Papers* and that this works well with respect to hostelries.

The earlier novels perhaps have a higher density of drinking places, and *Pickwick Papers* has by far the most. Mr Pickwick is a latter-day adventurer, and the novel has something of the picaresque about it, incorporating as it does five excursions, one of them taking in a sizeable chunk of England. Inns, taverns and alehouses form its fabric, and so the novel's eighteenth-century feel is reinforced, but with a nineteenth-century respectability excising anything verging on the bawdy. An example of how immersed in the culture of drinking places the novel is, and how ideal and reality are (casually or otherwise) matched, can be seen in the instance of The Bagman's Story.

Pickwick Papers has sometimes been criticised for its digressions into unrelated tales, and it is true to say that it does appear to lack a singular artistic purpose, an interpretation supported by the knowledge that this was Dickens's first novel and came out in serial form. It is not my intention to argue one way or another, that is, whether we can uncover a 'deeper' artistic intention and structure or whether it was simply the case that stories dependent upon drinkers, drinking and drinking places were inevitable given Dickens's early life and lifestyle. The Bagman's Story is one such unmotivated digression.[14] It tells of Tom Smart who, riding across Marlborough Downs on his way to Bristol, stops off at an inn. The narrative trope is typical – intemperate weather forces the character to take refuge, out of sympathy for himself and his horse, although in this instance the horse makes her own way to the inn. It is 'a strange old place' with 'a strong cheerful light in the bar-window' and the house appears to promise 'a rousing fire ... blazing within'. Having imagined the fire, five minutes later Tom finds himself 'ensconced' 'before a substantial matter-of-fact roaring fire, composed of something short of a bushel of coals'.[15] There is a comely landlady amidst another of Dickens's inviting descriptions of the food on offer and the idyllic bar. The only drawback to the whole scene, for Tom, is that a tall man in the bar is obviously intent upon the widowed landlady. Tom gets drunk, goes to bed, and hears the chair speak to him. It tells him that he deserves to install himself in the inn because the tall man is a rascal who is already married. The chair provides a letter as evidence of the latter point. When Tom wakes up the next morning the chair will no longer speak, but the letter remains – as if by 'imagining' the letter, just as he 'imagined' the inside of the inn, he has brought it into being. With the tall man discovered, all ends happily for Tom and his place at the bar is assured for evermore.

The same collection of elements – landlady, usurper, rightful claim – is echoed in the novel proper via the story of Sam Weller's father. Other similarities are that the potential usurper is defined by a physical characteristic that appears as slightly sinister (here it is Mr Stiggins's red nose), and that the man is to be revealed as a rascal. Wellers senior and junior plot to get Stiggins drunk before he gives a speech at a temperance meeting. The plan works, although Mr Weller does not so much inherit the pub as end his days a respectable man living 'at an excellent public-house near Shooter's Hill' after his wife has died.[16] This is a fitting conclusion for a man who thinks his parish is the Belle Savage, that is, the name of the famous coaching inn which he had occasion to use.[17] Whilst it is clear that the trajectories of these narratives find the landladies fairly invisible (a widowed landlady is evidently not 'complete' until she has a landlord-mate), for a man to close his life by 'ensconcing' himself in an inn or public house is to end his days in acceptable bliss. Mark Tapley, the hostler at the Blue Dragon in *Martin Chuzzlewit*, is a naturally happy man. Finding happiness too easy, he struggles to find miserable circumstances wherein there would at least be something admirable in being happy. His story ends when he resigns himself to happiness and he marries the widowed Mrs Lupin, landlady of the Blue Dragon. Perhaps in obeisance to Dickens's wishes, the name of the place is changed to the more realistic 'Jolly Tapley'.

At the other end of the scale, there is little evidence that a drinking house could represent something completely 'evil'. 'The Boot' in *Barnaby Rudge*, the meeting place of the rioters and a tavern which might have been described in less-than-flattering terms, is rendered as a lively place for goodfellows. Perhaps the meanest place represented is in *The Old Curiosity Shop* (1840–41). Quilp is the out-and-out villain of the novel, hounding Little Nell and her Grandfather throughout the length and breadth of England. Dickens goes to some lengths to mirror and heighten his character through his description of Quilp's special drinking retreat. When Quilp invites Swiveller there, Quilp paints it attractively as 'a little summer-house overlooking the river' where they can be 'snug and happy', but the narrator takes the occasion to show up Quilp for his usual deceiving self: 'The summer-house of which Mr Quilp had spoken was a rugged wooden box, rotten and bare to see, which overhung the river's mud, and threatened to slide down into it. The tavern to which it belonged was a crazy building, sapped and undermined by the rats, and only upheld by great bars of wood which were reared against its walls.'[18] The description of Quilp/tavern/summer-house continues in a similar fashion, although it is only a few pages later that we casually learn the place is called 'The Wilderness'.[19] The notion of evil-doing is enhanced by the continual reference to Quilp's favourite drink, a brand of gin called Scheidam, a particularly fiery and nasty spirit.

However, The Wilderness is specific to Quilp, a personification of his moral place within the human condition. It is *Oliver Twist* (1837–39) that offers a generic and substantial representation of the drinking place. When Oliver runs away to London the novel charts his decline in fortunes through its mapping of drinking houses. After his one piece of luck, when he is saved from starvation by 'a good-hearted turnpike-man, and a benevolent old lady',[20] his ensuing fate is symbolically sealed in Barnet: 'He had been crouching on the step for some time, wondering at the great number of public-houses (every other house in Barnet was a tavern, large or small), gazing listlessly at the coaches as they passed through.'[21] His new world is transforming itself into that of low life, and it is at this juncture the Artful Dodger appears. He immediately buys Oliver some food, takes him into a nearby small public house and orders him a pot of beer.[22] From Barnet Oliver is taken to the shadier parts of London (Saffron Hill the Great), where the narrator comments: 'The sole places that seemed to prosper amid the general blight of the place, were the public-houses.'[23] When Bill Sikes appears in his natural habitat, the description of the drinking place symbolises the end of the line for Oliver's social descent:

> In the obscure parlour of a low public-house, in the filthiest part of Little Saffron Hill; a dark and gloomy den, where a flaring gas-light burnt all day in the winter-time; and where no ray of sun ever shone in the summer: there sat, brooding over a little pewter measure and a small glass, strongly impregnated with the smell of liquor, a man in a velveteen coat, drab shorts, half-boots, and stockings, who even by that dim light no experienced agent of police would have hesitated for one instant to recognize as Mr William Sikes.[24]

Yet even here we find some vestige of human warmth, for it is in the same place that Nancy, when drunk, confesses her sympathy for Oliver, and so his happy ending is guaranteed.[25] Dickens's own sympathy for the difficulty of drinking houses may be reclaimed within the novel when Noah Claypole and Charlotte Sowerby – Oliver's adversaries at the undertakers early on in the novel – are sighted towards the end of the book playing a trick on publicans to earn some money. During church time Noah and Charlotte 'walk out', and when one of them faints in front of a public house they are to be revived with brandy sold to them by the landlord. The following day the publican is informed upon for having sold out of hours, and Noah and Charlotte pocket half the fine.[26] The public house is thus made to look the innocent victim.

Perhaps then it is a fact that in Dickens's novels even the most miserable drinking place will at least offer some feeling of sodality that prevents it from functioning as a house of out-and-out evil. After all, Dickens conflates the role of host and the role of author in his Preface to *The Old Curiosity Shop*, an idea it self-consciously takes from the opening comments of Fielding's *Tom Jones*.[27] It is interesting to see that when Dickens wants to represent utter desolation he has recourse not to an alehouse, gin palace or beer-house, but rather to a brewery. The premise to one of his novels is that a man offers to marry a woman, not for love, as it later materialises, but as part of a plan to make money out of her half-brother's brewery. Jilted by him into vengeful justice, she makes it her life's work to blight the lives of others. It is the brewery that underpins the novel, and its empty futility casts a gloom over the whole book. If it weren't for the brewery we wouldn't have the novel. 'While we waited at the gate, I peeped in … and saw that at the side of the house there was a large brewery. No brewing was going on in it, and none seemed to have gone on for a long long time.'[28] However, readers do not recall the brewery or its founding position within the plot. What readers remember is the house to which it is connected. For most it is Magwitch on the marshes, Joe's 'what larks Pip?', but mainly the thwarted love of Pip for the cruelly beautiful Estella for which they remember *Great Expectations*. Yet it is in the deserted brewery that Pip envisions Miss Havisham hanging from a beam, and the empty brewery most eminently stands for Pip's ruined heart.[29]

As if to mirror the failure of Miss Havisham's life, there is also a leitmotif of tracing Pip's own fortunes through the spaces of drinking houses. He celebrates his apprenticeship at the Blue Boar, and learns of his 'great expectations' at the Three Jolly Bargemen. When Pip moves to London, he is to stay at Barnard's Inn, and expects it to be some great hotel, a metropolitan version of the Blue Boar in his own village,[30] only to find it dingy and rotting. It is his first disabusement of 'great expectations'.[31] (Pip is not the only one to make the mistake. When Biddy writes to tell him that Joe is coming up to London, she believes he is stopping at Barnard's Hotel.)[32] When Pip returns to the village as a gentleman he feels it is beneath him to stay at Joe Gargery's dwelling. Instead he puts up at the best room in the Blue Boar. When Pip meets his social comeuppance this is disseminated through gossip at the Blue Boar, and the realisation that he has 'fallen' is brought home to Pip himself when he is unable to get 'his' room at the inn.

Dickens's even-handed ambiguousness towards drinking places is carried over into the understanding of alcoholic drink[33] and drunkenness. If it seems appropriate that Quilp should be partial to gin because of its fiery and perhaps too powerful nature, Dickens is quite capable of using the same drink for a more congenial portrayal. Perhaps there is something intentionally disquieting in *Oliver Twist* when Mrs Mann uses 'daffy' (gin and senna) to stop children suffering,[34] and, more particularly, the life of Sairey Gamp, 'a female functionary, a nurse, and watcher, and performer of nameless offices about the persons of the dead' in *Martin Chuzzlewit*.[35] Her abilities are unquestionable, and the novel treats her obvious drinking habits in a comic, sympathetic light. She invents dialogue to prevent any possible criticism of her capacity for drink or work. Mrs Harris allegedly tells Gamp: 'never did I think till I know'd you, as any women could sick-nurse and monthly likeways, on the little that you takes to drink.'[36]

But in the harsh world of *Hard Times* (1854) one of the burdens the earnest Stephen Blackpool has to bear is that of a drunkard wife who receives virtually no sympathetic comment from the narrator. *Pickwick Papers* in one of its 'irrelevant' stories – The Stroller's Tale – also includes the story of a habitual drunkard, a 'low pantomime actor': 'The public-house had a fascination for him which he could not resist. Neglected disease and hopeless poverty were as certain to be his portion as death itself, if he persevered in the same course; yet he *did* persevere, and the result may be guessed.'[37] He is so badly addicted in fact that he is said to have 'the horrors', that is, *delirium tremens*. He hallucinates and believes himself in hell.[38] In a novel which is a veritable hymn to drink and sociable drunkenness, if there is any moral to The Stroller's Tale, it certainly does not impinge upon the broader narrative.

In the main, drunkenness is indulged. Mr Micawber in *David Copperfield* (1849-50) is shown to be an expert in the making of punch, and there is a good-humoured escapism in the conviviality of these scenes – punch revives him and is also the fitting drink to celebrate his leaving of England.[39] Drink, and even drunkenness (notwithstanding habitual drunkards), do not carry the moral baggage that they would do for much of the nineteenth century. *Great Expectations* does provide one of those scenes which in other circumstances might be used as a warning against inebriation, yet the danger of intoxicating liquors is here specific to the scene. When Pip is cornered by Orlick and about to lose his life, Dickens heightens the tension by making Orlick drunk: 'He drank again, and became more ferocious. I saw by his tilting of the bottle that there was no great quantity left in it. I distinctly understood that he was working himself up with its contents, to make an end of me. I knew that every drop it held, was a drop of my life.'[40] Pip also realises that he has seen Orlick slouching about the alehouses – which serves to make Orlick's behaviour all the more disreputable, although in other works Dickens is quite happy to describe the alehouse in an attractive fashion.

The ghost of England present

In discussion of Dickens so far there has been little that could not have derived from the previous century. The scale and detail of description are Dickens's own, but what developments there had been in between time are not his concern. It was no shock to be told that in poverty-stricken areas, such as where Bill Sikes drinks, drinking dens were the only flourishing trade. The glory of inns had long been extolled, for their services to wayfarers and for their place in the English tradition. When Pip joins a club called the Finches of the Grove[41] we do get a humorous account of their actions, and the pointlessness of the club, but there is a weariness to it which is perhaps not only Pip's but a letting go of the previous century's pastimes.

The extensive references to 'public houses'[42] throughout Dickens's oeuvre do however serve notice that we have now entered the period when the drinking house comes closer to our own day, for when people think of the traditional English pub they are usually imagining something like a Victorian public house. The more fervent drive in the nineteenth century to impose a certain middle-class notion of respectability onto all and sundry is the main difference perhaps. This had clear repercussions in the field of drinking and drinking houses, and Dickens's period of writing covers a time when the temperance movement, begun in the 1820s, gained in strength and support. Despite this considerable mobilisation, the government continued to rake in profits from the trade. And despite the numerous bills offered up, no 'temperance' legislation was forthcoming in the nineteenth century. With the huge increase in urban centres of population and slum conditions, drunkenness continued to be the most convenient escape from a harsh environment (a bottle of gin was reputed to be the quickest way out of Manchester). Drink-related legislation had been consolidated in 1828, and then everything was opened up in 1830 with the Beer Act, when anyone for a small fee could sell beer. Dickens makes reference to the consequent 'beer-houses', placing them at the bottom of the social ladder when he describes the entry of Little Nell and Grandfather into a typical village: 'The farm-yard passed, then came the little inn; the humbler beer-shop, and the village tradesman's; then the lawyer's and the parson's, at whose dread names the beer-shop trembled.'[43]

This is also the period of the gin palaces, glittering attractions far removed from the seedy efficiency of the eighteenth-century gin shop. It is difficult to say how much worse or better things were than the eighteenth century or beginning of the nineteenth. Hogarth's *Gin Lane* of 1751 had played a major part in putting pressure on the government to take action. A hundred years later George Cruikshank was moved to produce a cartoon with the same target, called 'The Gin Juggernaut, or the worship of the Great Spirit – Its devotees destroying themselves – Its progress is marked with desolation, misery, and crime.'[44] In 1848 he produced 'The Bottle' and 'The Drunkard's Children', aimed at gin palaces and beer shops. '"The Bottle" pictures were instantly a huge success and sold in immense numbers, no less than 100,000 copies at a shilling each being sold within the space of a few days. "The Bottle" was at once dramatised, and played simultaneously at eight London theatres.'[45] It is difficult to argue that anything had changed for the large majority. The move to cities and large towns gave for a more rootless population and a greater (another?) reason for drinking, that is all. Dickens's sympathy for the lower orders is evident in his definitive description of the gin palace in *Sketches by Boz* – all glittering surfaces, a place to be that is better than home. He is adamant that the temperance movement is wrongheaded, for nobody can blame those who are poverty-stricken resorting to the comforts of cheap liquor: 'Gin-drinking is a great vice in England, but poverty is a greater; and until you can cure it, or persuade a half-famished wretch not to seek relief in the temporary oblivion of his own misery, with the pittance which, divided among his family, would just furnish a morsel of bread for each, gin-shops will increase in number and splendour.'[46]

But it is also noticeable that a gin palace would not provide any kind of narrative hook for Dickens. It can only be viewed sociologically, as if somehow places devoted to gin-drinking continue to remain outside the literary remit. Similarly it is noticeable that no beer shop appears in his work. I can only surmise that inns, taverns, alehouses, and even public houses as a place somewhere between taverns and alehouses, came with a ready-made literary template that Dickens could manipulate however he saw fit, or that he did not 'feel' for gin palaces as he did these other places. A beer shop, gin shop or gin palace had no literary heritage, low-life or otherwise.

It is also curious that the pressure of temperance was felt in his first novel and then did not reappear in any substantial form. One of the great set-pieces in *Pickwick Papers* is the dethroning of Stiggins – the would-be wooer of Mrs Weller – as a drinking hypocrite. The narrator's sympathies appear self-evident, for at the United Grand Junction Ebenezer Temperance Association (Brick Lane Branch) a list of recent converts includes a woman who believes the loss of one eye may have been due to excessive drinking and a man who believes his second-hand wooden legs last longer now that he has given up drinking gin and water. This is followed by a temperance song which begins 'Row along, thinking of nothing at all', a sentiment which the narrator believes sums up the mental attitude of temperance followers.[47] Thanks to the work of Sam, Stiggins turns up so inebriated he declares it is the meeting which is drunk. In *The Old Curiosity Shop*, Quilp's side-kick Swiveller, with a tongue-in-cheek aside, gives a pot-boy the standard temperance advice: 'lead a sober and temperate life, and abstain from all intoxicating and exciting liquors'.[48]

Pickwick Papers is also the novel in which we see a satire upon election practices. The corruption involved in electing members to Parliament was common knowledge. 'Treating' of potential voters and those without the vote who could nevertheless use mob intimidation was a tradition by the 1830s, having begun in the later Stuart period.[49] Hogarth's print of *An Election* is inevitably situated at a hostelry, whilst in his *Canvassing for Votes* (1757) electioneering activity takes place outside three inns. There is a joke in *She Stoops to Conquer*, when Marlow and Hastings still believe Hardcastle to be the landlord of an inn, that he must be busy because there is an election afoot. Hardcastle replies that that business has gone, 'since our betters have hit upon the expedient of electing each other'. In Smollett's *Launcelot Greaves* the hero is awoken at an inn by the sound of electioneering.[50] But the most extensive description of treating is in *Pickwick Papers*.

The Pickwickians, when they arrive at a place called Eatanswill, find themselves in the midst of an election, Slumkey vs Fizkin, Blues vs Buffs. '"Who is Slumkey?" whispered Mr Tupman. "I don't know," replied Mr Pickwick in the same tone. "Hush. Don't ask any questions. It's always best on these occasions to do what the mob do." "But suppose there are two mobs?" suggested Mr Snodgrass. "Shout with the largest," replied Mr Pickwick. Volumes could not have said more.'[51] The role of the hostelries in all this emerges when Mr Perker, Slumkey's agent, boasts: 'We have opened all the public-houses in the place, and left our adversary nothing but beer-shops – masterly stroke of policy that, my dear sir, eh?' It would evidently not be much of a treat to be treated at a beer-house. Another of the underhand schemes in electioneering is divulged by Sam Weller to the incredulous Pickwick: some of the voters are drugged by putting laudanum in the drinks.[52] But actually Dickens has nothing to say about the role of the inns themselves. As with so many of the representations, they are merely fulfilling one of their numerous social functions. It is to *Barnaby Rudge* we must turn in order to find an inn taking on a much more substantial place within the fiction.

Barnaby Rudge

> 'There are no inns,' rejoined Mr Willet, with a strong emphasis on the plural number; 'but there's a Inn – one Inn – the Maypole Inn. That's a Inn indeed. You won't see the like of that Inn often.'[53]

> the Maypole was an old building, with more gable ends than a lazy man would care to count on a sunny day; huge zig-zag chimneys, out of which it seemed as though even smoke could not choose but come in more than naturally fantastic shapes, imparted to it in its tortuous progress; and vast stables, gloomy, ruinous, and empty.[54]

> With its overhanging stories, drowsy little panes of glass, and front bulging out and projecting over the pathway, the old house looked as if it were nodding in its sleep. Indeed, it needed no great stretch of fancy to detect in it other resemblances to humanity.[55]

Barnaby Rudge is one of the least known of Dickens's novels, and also regarded as one of the least successful in artistic terms. It is one of the two historical novels he wrote, the other being *A Tale of Two Cities*. *Barnaby Rudge* is set at the time of the 'no popery' Gordon riots of 1780, a remarkable event in English history when anti-Catholic sentiment was marshalled by Lord George Gordon to counteract more lenient religious legislation. The riots and looting were serious, leaving London shocked in the wake of, amongst other things, the storming of a prison and liberation of its prisoners. The title of the novel refers to a character who is caught up in the events. The scenes are split between The Maypole Inn of Chigwell, some twelve miles from the centre of London, and the site of the riots themselves in London. The book has often been read as aimed at the activities of the Chartists at the time of Dickens's writing, a warning from history against the dangers of radical change.[56]

The novel begins with a description of the Maypole Inn and its inhabitants. It represents the solid, cosy past, but also the dangers of such conservatism. The inn sign is a young, thirty-foot ash – the 'Maypole' – the perfect sign of olde England, since the prohibition of maypoles had been one of the major flashpoints between the newer Puritan demands and the older festival culture. His description of it alerts the reader to its connection with the national, historical (military) past by the description of the ash as 'straight as any arrow that ever English yeoman drew'.[57] Dickens also uses the sign to draw another contrast between a past and a present – the past of 1775 in which year the novel begins, and the present time in which he is writing, some sixty years later, to note a greater literacy on the part of the general populace, since the sign is iconic rather than written, a perception that civilisation was indeed improved since the eighteenth century.

The Maypole's landlord is John Willet, 'a burly, large-headed man with a fat face'[58] and his customers have occupations suggestive of cosy village life – the parish-clerk and bell-ringer, the general chandler and post-office keeper, and the ranger.[59] When Gabriel Varden arrives one particular evening, it could be Benjamin the Waggoner[60] – he has promised to come straight home but the 'delicious perspective of warmth and brightness' within The Maypole is irresistible and the 'honest locksmith' convinces himself that 'the merciful man is merciful to his beast. I'll get out for a little while.'[61] The following sentiment, 'how unnatural it seemed for a sober man to be plodding wearily along through miry roads', could also have easily been lifted from the Wordsworth poem. The absolute power of The Maypole is asserted later in the novel when the extreme Protestant, Martha Varden (Gabriel's wife), who regards the inn as a poacher of Christian men, is overcome by its charm when she finally enters what the narrator has just described as 'the very snuggest, cosiest, and completest bar, that ever the wit of man devised'.[62]

In his description of The Maypole Inn Dickens consolidates his scene-setting by dating the building to the time of Henry VIII and furnishing it with the legend – as all good old inns should have – that Queen Elizabeth once slept there. Legend also has it that she cuffed an unfortunate page on her short sojourn at the inn. This use of folklore prepares the reader for a critical appreciation of history-writing; although some people dispute the story, the doubters are always shouted down by the majority, 'and all true believers exulted as in a victory'.[63] There is no ambivalence here towards the attitude under passing scrutiny – the power of the majority gets to dictate what is true. This incidental notice of mob rule will be taken up more seriously with the onset of the riots.

The novel is experimental in a couple of ways. Barnaby is a simple-minded soul who is easily led. The book therefore has no moral centre from which to judge the events, since Barnaby himself is not only caught up in the riots, but plays an active part. He is not therefore a basically decent character who through force of circumstances is compromised into acting in an unethical or immoral way. He has a basic instinct of empathy, but no discriminating moral judgement. Part of the book's experimentalism is to refuse the solid moral ground that his other novels provide in the form of characters such as Esther in *Bleak House*, Little Dorrit or Nicholas Nickleby. This adds to the uncertain understanding of the riots.

The structure of the novel is also quite daring, and perhaps accounts for its relative lack of popularity. Approximately just under half of the novel is given over to a very slow build-up, centring itself upon the sleepiness of olde England. As such, these pages are themselves somewhat soporific. Dickens attempts to inject some narrative interest into them by offering a mystery told by one of the Maypole regulars, Solomon Daisy, and through the conflict between the landlord of The Maypole and his son. But these are relatively unconvincing, even if the latter can be defended on the grounds that Dickens is homologically working 'tyranny' into the novel as a theme, with the rebellion of the son Joe like the rebellion of the apprentices during the riots. These pages lull the reader into the false security that The Maypole stands for. Only twelve miles from London, yet, as the novel will show, it is another world away. Dickens makes a point of placing The Maypole as 'measured' in accordance with the distance it stands from the Standard in Cornhill (as was), the 'centre' of London.[64]

When the scene moves from The Maypole to Gabriel's shop in Clerkenwell we are given a scrupulously tidy and neat place. It bespeaks a frugal, clean-living, respectable existence – an ideal of town/city dwelling for the respectable lower classes. This stands as a more feasible mode of existence in modern England than The Maypole, especially when contrasted with the notion that somehow The Maypole is no longer a 'home' since no children are born there, and Joe has left (see below). However, there is a viper in the midst of Varden's Clerkenwell residence in the form of a rebellious apprentice, Sim Tappertit. Although the main character does not provide a moral centre, Gabriel – the 'honest locksmith' – and his model house do represent some kind of centring. In addition, the usually rather ambivalent narratorial voice here becomes quite sarcastic when dealing with the clandestine Knights Prentice meeting that Sim attends, for he notes that the apprentices have gradually lost their 'privileges' – the privilege to have frequent holidays, beat people's heads and commit the occasional murder.[65] The reactionary apprentices will resist change, unless it restores these 'good old English customs'. So although their rebelliousness compares unfavourably with the relatively quiet Maypole, both spaces represent a moribund traditionalism.

When the narrator identifies the allure of Lord George Gordon's cause, he couches it in terms of its mystery and vagueness, elements which play upon old desires and prejudices, the very elements that compose The Maypole and the demands of the apprentices. If the target is really 'conservatism', then this can hardly be seen as an attack on the Chartists. The unreformed past is likewise deplored in the picture of Mr Dennis, the hangman: 'My work, is sound, Protestant, constitutional, English work. Is it, or is it not?',[66] and in a not uncommon prejudice, the Catholic way of execution, 'boiling and roasting', is obviously barbaric.[67] The novel shows that this vision of England is distasteful and probably wrong-headed. Another example of the ideology the novel advances is when Barnaby and his mother meet a Justice of the Peace, a man who has the character of a veritable John Bull: 'He was warmly attached to church and state, and never appointed to the living in his gift any but a three-bottle man and a first-rate fox-hunter.'[68] This could be Fielding's Squire Western of *Tom Jones*, but here there is nothing comically redeeming. Thus another component of 'England' and 'Englishness' is disposed of. However, perhaps because the novel is set in the past, it is unable overtly to offer the kind of benevolent paternalist resolutions found in those novels Dickens wrote with nineteenth-century social concerns.

Covertly, the England that is desirable for readers of *Barnaby Rudge* again belongs to Gabriel Varden, for having described his house, his locksmith workshop 'The Golden Key' is next presented in all its rosiness. We even get a personification of drink to encourage our approval: 'Toby looked on from a tall bench hard by; one beaming smile, from his broad nut-brown face down to the slack-baked buckles in his shoes.' – 'Gabriel lifted Toby to his mouth, and took a hearty draught.'[69]

Yet we may have already missed the symbolism of The Maypole, for it is quite possible that the novel intends us to treat its centrality as in some way already a decline from a better order. There is a hint of this earlier on when the idea that the nearby mansion – the Warren – could be a 'public house',[70] an echo of the trope of mistaking mansions for inns. This is the other side of the coin, that as desirable as inns might be in the context of representing the best that survives of olde England, they are also to be considered as the modern usurpers of the older mansions, a sign that customary England can no longer be sustained: 'It was no longer a home; children were never born and bred there; the fireside had become mercenary – a something to be bought and sold – a very courtezan: let who would die, or sit beside, or leave it, it was still the same – it missed nobody, cared for nobody, had equal warmth and smiles for all. God help the man whose heart ever changes with the world, as an old mansion when it becomes an inn.'[71] The focus on The Maypole in this context should tell us from the outset that something is rotten in the state of England.

Drinking places and homes are the cognitive anchor-points for the novel. We have already seen The Maypole and Varden's house. The resort of Gordon's active supporters is The Boot, the name itself giving an indication of its symbolic role within the novel – a peremptory kick. As an item of footwear, perhaps its single nature indicates a certain uselessness. It is described as 'a lone house of public entertainment' situated in an isolated spot.[72] Another space is that of Barnaby's and his mother's. They live in a country idyll: 'Barnaby's enjoyments were, to walk, and run, and leap, till he was tired; then to lie down in the long grass, or by the growing corn, or in the shade of some tall tree, looking upward at the light clouds as they floated over the blue surface of the sky, and listening to the lark as she poured out her brilliant song.'[73] They live in nothing more than a hut, and the rural simplicity is a mirror image of the simple town house of Gabriel. Although there is no specific argument against luxury, the same idea runs through – the barely sufficient is ample for most humble folks.

Once the acceptable private space of homes and the public spaces of inns and taverns have been set up, the scene is set for a space that is out of bounds – the city streets which the rioters will overrun. The symbolic end of olde England occurs when the rioters attack The Maypole and destroy its inner sanctum, the Bar, whilst John Willet can only look on stupefied.[74] They tie him up, whilst, temporarily out of his senses, all he can mutter is that there is an 'ordinary' to run every Sunday at two o'clock.[75] When the regular Solomon Daisy later sees the destruction the sense of an ending is complete: 'Oh dear old Johnny, here's a change! That the Maypole bar should come to this, and we should live to see it! The old Warren too, Johnny – Mr Haredale – oh, Johnny, what a piteous sight this is!'[76] Of course, the reader's sympathies lie with those who have become victims at the hands of rioters, but the logic of the novel is that these were things that had to be cleared away, one way or another. The Maypole is gone, and so is its adjunct the Warren.

The destruction of The Maypole is of a readily understood space, 'olde England', but done for reasons which are incomprehensible. Its own rambling existence is justified by 'customary usage' rather than 'logic', and this perhaps partly explains its demise, an eruption of those 'unreasonable' and 'traditional' elements that it embodies, if in a different form. But the greatest incomprehension is to witness mob action in the 'uncharted' space of the streets, and one of the great technical achievements of *Barnaby Rudge* is its description of the mob and its movement. Dickens's overriding image is a typical one of fluidity: 'A mob is usually a creature of very mysterious existence, particularly in a large city. Where it comes from or whither it goes, few men can tell. Assembling and dispersing with equal suddenness, it is as difficult to follow to its various sources as the sea itself; nor does the parallel stop here, for the ocean is not more fickle and uncertain, more terrible when roused, more unreasonable, or more cruel.'[77] Similarly, when they storm the Warren after having demolished The Maypole, 'the crowd poured in like water'.[78]

The liquid similes are developed in a more complex manner when it comes to a description of the setting alight of the distillery, when the image of a mob inflamed by drink and moving from one place to the next as if water, is mixed with the fired liquor running free from the building. The two are combined and confused to produce a vision of hell. The vintner's house and surrounding buildings are ablaze, whilst the dust, smoke and fiery particles obliterate the stars, moon and sky:

> But there was a worse spectacle than this – worse by far than fire and smoke, or even the rabble's unappeasable and maniac rage. The gutters of the street, and every crack and fissure in the stones, ran with scorching spirit, which being dammed up by busy hands, overflowed the road and pavement, and formed a great pool, into which the people dropped down dead by dozens. They lay in heaps all round this fearful pond, husbands and wives, fathers and sons, mothers and daughters, women with children in their arms and babies at their breasts, and drank until they died. While some stooped with their lips to the brink and never raised their heads again, others sprang up from their fiery draught, and danced, half in a mad triumph, and half in the agony of suffocation, until they fell, and steeped their corpses in the liquor that had killed them. Nor was even this the worst or most appalling kind of death that happened on this fatal night. From the burning cellars, where they drank out of hats, pails, buckets, tubs, and shoes, some men were drawn, alive, but all alight from head to foot; who, in their unendurable anguish and suffering, making for anything that had the look of water, rolled, hissing, in this hideous lake, and splashed up liquid fire which lapped in all it met with as it ran along the surface, and neither spared the living nor the dead. On this last night of the great riots – for the last night it was – the wretched victims of a senseless outcry, became themselves the dust and ashes of the flames they had kindled, and strewed in the public streets of London.[79]

The culmination of the riots is the conflagration of anarchic spirit and hard liquor, as if drink has exploded the city and its people.[80] Dickens folds into the passage the idea of poetic justice – that those who are so besotted with whatever inflames (liquor, rebellion) should die by it. This is the contrast that the time spent in The Maypole has set up. As an inn it has functioned as a public house in the sense that it provides a public forum in a domestic setting. Drinking there does not inflame, it provides all those homely English comforts – fire, food, conversation – that seem to be desirable. Here, at the end of the Gordon riots, we have a purely public spectacle free from all domestic constraints. The reader is left with only the Varden residence as any kind of appropriate space.

When the dust has settled and the novel rounds up events and gives us the lives of its characters, it installs Joe Willet and Dolly Varden as proprietors of The Maypole. Perhaps chained to its own rhetoric, the Maypole partly reverts to an ideal place, with many small Joes and Dollys running wild there. However, the narrative is obviously keen to declare that the Riots did after all signify some irrevocable loss: 'It was a long time, too, before there was such a country inn as the Maypole, in all England: indeed it is a great question whether there has ever been such another to this hour, or ever will be.'[81] This despite the fact that an image of olde England is snuck back in with the litany of 'feastings and christenings, and revellings at Christmas, and celebrations of birthdays, wedding-days, and all manner of days, both at the Maypole and the Golden Key', by which latter joining the novel has the best of both worlds – a more alert Maypole, symbol of the past, and the ever-lauded Golden Key, symbol of the honest workman who knows his place. In essence this provides a modified, more caring conservatism.

Notes

1 Charles Dickens, *The Pickwick Papers* (London, Penguin, 1986 [1836–37]), p. 196.
2 *Ibid*.
3 Charles Dickens, *Dombey and Son* (London, Penguin, 1985 [1846–48]), p. 121.
4 Dickens, *Pickwick*, p. 161.
5 Quoted in Jacob Larwood and John Camden Hotlen, *English Inn Signs*, revised and modernised (London, Chatto and Windus, 1951 [1866]), p. 12.
6 Charles Dickens, *Martin Chuzzlewit* (London, Penguin, 1986 [1843–44]), p. 74.
7 *Ibid*., p. 59.
8 Charles Dickens, *Barnaby Rudge* (London, Penguin, 1997 [1841], p. 299.
9 Larwood, *Signs*, does not list a Blue Dragon, nor does Eric R. Delderfield's *Introduction to Inn Signs* (Newton Abbot, David & Charles, 1969).
10 The Blue Boar was 'one of the badges of Richard Duke of York, father of Edward IV' and the Red Lion is probably from Edward III's badge, although it also has a general (mistaken) association with the three red lions of the national coat of arms, which 'in any case … are properly leopards', Larwood, *Signs*, pp. 70, 72.
11 The Saracen's Head in Dickens, *Pickwick*, p. 812.
12 Dickens, *Chuzzlewit*, p. 621.
13 The Maypole Inn in *Barnaby Rudge*, 'with more gable ends than a lazy man would care to count on a summer's day', has Ye Olde King's Head at Chigwell as its basis. One commentator notes: 'The laziest man, on the hottest day, easily could count those gables, which number three large ones, and a kind of small would-be-a-gable if it could, so to say', Charles G. Harper, quoted in Denzil Batchelor, *The English Inn* (London, Batsford, 1964), p. 137. Batchelor himself counts four-and-a-half gables from Harper's own sketch. Comprehensive coverage of the real and the fictional in Dickens can be found in two works by W. B. Matz, *Dickensian Inns and Taverns* (London, Cecil Palmer, 1922), and *The Inns and Taverns of 'Pickwick' with Some Observations on their Other Associations* (London, Cecil Palmer, 1921).
14 Dickens, *Pickwick*, pp. 259ff.
15 *Ibid*., p. 261.
16 *Ibid*., p. 871.
17 *Ibid*., p. 200.
18 Charles Dickens, *The Old Curiosity Shop* (London, Penguin, 1985 [1840–41]), p. 225.
19 *Ibid*., p. 236.
20 Charles Dickens, *Oliver Twist* (London, Penguin, 1985 [1837–39]), p. 99.

21 *Ibid.*, p. 100.
22 *Ibid.*, p. 101.
23 *Ibid.*, p. 103.
24 *Ibid.*, p. 152.
25 *Ibid.*, pp. 239–40.
26 *Ibid.*, p. 477.
27 Dickens, *Curiosity*, p. 39.
28 Charles Dickens, *Great Expectations* (Harmondsworth, Penguin, 1980 [1860–61]), p. 85.
29 *Ibid.*, p. 413.
30 *Ibid.*, p. 196.
31 *Ibid.*, p. 197.
32 *Ibid.*, p. 239.
33 For those interested in trying out some of the drinks, Cedric Dickens, Dickens's great-grandson, provides an entertaining list, with ingredients, in *Drinking with Dickens* (Goring-on-Thames, England, Elvendon Press, 1980).
34 Dickens, *Oliver*, p. 51.
35 Dickens, *Chuzzlewit*, p. 374.
36 *Ibid.*, p. 473.
37 Dickens, *Pickwick*, 'The Stroller's Tale', pp. 105ff.
38 *Ibid.*, p. 110. Magwitch in *Great Expectations* talks of a man dying of the horrors, p. 326.
39 Charles Dickens, *David Copperfield* (London, Penguin, 1996 [1849–50]), p. 383, pp. 739–40.
40 Dickens, *Expectations*, pp. 437–8.
41 *Ibid.*, p. 292.
42 According to Peter Clark, *The English Alehouse: A Social History 1200–1830* (Harlow, Longman, 1983), the derivation of the term 'public house' is unclear. It comes into common usage some time around the end of the seventeenth century, and is possibly an abbreviation for 'public alehouse' to distinguish it from 'private alehouse', although the term could also cover taverns and smaller inns as well as alehouses, p. 195.
43 Dickens, *Curiosity*, p. 176.
44 Frederick W. Hackwood, *Inns, Ales, and Drinking Customs of Old England* (London, T. Fisher Unwin, 1910), p. 140.
45 *Ibid.*
46 Charles Dickens, 'Gin-Shops', in *Sketches by Boz* (London, Penguin, 1995 [1836; 1839]), p. 220.
47 Dickens, *Pickwick*, pp. 547–9.
48 Dickens, *Curiosity*, p. 371.
49 Clark, *Alehouse*, p. 237.
50 Tobias Smollett, *The Life and Adventures of Sir Launcelot Greaves* (London, Oxford University Press, 1973 [1760–61]), p. 66.
51 Dickens, *Pickwick*, p. 239.
52 *Ibid.*, p. 246.
53 Dickens, *Barnaby*, p. 332.
54 *Ibid.*, p. 43.
55 *Ibid.*, p. 44.

56 *Ibid.*, Gordon Spence's introduction to the Penguin edition discusses this feature, pp. 19–23.
57 *Ibid.*, p. 43.
58 *Ibid.*, p. 45.
59 *Ibid.*, p. 48.
60 It is quite feasible that Dickens is drawing upon the poem. Gordon Spence notes that Barnaby's characterisation partly derives from Wordsworth's 'The Idiot Boy', *ibid.*, Introduction, p. 15.
61 *Ibid.*, p. 67.
62 *Ibid.*, p. 209.
63 *Ibid.*, p. 43. Compare this with the more extensive treatment of history-writing via 'inn-tales' and 'inn-conversation' in George Eliot's *Silas Marner* in the following chapter.
64 *Ibid.*, p. 43.
65 *Ibid.*, p. 115.
66 *Ibid.*, p. 354.
67 *Ibid.*, p. 355.
68 *Ibid.*, p. 435.
69 *Ibid.*, p. 382.
70 *Ibid.*, p. 49.
71 *Ibid.*, p. 128.
72 *Ibid.*, p. 362.
73 *Ibid.*, pp. 416–17.
74 *Ibid.*, p. 497.
75 *Ibid.*, p. 498.
76 *Ibid.*, p. 512.
77 *Ibid.*, p. 475.
78 *Ibid.*, p. 506.
79 *Ibid.*, p. 618.
80 Drink is given as a prime cause of the riots by Dorothy M. George, *London Life in the Eighteenth Century* (Harmondsworth, Penguin (Peregrine), 1966 [1925]), with anti-Catholic sentiment playing second fiddle, p. 125.
81 Dickens, *Barnaby*, p. 735.

10

Of Rainbows and Fingers

Silas Marner

> The Rainbow, in Marner's view, was a place of luxurious resort for rich and stout husbands, whose wives had superfluous stores of linen; it was the place where he was likely to find the powers and dignities of Raveloe, and where he could most speedily make his loss public.[1]

In choosing someone of no, or at most, limited, culpability to carry the burden of the story, *Barnaby Rudge* evades the ascription of blame to an identifiable agent. The novel ends with Barnaby's raven 'Grip' cawing 'I'm a devil, I'm a devil, *I*'m a devil!' It has no cognisance of the meaning of these words – just as, in a way, Barnaby has no real awareness of his actions. This lets everyone off the hook. The riots are an aberration, an upsurge of vague, primitive, irrational fears; like Gordon himself within the novel and history, a singularity. There is an intriguing interplay between the way the novel itself limns these elements, and Dickens's Preface, in which he tells the story of how he came by the two ravens upon which Grip is based. The first had been a raven of '"good gifts", which he improved by study and attention in a most exemplary manner'. The second was acquired by a friend from a village public house when the first had died. Dickens says the second raven was older and more gifted, which, in the context of the novel, the reader might interpret as more 'traditional'. Presumably as a consequence of its formative environment, although Dickens does not make it explicit, this raven was only at its best when in the presence of a drunken man. However, never having had a drunken man to hand, Dickens was never able to verify this ability.

It is a tantalising context for the novel. Is Dickens telling the story to show that he is always in the midst of sobriety (or at least temperance)? In other words, is he saying that he never places himself in a position akin to those in the novel, and will thus never be prey to that kind of aberration? It is not clear whether he does it out of moral rectitude or fear that there is a danger of becoming addicted. More importantly, it is also a story of how he refuses some kind of objective verification to the tale that comes with the ravens, as if story-telling (for which read 'history') is not open to 'sober' verification. The truth of the matter lies somewhere in the taking on trust of such matters. The death of the bird has two possible causes: 'It may have been that he was too bright a genius to live long, or it may have been that he took some pernicious substance into his bill, and thence into his maw.'[2] The second, prosaic explanation is the more acceptable, but the first is a more suggestive, more poetic, cultural explanation. Interpretations and causes remain open-ended when dealing with the past, even if, on the balance of probability, one explanation lacks a logical persuasive force.

The writing of history, 'historiography', became a preoccupation with the nineteenth century, partly as a result of the inroads made into standard Christian belief, as underwritten by the Bible. With Lyell's *Principles of Geology* (1830–33), which showed the world to be somewhat older than the six thousand years a literal reading of the Bible would vouchsafe, the method of writing 'history' was up for grabs. Since, as we have already seen, the drinking house could be used as shorthand for England's past, it was only natural that, above and beyond Dickens's use of The Maypole as a means to historical understanding of England's history, a hostelry would at some stage be used in the debate about historiography. As David Carroll identifies, George Eliot uses The Rainbow, the public house in *Silas Marner* (1861), for just such a purpose. Although the arguments around historiography had a European dimension, it could not but fail to affect the construction of national identity, the writing of England and Englishness. The inn, tavern, village public house or alehouse, then become caught up in the new way of perceiving olde England – not just as olde England, but as a self-conscious part in writing the history of England.

The story of Silas is of a weaver who is forced out of a narrow religious community when he is wrongly accused of theft. Like *Barnaby Rudge* it is a historical novel, set about eighty years previously, and also like *Barnaby Rudge*, Wordsworth's rustics stand at the back of this depiction of a simple man immersed in circumstances beyond his mental ken. As with Dickens's novel, it is an opportunity to throw into relief the modern world against a more traditionally minded one. After leaving the community of Lantern Yard, Silas finds himself employment as a weaver in Raveloe, where his self-imposed isolation invites some suspicion but not outright hostility. Eliot introduces the ideological terrain of the novel when she compares Raveloe with Lantern Yard: 'Raveloe lay low among the bushy trees and the rutted lanes, aloof from the currents of industrial energy and Puritan earnestness: they ate and drank freely, accepting gout and apoplexy as things that ran mysteriously in respectable families, and the poor thought that the rich were entirely in the right of it to lead a jolly life; besides, their feasting caused a multiplication of orts, which were the heirlooms of the poor.'[3] It is the olde England of customary obligation and acceptance of the Great Chain of Being, everybody in their place and knowing their place within the social hierarchy, with the lower orders gratefully receiving the scraps ('orts') of their betters. The modern world of Puritan sobriety and industriousness – the perceived dynamo behind the industrial revolution – is the one that festive England is losing out to, but which Raveloe has yet to be affected by.

Once in Raveloe, the narrative tells us that Silas spends his time weaving and counting the gold he accumulates. Each night he lays out the money he is hoarding. The grand historical scheme is evident: religious belief has given way to worship of Mammon. Silas returns one day to find all his money gone. There is no cast-iron explanation for its disappearance. It could have been stolen by a tinker or whisked away by supernatural powers. Later, one night, whilst Silas is undergoing one of his cataleptic fits, the two-year-old child of a dying mother wanders into his house. Her golden curls are to his eye at first the gold sovereigns that have vanished. In this manner does Eliot give the story a mythical dimension – the golden pieces are replaced by golden curls, the money by a child. Marner responds by bringing up the child. Lavishing love upon it, it becomes a symbol of his love, and, on a broader scale, of a humanist world view at the expense of an explicitly religious one.

It is after five chapters of fairly unremitting gloom that takes in both Silas's miserable history and the self-lacerating lives of the brothers Dunstan and Godfrey Cass, the village nobility, that Silas's money goes missing, stolen from him by an unknown force. Silas rushes out of his house in a dither, not knowing what to do, but soon aware that the place he must go to redress the wrong is The Rainbow. At this point the narrator describes The Rainbow in a mildly satirical fashion as an image of olde England – Squire Cass usually drinks there, in the more select parlour, enjoying 'the double pleasure of conviviality and condescension'.[4] Even though the higher ranks are at a birthday party elsewhere on this particular night, there is still an element of social differentiation between the superior spirits-and-water drinkers and the lower beer drinkers.[5] Silas's entrance into The Rainbow will be his (and our) first meeting with the rank and file of Raveloe society. Just as Silas slackens his pace as he approaches The Rainbow, the narrative pace at the end of Chapter 5 slows to the largo of a lazy village public house. The narrative drive leads us to expect that the beginning of Chapter 6 will continue with the arrival of Silas, but in fact we have a whole chapter whereby we eavesdrop upon public-house chatter about cows and choir-singing.

From textual historical evidence, it is likely that this Chapter 6 was an afterthought.[6] The aimless conversation is certainly not crucial from the narrative point of view, nor is the chapter as a whole, since Silas does not even appear in it. Emotionally it is not essential since Silas's isolation from the community has already been made perfectly clear, and a cynical reader may even feel that he has done well to avoid such company. By illustrating the usual evening routine it does show precisely into what kind of culture Silas is to be immersed. It could clearly have been omitted, especially since the softening of Raveloe towards him occurs in the following chapter, when, after Silas has told of his misfortune, they see him as someone prone to the trials and tribulations of ordinary mortals, but this is still not necessary from the narrative point of view since the subsequent raising of Eppie is more than sufficient in itself to ensure his future within the community.

We can assume that the chapter was necessary for other reasons. The broad view it offers of the lower strata of Raveloe society is what 'anchors' both Silas and the novel. It contrasts with the scenes of upper-society revelry – a couple of parties – full of their own brand of inanity. At the end of the novel, when Godfrey declares to Silas and Eppie that he is in fact Eppie's father and that he and his (second) wife would now like to make amends by taking her into their home, Eppie rejects them, preferring to live amongst plain, hard-working, rustic folk. The higher Raveloe order is thus, in this structural scheme, deemed to be sterile. True growth – and Silas himself uses the image of trees having grown, and the narrator talks of being aware of 'roots' – can only come from proper soil, such as Silas's unconditional love, and the support of the community at large (with its heart at The Rainbow). Godfrey's failure to acknowledge his marriage or child damn him from the outset.

It is the life of the village public house which more than anything else represents the older, communal England in the face of those modern, materialist pressures hovering outside. When Silas's gold is stolen the only place he can think of going to is The Rainbow. Once there, and once he has told his story of the lost money, Raveloe folds him into their concerns. They debate at length the possibilities of how the money could possibly have gone. David Carroll comments:

> the lengthy discussion there about the existence of ghosts runs, in its own idiomatic way, through the whole gamut of arguments, from historical evidence, experience, experiment, to analogy and belief. Similarly, the debate over Silas's lost gold is a parody of the continuing contemporaneous disputes in theology and history over the nature of evidence and its interpretation. But here in Raveloe the village consensus is always achieved through the ritual of debate, argument, disagreement and reconciliation; and it is by this means that the approved version of the legend of Silas Marner is eventually established in the community.[7]

Whilst dealing with this process of myth-making, of accommodating what is singular into accepted patterns of (folk) thought, Eliot observes that newer ideas or faiths discard this kind of past at their own peril. The Rainbow community, symbolising as it does the whole spectrum of (male) community life (the upper classes drink there as well as the lower – in fact, they cannot find a life elsewhere in the early part of the novel), represents the roots of England. Structurally, the close of the book is like that of *Barnaby Rudge*. We end with the future, that is, the marriage of Eppie, Silas's foster child, and family life – it returns us to the community of The Rainbow, for the wedding guests end up there for their celebration. This implies that the old idea of community, 'the roots', is centred in the village drinking house. It is also an implicit recognition that it functions as this kind of institution for working out its communal (local) myths, as opposed to the received myths of the church (Silas notices how godless the community is compared to the one at Lantern Yard). For all the portrayals of the regulars at both The Maypole and The Rainbow as limited intellects prone to folk world views, these views are also portrayed – for all their lack of scientific rigour – as 'common sense' in the older meaning of 'communal sense', that is, understanding as validated by the majority.

Felix Holt

> 'But, Sir, to judge of these things a man must know the English voter and the English publican.'

Silas Marner was not the first piece in which Eliot had found use for the inn. In a narrative which is concerned with the effects of a drunken husband, 'Janet's Repentance' in *Scenes of Clerical Life* begins significantly at the Red Lion. It is a convenient place to introduce the male characters of the village, expose the ideological horizons (this time concerning religion) of its citizens, and contrast the past with the present. But it is perhaps in *Felix Holt* (1866), a work which embodies features of both her own *Silas Marner* and Dickens's *Barnaby Rudge*, where Eliot most significantly moulded a narrative around drinking houses.

The body of the story concerns the young man of the title, a watch-maker enthused with Radical ideas who devotes his life to improving the lives of the working classes. His Radicalism is contrasted with that of the Liberal candidate whose family is part of the local aristocracy. The woman who has to choose between the man who has avowed eternal poverty for himself and the rich man who would be a Member of Parliament is Esther. The dramatic climax of the novel occurs, as in *Barnaby Rudge*, when the protagonist gets caught up in a drunken mob riot, although in this instance it is at an election, and is jailed for four years for manslaughter. The narrative similarities to *Silas Marner* are many. Like Eppie, Esther discovers she is a foster-child, and, also like Eppie, that she can lay claim to wealth. Her response to the latter also follows in Eppie's footsteps when she rejects the offer of riches in favour of the nobler life of the lower classes.[8]

The historical context of the novel is that the election in Treby Magna takes place just after the Reform Act of 1832, and the novel gives the event's significance a broad historical sweep. The epigram to Eliot's own Introduction to the novel is from Drayton's *Polyolbion*, an early seventeenth-century chorographical poem – that is, a historical mapping of England and Wales.⁹ The epigram automatically suggests an older version of England, and a foil against which the events of the novel and the state of Reform England can be viewed. After the epigram the Introductory text begins with a discussion of the passing away of the once great coaching inns. The juxtaposition of lines from Drayton with a paragraph on England in the days before the railroad had arrived therefore links the picture of England at the time of the Reform Act with Tudor and Stuart times: 'Five-and-thirty years ago the glory had not yet departed from the old coach roads: the great roadside inns were still brilliant with well-polished tankards, the smiling glances of pretty barmaids, and the repartees of jocose ostlers.'¹⁰ Pre-Reform England therefore has a direct link with olde England, although this is far from an unqualified nostalgic endorsement of the imagined national past we have seen in other writers, and given Eliot's comments early on in her career on the false picture often painted of rural life with its 'jovial farmers', some of its tongue is in its cheek. But it offers up these golden years nevertheless, balanced against what is thankfully departed from the past – 'pocket boroughs', an unrepresented Birmingham, 'unrepealed corn-laws'.¹¹

Eliot proceeds to offer her own prose chorography by imagining a journey with a coachman. The horror of modern life is forcefully rendered when the coachman, now bitter at the predominance of trains, finds the appropriate image for a nation desolated: '"Why, every inn on the road would be shut up!" and at that word the coachman looked before him with the blank gaze of one who had driven his coach to the outermost edge of the universe, and saw his leaders plunging into the abyss.'¹² But we are also made aware of the miners in the landscape, men who, significantly, are not dependent upon landowners for their livelihood. They spend their high wages at the alehouse with their friends from the Benefit Club. Pre-Reform England is both olde England and a newer industrial England, although the latter will carry over into the England post-1832. The language of the prose suggests that there is something comforting about the old coaching inns of customary England, whilst there is something distinctly undesirable about the resorts of the newer workers – 'high' wages can only mean that the miners are paid over and above what their labour deserves. Their spending of it at the alehouse is reminiscent of the eighteenth-century arguments against luxury. Too much money can only lead to idle drunkenness.

These subtexts are fully explored in a chapter which, as with The Rainbow in *Silas Marner*, uses as a centre-piece a drinking place. Chapter 11 starts with an image of Felix walking on a Sunday afternoon to the hamlet of Sproxton. His walk takes him across Sir Maximus Debarry's Park, some common ground, and the rest of the journey alongside a canal. There is a subtle mapping of the various spaces: the olde England land of Debarry, the 'common' land of the people, and the mark of commerce amidst meadows and pastures, its more recent, industrial aspect emphasised by the remark that this branch of the canal leads straight to the coal-pits (and Eliot's audience would probably have known that the canal's main trunk was linked to London, the centre of power).

After sketching England's chequered land, Sproxton is then mapped through the public houses there. The main house is known as Chubb's, after the landlord, but also as the Sugar Loaf or the New Pits. The latter name indicates its recent centrality to the district. The narrator contrasts this with another 'nucleus', the Old Pits, a place much less frequented. A third hostelry exists, the Blue Cow, inferior to both but 'equal, of course, in the fundamental attributes of humanity, such as a desire for beer, but not equal in ability to pay for it'.[13]

Eliot then leaves Holt in the background and uses Chubb as an example of how the new voting system continues to have a number of weaknesses. Chubb's character is assassinated. He is not the jovial host of the Bonniface type, but a 'thin, sallow' somewhat emotionless man. The implication is then that this is not olde England inn territory, but a newer, cheerless version, coincident with Reform. The character assassination continues. Chubb is a man who has chosen to run the Sugar Loaf as his easiest employment option, speculating that a 'public' in the middle of the miners' high wages cannot fail but do well. It is made clear that Chubb himself has an aversion to 'proper' work. Secondly, he is shown to be of limited intellectual ability – everything in his mind is either an 'idee' or 'humbug'.[14] Worryingly for the novel, this man, as a forty-shilling freeholder, now has the vote.[15]

If the type of landlord has changed in the age of Reform, from the olde England version to a less attractive modern version, more seriously, the mode of patronage has also changed. A landlord would at one time have probably been bound to the local landowner, in the time of customary obligation, but now Chubb's rent goes to the same company that runs the pit. Even though paying rent to a landowner amounted to a cash contract, its olde England image had the patina of giving the lord his due in return for paternalist guardianship. Paying rent to a coal company can be nothing other than the new capitalist mode, with the cash nexus the only consideration. Furthermore, this manner of affairs affects the way Chubb will vote. His philosophical-political outlook, again no doubt in keeping with the capitalist times, is that the state works for the benefit of the individual, and the individual in this instance is Chubb. Chubb looks about to see who can upset his life the most, and it is the middleman for the company, Peter Garstin. Hence Chubb will cast his vote according to this criterion, for the Whigs (although see below).

Election corruption is compounded when Chubb learns, from a cousin who runs a drinking house in another county (as if all such knowledge comes through the inns and pubs), that even non-voters can be useful at 'Nominations and Elections'. With characteristic humour, the narrator observes: 'He approved of that; it entered into his political "idee"; and indeed he would have been for extending the franchise to this class – at least in Sproxton. If any one had observed that you must draw a line somewhere, Mr Chubb would have concurred at once, and would have given permission to draw it at a radius of two mile from his own tap.'[16] This is all a far cry from the halcyon days of roadside inns painted in the Introduction, and is a harsh measure of England's transformation into a middle-class nation.

Another change is identified by way of the activities of Felix Holt. The landlord is convinced that Felix is an electioneering agent from Felix's past visits to his pub. Felix's actual mission at the Sugar Loaf is to convince the miners to go to a meeting on Saturday where he will attempt to persuade them that they should give up some of their drinking in favour of education, especially for the education of their children. His idea is that they could club together to pay for a schoolteacher. This is a distinct difference from the ideological battles we have previously seen fought out in the drinking house. The overriding aim here is not religious, or moral, or even essentially political (in the narrower sense). The fact that the miners are spending their money in the alehouse is not a sign of moral turpitude or idle labour, they are simply not making the most of their lives. It is the great nineteenth-century aim of self-improvement, a motive sometimes imposed from above by the middle classes, but also very much a part of certain sections of the working classes. This, I think, distinguishes *Felix Holt*'s use of the drinking place from those in *Silas Marner* and *Barnaby Rudge*. Although Eliot was probably mainly drawing upon Samuel Bamford's *Passages in the Life of a Radical* (1840),[17] which she read in preparation for this novel, she may also have had in mind the life of the Radical Francis Place.[18] The pamphlet he published – *Improvement of the Working People: Drunkenness – Education* (1834), in which the two are obviously contrasted as mutually exclusive, is precisely the social problem Felix tackles. In any case, Felix's vision of improvement of the working classes is clearly within this nineteenth-century paradigm.

The landlord indulges Felix in conversation, even though Felix does not drink much. Chubb tries to sound him out for his political affiliations, and declares himself to be an independent (since he lives on nobody's land) and will vote for the one who treats him the 'handsomest'.[19] This connection between drink and electioneering we have seen already in *Pickwick Papers*. The link has now been brought to Sproxton since it has recently entered into the election process, following the Reform. One miner has heard that free beer is to be had during the approach to elections.[20]

The election agent for Harold Transome, Mr Johnson, appears at Chubb's, and after some private dialogue with Chubb in the parlour, emerges to 'treat' the whole place. For the customers, this is the first real sign that the election has come to Sproxton.[21] Felix exits the place before he loses his temper at Johnson's particular line of Radicalism, which has no real interest in the miners' welfare (such as education) and Johnson goes on to promise beer and free holidays if his man gets in. Although non-voters, he says that the miners of Sproxton can help his man – Transome – by 'hurrahing' him when necessary. He emphasises that if Transome gets in, 'it will be the better for every good fellow who takes his pot at the Sugar Loaf'.[22] The issue of treating sets the scene for the riot at the election, by the drunken mob supportive of Harold Transome.

Chubb's has a clientele of a definite social caste, and the use of a single space helps to consolidate the idea that these men represent in toto one particular element. The novel is quite fond of chess metaphors, and so what Chubb's represents can be seen as a chess piece in the election game. The build-up of pieces through drinking-houses continues when Eliot contrasts the different hostelries to delineate the social players and political parties involved. At the apex, but possibly 'old' apex, is the Marquis of Granby, a Tory house. Even those who have changed their political colours are not able to give up the good food there – another sign of the reality behind the political rhetoric. Other places in the market town are mentioned. The poorer farmers stay at The Ram Inn and the Seven Stars. (When the electioneering moves to Duffield the novel again uses different houses to distinguish the different alliances: Crown for Debarry; Three Cranes for Garstin; Fox and Hounds for Transome.)[23] The Ram is also contrasted to the Marquis as more 'plebeian' with respect to the 'venerable Marquis of Granby'.[24] The nature of the 'plebeian' as a political force is picked up in a scene where the hustings are played out in front of this hostelry, whilst the Tory crowd congregates about the Marquis. The social distinctions attached to these drinking places thereby become markers of political ideology, as if the newer politics is a lower-class politics. The Marquis is the place where the higher echelons of society mix, and in one chapter Eliot uses it, as she had used the Red Lion in 'Janet's Repentance' and The Rainbow in *Silas Marner*, to allow a conversation to proceed which throws up various shades of opinion about issues relevant to the novel. In *Silas Marner* it had been the different interpretative models available to a community, here it is the different political opinions.[25]

When the riot comes, the mob's reign over space is similar to that in the riot scene in *Barnaby Rudge*, although the focus in *Felix Holt* on public-house space is much greater. The Seven Stars is attacked and laid waste after the Riot Act has been read out from The Ram. The final target for the mob is Treby Manor, just as the Warren had been in *Barnaby*, the symbol of olde England, of inherited privilege. Felix is found guilty, and whilst he is in prison the novel switches to the blossoming romance between Harold Transome and Esther Lyon. Structurally, the novel moves from the public space (often symbolised by the 'public' house) to the private sphere of domesticity. Drinking houses fall by the wayside after the riot. But drink has clearly been the problem, and specifically the drunken lower classes on high wages. At one point in the novel, where Felix explicates his Radical ideology, he explains that it is not simply good enough to extend the franchise to one and all, since an uneducated voter can only produce harm. The analogy he uses is plain enough: Felix labours the point that a drunken majority of voters gives the wrong kind of power in comparison to the minority of sober voters.[26] The implications for the rest of the novel's politics are evident; a vote is only as good as the education of the voter, hence the running battle between drink and education that Felix fights and that the novel's movement – towards a drunken climax, to be replaced thereafter by the story of Esther's romantic turmoil – reinforces.

Sobriety and drunkenness are built into the complex legal plot that dominates much of the novel. Esther's claim to the Transome estate comes into play when the last in the Transome line, the old 'tosspot' Tommy Trounsem, dies in the riot, drunk.[27] (Even the transformation of the name, from Transome to Trounsem, suggests a certain inebriety.) The move from the public first part of the novel, where drunkenness is a general trait of a certain section of the working class, to the private space of the second half, is therefore effected through the life of the significantly named drunk. There is a certain sense of poetic justice in that Harold loses his estate because the last in the family line is a drunkard. Harold is partly culpable for the riots since, even though aware of the actions of his election agents in their encouragement of drunken support, he has done little to prevent it. The poetic justice works at the structural level of social comment within the book as well. Julian Transome's original legal provisions to ensure continuity for his estate, no doubt partly an insurance against the kind of dissolution his son engaged in, actually works to good effect some hundred years down the line, when the (eventually) worthy Esther is set to inherit the estates with the failure of the drunken Transomes/Trounsems. Since the last in the line is Tommy Trounsem, there is a clear echo of the original family prodigal, Thomas Transome. However, the rejection of such inheritance by Esther suggests that these are games for the dissolute upper classes. Esther and Felix, united in the end, represent the middle way between this latter society and the high-earning (that is, in their own sense, luxurious and dissolute) working classes. Esther and Felix represent the respectable working class that is satisfied with its life of thrift and hard work. These symbolic counters are best embodied in Felix's vocation. He is a watch-maker. More than his radical persona, perhaps, his vocation (with its Protestant associations) gives the underlying ideology – the sense of purpose and good works is manifest in the proper attention to time, as opposed to the variations of idle time that both the end of the Transome line – down to public-house drinking – and drink and drinking houses in general, represent.

The Mayor of Casterbridge

> 'I don't drink,' he said in a low, halting, apologetic voice. 'You hear, Susan? – I don't drink now – I haven't since that night.' Those were his first words.

The role of time redeemed, and the symbolic uses of drinking houses, are evident in Thomas Hardy's *The Mayor of Casterbridge* (1886). They are more closely and complexly interwoven into the text than in *Felix Holt* because 'drink' itself is cast as one of the major players in the novel. The century's medical and social background against which *The Mayor of Casterbridge* might be seen is particularly acute for the novel, since, although set sometime in the past, Henchard's problem with drink is an intriguing mix of the social, medical, philosophical and psychological outlook of the time of Hardy's writing. Whilst it could be argued that the novels by Dickens and Eliot which I have discussed also fall within this historical context, the psychological aspects of Henchard's case coupled with ideas of work-discipline (which are not overtly present in these other nineteenth-century novels) give leeway for thinking of it as a treatment more in tune with the effect social change had on drinking houses and their representation, although superficially any of the hostelries in *Casterbridge* could (arguably) have appeared in these other novels.

The story of Henchard in *The Mayor of Casterbridge* is a simple temperance narrative whose outline would have been familiar fare to the public ever since the temperance movement had taken off in the 1820s. The moral of such stories was always the same, and those we have seen time and time again: drunkenness would lead to disease, poverty and despair, whereas sobriety, thrift and hard work would lead to rewards. Why the drink problems of the nineteenth century should have led to the creation of a very powerful campaigning movement, whereas the drink problems of the eighteenth century prompted no such general response, is a question for social historians, but the fact is that people in the nineteenth century would have been bombarded with literature about the evils of drink, and that, even though the arguments were similar to those of the eighteenth century, there was an environment which was more receptive to them. Dickens's early skit on a temperance meeting in *Pickwick Papers* (seen in the last chapter) is a good indication of how quickly the temperance movement took hold.

It was in 1830 that the Beer Act came into force and exacerbated any existing problems with drink and drunkenness. For the price of two guineas paid to the Excise anyone could sell beer. This was not simply a freeing up of trade for the sake of *laissez-faire* economic philosophy, it was in part a measure to control the consumption of alcohol through encouraging people to switch from spirits to weaker alcoholic beverages. If beer were sold separately, people would not get so drunk, so the thinking went. It would also, according to the free-traders, 'advance morality' and 'national prosperity',[29] and would even help promote democracy.[30] Another factor behind the Beer Act may have been an attempt to win popularity for a faltering government.[31] It was also seen as a gesture towards the ending of hierarchical privilege – the tax on beer then seen as an indirect tax on the poor, as Thomas Paine had once complained.[32] Before the Act came into force the licensing system gave magistrates sole control over the renewal of licences each year, a power that was seen as an outdated preserve of the upper classes which some thought should be overturned.[33]

For the rest of the century the drink question vexed Victorian society, embodying the age's struggle to come to terms with itself, the desire to control free trade in beer not the least of the parodoxes generated. If there was an argument that tax on alcohol hit the poor in the same way that expensive bread did, the Chartists could later argue that the government reduced taxes on alcohol to keep the working classes drinking rather than thinking[34] (which is Felix Holt's belief); if it could be argued that drinking was good for the economy 'and would save English agriculture',[35] it could also be argued by temperance reformers that the trade in drink led to 'trade depression'.[36] For the medical profession, intemperance might be the cause of ninety per cent of all insanity, or, conversely, 'there was a direct correlation between the amount of beer and wine insane patients consumed and the speed of their recovery'.[37] Temperance reformers blamed moral failing when someone turned to drink, whereas the socialists blamed the poverty-stricken environment, and thus absolved individual responsibility. In turn the socialists had to answer the argument that drinking was at its most virulent when times were most prosperous.[38] The temperance movement itself became riven with opposing aims and philosophies, especially that between the 'moral suasionists', who had given the main impetus to the movement in the 1830s, and 'the legal suppressionists' ('prohibitionists'), whose United Kingdom Alliance for the Suppression of the Traffic in all Intoxicating Liquours (UKA) was formed in 1853. For the UKA it was the government's duty to stop the trade in drink, in other words, it was primarily a legal issue, although it is also true that they could argue the government shirked its moral responsibility by not prohibiting drink traffic. For the moral suasionists, on the other hand, it was a question of individual agency. As Joseph Livesey, founder of the English Total Abstinence Movement put it, 'the evil is in the drink, not in the trade'. Although the effect upon legislation by the activities of the temperance movement was not great, its power filtered through in other ways, (adversely) powerful enough by the end of the century to contribute (allegedly) to the defeat of the Liberal Party in 1895, after the Liberals had formally aligned themselves with the temperance campaigners in 1890.[39] Before then the argument had not been drawn up along party lines, although even in 1874 Gladstone was blaming drink for his defeat at the general election.[40]

We have seen that, notwithstanding the kind of drunkenness associated with dram-drinking, the drunkenness of the eighteenth century attracted little reproof. According to Lilian Lewis Shiman the change in attitude arose in the nineteenth century, where 'The "work discipline" concept brought into being by industrialisation transformed drunkenness from a personal state of excess sociability into an anti-social vice'[41] (although, as we have seen, the introduction of new work patterns and ideology had been emerging since the Reformation; it might be more accurate to say that industrial capitalism accelerated the transformation). The change in attitude towards drunkenness is identifiable in novels. Indeed, Mairi McCormick turns to fiction for a record of first depictions of alcoholics because they are not available in medical records. 'First representations of the gamma alcoholic in the English novel' can be found in fiction from 1830 onwards, whereas gamma alcoholism was still not recognised 'in 1850 by the learned professions',[42] although it should be noted that at the beginning of the century Thomas Trotter's *An Essay Medical, Philosophical, and Chemical on Drunkenness and its Effects on the Human Body* (1804) discussed the physical and psychological effects of habitual drinking, as well as the treatment of it, in a manner very close to the concept of alcoholism McCormick is drawing upon.[43]

Elsewhere, John Peck notes the change in attitude towards drink and drunkenness occurring within the space of a few years. Thackeray's 1848 novel *Vanity Fair*, 'an astonishing drinks manual of the early nineteenth century', 'seems entirely free of any air of moral condemnation' amongst all of the drinking, whereas *The Newcomes*, published only seven years later, is on the defensive, thanks to the general change in social attitudes.[44] The social consequences of habitual drunkenness upon the lives of characters involved becomes more realistically integrated into narratives. Anne Brontë's *The Tenant of Wildfell Hall* (1848) covers the life of a mother and child attempting to escape a drunken, physically abusive husband. The heroine of Eliot's 'Janet's Repentance' is likewise seen escaping a brutish, sottish husband, whilst Janet herself has turned to alcohol to numb her sensibilities. Eventually Janet breaks free, and with the help of a saintly evangelist stops drinking. If Janet fits within a scheme of forgiveness, Dickens shows that for some there is no stronger resentment than towards those who have blighted a life through drink. Jenny Wren's fantasy of revenge upon her drunken father in *Our Mutual Friend* (1864–65) is to imagine her father asleep as she spoons boiling liquor into his gaping mouth.[45] For sheer horror at drunkenness, as if prose had taken a hundred years to catch up with Hogarth's pictorial skills, Charles Kingsley's *Alton Locke* (1850) has the hero, whilst in the depths of despair, dragged to a drunkard's house, only to see the man's neglected wife and children dead and in the process of being eaten by rats. We are in no doubt that this is the evil that Chartism is fighting: 'Ugh! it was the very mouth of hell, that room.'[46]

As well as the role of the state in trade and morality, drunkenness in the nineteenth century was also a distinctly class issue, as has already been suggested. The temperance movement is (and was) often seen as a body which foisted middle-class interests upon the lower classes. More accurately, there was an alliance between certain sections of the middle classes and the respectable working classes as regards temperance, with a kind of closing of the circle whereby the debauched leisure classes were on a par with the lower orders when it came to loutish drinking habits[47] (perhaps an implication in *Felix Holt*, ironically conflated in the figure of Tommy Trounsem, who is both dissolute upper class and dissolute lower class). But with the Drink Question what was also at stake was the limit of reason: 'as rationalistic movements growing out of the enlightenment, abstainers and free licensers had fears in common: of traditionalist class privilege (consolidated through the licensing system), and of urban populations maddened by gin'.[48] The use of reason meant that anything connected with the old, medieval hierarchy had to go, and that the masses should be kept within reason at all times – hence the ban on alcohol at the Great Exhibition in 1851, 'following pressure from temperance campaigners'.[49] Drunkenness and insanity were also quite commonly linked, most likely because the symptoms were regarded as similar.[50] Why would a rational person drink, when all it could lead to was 'crime, pauperism, disease, insanity'?[51]

The increased role of social engineering in the nineteenth century can be seen as the application of reason to society; an appeal to individual agency in a world which, as it became more anonymous for any one individual, was now tending to grant psychological uniqueness to those very same individuals. Coupled with this is the nineteenth-century belief that moral and financial well-being were compatible and achievable through self-discipline. The issue of drink sets us firmly and squarely into the middle of discussions concerning industrialisation, class perception and the rise of mass entertainment. For Brian Harrison in *Drink and the Victorians* 'the history of the temperance movement … [is] of the greatest historical interest if one wishes to understand how we differ from the Victorians'.[52] He also points out that 'Whereas the twentieth century idolizes "heroes of consumption", the nineteenth idolized "heroes of abstinence".'[53] It is in the midst of this nineteenth-century temperance context that we might look at *The Mayor of Casterbridge*.

The narrator of Hardy's novel informs us towards the end that Casterbridge has for many years been an assize town.[54] In the course of the novel's events it is the nature of man that is measured in Casterbridge, as one might do with bread and ale – the two are linked in the minds of the Casterbridge inhabitants, as when someone tells Susan Henchard 'There's less good bread than good beer in Casterbridge now'[55] – and Hardy's measure of man is his measure of Henchard. In its own way, then, *The Mayor of Casterbridge* is a measure of Victorian society, and Hardy has used the framework of what appears to be a straightforward temperance narrative with which to do it. Henchard's drunkenness leads to the break-up of the family unit, literally, when he sells his wife at a fair after too much to drink. He repents, swears to abstain from strong liquor, and subsequently becomes a successful business man who enjoys the high social status in the local community that this brings. His later decline is exacerbated by his return to drink. Nothing could be more certain. Drink is the ruin of domesticity and prosperity, whereas temperance enables a man to devote his energies to the pursuit of wealth, respectability and high moral standing. How accurate is this interpretation?

We can provisionally discount the temperance interpretation that would see the initial scenario as a case where the husband's drinking is to blame for the family's poverty since Henchard has in fact come looking for work. That Henchard does drink is made clear, but it is also stated later that Henchard 'had been given to bouts only, and was not a habitual drunkard'.[56] The fact that Henchard is not an alcoholic places him firmly within the social fabric rather than making him a more extreme case, that of the addict. This is especially so since, as Barr notes, '[agricultural] work was sporadic and seasonal, and [the workers] had tended to fill in the gaps with drink. They did not take regular holidays, but indulged in random drinking sprees.'[57] It is also worth noting that Susan takes a milder version of the rum-laced furmity when Henchard drinks at the fair, without the same consequent desire to drink until drunk; in other words, the liquor is not seen as inherently addictive.[58] Nor is this the result of the trade in drink itself. The first tent is licensed whereas the second provides smuggled spirit, a state of affairs suggesting that no matter what, people will want to drink and that there will be ways and means to drink regardless of the law of the land. It also scotches the idea that by making alternative refreshments available (as the temperance movement often advocated) the desire for drink can be displaced. There is neither a defence of drink nor a castigation of drink, yet drink lies at the heart of the story.

The morning after selling his wife Henchard regrets his actions, but before searching for her he wishes to register an oath, 'a greater oath than he had ever sworn before: and to do it properly he required a fit place and imagery; for there was something fetichistic in this man's beliefs'.[59] The fit place is the church where he declares 'I, Michael Henchard ... do take an oath before God here in this solemn place that I will avoid all strong liquors for the space of twenty-one years to come, being a year for every year that I have lived. And this I swear upon the book before me.'[60] The oath is rough and ready but does suggest an acquaintance with temperance oaths,[61] but it is also similar in its combination of elements – revelry, repentance, redemption – with Hal's rejection of his former life.

There is the notion embedded in Henchard's action that by abstaining for exactly the same time period he has already lived he is in some way redeeming time, making himself morally useful. By making himself morally useful he is thus symbolically placed at the centre of Victorian society, since, as Harrison argues, the Victorians placed stress on 'individual moral effort'.[62] Henchard's act is symbolically central in another way. It has been argued that the rise of capitalism shifted the state's understanding of time into a conceptualisation which was (is) antagonistic to personal time (or the older, task-oriented agricultural time). In redeeming time there is a sense in which Henchard is allying himself with industrial capitalism (and the same could be argued about Felix Holt).[63] Further to this, the refusal to drink takes him out of the pattern of behaviour where drinking had been essential to social bonding in 'pre-industrial artisan society' and into the 'purely market economy' of industrialisation.[64] The swearing of the oath in a church gives the story some religious context, and follows the narrative paradigm of 'abstinence' campaigners by offering paradise on earth after the repentance of the sinner.[65] Initially what is at issue, it seems, is the question of character, and since we are at this point in the essay dealing with the measure of man, we might analyse Henchard's character in some detail.

There are a number of ways of looking at the 'idea' of 'man' at this period. There is the residual idea of universal man, with his universal faults, essentially the 'classic ideal', with states of affairs to a large extent preordained. Arguably, however, the dominant notion is that of man as an autonomous agent, with his life in his own hands (Protestantism). And then there is the emerging notion of man as a product of his environment (the socialist view). We might see a mixture of all three in the novel. The world the characters inhabit is fatalistic in tone, the drama of human affairs played out in an indifferent universe. Hardy even places some of the action in a Roman amphitheatre as if to underscore the point. But against this there also appears to be a sense in which people have their futures in their own hands, as in the success of Donald Farfrae, Henchard's friend turned rival. The narrator puts part of this success down to Farfrae's background, northern energy against a more easy-going south. But it is 'with the instinct of a perverse character' that Henchard espies the furmity woman's trick of lacing the drinks with something stronger.[66] Why should this be perverse? It is as if Henchard deliberately seeks out what is not natural or, possibly, what the order of things hides, as if he wants to go against what is natural. But whether 'character' is 'natural' or not is a moot point. The narrator states: 'Character is Fate, said Novalis, and Farfrae's character was just the reverse of Henchard's, who might not inaptly be described as Faust has been described – as a vehement gloomy being who had quitted the ways of vulgar men without light to guide him on a better way'.[67] According to the narrative's logic Henchard's character is his destiny, and it is thus his perversity which will determine his life.[68]

The drinking leads him to sell his wife, which, although he has talked about doing before, he has never done. Here it would seem that drink is very much to blame since it is the spur for an action that has only been a 'harmless' jest in the past. But as a drinking man he is also very much a part of his culture. It is the consequent renunciation of drink which sets him apart from the rest of Casterbridge. In other words, his refusal to drink is what makes him so unusual, a genuine sign of his perversity. Drinking is the norm, as the amount of time spent in the public houses in Casterbridge attests to. There is a grim irony at work. Henchard swears his pledge in a church, before God. He is making his pact with God to abstain, which contrasts with the Faustian reference attached to him and the implication of a pact with the Devil. The logic of this would be that, indeed, as temperance reformers consistently argued, drink is evil.

Hardy then skips the next nineteen years when Henchard becomes prosperous and mayor and magistrate. The good times, under God's aegis, are of no interest. What does interest the author (and us) is watching Henchard slide back to destitution. During these nineteen years Henchard has mastered his own perversity. He has been the Victorian ideal man of action, raising himself up from nothing, the autonomous agent. It is as if the novel is saying the Victorian dream of the hero as self-made man is possible, and to reiterate the point Farfrae does the same. Nor does the latter have to go to America to make his fortune as was his original plan. More importantly, he has not had to renounce drink. On the one hand Hardy gives us a picture of men who can take their lives in their own hands and prosper, rise to the top, that is, the Victorian ideal masculine self-image, but on the other hand he can show that for no good reason at all prosperity is in the lap of the gods. Now of course this might simply be chalked up to Hardy's pessimism, fatalism or scepticism, depending on which shade we prefer, and I would not argue against this. But in addition I think we might also pick out something else. By renouncing drink Henchard also renounces his society. It has been argued that the kind of personality which had the strength to carry out such an oath also had the kind of will power to succeed in business.[69] But such will power is not natural to Henchard since he must hold down his natural (drinking) character in order to persevere in the world of successful commerce.[70]

In some ways, the universe's indifference to human striving is mirrored in the narrative's attitude to drink and the nature of drink. Henchard's lot is not much different from others when we first meet him, and it is noteworthy that we do not find out his name until he swears the oath (the morning after the night before he wonders whether he gave his name out to the crowd in the tent and is relieved to remember he had not[71]). He is thus not named as an individual self until he goes against his natural self, that is, he is not a unique individual until he has transformed his being into a kind of self-consciousness, or consciousness of the self of Michael Henchard. By naming himself as an abstainer he separates himself from his immediate society. His first words to Susan on their reunion are 'I don't drink', the one guarantee he can give to his wife that he has changed character. Drink is throughout symbolic of his volcanic nature, since its own effects are unstable, and to renounce this is to renounce his nature. In contemplating what might have happened to Henchard before she finds out he is still alive, Susan thinks: 'He had possibly drunk himself into his tomb. But he might, on the other hand, have had too much sense to do so' because he was not 'a habitual drunkard'.[72] It is in his nature to be inconsistent since consistency would mean being habitually drunk or a teetotaller. Stirling Haig believes that rather than the characters being fixed, as 'character is fate' would suggest, 'the characters are portrayed in a constant state of suspension marked by fluidity and rootlessness'[73] and traces this in the motif of 'water' used throughout the novel. He makes the interesting observation that 'Henchard is either up or down, which is to say *dry* or *wet*'.[74] For our own purposes we can see that this is in accord with the idea of trying to fix life in some way (through the Victorian archetype rather than giving in to the vagaries of self). To be dry (sober) is to be fixed, to be wet is to be prey to contingency. But I also think it points to the distinction between character and self. The former is 'assumed' by Henchard as he rises to the top, the latter is what he emerges from and slips back into. Character is fate only in the sense that if Henchard adopts a Victorian character his fate is sealed (he becomes the successful business man), but without character he is back with his existential, contingent self – fluid, 'wet'. It is perhaps the novel's own confusion between 'character' and 'self' that has led to the many discussions on the significance of the narrator's comment that 'character is fate'.

With respect to self rather than character, late on in the narrative we are given a small insight into the novel's view of the psychology of the mind, and this also helps explain why drink may or may not be regarded as 'evil' in the novel and the society it describes. When Henchard discovers that Elizabeth-Jane is to marry the one man he would wish her not to, Farfrae, he thinks of wrecking the whole plan by telling Farfrae that Elizabeth is 'legally, nobody's child'. Such information in a society built upon respectability would be devastating. This is how the narrator understands human psychology: 'There is an outer chamber of the brain in which thoughts unowned, unsolicited, and of noxious kind, are sometimes allowed to wander for a moment prior to being sent off whence they came. One of these thoughts sailed into Henchard's ken now.' Henchard dismisses it with: 'God forbid such a thing! Why should I still be subject to these visitations of the devil, when I try so hard to keep him away?'.[75] It is evident that Henchard's struggle with moral self-worth is a struggle with what he chooses to see as the work of the Devil, the temptation to do evil. The temperance oath has thus been part of this longer struggle. Looking back at his life from this particular psychological viewpoint it can be seen that drink was the catalyst to allow 'these visitations of the devil' to come to the fore, but also the 'twenty-one years' is to be seen as a self-imposed sentence since once it is over he feels he can drink 'with a good conscience'.[76] On the day the pledge is over, Henchard also says that he means 'to enjoy myself', making clear the distinction that business is not pleasure. The twenty-one years thus represent the novel's version of Victorian earnestness.

Hardy has taken what might be seen as the biggest threat and/or temptation to individual will power in Victorian society and shown that that society will neither be dragged down by drink nor dragged up by teetotalism. The intersection of drink and a particular personality might have dire consequences, but even here the argument against drink is not allowed much leeway. The novel refuses to allow drink to be the scapegoat for all society's troubles, as many avowed.

The society that Henchard takes himself out of is quite clearly differentiated along class lines, or, to be more precise, along a hierarchical line of social respectability, through symbolic use of the three public houses, the King's Arms, the Three Mariners, and Peter's Finger.[77] At the top of the heap is the King's Arms. It is here that Susan first sees Henchard when she arrives in Casterbridge, where he is presiding over the Great Public Dinner as mayor. Not only is the hotel at the top of the social ladder, it is representative of what we might call 'official England', associated through its name to the monarchy, through its function to the official business in Casterbridge and, through an 'incidental' descriptive touch, to Englishness: the band is playing 'The Roast Beef of Olde England' directly in front of it.[78] Having risen therefore to the top of middle-class society, Henchard takes his place at the head of Casterbridge's version of the state and monarchy. By redeeming his time into moral time, that is, capitalist time, he gets his just rewards. By turning himself into Victorian man he places himself at the head of Victorian society, at the expense of sociability and pleasure (unofficial Victorian society) as Susan notices his wine glasses are empty.[79] The narrator makes a point of detailing the ritual of social drinking of which Henchard takes no part.[80] It is at this function someone points up that Henchard is responsible for the recent bad wheat/bread in the town and asks what he is to do about it:

> 'But what are you going to do to repay us for the past?' inquired the man who had before spoken, and who seemed to be a baker or miller. 'Will you replace the grown flour we've still got by sound grain?'
> Henchard's face had become still more stern at these interruptions, and he drank from his tumbler of water as if to calm himself or gain time. Instead of vouchsafing a direct reply, he stiffly observed—
> 'If anybody will tell me how to turn grown wheat into wholesome wheat I'll take it back with pleasure. But it can't be done.'[81]

Hardy is piling on the ironies in this section. The lightest hint of irony is the narrator's uncertainty as to whether Henchard takes water to calm himself, in implicit contradistinction to (the missing) alcohol which would inflame him and exacerbate his irascibility, or whether it is used to gain time, and is thus a twist on Henchard's oath to redeem time.

Repaying the past is of course what Henchard's temperance oath represents, the attempt to redeem the past through making himself into a wholesome character. Yet this is in the face of his observation that in nature such a thing is not possible. It is Farfrae who shows him how to restore the overgrown wheat. Henchard declares: 'It's complete!—quite restored, or—well—nearly.' Farfrae returns with: 'Quite enough restored to make good seconds out of it ... To fetch it back entirely is impossible; Nature won't stand so much as that, but heere you go a great way towards it.'[82] There is an implicit warning, that by tampering with nature (Henchard's oath goes against his own nature) there is a limit on how much it is possible to achieve. With Henchard's later reversion to bad ways the novel appears to bear out the observation that nature will only stand so much, that the restoration of a good (Edenic?) nature is only a temporary measure (the significance of Henchard's 'redemptive' oath fittingly in the church suggestive in the light of this of atonement for the Fall). Man's nature is thus more akin to Henchard's pre-oath days, and, by implication, Victorian society's moral worth is, and can only be, 'temporary'.

As the narrative shows Henchard spiritually separate from his social environment through his teetotalism, it also shows how drink bonds that society, showing that the teetotaller's lot is a lonely one. He briefly leaves the dinner at the Hotel to look for Farfrae. When he returns 'The Corporation, private residents, and major and minor tradesmen had, in fact, gone in for comforting beverages to such an extent that they had quite forgotten, not only the Mayor, but all those vast political, religious, and social differences which they felt necessary to maintain in the daytime, and which separated them like iron grills.'[83] So, far from drink being represented as the evil in society, it is the bringer in this instance of a conviviality that crosses all social divides. Henchard at this time is not a part of it.

After Farfrae has passed a message to Henchard to the effect that he knows of a process to restore the taste of grown wheat, Henchard automatically assumes Farfrae has put up at the most respectable place, the King's Arms. However, Henchard is informed that Farfrae has gone to the Three Mariners. The name of the pub itself suggests a more down-to-earth crowd, defined by its homage to an occupation rather than the monarchy, although like the King's Arms it can still claim to be part of English tradition, since it dates back to Elizabethan times. It is also the case that the narrator, in a rare value judgement,[84] approves of the place: 'This ancient house of accommodation for man and beast, now, unfortunately, pulled down,'[85], and further: 'The good stabling and the good ale of the Mariners ... [were] perseveringly sought out by the sagacious old heads who knew what was what in Casterbridge.'[86] 'Inside these illuminated holes [windows], at a distance of about three inches, were ranged at this hour, as every passer knew, the ruddy polls of Billy Wills the glazier, Smart the shoe-maker, Buzzford the general dealer, and others of a secondary set of worthies, of a grade somewhat below that of the diners at the King's Arms, each with his yard of clay.'[87] It is an instance of that listing of occupations we have seen from Langland onwards, a way of showing a 'community'. The complete range of Casterbridge society is given through this place, those attending the public dinner at the King's Arms (and later rounded off with a description of the public house at the lowest end of the social scale, Peter's Finger). What differentiates these from those at the King's Arms, apart from the obvious 'secondary' social standing, is that this is not a special occasion, that these are regulars, frittering away their time without regard for the demands of state or governance. There is no sense of progression, of Enlightenment reason channelled into the success of capitalism, there is only sameness. That the Three Mariners has disappeared by the time the narrative is related perhaps vouchsafes for the disappearance of the older way of life and rhythm that the thrusting Victorian dynamos and their investment in 'time' have usurped, men like the sober Henchard and Farfrae, along with the new machinery. Not only then is drink the great social leveller, as described in the King's Arms, it is the representative, in its middle social setting, of the link with the traditional, unofficial past.

The issue of respectability as crucial to Victorian society is further enhanced in a couple of ways. When Henchard seeks Farfrae in the Three Mariners, he deliberately tones down his appearance before entering. When Elizabeth-Jane and Susan arrive in Casterbridge, on looking for a respectable place they decide to follow Farfrae who himself looks respectable. They must choose somewhere respectable even if they cannot afford it, although there is also the worry that the Three Mariners is not respectable enough and would be an embarrassment to Henchard if he discovered they had stayed there. Once there Elizabeth-Jane has to work to pay off some of the cost of their lodging, a fact that returns to haunt her when her own maid later on brings up the incident to humble her in front of Henchard.

In completing the panoramic view of the social strata of Casterbridge the story finally takes us to the region inhabited by the lower classes, where vice runs freely 'in and out of certain doors of the neighbourhood'.[88] At the heart of it is Mixen Lane, 'the inn called Peter's Finger was the church' – again the connection between religion and alcohol not too metaphorically distant, not the least because 'Peter's Finger' is a religious sign. 'It was centrally situate, as such places should be, and bore about the same social relation to the Three Mariners as the latter bore to the King's Arms.'[89] (There is the suggestion of a joke on Hardy's part, with the main body of people 'the three mariners' and either end of society represented by the body's extremities, arms and fingers.) It is in Peter's Finger where we find that the furmity woman mixes with poachers and others. The narrator observes that nothing has changed in the time that both Henchard and Farfrae have been mayors. It is as if the story has given us the drama of public Victorian society by showing us the only area where it is actually capable of dramatic movement, in the new middling classes, with the upper and lower classes static. (Farfrae has the chance to be a 'gentleman', that is, the opportunity to live off residual wealth thanks to Lucetta's money, but refuses it, as if there were no life there, the only action available being that of monetary mobility and respectability, the cut and thrust of the marketplace.) At the other end, the life of the inhabitants of the Three Mariners appears changeless, as does the kind of life enjoyed by the frequenters of Peter's Finger. Like those who enjoy hereditary wealth, their lives are untouched by the Victorian great and good. Symbolically the function of those linked to Peter's Finger is to disrupt this Victorian edifice. The mere existence of Mixen Lane and Peter's Finger shows a distinct lack of civic progress and the unreachable nature of certain sections of society. We are taken there to show the hatching of the skimmity-ride, an old tradition whereby a couple of worthies are mocked by a ride through town of their effigies. The discovery of love letters between Lucetta and Henchard is the occasion for this year's mockery. It leads to Lucetta's death and Henchard's confrontation with his own image and death when he sees the discarded dummy of himself float past on a river. Hardy also juxtaposes the preparations for the skimmity-ride with the preparations for the royal visit to emphasise the undermining of the received image of what is worthy and what is not. By doing so he closes that social circle whereby the habits of the upper classes are comparable to those of the lower. It is perhaps noticeable that Jopp is distracted from going about his errands by the temptation of the public house, drawn into the idle time that Peter's Finger offers. In all three public houses drink is simply there, and, for better or for worse, it brings their societies together. In a Victorian novel where the overwhelming tone is one of equanimity in the face of human striving, it is perhaps unsurprising that both at the level of character and of social observation, drink is everywhere, yet unfathomable.

Any Victorian looking for a definitive answer to the Drink Question would be stimied by *The Mayor of Casterbridge*, but for other readers it provides an intriguing overview of the interplay between Victorian ideology, psychology and the public house. The one man who ostensibly uses his reason, maintains his 'senses' by not drinking and thus attains 'character' rather than wallowing in an unreconstructed self, fails according to those very criteria which would judge whether he were successful or not. There is no sustained reason in the novel not to drink, although there may be reason enough not to drink to excess; whilst there are plenty of good reasons to take to drink, not least for sociability, serenity, pleasure and social status – all the reasons that those who did use the nineteenth-century pub would instinctively be aware of. Susan drinks, Farfrae drinks, all the worthies drink, and all the lower orders drink. To be seen in a public house can be the sign of greatest achievement – Henchard at the King's Arms – or of social sliding – Henchard's visit to the Three Mariners to find Farfrae; Susan's and

Elizabeth's stay there. Or it can designate mutual membership of the margins of society. The temperance movement did nothing to change these values.

Notes

1 George Eliot, *Silas Marner* (London, Penguin, 1996 [1861]), p. 45.
2 Charles Dickens, *Barnaby Rudge* (London, Penguin, 1997 [1841]), p. 40.
3 Eliot, *Silas*, p. 23.
4 *Ibid.*, p. 45.
5 *Ibid.*, pp. 45 and 46.
6 *Ibid.*, n. 2 to p. 45: 'At this point in the manuscript, a deleted sentence ... suggests that George Eliot only introduced Chapter 6, the lengthy conversation in the Rainbow, as a second thought.'
7 *Ibid.*, Introduction, p. xi.
8 There are other similarities. The disreputable lawyer Jermyn reveals his own fatherhood late in the novel, as Eppie's father does, and Eliot enjoys contrasting the present with the past (or, as discussed below, different pasts).
9 Richard Helgerson's *Forms of Nationhood: The Elizabethan Writing of England* (Chicago, The University of Chicago Press, 1992) discusses this work in detail.
10 George Eliot, *Felix Holt: The Radical* (London, Penguin, 1995 [1866]), p. 3.
11 *Ibid.*
12 *Ibid.*, p. 8.
13 *Ibid.*, p. 127.
14 *Ibid.*, p. 128.
15 *Ibid.*: 'following the 1832 Reform Bill, the main electoral qualifications in the counties were the tenure of a forty-shilling freehold, a £10 copyhold, a £10 leasehold (where the lease was a least sixty years), a £50 leasehold (where the lease was not less than twenty years), and those with tenancy of land or tenements who paid at least £50 a year in rent', n. 1, ch. 10.
16 *Ibid.*, p. 130.
17 *Ibid.*, Lynda Mugglestone, Introduction, p. xviii. Bamford was hardly an abstemious man. There is a story told of him leaving a list of known Radicals with a landlord as guarantee that he would pay his reckoning the following day, something he was sure to redeem. The story appeared in the *Manchester Mercury*, 22 February 1820; W. H. Chaloner's Introduction to *The Autobiography of Samuel Bamford*, vol. 1: *Early Days* (London, Frank Cass, 1967, pp. 17–18).
19 Unfortunately there is not the space to discuss Place in more detail. In his *Autobiography* he often contrasts the more sober 1820s with the drink-sodden 1770s and after: *The Autobiography of Francis Place (1771–1854)*, ed. Mary Thrale (London, Cambridge University Press, 1972). He ascribes the change to better manners and more education amongst the working class partly to his own efforts. As Dudley Miles notes in *Francis Place: The Life of a Remarkable Radical, 1771–1854* (Brighton, Sussex, The Harvester Press, 1988), the attack on Place by E. P. Thompson in *The Making of the English Working Class* (London, Penguin, 1991) marked the downturn in his reputation amongst historians, p. 4.
19 Eliot, *Holt*, p. 132.

20 *Ibid.*, p. 134.
21 *Ibid.*, p. 135.
22 *Ibid.*, p. 141.
23 *Ibid.*, p. 287.
24 *Ibid.*, p. 198.
25 *Ibid.*, pp. 207ff.
26 *Ibid.*, pp. 293–4.
27 The estate had been settled upon the male heirs of the Transomes in 1729 by Julian Transome, but the estate had been sold to the Durfeys by his dissolute son Thomas in order to pay a debt, before he took possession of it. (Harold Transome is in fact a Durfey – the Durfeys simply took on the name of Transome.) However, if the true Transome line ends, to ensure continuity, Julian Transome had ensured that the estates were to go to the Bycliffes, which, it materialises, is what Esther is.
28 A version of this section is published as 'The Reason for Drinking in Hardy's *The Mayor of Casterbridge*' in *Varieties of Victorianism. The Uses of the Past*, ed. Gary Day (Houndmills, Basingstoke, Macmillan, 1998), pp. 142–60.
29 Brian Harrison, *Drink and the Victorians: The Temperance Question in England 1815–1872*, 2nd edition (Keele, Staffordshire, Keele University Press, 1994 [1971]), p. 63.
30 Henry Carter, *The English Temperance Movement: A Study in Objectives* (London, Hogarth Press, 1933), p. 25.
31 Harrison, *Drink*, pp. 72–4.
32 *Ibid.*, p. 69.
33 Carter, *Temperance*, calls the Beer Act a 'Parliamentary Blunder' (p. 16) and 'a disastrous experiment' (p. 18) in that it led to a massive increase in the consumption of drink. Harrison, *Drink*, is much more circumspect, and argues that what figures we do have suggest only a moderate increase in consumption after the Act came into force (pp. 79–80). He argues that the notion of the Beer Act as an unmitigated disaster lies with the *History of Liquor Licensing* (1903) by the Webbs, who for personal reasons were attracted to the 'debauchery theory' (p. 84).
34 Andrew Barr, *Drink: An Informal Social History* (London, Bantam, 1995), pp. 10–11.
35 Carter, *Temperance*, p. 25.
36 Lilian Lewis Shiman, *Crusade against Drink in Victorian England* (Basingstoke and New York, Macmillan and St. Martin's Press, 1988), p. 209.
37 Peter McCandless, '"Curses of Civilization": Insanity and Drunkenness in Victorian Britain', *British Journal of Addiction*, 79 (1984), 51.
38 Shiman, *Crusade*, pp. 209–10.
39 For discussion of the temperance movements see Harrison's *Drink* and Shiman's *Crusade*. Carter's *The English Temperance Movement* is an interesting account biased in favour of the 'moral suasionists' headed by Livesey.
40 Barr, *Drink*, p. 139.
41 Shiman, *Crusade*, p. 2.
42 Mairi McCormick, 'First Representations of the Gamma Alcoholic in the English Novel', *Quarterly Journal of Studies on Alcoholism*, 30 (1969), 959. 'Gamma alcoholism means that species of alcoholism in which (1) acquired increased

tissue tolerance to alcohol, (2) adaptive cell metabolism, (3) withdrawal symptoms and "craving," i.e., physical dependence, and (4) loss of control are involved', E. M. Jellinek, quoted in McCormick, p. 960. The first 'real use of the word' alcoholic is by W. Marcet in 1860 – from John Peck's 'Thackeray and Drink: *Vanity Fair* and *The Newcomes*', *Dionysos*, 4:1 (1992), 18, n. 4.
43 Thomas Trotter, *An Essay Medical, Philosophical, and Chemical on Drunkenness and its Effects on the Human Body*, ed. Roy Porter (London, Routledge, 1988 [1804]).
44 Peck, 'Thackeray', pp. 14 and 16.
45 Charles Dickens, *Our Mutual Friend* (London, Penguin, 1985 [1864–65]), p. 294. In *Hard Times* Dickens gives the hero, Stephen Blackpool, a drunken wife. Resentment is tempered and directed at the class-biased divorce laws, in keeping with the novel's themes.
46 Charles Kingsley, *Alton Locke* (London, Collins, n.d. [1850]), p. 399.
47 Harrison, *Drink*, p. 141.
48 *Ibid.*, p. 63.
49 Barr, *Drink*, pp. 37–8.
50 McCandless, 'Curses', especially pp. 49–50.
51 Joseph Livesey, quoted in Carter, *Temperance*, p. 15.
52 Harrison, *Drink*, p. 11.
53 *Ibid.*, p. 28.
54 Thomas Hardy, *The Mayor of Casterbridge* (London, Penguin, 1994 [1886]), p. 378.
55 *Ibid.*, p. 33.
56 *Ibid.*, p. 29.
57 Barr, *Drink*, p. 36.
58 This was a belief of the temperance reformers, Harrison, *Drink*, p. 23.
59 Hardy, *Mayor*, pp. 17–18.
60 *Ibid.*, p. 18.
61 Carter, *Temperance*, reprints some temperance pledges in his book, Appendix 1.
62 Harrison, *Drink*, p. 39.
63 Although at other points in the narrative Henchard is representative of the traditional way of life in comparison to Farfrae's efficient new methods, illustrated amongst other things by Farfrae's introduction of the 'seed drill' and Henchard's dismissal of it.
64 Barr, *Drink*, pp. 174–5.
65 Harrison, *Drink*, p. 42.
66 Hardy, *Mayor*, p. 6.
67 *Ibid.*, p. 131. 'Note also that in Marlowe's play, Dr Faustus is given 21 years of luxury in exchange for his soul. Henchard has vowed 21 years of abstinence and so is a kind of inverse Dr Faustus.' Peter Smith, in correspondence.
68 There is something similar in the figure of Jude in *Jude the Obscure*. Jude's two weaknesses are for women and drink, although only the former brings him down. *The Mayor of Casterbridge* offers the consequences of the second part of this equation.
69 Shiman, *Crusade*, p. 30.
70 I am not arguing that there is such a thing as a 'natural character' given to us from birth, but this is the way it operates in the novel.

71 Hardy, *Mayor*, p. 17.
72 *Ibid.*, p. 29.
73 Stirling Haig, '"By the Rivers of Babylon": Water and Exile in *The Mayor of Casterbridge*', *The Thomas Hardy Yearbook*, 11 (1984), p. 56.
74 *Ibid.*
75 Hardy, *Mayor*, p. 354.
76 *Ibid.*, p. 270.
77 We have seen in *Felix Holt* how convenient it is to use two or three hostelries as a means of classifying social distinctions.
78 Hardy, *Mayor.*, p. 35.
79 *Ibid.*, p. 37.
80 *Ibid.*, p. 38.
81 *Ibid.*, p. 41.
82 *Ibid.*, p. 53.
83 *Ibid.*, p. 45.
84 Most judgements are reserved for nostalgic comments. This also applies to the changing fortunes of the brewing industry in the face of monopolisation.
85 *Ibid.*, pp. 45–6.
86 *Ibid.*, p. 47.
87 *Ibid.*, p. 46.
88 *Ibid.*, p. 293.
89 *Ibid.*, p. 295.

11

Our mutual wasteland

'Sir,

   The Committee of the Imperial Commission of Liquor Control is directed to draw your attention to the fact that you have disregarded the Committee's communications under section 5A of the Act for the Regulation of Places of Public Entertainment; and that you are now under section 47C of the Act amending the Act for the Regulation of Places of Public entertainment aforesaid. The charges on which prosecution will be founded are as follows.'

G. K. Chesterton, *The Flying Inn*[1]

The ordinary pub-goer has no official existence. It is typical that the *New English Dictionary* gives no pub use of the word 'vault' and that for the *Encyclopædia Britannica* the pub only exists in relation to the liquor laws (to which one-eighth of a paragraph is devoted) and the legal aspect of public house Trusts.

Mass Observation, *The Pub and the People*[2]

It is only possible to utilise inns, taverns and alehouses as symbols because they are ready-made history, versions of England encapsulated. With George Eliot, Dickens and Hardy there is constantly a feeling, even when set in a contemporary England, that these places are historically redolent. When Dickens in his Preface to *Oliver Twist* bemoans how literature of the past has made the criminal underworld and lower-class life look attractive, he is calling for a greater realism, one that disposes of romanticising, and in the creation of the Three Cripples, Bill Sikes's pub, this is no doubt what he had in mind. But with time, successive generations have had to cope with Dickens's own influence, how to make these places un-Dickensian if they want to work as realists. Inns in the second half of the nineteenth century can only be primarily symbolic, since with changing circumstances their unique social function of providing refreshment and accommodation is superseded by the impact of trains on coach transport, and the emergence of lodging houses and hotels. 'Inn' therefore more likely exists as a rhetorical idea – as Eliot uses it in *Felix Holt* – than a reference to something real. When the hero of H. G. Wells's *The History of Mr Polly* (1910) finally achieves peace, away from the sordid reality of being a tradesman, it is at The Potwell Inn, a place of beauty in the English imagination. In G. K. Chesterton's *The Flying Inn* (1914), the landlord of 'The Old Ship' is threatened with having his establishment closed down. Thanks to a loophole in the law he discovers that he can sell ale wherever he puts up his sign. So sign in hand, he defies the state by becoming a peripatetic landlord. Thus England, in the form of the 'inn', is dying, but stolid English virtues survive in the determination to hang onto the 'inn'. That it must 'fly' is a sign of its demise.

On the other hand, however, the public house has yet to come into its literary own. For all the numerous descriptions of drinking-houses, some of which he terms 'public houses', the world of 'the pub' is not what Dickens is after, although the Six Jolly Fellowship Porters in *Our Mutual Friend* is a possible exception. It is partly to do with the eyes through which we get the narratives. There are no 'inside' pictures, no first-person accounts of the everyday environment. Perhaps Eliot's Rainbow in *Silas Marner* and the Red Lion in 'Janet's Repentance' are a little closer in that they attempt relatively inconsequential conversations. But their role is within the larger narratives, sites of folk wisdom to be contrasted with pressures to see the world as a more modern place.

This is not intended to make realistic accuracy the benchmark of quality in this area of literature. Like any other material, the drinking house is to be manipulated for artistic ends. Nor should the goal of realism be seen as a lesser ambition, as it sometimes has been by critics. The technologies required to succeed in literary realism can be every bit as complicated as the more 'difficult' (to read) modes of writing. The issue becomes acute when the artistic avant-garde at the end of the nineteenth century and beginning of the twentieth sought to cast off the baggy, moralistic, paternalistic, prissy art of the Victorians (although, confusingly, sometimes it had nothing older than Edwardian literature in its sights). It was a turn away from realism, or the previous idea(s) of realism, in favour of new ways of understanding what should be counted as 'real', and the determinedly modern artists experimented with new ways of how this could be achieved. This diverse 'new' is now known collectively as modernism. If anything can be said to connect the likes of a majority of these musicians, painters, sculptors and writers, it is perhaps the move inwards towards the psychological and individualistic. Modernism breaks away from the social panoramas of Dickens and Eliot, where people may have inhabited the different worlds of rich and poor, town and country, yet could still acknowledge their mutual existence. In the more psychologically orientated world of modernist art, the tendency is to construct each individual's world as self-contained, with little or no connection to any other person's world. An individual psyche then becomes an unknowable island. What is 'real' therefore is no longer what comes under general social observation but what is perceived within each individual's mental landscape.

This is partly to do with the rise of psychology and (a little later) psychoanalysis. They impinge both upon the literature discussed here, and upon the perception of 'alcohol' as a socially sanctioned drug. No longer categorised as 'habitual drunkards' but rather as 'alcoholics', their drunkenness or addiction is no longer necessarily the consequence of moral failings or difficult social environments. The problem of drunkenness comes to be seen by some as sited within the individual's psychology and physiology – it becomes medicalised and psychologised. The mixture of a medicalisation of drunkenness and new artistic ventures should lead to a change in the representation of drinking houses. Theoretically, if this argument is followed, the idea of the public house as a social space must provide something of a challenge to the newer literary culture bent on exposing the inner workings of the mind, and a social culture bent on limning the serious drinker as an autonomous psychological problem. The drinking-house space thus far has been 'social', but if the newer art forms are more interested in individual perception, where does that leave the public house?

London is once more the centre of our enquiry. It was the centre of imperialism at the beginning of the twentieth century, and one of the centres of artistic interest. However, if we concentrated on 'English' modernist writing, we would find scant material related to drinkers and drinking houses (if we could include Hemingway and Joyce we would have ample material). It is a curious fact, and again possibly due to the social base of the major writers and a sense of what is fitting for literature. Virginia Woolf's Mrs Dalloway notices a drunk on her ambles through London, comically seeing him as a symbol of freedom over and beyond any kind of Parliamentary legislation, but her novels advance the domestic environment alone. Conrad's *The Secret Agent* ends with the poisonous professor in a beer hall, and *Lord Jim* has a character experience the DTs (he sees pink toads scurrying over his bed). Alone amongst those modernist writers choosing English scenery it is T. S. Eliot who found space for a significant pub scene. In *The Waste Land* (1922) a pub is observed through American middling-class eyes (dealt with below). Joyce's scenes are perhaps what we would expect – inside the heads of people inside pubs. For the English writers or writers of the English scene, however, it was those who had commitments to the 'social' world, and a realistic representation of it, who continued to find the pub a fruitful area. And in retrospect perhaps this was what was needed to bring the pub into its own, 'inside' jobs which would divest the pub of the olde England cognates of inns, taverns, ordinaries and alehouses.[3] And once again, we must turn aside from the main literary stream into some minor tributaries to find pub representations.

We begin with Arthur Morrison, whose tales of East End life naturally covered pub life, through A. E. Coppard's 'The Black Dog' (1923), and end the chapter with some of the best evocations to be found – in John Hampson's *Saturday Night at the Greyhound* (1931) and the work of Patrick

Hamilton in the 1930s and 1940s. In the midst of it all is T. S. Eliot's high-literary slice of East End life in *The Waste Land*.

Arthur Morrison – 'The Red Cow Group'

Jack London's *The People of the Abyss* (1903), a journalistic exposé of London at the beginning of the twentieth century, focuses on East London, where the working classes were concentrated. Drink and the pub play a large part, as does his sense that here we have the greatest nation on earth, and yet much of its populace is worse off than a hobo in America, who at least has the freedom of the countryside. London at the turn of the twentieth century is an overcrowded slum, and not surprisingly, drink and drunkenness rules the common lot: 'The English working classes may be said to be soaked in beer. They are made dull and sodden by it' – 'The public-house is ubiquitous. It flourishes on every corner and between corners, and it is frequented almost as much by women as by men.'[4] Jack London's vision of the world's number one metropolis is one echoed in the world of Arthur Morrison (1863–1945), a graduate of Walter Besant's 'People's Palace'. Morrison eschews the overtly cultural-literary influences when he plunges the reader into London's East End in the novels *A Child of the Jago* (1896), *The Hole in the Wall* (1902) and the collection *Tales of Mean Streets* (1894). Like other minor writers we have encountered throughout *The Pub in Literature*, his quality of description for the drinking place is simply not to be found in the work of better-known luminaries. Of course, by the end of the nineteenth century we are talking about a different type of writing – it is self-consciously working class, and one of the features of such writing is to refuse to play the 'literary' game, aiming instead for a pristine, photographic image that has not been touched up by literary pretensions. Such fidelity to what is real life (which usually means 'lower-class' lives rather than middle-class ones) has been a rallying call of these writers, whether they accepted the name of 'realist' or not (Morrison did not, whilst still arguing that it was his duty to represent what he had seen[5]). As the argument goes, each generation finds its own realism – and that is the skill.

Morrison's work is thoroughly permeated with alcohol and pubs. The title of the novel *The Hole in the Wall* itself is the name of the pub where the young Stephen is brought up by his grandfather. The narrative switches between Stephen's first-person narrative and a third-person voice, rather in the manner of Dickens's *Bleak House*. It uses the tricks of detective fiction (which Morrison also wrote) to sustain narrative interest, but lacks the density of the short stories in *Mean Streets*.

The Introduction to *Mean Streets* paints an overwhelmingly gloomy picture of the East End, beginning with the stereotypical impressions people have of it: 'It is down through Cornhill and out beyond Leadenhall Street and Aldgate Pump, one will say: a shocking place, where he once went with a curate; an evil plexus of slums that hide human creeping things; where filthy men and women live on penn'orths of gin, where collars and clean shirts are decencies unknown, where every citizen wears a black eye, and none ever combs his hair.'[6] He does not directly dispute these images, seeing each notion as 'but the distorted shadow of a minor feature',[7] but takes the reader into the particular lives of East Enders. The mainstays are poverty, drunkenness, everyday violence, few aspirations and little joy – a truth that was a 'meat too strong' for some critics.[8]

The world described in the Introduction continues in the short stories. The first, 'Lizerhunt', follows Elizabeth Hunt's life. It begins with courting – 'walking out' followed by the more serious 'keeping company' – and ends in marriage to a husband brutal to both her and his own mother. When the mother dies, the little money they had from her 'mangling' (taking in washing) goes. The father takes no interest in the child, and the tale ends with him telling her to get money from the streets however she can (i.e., prostitution). The second tale, 'Without Visible Means', follows some out-of-work Londoners as they tramp beyond the capital looking for employment. It is a pinched world. When Joey's bag of tools is stolen by one of the other men, he is pushed over the edge and starts to ramble continually that he has been the background notes on an accordion throughout his life, played on by others. His health deteriorates rapidly. At the end of the tale, his last companion and he go into a tavern, the place where Christian compassion is once more to be tested, with poverty the new plague. The prose is matter-of-fact, like American naturalism or some socialist realism:

> They carried a twopenny loaf into the tap-room of a small tavern, and Dave had mild ale himself, but saw that Joey was served with stout with a penn'orth of gin in it. Soon the gin and the stout reached Joey's head, and drew it to the table. And he slept, leaving the rest of the shilling where it lay.
>
> Dave arose, and stuffed the last of the twopenny loaf into his pocket. He took a piece of chalk from the bagatelle board in the corner, and wrote this on the table: – '*dr. sir. for god sake take him to the work House.*'
>
> Then he gathered up the coppers where they lay, and stepped quietly into the street.[9]

'To Bow Bridge' follows the 'eleven-five tram-car from Stratford' to Bow – in the County of London closing hours are an hour later than everywhere else, and so the car consists of many attempting to take advantage of it. 'Three Rounds' is a story of Neddy Milton, whose only option in life is to succeed as a boxer. To break into the professional game he needs to win at the matches put on at the Prince Regent pub. He wins this match, but his poverty, lack of food and hence lack of fitness will probably work against him. Drink and the public house are the fabric of everyday life.

There is one story in the collection which is of particular interest to us. 'The Red Cow Group' is set in a pub, and the tale tells of how a normally passive drinking group are worked upon by an anarchist called 'Sotcher', when they briefly become The Red Cow Anarchist Group. It will be readily understood that the story has one feature we are already familiar with – the idea that the drinking house is a place of insurgent activity. Just as Morrison corrects the myth of the East End, he offers his own version of the gap between perception and reality to be found here. As with the activities in *Felix Holt*, the suggestion is that to get to the common Englishman you seek him out in a public house. In *Felix Holt* the pub was both the place where the English lower orders maintained their ignorance in favour of beer, and the place where they were easily manipulated and bribed for political ends. 'The Red Cow Group' unpicks the latter aspect.

Like the other stories (and Morrison's other social novels) there is a feeling that the lives lived are not to be escaped, that the lots endured will always be so. Blame is shared between the people themselves and the system that allows it. The story begins with this belief compressed into the pub environment, so that the pub becomes a microcosm of the East End. The reaction of the Red Cow regulars to any attempt to raise their consciousness solicits a sarcastic tone: '[The group] had long been plunged in a beery apathy, neither regarding nor caring for the fearful iniquities of the social system that oppressed them' and 'night after night they drank their beer and smoked their pipes, sunk in a stagnant ignorance of their manifold wrongs'.[10] In time-honoured tradition, the narrator lists the occupations of the regulars: a porter, a bankrupt tradesman, a bookmaker's runner, and the others making ends meet however they can 'out of the London heap in ways and places unspecified'.[11] Morrison shows that the medium of worth is not money but 'liquid measure': 'fourpence was never spoken of in the common way: it was a quart, and a quart was the monetary standard of the community'.[12] After Sotcher has convinced them that they are society's wronged, he casually tells them how they can make explosives. In his absence they vote for him to be the sole agent of destruction. When they find that he is unwilling, the tables are turned for it is his sort who have 'got to be suppressed'.[13] Sotcher proves himself to be a coward and attempts to wriggle out of the action. The group bind him and take him to a gas container, with a canister of explosive strapped to his body, and leave him there.[14] He is arrested for being drunk and disorderly. The concoction turns out to have been a harmless liquid. In the midst of social deprivation, and at the centre of the working-man's home from home, all that can be found is the apathy that perpetuates (or allows to be perpetuated) the same monotonous living. Far from being a time-bomb waiting to explode, the English working classes are drink-sodden and apolitical, and there is irony in their steadfast refusal to be cowed or swayed by others, the English trait of self-reliance turned in on itself.

T. S. Eliot – 'A Game of Chess'

> Postcard, coloured, showing two rednosed bulbous boozers leaning against bar-counter, holding up full glasses. Caption: "What are the vilest words in the dictionary, Bert?" "Dunno!" "TIME, GENTLEMEN, PLEASE!"[15]

> When Lil's husband got demobbed, I said —
> I didn't mince my words, I said to her myself,
> HURRY UP PLEASE ITS TIME
>
> T. S. Eliot, *The Waste Land*

'The Red Cow Group' ends with Sotcher in prison whilst, presumably, the Red Cow group returns to its beery indifference. In miniature the story represents the common perception, both in Morrison's work and elsewhere, that the lower orders are sunk in their ignorance. Despite the much vaunted 'improvement' in education and opportunities, (still) nothing much appears to have changed. T. S. Eliot uses the same notion for a section of *The Waste Land* (1922). Part II, 'A Game of Chess', contrasts two scenes – one from high society, a sterile relationship, set in the home – and one from the lower classes, set in a pub. The play of opposites is a stark echo of what we have seen before: the upper classes live their lives in private, the lower in public. The high-class setting is a boudoir, with a latter-day Belinda enthroned in front of a mirror, observed by an unsympathetic narrator. The two are familiar to each other in the manner of a couple, but he only appears to answer her questions inside his own head. His responses would, in any case, be inappropriate. To 'What are you thinking of?' his thoughts run on 'I think we are in rats' alley / Where the dead men lost their bones.'[16] Both his silence and the nature of his thoughts signify a profound lack of communication.

When the scene switches to the pub, there is the expectation that with the contrast will come a sense of community, in keeping with the nature of hostelries. Yet the apparent community within the public house is as sterile as that in the private room. What begins with the promise of a conversation – a woman directly addresses another person – in fact continues as a monologue which revolves around getting false teeth, the problems of abortion and how to keep your man when he returns from active service. The usual cud-chewing and pint-pot philosophy prevalent in drinking-house scenes, with its phatic binding, is here reduced to inanity:

> When Lil's husband got demobbed, I said —
> I didn't mince my words, I said to her myself,
> HURRY UP PLEASE ITS TIME
> Now Albert's coming back, make yourself a bit smart.
> He'll want to know what you done with that money he gave you
> To get yourself some teeth. He did, I was there.
> You have them all out, Lil, and get a nice set,
> He said, I swear, I can't bear to look at you.

And no more can't I, I said, and think of poor Albert,
He's been in the army four years, he wants a good time,
And if you don't give it him, there's others will, I said.
Oh is there, she said. Something o' that, I said.
Then I'll know who to thank, she said, and give me a straight look.
HURRY UP PLEASE ITS TIME[17]

The promised conversation emerges as an unconnected counterpoint between the woman's voice and that of the barman calling 'HURRY UP PLEASE ITS TIME'. There is communication breakdown at all possible intersections.

Although the time spent by the higher-class couple is shown to be no better than that of the lower pub classes, and is likewise measured out in arbitrary landmarks – 'The hot water at ten', 'a closed car at four' – their 'higher-order' time is not circumscribed, it is their own. The time in the pub however, that is, the time of the lower classes, is once more under the cosh. The scene has, in its own way, the conjunction of time and state we have continued to trace. The immediate reference point here is World War I, and the official voice of the pub calling time is once again the imposition of order onto disorder, the imposition of the state onto pleasure and idleness. To illustrate the shift in social awareness of 'pub time' it is necessary to take a brief detour into the liquor-licensing that the Great War inaugurated. It was during World War I that the legislation which settled public-house opening hours for much of the twentieth century was first drafted. Worried that English workers, particularly armaments and dock workers, would be more interested in getting drunk than in the defence of the realm, it was felt necessary to bring in legislation that would curb the hours of public drinking. The Parliamentary debates during World War I leading up to this legislation are very revealing. Lloyd George, then Chancellor of the Exchequer and soon to be Prime Minister, believed drink to be a greater threat than Germany and Austria (hyperbole or not, it placed drink at the forefront of concerns). One example, from May 1915, sees Lloyd George talking on the 'Defence of the Realm (Amendment – No. 3) Bill' as it goes through its second reading: 'Drink is the proved enemy of the strength and efficiency of the people of this country, and the nation, which has given to the Government boundless and encouraging confidence in all the measures against our foreign foes, expects that the Government will deal as strongly and as effectively with the enemy within our gates.'[18] It should also be noted that in these debates, which are really the culmination of the work throughout the nineteenth century of the temperance movement, class plays a large part. For example, Lord Robert Cecil, discussing 'Early Closing Regulations' in a Commons debate, notes: 'We hear a great deal about the evils of drink … but I see that the restaurants all over this city are open just the same as usual.'[19] However, the argument for legislation was won and alcohol sales were restricted in all districts to 5½ hours on weekdays when previously they had been, in London, 19½ hours, and in other towns 17 hours. These restrictions, which were only meant to be emergency measures for the duration of hostilities, in fact outlasted the war (with minor alterations) and were not relaxed until as late as 1961.

To return to 'A Game of Chess', it can be seen that the upper classes have their own sense of order through minor social events, their time is their own – as the jibe about 'restaurant' time in the above debate clearly demonstrates. At the other end of the scale, the lower classes have their time ordered for them, for the pub must shut – 'HURRY UP PLEASE ITS TIME'. In a poem which desperately seeks to order culture and itself, foretelling as it does closing time for western civilisation in a manner which embraces all sections of society, the class division of time and society nevertheless remains everywhere evident. Consciously or subconsciously, Eliot was tapping into another example of how the state has controlled the elements it has always feared – the lower orders. The use of a first-person voice in both parts, so that the reader is positioned within both classes, would appear to emphasise the shared nature of these two otherwise disparate social spaces. The poem's attempt to field a demotic and a 'proper' voice without favouring either one is an attempt to nullify or level notions of class distinction as the poem itself strives for spiritual transcendence. Of course, the charge of 'elitism' aimed at *The Waste Land* by critics re-enters through its 'difficulty' of interpretation – only the select few will 'understand' and carry culture forward.[20]

This reach for spiritual supremacy at the expense of social particularity may have been the reason Eliot removed the first fifty lines from an earlier (unpublished) version. Instead of 'April is the cruellest month, breeding / Lilacs out of the dead land', with its reference to the opening lines of Chaucer's *Canterbury Tales*, we would have been treated to the American equivalent of a pub crawl: 'First we had a couple of feelers down at Tom's place, / There was old Tom, boiled to the eyes, blind'.[21] (Since Chaucer's work begins with a group in a hostelry, critics would still have been free to interpret it as an oblique reference to the *Canterbury Tales*, with the decline in western civilisation measured by the gap between The Tabard and Tom's Place). In the unpublished lines the gang drinks illicitly in the back room of Tom's place and then goes for more drinks at the Opera Exchange. In the riot of the evening they lose 'Steve', who, we are told in parenthesis, materialised at another boozer called 'Myrtle's place'. Out of the brackets and back to the main action the narrator tells us that he has been accosted by a 'fly cop' looking to make trouble for them (shades of *London Spy*). A Mr Donovan turns up, squares it with the policeman, and the group moves on to the German Club. The neglected passage ends when the narrator stays up until sunrise before going home.

In the transition from draft to published item, the American environment is lost in favour of Europe. The language of the earlier draft is demotic, the lifestyle carefree and high-class, the feeling of decadence strong (for an

American audience especially, since this would have come in the middle of Prohibition). By omitting these lines and opening with the Chaucerian echoes instead, the origins of English literature rather than the current evasion of Prohibition is the anchor-point for the poem. Eliot was clearly enamoured of the idea of beginning the poem with a drunken splurge, but the eventual choice of opening with a reference to Chaucer rather than a booze-up serves to send out the right cultural signals. It is (possibly) another example of 'drink' being 'censored' in the name of literary decorum, so that the drinking scene that does occur is properly corralled within 'literature'. To return to the section 'A Game of Chess', the same slide in favour of the correct over the demotic, the sober over the drunk, occurs at the very end when they leave the pub. If the section had finished with the lines 'Goonight Bill. Goonight Lou. Goonight May. Goonight. / Ta ta. Goonight. Goonight' it would have stayed within the class argot, but a third narrative voice cleans up the language when it follows with 'Good night, ladies, good night, sweet ladies, good night, / good night.'[22] This transcendent viewpoint therefore pushes the pub back to some point far removed from the overall project to restore civilisation. Eliot's use of the pub in all this might seem slight, and my digression into liquor-licensing legislation might seem too broad a context, but this is the environment within which the twentieth-century English pub is understood. Its time is defined by the state because of fears at the beginning of the century that the majority of its inhabitants, like the wasters in *Henry IV Parts I and II* and *Henry V*, would not of their own free will be good citizens. The cultured, third voice of Part II ultimately takes the superior tone and waves goodbye to the demotic voice of the pub.

A. E. Coppard – 'The Black Dog'

In Arthur Morrison and in T. S. Eliot the public house works against some of the stereotyping that might have carried over from the days when inns and alehouses were the order of the day. In A. E. Coppard's short story 'The Black Dog'[23] the idea of the country pub (and the countryside) as idyll is laid to rest at a time when countryside hostelries were once more finding a clientele with the arrival of the car. Coppard's story concerns the Honourable Gerald Loughlin who has just met and been charmed by Orianda Crabbe at a Lady Tillington's house. He is due to leave the following day, but whilst waiting for the train decides it is too good an opportunity not to follow up. He impulsively makes his way back in a state of romantic vagueness. He stops off at a pub, 'the Three Pigeons', and this gives him a chance to reflect on things. The pub's name is surely a reference to Goldsmith's in *She Stoops to Conquer* since it is not a particularly common sign, and its emptiness might be a sign of literary desuetude (a feeling which grows as the tale goes on). The time spent here is used to introduce leitmotifs: 'This drowsiness was heaven, it made so clear his recollection of Orianda'[24] and his thoughts lead him further to think that there could be nothing better, 'just at this moment, than to be sitting with her in this empty inn'.[25] His mind runs on, fantasising how they would be together. He leaves the pub and walks to the church, inside which he imagines marrying her (another instance of pub and church in close proximity). The idea that he is searching for heaven on earth is continued when he struggles with his own romantic notions: 'not here, surely, the apple of Eden flourished', and the second idea, that this is a test of what place the modern world has for the Romantic imagination soon appears: 'Absurd! You *couldn't* fall in love with a person as sharply as all that, could you? But why not? Unless fancy was charged with the lightning of gods it was nothing at all.'[26]

Orianda finally turns up at one of the spots she had described to him. In their conversation he discovers her lower-class status, and pushing any thoughts of 'caste' aside he takes this to be part of her fascination. Orianda tells of how her mother left her father for another man, and that she herself went to live with her mother – a decision which was the wrong moral choice (since she believes her mother to have been at fault) but is another facet of her personality which fascinates Gerald: '"My dear girl," he burst out, "your mother and you were right, absolutely. I am sure life is enhanced not by amassing conventions, but by destroying them."'[27] So the tale continues to watch Gerald's moral world slowly crumble as he accommodates more ideas that are traditionally anathema to him and his class of 'gentleman'. He offers to take her back to her father, who, he learns, runs an inn/pub called 'the Black Dog'. He is thrilled at the idea of another world opening up to him, once again framing the adventure in romantic terms. She continues to be the rock on which his moral and his imaginative world slowly but surely shatters. She wants nothing of this and admonishes him with 'I don't want ... to grow into a world of any kind.'[28]

When they arrive at the Black Dog, a woman, Lizzie, is living with her father, and Orianda makes it clear to Gerald that she will oust Lizzie. When she says that she will lie to Lizzie in order to get rid of her, Loughlin admits that he does not like the scheme, that it lacks 'grandeur'. As if picking up his earlier imaginative thoughts she replies: 'Pooh! You shouldn't waste grandeur on clearing up a mess. This is a very dirty Eden.' The country-pub idyll continues to shade into a dystopia. She refuses to entertain the idea of marriage, saying that she wants 'a barbarian lover'. The barbarity of the countryside is displayed when one day he sees some men struggling to twist ropes around the horns and legs of a cow. When he gets close up he finds the men sawing off the crumpled horns to prevent them growing into the head and driving it mad.

Eventually Lizzie is forced to leave. Gerald drives her to the train station in a horse and trap, a detail which combines old and new. At the station, whilst Gerald is busy with her luggage, she rides off with the horse and trap and is not seen again. They cannot find her, and 'time resumed its sweet slow delightfulness, though its clarity was diminished and some of its enjoyment dimmed'.[29] It is borrowed time, for a few days later Lizzie is dragged out of a river:

> Then it was that Loughlin's soul discovered to him a mass of feelings – fine sympathy, futile sentiment, a passion for righteousness, morbid regrets – from which a tragic bias was born. After the dread ordeal of the inquest, which gave a passive verdict of Found Drowned, it was not possible for him to stem this disloyal tendency of his mind. It laid that drowned figure accusatively at the feet of his beloved girl, and no argument or sophistry could disperse the venal savour that clung to the house of "The Black Dog."

Even though Orianda grows 'more alluring than ever', he leaves, promising to write. 'In London he has not forgotten, but he cannot endure the thought of that countryside – to be far from the madding crowd is to be mad indeed.'[30]

The story comes full cycle. London is the centre from which all things are judged. The old England exists in the far-flung west country, but it is a dystopia whose symbol is the Black Dog. It is part of the tale's strength to throw up possible signs and connections (the Three Pigeons; 'Eden'; the father is the best ladder and hurdle maker in the district) and leave them in a suggestive framework. But of all it is the title of the story and the name of the inn that is most teasing. The sign is not uncommon and it is the most favourite of dog signs.[31] In rural districts it is speculated that the black dog was traditionally a spectral hound given to frightening the neighbourhood.[32] This would fit well with the story, also perhaps reinforcing the idea that it is a feature with which Orianda and her father are familiar, but with which townspeople (where the sign would have a different or no meaning) would be unaware. Also probably woven into the meaning of the tale is the fact that the black dog has often been used to represent the devil.[33] Given the opposing references to Eden from Gerald and from Orianda, the black dog would certainly signify evil. This really is full circle, since it is no longer the country that is simple and innocent, opposed to the wicked capital, rather, the countryside is the dark side of England, an unknowable place that is no longer the nation. Just as Gerald cannot break the codes of the countryside folk, the reader is unable to pin down the precise meaning of the black dog, whilst such a technique adds to the sense of unease that the Black Dog sign itself might signify, a recognition perhaps that England is no longer sure of itself as a leading nation.

John Hampson – *Saturday Night at The Greyhound*

Hampson's novel (1931) is one of the few pieces of literature to use the process of running a drinking house as a means to explore character. It also pays due respect to the fact that the normal working pattern, after the restriction of drinking hours in the 1921 Act, firmly engineered the leisure night to be on a Saturday evening. Readers might be more familiar with Alan Sillitoe's *Saturday Night and Sunday Morning* (1958) as the fictional depiction of this ritual and its significance, but Hampson was possibly the first to make structural and symbolic use of it. Whilst we might expect Saturday night to be represented as the up-dated version of pre-industrial festival England[34] – part of its strength is its refusal to offer such pub sociology, in favour of a more acute portrayal of the starkness underlying such a weekly 'festival'.

The novel is divided into three parts: Nightfall at The Greyhound, The Open House, and The House Closes. The first part takes the main characters in turn – Mrs Tapin – the pub's charwoman; Ivy Flack – the landlady; Tom – Ivy's brother; Clara – Mrs Tapin's daughter; and Fred Flack, the landlord who is having an affair with Clara. The section gives the life history of each as it builds up to opening the doors on Saturday night. Tom and Ivy have had a very good grounding in running public houses, having been brought up in one and worked in others. Mrs Tapin has schemed her way through life, getting pregnant by the old squire for material gain. Fred is a feckless, extremely handsome, happy-go-lucky type upon whose life the others depend. These characters are judged by their ability to make the pub workable in a district where the miners are loath to give over money they have had to squeeze out of the ground through hard labour. Part 2, which puts the reader into the present, switches between the various characters already introduced, and brings on two more characters, Roy Grovedon, the old squire's son, and Ruth Dorme, his 'fancy piece' from London. Ruth becomes interested in the unfolding drama of The Greyhound out of boredom. 'The House Closes' tracks the ineluctable downward spiral of events.

The novel manipulates a set of themes associated with drinking-house literature. The pub exists in contrast to the manor house, the two being linked through Mrs Tapin who chars at the pub and whose daughter Clara is the offspring of the lord of the manor. The interrelation between 'inn' and 'mansion' materialises when the squire's son comes up from London with his girlfriend Ruth and he asks her: '"Well, which shall it be? Inn or ancestral hall?" Ruth Dorme laughed and chose once more the Inn.'[35] It is another instance of provincial life enlivened, witnessed and judged by 'London'.

Clustered around the distinction between manor house and inn are notions of olde England vanishing (it is always vanishing, it has never vanished). Clara is the result of a liaison between her mother, Mrs Tapin, and the old squire. In those days it was possible to 'catch' the old squire in such a way and make him pay (he finds her a husband). Mrs Tapin wishes the same for her daughter, but in these changed times she realises that the young squire is not a possible catch, and that the only landlord on Clara's horizon is the worthless Fred. That olde England has given way to the commercial world is signified when we learn that although the old squire still owns virtually all the surrounding land, including the mine, he sold the pub to a major brewery during World War I. The lives of those running the pub therefore represent the newer environment, distinct from the old one of *noblesse oblige*.

Fred has at some point bought a greyhound, called Pertinax, suggestive of 'dogged resolution' and 'obstinacy' ('pertinacious'), and of 'relevance' ('pertinence'). The novel uses this dog and the pub's name to explore the different attitudes of the central characters. Attitudes to the pub and the dog are conflated, and, ultimately, since both represent 'life', it allows the novel to explore their attitudes to existence. Mrs Tapin simply hates all dogs because the men lavish more attention on them than on women, a fact which encapsulates her life, since she has borne the old squire's child (Clara) and been married off to a man she despises (and it is apparent that Asa Tapin does prefer whippets to women). Tom sees the 'greyhound' as a symbol of the difficult existence eked out by the villagers and miners – something he admires but would not wish upon himself. Fred has been duped into buying a greyhound that is a useless runner, a symbol of his constant misjudgement and his desire to be accepted into male social life. Ivy sees Pertinax as a mascot, believing her fortunes are tied up in it. The symbolic logic is worked out perfectly when Mrs Tapin stabs the dog to death, foreshadowing the demise of the pub that night when it is raided for serving after hours, following up a tip-off from the vengeful Mrs Tapin herself.

The inn sign is concretised through the greyhound that the landlord has bought for an extortionate fee from one of the villagers. A greyhound is not like most other dogs, with their unconditional love. The greyhound symbolises the lean existence that the villagers live, a hard, compassionless life, rather like that portrayed in Coppard's story. Again, like Coppard's story, London is the implied centre, and the gentry are the implicit guardians of the nation, yet they are shadowy figures, and by placing these public-house microcosms at the centre of the narratives London's centrality is recast as out of touch with the heart of the nation. What is also observable in the Black Dog and The Greyhound is the uncertain moral landscape, since the idea of old England, with or without the final 'e', is one of an antiquated moral framework. *Saturday Night at The Greyhound*, like 'The Red Cow Group' and 'The Black Dog', adopts a rather neutral moral tone, in keeping with its unsparing outlook. Even if, in Coppard's tale, the Honourable Gerald is indeed honourable, his values stand little chance.

Patrick Hamilton's whole poisoned nightmarish circle of the idle tipler's existence

The moral uncertainty which pervades 'The Black Dog', a consequence perhaps of the aftermath of World War I, becomes especially acute when we view the events of Munich before World War II. On Thursday 22 September 1938, Chamberlain and his personal adviser, Sir Horace Wilson, arrived on the east bank of the Rhine opposite Godesberg, where they were due to meet Hitler. This proved to be the last meeting before the Munich Conference. They were going to tell Hitler the good news that Beně's Czech government had agreed to Hitler's terms and would allow the secession of the mainly German Sudetenland from Czechoslovakia. The French and British governments believed that this arrangement would prevent a second world war. Indeed, Chamberlain had just stated to journalists before setting off from Heston, England, that the context of his meeting with Hitler was that it should lead to a better understanding between the British and German peoples, which in itself would be the foundation of a European peace.[36]

At that point in time the British people felt slightly uneasy about the treatment of the Czechs, and Chamberlain 'had actually been booed when he left Britain that morning'.[37] When Chamberlain had arrived back from Germany just a few days earlier after his first meeting with Hitler, he had been greeted by a crowd of hundreds at the airport and given an ovation. 'A Mass Observation Poll taken before he left for Godesberg had found 40 percent of those questioned opposed to his policy over Czechoslovakia and only 22 percent in favour, though a further 28 percent were undecided.'[38]

The agreement reached at the Munich Conference a few days later between Germany, Britain, France and Italy was, on the face of it, a better agreement than that of the Godesberg memorandum. The improvement rested on the fact that the Germans would not now take the Sudetenland by force from the Czechoslovakian government. Instead, there would be an orderly handover of the territories, supervised by an International Commission. Chamberlain's overriding concern remained the same, however: more important than the Czech Sudeten issue was the bilateral agreement he had secured from Hitler that Britain and Germany would not go to war. This was the famous piece of paper he waved ecstatically on his return to England, where he was greeted as a hero of great personal courage and stamina, a statesman who had saved the day at the eleventh hour. The press was virtually unanimous in its praise of his achievement. The whole country was relieved that war had been avoided. The Czechs had not been invited to the negotiations about their own country and felt betrayed by both the French and the British.

Hangover Square covers the period from the Christmas after Munich through to the declaration of war on 3 September 1939. The novel was published in 1941 and was thus in the thick of the war that Munich failed to prevent, whilst still within spitting distance of that agreement. These are the thoughts of *Hangover Square*'s central character, George Harvey Bone, as he wanders through London:

> He just couldn't stand Munich. Somewhere at the back of his mind it was weighing on him: it had become part of his general feeling of disgrace, of the shame in which he in particular, and the world generally, was steeped. He still couldn't get over the feeling that there was something *indecent* about it – Adolf, and Musso and Neville all grinning together, and all that aeroplane-taking and cheering on balconies.[39]

Bone is a weak man, besotted with the worthless Netta and caught up in the endless drinking their circle indulges in. George is also a schizophrenic, prone to what he and his toping acquaintances call dead moods. At these times his connection with reality is tenuous and his desire to murder Netta is uppermost in his mind. The novel parallels George's addiction, its social significance and its consequences, with the run-up to the outbreak of World War II.

Hamilton is regarded as a minor writer, perhaps better known for his play *Gas Light* (1939) and the play that Hitchcock turned into a film of the same name, *Rope* (1929). His novels tend to have period interest rather than being read for their own sake, except perhaps *Hangover Square*, which incorporates a dramatic tension not evident in his *Twenty Thousand Streets under the Sky* trilogy of the 1930s. That trilogy and *Hangover Square* both describe milieux which show people as alienated from each other, although the characters themselves never appear to articulate an out-and-out existential despair. Hamilton has been most praised for his description of pubs and drinking, and this is probably the best side to his writing. He is also excellent at describing the psychological effects of alcohol, particularly the way that drink dissipates will power, and deserves more credit for this than he has been given. Where the writing is at its weakest is when it gives the author's social message. Here is the conclusion, as Hamilton terms it, to *The Siege of Pleasure*, the second novel in the trilogy *Twenty Thousand Streets under the Sky*. The conclusion also serves as a plot summary:

> Conclusion
> 'All through a glass of port,' Jenny, the girl of the streets, had said. She had said it in jest, but who shall decline to surmise that she had stumbled upon the literal truth?
> If Jenny had not taken that first glass she would not have taken the second, and if she had not taken the second she would not have taken the third, and if she had not taken the third she would not then and there have resolved to abandon herself to the pleasures and perils of drink. And if she had not done that, she would not have become involved in the events which lost her her job, and set her going down the paths of destruction.

> Probably there was never any doubt of Jenny's social destiny, but can it not at least be said that that glass of port unlocked her destiny?[40]

Drink is a social evil in a preordained social system over which she has no control, and the narrator is at rather crude pains to point this out. The commentary is never as bald as this in *Hangover Square*. What *Hangover Square* tends to do to gain an outside view on George, who is mainly described through free indirect discourse, is to shift narrative perspective and see him through the eyes of other characters. The problem with *Hangover Square* in terms of interpretation is really one of overdetermination: Hamilton appears to want addiction to stand for everything and in all ways.

George is hopelessly in love with Netta, who strings him along for what money she can get out of him. The tart without a heart and the weak male who falls for her is a theme found elsewhere in Hamilton's work. This element of fixation in the novel appears to operate in at least two ways. The first is the purely personal, how unreciprocated love is destructive. It is the melodramatic element which does not resonate in any particular manner with Hamilton's other, perhaps larger, concerns. He scatters the text with quotations from Milton's *Samson Agonistes* to help the reader follow the idea of man brought down by woman. This then shades into a second idea which does have political consequences. Netta is attractive and bewitching, but hollow and cruel. She in turn falls for a man named Peter, who, like herself, is attractive and bewitching, hollow and cruel. The novel makes the association between these personal qualities and the allure of Fascism, and George comes to realise that both Netta and Peter admire Mussolini and Fascist qualities in general. Peter's dangerous aura also comes from the fact that he has been in prison for killing a man whilst drink-driving.

Moving on from the addiction of personal attraction to George's addiction to social drinking we find that he does not actually like drinking and would like to stop it. The reason he does drink is that it gives him access to a social environment where he is more welcome than anywhere else. This is 'the community' the pub so often stands for, here turned on its head. Drunkenness is also an escape from a reality which has nothing to offer him. This is one of the areas where the novel is overdetermined, since drink functions in the same way that the schizophrenia does, it serves to give George two mental states, and in the drunken state, just as in the schizophrenic state, he is not in control of his actions. Aesthetically, the novel could probably have worked just as well without the added weight of a mental illness: the schizophrenia functions within the novel as a more extreme version of drunkenness.

George's unhappiness with his drinking is linked symbolically with the significance of Munich. The unease he feels at his own lifestyle is mirrored in the unease he feels at the shame of the Munich agreement, and both nag away at the back of his mind. His own lifestyle is thus a mirror image of the behaviour of the British government (and, by extension, the nation) at that particular time, behaving badly but unable to stop the moral rot. Addiction is thus a personal moral failing analogous to Britain's own moral shortcomings at Munich. To take it one step further, what the British government is addicted to is the policy of appeasement. George's personal weakness for social drinking and the social status quo he finds himself involved in is thus the weakness of Chamberlain's government, addicted as it is to trying to maintain a harmonious Europe with as little cost to itself as possible. There is something morally shameful on both counts.

Greater than George's addiction to drink is his addiction to the social scene. George is shown to be different from those with whom he mixes (although early on in the novel there is a comment that there are thousands of men like George haunting bars, and it is suggested that Mickey, one of the circle's drinkers, might have similar longings to escape). However, in the main, in contrast to George, the circle of idle tipplers *wants* to drink. This is made obvious when George attempts to convince Netta to give up the 'racket' of the daily drunk.

> 'Tell me, Netta,' he began again. 'Don't you *ever* feel you want to get away from this racket?'
>
> 'What racket?'
>
> 'Oh – just the racket generally. Boozing, doing nothing. It's all such a waste. Don't you ever want to cut it all out?'
>
> 'Cut what out? Drinking?'
>
> 'Yes. Drinking. *I'd* cut it out if I could only get my life straight – if only things made sense.'
>
> 'This is a new departure, George,' she said. 'You as a temperance expert. How long have you been like this?'
>
> 'Always. I hate drinking really.'
>
> 'Yes. That's the impression I got.'
>
> 'No. Don't be sarcastic. It's the truth. It's only because of this life one leads. Don't you ever feel the same? Don't you ever wake up in the early hours of the morning and feel the same?'
>
> 'Alcoholic remorse?'
>
> 'No. Not alcoholic remorse. Just wanting to get things straight. You *must* know what I mean. You must feel something of what I feel. *You* can't be content going on living the life you lead.'

Netta doesn't know what he means, or chooses not to. George dreams of some idyllic life where they will be happy ever after. This comes in the shape of a chicken farm or the place Maidenhead. The novel attempts to have it both ways. The hedonism of the idle tipplers' circle represents British behaviour at the time of Munich and after, in the sense that hedonism is an activity that follows its own desires without much thought for others. Munich shows Britain keen to preserve its Empire, with no concern for 'a quarrel in a far away country between people of whom we know nothing', as Chamberlain succinctly put it. The self-absorption of Bone's circle is similar to Britain's constant refusal to take part in any activities that do not directly ('intimately') affect her, for example militarisation of the Rhineland and invasion of Czechoslovakia. But the novel also shows George's sense of disgrace as the line taken by the liberal press which, to quote George, 'was getting pretty hot against Munich'.[41] The novel is undecided whether the 'whole poisoned nightmarish circle of the idle tippler's existence' is the metaphorical presentation of Britain at the time of Munich, or whether it is George's weak personal stance, addiction with a conscience, a kind of liberal guilt without much clue as to what might redeem it, which is the apt metaphor.

In a sense the metaphor is the view which incorporates both, a mixture of people who retain a moral framework, like George, and the more frequently encountered reckless hedonists. The narrator says of George: 'He didn't pretend to be any better. He hated himself for the life he led – the life in common with them. Drunken, lazy, impecunious, neurotic, arrogant, pub-crawling cheap lot of swine – that was what they all were. Including him and Netta.'[42] Together, the 'pub-crawling cheap lot of swine' form the microcosmic Britain. The main moral problem with such behaviour is the charge of recklessness, which in Hamilton's work takes on something of a social and philosophic moral problem, and it is this which is at the heart of the matter for him. He presents the consequences of their recklessness in two ways. Firstly is the idea of the drunken driver, and secondly there is George's killing of Netta.

In a footnote to his essay on Hamilton, Peter Widdowson remarks on how Hamilton used the motif of the drunken driver in a number of pieces.[43] Hamilton's radio play, *To The Public Danger*, hinges upon a car-ride by four inebriates who knock somebody down in the dark. Instead of stopping they blithely continue, with only one of the four adamant that they should go back and see what they have done. Eventually the moralist extricates himself from the other three, who drive off, only to crash into a tree and kill themselves. Ironically, and with some poetic justice the play suggests, it turns out that what they had in fact driven over was not a person but a couple of bikes with a sack of potatoes thrown over. Operating in a similar vein to *The Siege of Pleasure* Conclusion already discussed, To the Public Danger ends with the coroner giving his verdict on the deaths. The coroner is here describing the actions of the man who wanted to go back to the scene of the accident. The play was broadcast on 25 February 1939, and it is hard not to see these comments again in the light of a Britain coming to terms with Munich.

> In standing up for a principle, in seeking to save a life, this young man made his way, fought his way, from that car, and thereby saved his own life. He saved also, something which some of us may think just as precious – I mean his honour – an honour which he may now carry

> unblemished through that same life which he has saved for himself. We congratulate him …
>
> In a case of this sort, with the strange and ironical circumstances which attended it, there is bound, I know, to be a great amount of publicity in the newspapers. If that publicity can serve to call still more and more attention to the danger, the tragedy, the misery to human beings which is caused, which is being caused to-day and every day by people entering that instrument of death, the motor-car, in incomplete possession of their senses, under any influence, of drink or otherwise, however small – if that can be done, then some little good may yet come of this, and other lives be saved where these three have been wasted.[44]

The first issue signalled here by drunk-driving is that of honour, which can be quite easily tied in with Munich, and Chamberlain's claim that at Munich he achieved peace with honour. The role of honour is less obvious in *Hangover Square*, although of course it is its lack which is what leads to the feeling of shame. The second issue around drink-driving is blatantly that concerning the consequences of recklessness.

As already mentioned, in *Hangover Square* Netta is attracted to Peter, who has Fascistic sympathies. What she likes about him is his past: he has been in jail for assaulting and wounding someone at a political meeting, and he has also been incarcerated for killing someone while drink-driving: 'Both provided something bloody, brutal, and unusual which gave him a halo of originality.'[45] As for Netta's attraction to all things Fascist: 'It might be said that this feeling for violence and brutality, for the pageant and panorama of fascism on the Continent, formed her principal disinterested aesthetic pleasure.'[46] For Netta the attraction of Fascism is its brutality and violence, and this is manifest in the reckless danger of drink-driving which, in the case of the Fascistic Peter, has at one time resulted in the death of a pedestrian.

This brings us back to the circle addicted to drink. The predominant problem of addiction as offered by the novel is that actions are performed whilst under the influence which are dangerous to the very fabric of society. The analogy between the poisoned circle and Britain's behaviour at Munich then becomes one of the drunken driver, reckless, incapable of measuring the consequences or even caring for them. This is one of the subtler themes of the novel, especially when it can be seen that for Hamilton it is not just a social comment but it also bespeaks an aesthetic sensibility.

Historically there can only be one ending to Munich, and that is the Second World War. The logic of this is that the novel must find its own correlative for such a climax. So on the day that war breaks out, George kills both Netta and Peter whilst the wireless plays Chamberlain's Declaration speech to the nation. The novel juxtaposes George's thoughts and actions with Chamberlain's words. George then goes to Maidenhead, his idea of heaven. But of course, it is all an illusion. Maidenhead is no heaven. In his suicide note that George sends to the Maidenhead coroner, he says: 'I know that I have done wrong, but I am not well. I do not really know what I am doing. I thought I was right, but now I am wrong about Maidenhead, I may be wrong. Please remember my cat.'[47]

The novel has painted itself into a corner somewhat by this point. George Harvey Bone, an alcoholic schizophrenic, has had to carry the symbolic weight of Munich from Christmas 1938 up to 3 September 1939. His concluding note, which spares us the pontificating of a coroner, as in the radio play, shows that George is completely confused. He thought there was a decent mode of existence to be had, symbolised by Maidenhead, but comes to find that this is not possible. He has killed people, knows that in some way this is wrong, but is not sure. His one defence is that he is ill, ill in the sense that he is not in control of his actions. This may be the logical conclusion of the idle tippler's existence – and the narrative has George polish off three-quarters of a bottle of whisky as he writes his suicide note. But his confusion may also be the result of his schizophrenia – the problem again of the novel's overdetermination. Yet it may also be that schizophrenia is the novel's way of showing that drink leads to a mental state akin to schizophrenia, and that this is the psyche of a British nation that could countenance both the shame of Munich and the recklessness of war when it eventually came. The apt symbol that Hamilton finds is the daily round of idle pub-drinking.

Notes

1 G. K. Chesterton, *The Flying Inn* (London, Methuen, 1954 [1914]), p. 33.
2 Mass Observation, *The Pub and the People: A Worktown Study by Mass Observation* (London, Victor Gollancz, 1943), p. 340.
3 The authors of *The Pub and the People*, the sociological and cultural exploration of the life of pubs at the end of the 1930s, note a similar problem for their field: there are 'very few' books 'that contain accurate descriptive material about pubs', mainly because most commentators (sociologists and temperance men) were not often pub-goers: Mass Observation, *Pub*, pp. 339–40. They also note that: 'Amongst contemporary novels there are plenty of pub scenes also, the most outstanding being Joyce's pub stuff in *Ulysses*, and a short story in *New Writing* (1938) by H. T. Hopkinson. But no one – say an educated Indian – ignorant of the pub, reading modern novels would be able to get from them any understanding of what the pub really is and who uses it,' p. 341. Surprisingly, they do not list Hampson's novel or Hamilton's work, both very popular writers in the 1930s, and both with some literary acclaim.
4 Jack London, *The People of the Abyss* (London, Journeyman Press, 1980 [1903]), p. 120.
5 Arthur Morrison, Preface to the 3rd edition of *A Child of the Jago* (Woodbridge, Suffolk, The Boydell Press, 1982 [1896]), pp. 37–8.
6 Arthur Morrison, *Tales of Mean Streets* (London, Methuen, 1896 [1894]), pp. 7–8.
7 Ibid., p. 8.

8   Morrison, Preface to *Child*, p. 38.
9   Morrison, *Streets*, p. 82.
10 *Ibid.*, pp. 173 and 174.
11 *Ibid.*, p. 174.
12 *Ibid.*, p. 175.
13 *Ibid.*, p. 192.
14 Joseph Conrad was to use the idea of revolutionaries blowing up Greenwich as a symbolic act in *The Secret Agent*, a few years later than Morrison's story.
15 Quoted in Mass Observation, *Pub*, p. 147.
16 T. S. Eliot, *The Waste Land*, in *Collected Poems 1909–1962* (London, Faber, 1974), ll. 113 and 115–16.
17 *Ibid.*, ll.139–52.
18 10 May 1915, *Official Report. Parliamentary Debates*, 1376–7.
19 1 March 1915.
20 Eliot asked John Quinn to prepare a contract for the then untitled *Waste Land*. When he read it he replied in a letter: 'It is for the elect or the remnant or the select few or the superior guys, or any word that you may choose, for the small numbers of readers that it is certain to have.' Quoted in *The Waste Land: A Facsimile and Transcript of the Original Drafts Including the Annotations of Ezra Pound*, ed. Valerie Eliot, (London, Faber, 1971), p. xxiii.
21 V. Eliot, *Waste*, ll.1–2, unpublished typescript, p. 5.
22 Eliot, *Waste*, ll. 170–2.
23 A. E. Coppard, 'The Black Dog', in *The Black Dog and Other Stories* (London, Jonathan Cape), 1923.
24 *Ibid.*, p. 15.
25 *Ibid.*, p. 16.
26 *Ibid.*, p. 17.
27 *Ibid.*, p. 22.
28 *Ibid.*, p. 23.
29 *Ibid.*, p. 47.
30 *Ibid.*, p. 48.
31 Jacob Larwood and John Camden Hotten, *English Inn Signs*, revised and modernised, (London, Chatto and Windus, 1951 [1866]) list a few, p. 126.
32 *Ibid*
33 *Brewer's Dictionary of Phrase and Fable*, revised edition (Ivor H. Evans) (London, Cassell, 1970), 'Black Dog'.
34 As described in *The Pub and the People*: 'Saturday night is what is left in our culture of the old orgy, the recurring unrepression. It is a small weekly edition of the major Easter, Christmas, New Year and Whitsun orgies, the great religious festivals, pre-Christian and taken over by Christianity, key points in the cycle of the Industrial year today, days that to the majority of Worktowners no long have any more conscious religious significance than does Sunday, but days of release from the factory routine,' Mass Observation, *Pub*, p. 122.
35 John Hampson, *Saturday Night at The Greyhound* (London, Penguin, 1937 [1931]), p. 134.
36 Robert Kee, *Munich: The Eleventh Hour* (London, Hamilton, 1988), p. 173.
37 *Ibid.*, p. 174.
38 *Ibid.*, p. 180.

39 Patrick Hamilton, *Hangover Square: A Story of Darkest Earl's Court* (London, Penguin, 1974 [1941]), p. 58.
40 Patrick Hamilton, *The Siege of Pleasure*, in *Twenty Thousand Streets under the Sky* (London, Constable, 1935), p. 161.
41 Patrick Hamilton, *Hangover*, p. 58.
42 *Ibid.*, p. 29.
43 P. J. Widdowson, 'The Saloon Bar Society: Patrick Hamilton's Fiction in the 1930s', in *The 1930s: A Challenge to Orthodoxy*, ed. John Lucas (Sussex, Harvester Press, 1978), pp. 117–37, p. 137, n.27.
44 Patrick Hamilton, *Money with Menaces* and *To The Public Danger* (London, Constable, 1939), pp. 90–1.
45 Hamilton, *Hangover*, p. 128.
46 *Ibid.*, pp. 129–30.
47 *Ibid.*, p. 280.

12

Kegged

> Everyone is interested in people, especially if they are behaving discreditably. And here is a book that is a magic casement on a foaming fairyland of ale and cakes. It brings home, with the clarity of a dream, a world where there were lights and thoughtlessness and, above all, an absolute stress on private life.
>
> You walk back into a warm bright room and marvel that in 1938 we never knew that those spittoons were in Arcadia.
>
> Mass observation, *The Pub and the People*[1]

> My favourite public house, 'The Moon under Water', is only two minutes from a bus stop, but it is on a side-street, and drunks and rowdies never seem to find their way there, even on Saturday nights.
>
> George Orwell, 'The Moon Under Water'[2]

Reading an Orwell novel such as *Keep the Aspidistra Flying* (1936) might lead the reader to think that like much else in depressed 1930s England the pub was as joyless a place as the world outside. In Orwell's novel the simple act of buying a drink is a means with which to uncover the whole sorry class structure of the English nation. Gordon Comstock, an impoverished 'poet', imagines spending his half-day off visiting the champagne socialist, Ravelston, only to come out against it: 'how could he go and see Ravelston when he had no money? Ravelston would be sure to say "Let's go to a pub," or something! He couldn't let Ravelston pay for his drinks. His friendship with Ravelston was only possible on the understanding that he paid his share of everything.'[3] Turn to a couple of his essays, however, and the picture is different. During the war Orwell reviewed the Mass Observation publication *The Pub and the People*, a sociological study of a Northern working-class town's favourite habitat, and bemoaned that the pub was on the decline 'because the whole trend of the age is away from creative communal amusements and towards solitary mechanical ones' (cinema and radio).[4] Such a comment showed that cultural commentators still hankered after the organic community, and could find its existence or demise in the pub. As in *Hangover Square*, the symbol of the public house pulls in different directions: a sign of (actual or wished for) community on the one hand, and on the other, the most obvious sign that England is wrong at its core. In 'The Moon under Water', published the year after the war ended, Orwell offers his version of the wished-for English drinking house. The sentiments in this description have lasted until the end of the twentieth century as the dominant ideal of what the English pub is (and, in the short-term English imagination, had been, for centuries).

His favourite hostelry, 'The Moon under Water'[5] is 'uncompromisingly Victorian' he tells us, not 'modern', in its decor and architecture, with separate rooms: public bar, saloon bar, ladies' bar, discreet off-licence, and upstairs dining room where you can eat lunch, not dinner, with draught stout. The mugs are china, now thirty years out of date, but they make the beer taste better than liquor in handleless glasses. The surprising garden at the back is its best feature, 'because it allows whole families to go there instead of Mum having to stay at home and mind the baby while Dad goes out alone'. However, Orwell is toying with us: 'But now is the time to reveal something which the discerning and disillusioned reader will probably have guessed already. There is no such place as "The Moon under Water".' He tells us that some places he knows come close, and that one pub has as many as eight of the ten necessary qualities. It is rather like the game played by Coppard – utilising a pub to imagine the ideal, only to burst the bubble. The quiet family values are, however, installed, and the suggestion that a number of places come close offers the hope that England is not so bad after all. The essay came out in the *Evening Standard*, 9 February 1946, and was no doubt an attempt to cheer up a nation that was looking for signs of victory after the long hard slog of the Second World War. In the Review essay he had argued that the value of the pub was its communal atmosphere; going to the pub had very little to do with drunkenness, and this is also his argument in 'The Moon under Water'.

Both Orwell's essay and the authorial presence in *The Pub and the People* look backwards. The latter, in particular, with its distillation of the working-class pub experience, treats its subjects anthropologically. But in the 1950s at the forefront of English literature was a new brand of writer, male authors from the working or lower middle classes, describing provincial life, writers who gained the moniker 'Angry Young Men'. For them, angry or not, the pub was a fact of existence, not an object of curiosity. More than that, it was a desirable place to be and hardly needed to be defended against middle-class disapproval.

What has been cast as 'seminal' in its influence on the Angry Young Men was William Cooper's *Scenes from Provincial Life* (1950). The central couple spend their Sundays at the Dog and Duck in pre-war England, and their break-up 'scene' is titled 'Conclusion in a Public-House', although in true English 'liberal' style there is no conclusion at all. In the very ordinariness of English life that the novel offers, these aspects of the landscape are thoroughly unremarkable.⁶ Not that the pub loses its class connotations. In Kingsley Amis's *Lucky Jim* (1954) the down-at-heel lecturer Jim Dixon escapes from the pretentious musical evening of Professor Welch to the local pub. His delight there is enhanced when he discovers that the pub stays open till 10.30 rather than the 10.00 he had assumed.⁷ Where once the narrative might have placed such an action (if it were allowed in at all) under a cloud, now the dominant social world finds such actions comically congenial and culturally laudable. In this environment of post-war Britain, the pub has no moral taint to it. Nor is it unfamiliar to the readers of the literature (as, presumably, it was to the southern readers of *The Pub and the People*). Archie Rice in John Osborne's play *The Entertainer* (1957) cannot go to Canada because they do not serve draught Bass in Toronto.⁸ It is a perfectly reasonable excuse (to the audience if not for his relations). John Braine's quintessential 1950s' novel *Room at the Top* (1957) finds working-class (clerical-class) Joe Lampton chasing the posh Susan. At the cinema in the intermission they go to the bar where Susan observes, as she looks warily about the room: 'Mummy would be awfully cross if she knew I was here – She thinks pubs are low.'⁹ But the 'centre' is now the provinces and the lower classes, not London and not big money (even if Joe opts for the material girl in the end), and Susan's comment places her on the outside of the cultural centre. People spend their time in pubs naturally and willingly, they do not have to be dragged either into or out of them.

Such is the case in Alan Sillitoe's *Saturday Night and Sunday Morning* (1958). The difference pre- and post-war literature can be seen by comparing it with *Saturday Night at The Greyhound*. In Sillitoe's novel the world remains enclosed within that of the working class whose weekly routine ends with the Saturday night drinking binge. There is no introduction of 'the monied' or 'upper class' with which to contrast this world, as happens in Hampson's novel. At the end of *Saturday Night at The Greyhound* Ruth is arrested and can only laugh at the events. The narrator comments: 'From her side it was comedy, for the Flacks tragedy.'¹⁰ In other words, the story can be interpreted from two opposed class points-of-view. With Sillitoe's first novel there is no such dual perspective, the narrator's voice is clearly complicit with that of the male working class.

This is evident in the opening scene at the White Horse, where the description of Arthur Seaton's drunkenness – 'eleven pints of beer and seven small gins playing hide-and-seek inside his stomach' – is barely distinguishable from the narrator's own viewpoint. The address to 'you' embraces reader, narrator and Arthur:

> For it was Saturday night, the best and bingiest glad-time of the week, one of the fifty-two holidays in the slow-turning Big Wheel of the year, a violent preamble to a prostrate Sabbath. Piled-up passions were exploded on Saturday night, and the effect of a week's monotonous graft in the factory was swilled out of your system in a burst of goodwill. You

followed the motto of 'be drunk and be happy', kept your crafty arms around female waists, and felt the beer going beneficially down into the elastic capacity of your guts.[11]

The novel weaves in and out of Arthur's thoughts and the lives of those with whom he comes into contact. He sleeps with another man's wife without guilt, rides his luck at the factory and earns enough money to keep a wardrobe full of teddy-boy suits. At the end he settles down to a domestic life after acquaintances of the husband beat him up. The binary structure of the novel plays out the symbolism of the weekly ritual. Part 1 is the festival life of Saturday night, a period of sheer irresponsibility – best symbolised when Brenda becomes pregnant, much to Arthur's indifference (gin and a hot bath will cure that). Saturday is always sexually charged, and so this section covers Arthur's sexual exploits – he is in the pub with Brenda at the beginning. Part 2, Sunday morning, is when Arthur wakes up to some kind of a planned life. He asks the 'good' girl Doreen to marry him, and the sense of the novel is that this represents the 'endpoint' of Arthur's life. The second part is noticeably shorter. It is rather like the ending of a *Bildungsroman*: once the main character is married off all interest is lost – as might be expected of an 'angry young man' with nothing in particular to be angry about and no more women to chase.

Although lumped together, novels such as *Scenes from Provincial Life* and *Lucky Jim* differ from novels such as *Saturday Night and Sunday Morning*, *Room at the Top* and David Storey's *This Sporting Life* (1960) in the class base of the protagonists. The former have middle-class anti-authority heroes whereas the latter have working-class angry young men. Thus Arthur Seaton is at home in his pubs, but, unless a certain type of pub – for example a country or suburban pub – Amis's Jim Dixon and Wain's Charles Lumley are types of interloper who tend to 'slip out for a couple'. For them, binge drinking is not the norm, hence the enormity of Dixon's hangover. The difference between the two is interestingly and self-consciously delineated in another 'seminal' novel of the 1950s, John Wain's *Hurry on Down* (1953).

Charles Lumley has finished university and is struggling to find his place in the world. In common with other disgruntled young males of this literary period he is dissatisfied with existing structures of life, and throughout the novel we see him explore and dismiss possible roles – the standard middle-class life with girlfriend Sheila, the Romantic life with Veronica, and a series of differently styled jobs – drugs runner, bouncer, chauffeur. Towards the start of the novel he attempts some kind of meeting with Sheila, only to find Sheila's sister and brother-in-law there. They heartily disapprove of his drifting through life, and the scene climaxes when Charles attempts to throw the washing-up bowl over Robert. Charles escapes to a nearby pub.

Initially the pub is quiet and he finds himself listening to some inane banter between the landlord and a drinker. As the pub fills up and Charles gets drunker, he finds himself having to move out of the way of the incoming groups. His outsider status is confirmed when someone gets served at the bar before he does. He realises that the pub is 'predominantly working class in atmosphere' and consequently 'peopled by raw, angular personalities who had been encouraged by life to develop their sharp edges'.[12] When the landlord asks him to move away from the bar now that he has been served, Charles shrieks, 'I haven't been served! I want a gin and a glass of stout!', causing the pub to go silent. The 'all-important fact' is 'brought home' – he is 'imprisoned in his class', educated for a world that the 'jungle' of the 1950s has done away with. Further, he hates his own class. His ignominy (and fall from class) is complete when a man at the bar asks for a light. The drunken Charles struggles to open a box of matches and then light one, eventually thrusting 'the burning match out to the full extent of his arm. Immediately the face ceased to be a face, and became a purple sphere of fury with two vast coloured eyes. As the match sank sizzling into his limp moustache, and the flame flickered for an instant up his nostrils, the man started back with a hoarse cry of pain and anger.'[13] Charles has done the worst thing a man from his class could do: 'He had been the cause of a disturbance! He had broken the sacred law of self-effacing, mute compliance – he had made, the phrase ran, an *exhibition of himself*!'[14] Charles leaves. Wain uses the pub as a tool to bring to the surface the whole middle-class structure within which Charles is locked, setting up the rest of the novel for a sequence of attempted escapes. The plot trajectory remains middle-class, with the sense, as with the other novels, that the working classes are destined to remain 'fixed' in social and geographical locations, symbolised by a town or city pub, whereas the middle classes are mobile and have choices, no matter how much they might despise their own class.

Outsiders inside

> 'Hey, Doris, man,' she says, 'how are you doing and how are you getting on with the English?' 'Well,' I say, 'the thing is, I don't think I've met any. London is full of foreigners.' 'Hell, yes, I know what you mean. But I met an Englishman last night.' 'You didn't?' 'I did. In a pub. And he's the real thing.'
>
> Doris Lessing, *In Pursuit of the English*[15]

With the acceptance (return) to a predominantly realistic mode for English fiction from the 1950s onwards (an occasional allegory notwithstanding), the pub faded into the background of the everyday fabric, taken for granted. In social worlds the pub also became more acceptable to more classes, although still retaining something of its working-class aura. Its centrality to English lower-class culture became enshrined in two British soaps in particular: 'the Rover's Return' in *Coronation Street*, which started in 1960, and 'the Queen Vic' in *EastEnders*, which started in 1985. It seemed only natural to use a pub as the focal point for 'local' communities, although of course with an increasingly multicultural Britain their value as proper 'social centres' has always been debatable, particularly in *Coronation Street*. However, when a soap attempted to exist without a pub, most noticeably *Brookside* (started in 1982), it struggled to find natural meeting places for its cast, and the latter eventually had to create 'Bar Brookie' as a surrogate public house for the unfeasibly temperate inhabitants.

Nor should we forget the change in English drinking habits. From the 1970s lager gained hugely in popularity, and much like other arguments we have seen throughout history, this 'foreign' drink attracted much highly prejudiced criticism: it was un-English, it was drunk by the young; it led directly to a particular kind of violence called lager-loutism, with its association in the 1970s and 1980s of football hooliganism and Spanish-holiday yobbism. Lager was also part of the trend towards kegged beer, that is, beer delivered to the customer through artificially gassy means, and since its foundation in 1971 the Campaign for Real Ale has worked tirelessly to raise the public consciousness to appreciate the value of beer produced and delivered to the consumer without artificial aids. In the late 1980s, wine became increasingly acceptable to a larger proportion of the public. But drinking customs and associations died hard, and in the latter part of the 1990s the stand-up comedian Al Murray ('Pub Landlord') devoted a whole show to drink-related prejudices. It was called '… and a glass of white wine for the lady'.[16] Women, of course, do not drink pints. The landlord ruthlessly sought out members of the audience whose drinking practices did not measure up to his own high standards.

The popularity and convenience of the public-house setting has not abated in literature and drama. Robert Rankin, a fantasy writer, set his Brentford trilogy in the Flying Swan pub, where a character materialises in the first novel, *The Antipope* (1981), with a whiff of sulphur to spook the regulars.[17] The theatre group 'Told by an Idiot' in collaboration with Biyi Bandele proffered *Happy Birthday, Mister Deka D*.[18] The play is set in an absurdist always closed/always open public house. The hero of the title sits silently in the middle of crazed floorboards celebrating his birthday every day, unaware of the barmaid and ex-lover who awkwardly and tangentially discuss their own fractured lives (1999). Two novels by Irish writers have used the English pub as an integral part of their stories: Michael Curtin's *The League Against Christmas* (1989) and J. M. O'Neill's *Duffy is Dead* (1987). Both offer the outsider's insider view of pub life, and both use it as a fitting place to explore ideas of 'humanity', particularly the latter.

In Curtin's novel the pub as an escape against reality is brought into interesting conflict with another supposed bastion of goodwill and escapism, Christmas. A group of five people gradually accumulate to make up a whist group in the King's Arms pub in Shepherd's Bush: Percy Bateman, an itinerant Irishman; Kenneth Foster – chartered accountant; Ellis – ex-London Area Manger of NatWest Finance; Ernie Gosling, potman at the King's Arms; Diana Hayhurst, in charge of a woman's magazine called *Unipolitan*. Bateman harbours a deep-seated grudge against his father and the Irish village he grew up in; Foster has a secret desire to wear women's clothes; Ellis carries a piece of lino with him wherever he goes, eschewing all other floor coverings; Gosling, at sixty, discovers his vocation as a potman; Diana Hayhurst, to keep her magazine in tune with her readers, seeks out unreconstructed men and prints the opposite of whatever opinions they hold – hence her glee at finding a group of four rum males in the King's Arms – 'Over her dead body ... would the man's viewpoint get into *Unipolitan*.'[19]

Curtin's pub is thus a convenient means of bringing together a disparate group of people who have all fared differently under Thatcher's regime. The tone of the novel is fairly even-handed about the impact of Thatcherite economics, some people having done well, others having lost their jobs. However, the mean-spirited desire to launch an attack on Christmas might be seen as of a piece with Thatcherism, such as when Foster contemplates why Ellis should carry around a piece of lino: '[Ellis] liked to step on something cold in the morning. Some people did like a touch of cold, the Prime Minister herself attributed her capacity for hard work and long hours in part to the aid of a lack of warmth in staying alert.'[20] This 'coldness' aligns itself with the desire to spoil Christmas.

Duffy is Dead (1987) follows the end of an Irishman's reign as landlord of a London pub, seemingly precipitated by the death of the enigmatic Duffy. Part of the subtlety of this and Curtin's novel is the way in which they use and transform elements we have already encountered. In *Duffy is Dead* Calnan is the bibulous landlord of the Trade Winds in Dalston, London. He is fat, Irish, savagely ugly and world-weary, but not so jaundiced as to refuse a good practical joke when the occasion presents itself. The pub he manages is ruinously dilapidated. At twenty-five to four one morning he is woken by a phone call from Mackessy, one of the bar-fly regulars, to be told that 'Duffy is dead'. Both Mackessy and his side-kick Neelan are so devastated by the news that they demand that Calnan open up so that they can drown their sorrows.

> 'It's a shock for you, Cal, I know. But I thought I'd give it to you straight from the shoulder. Best in the end.'
> 'You're looking for a drink, aren't you?' Calnan said.
> 'Well, I wouldn't say no. And Neelan needs a few shots. We're at the Archway. The Spades have a mini-shop across the road. We could be down to you in ten minutes.'
> Calnan's silence was consent. He rang off: death opened groaning sluice-gates of insincerity. Duffy, dead, owed him ten pounds, he remembered.[21]

Mackessy and Neelan suggest that the pub should raise a funeral fund. After a brawl in the pub they pocket the proceeds they claim have been stolen, and it is then up to Calnan somehow to save the day, whilst not appearing to be a soft touch. He uses the 'physiotherapist' Cassie across the road to lead Mackessy on, and whilst Mackessy is amorously engaged he steals the money back. Throughout the novel, whilst Calnan is footing the funeral expenses, he plays an elaborate joke on the hapless twosome, kidding them that some rich American friend of Duffy's is paying. Generosity is a weakness in a harsh environment, but without it life has no value. Because the public house is traditionally, mythically, some kind of refuge from the world at large, regardless of its function in the marketplace, O'Neill can use its symbolism to adjudge just how much succour and sustenance remains in a modern metropolis.

In O'Neill's novel the changed English landscape is finally recognised in literature of the pub, helped by its central character's being Irish (similarly in Curtin's novel, the pub harbours a cast of 'Irish and non-Europeans'). Multiracial England has a large majority, like the Irish, who are both inside and outside; insiders from birth, but outsiders because of the racist culture that surrounds them. In *Duffy is Dead* allegiances are formed partly out of economic necessity, partly out of gruff acceptance, and occasionally out of genuine fellow-feeling. But outsider status is confirmed when Calnan shows disrespect to some 'rozzers' (policemen) who pick on him as he urinates in a graveyard. Because he is Irish they have his pub raided as a suspected IRA den. The brewery does not like the attention the pub receives from the police, who disclose to the brewery Calnan's previous criminal record, a fact he had not declared in his application for the licence. That leads to the end of his tenancy at the close of the novel.

The main emotional thrust of *Duffy is Dead* is the battle of wills between Calnan and the transparently cunning Mackessy and Neelan. The pub is the site where, as we have seen before, the milk of human kindness is tested. To be too generous to the likes of Mackessy and Neelan would be sure disaster for a landlord, as it is for Fred Flack in *Saturday Night at The Greyhound*. As Calnan uncovers another side to Duffy's life, not just a waster like them – forced into retirement when he hurt his hand feeding the ducks[22] and consequently the 'contented foster child of the State for almost all his days'[23] – but also known as Roderick Hodder O'Callaghan Davis, a friend of the rich in Stoke Newington in his capacity as a 'gifted medium', Calnan's 'humanity' is 'held on a thread over a black hole of space'.[24] The goodness of human nature, in those who are scheming spongers – such as the bar-flies – and in those who must eke out an existence in difficult circumstances – Calnan – is under strain, much as when the hostelry is the testing ground in Dekker's time of plague, or in John Taylor's *Pennyless Pilgrimage* (1618). 'Mean city streets left marks on man and beast' as the narrator comments at one point.[25] But Calnan, as a publican, is expected to suffer financial loss: 'Part of the game', Mackessy says.²⁶ Calnan himself has some sense of the landlord as a pastoral figure tending to a wayward flock: 'morning taprooms were acts of contrition, imperfect, but needing forgiveness',²⁷ and even the parish priest suggests this role for Calnan: 'The Landlord of the Inn is observed, you know. His house is a landmark. A respected man. People follow.'²⁸ And Calnan as publican knows just how difficult his part in society is: 'winning plaudits for kindness or humanity were symptoms of disease, softening bone, wasting tissue. Great publicans were cast-iron vegetables.'²⁹ The question 'Am I my brother's keeper?' is never far away; the fact that Calnan keeps the worst cleaner in London on his books, because he cannot bear to contemplate the man's existence if he were unemployed, is the book's answer to that implied question.

The notion that Duffy lives in modern plague times simmers carefully throughout the narrative. Brennan's public announcement that 'Duffy is dead', 'like a bellman in plague',³⁰ casts Duffy as a plague victim. Because they are all of Duffy's circle, they are likewise susceptible to this 'plague'. The connection with London's plagues of old is brought out when Cal is musing in his cellar. He remembers a visit from the brewery surveyor and their conversation.

> 'Ailing publicans,' he said, 'escape to their cellars. They sit, drain their precious flasks, find peace, listen to the shuffling feet above them.'
> 'A kind of early grave,' Calnan said.
> 'Peace, Calnan.'
> Calnan had shown him loose masonry where behind the stonework two yellowed stumps of bone protruded like gross blind creatures born in darkness.
> 'Plague bones,' he had said. 'We demolish old piles and there they are, hundreds of them. Plague pits, you know. A couple of miles of grassy fields from the City to here, once. Dig a hole out there, haul cadavers out by the cartload.'³¹

Remembering this, Calnan carefully digs out the bones and packages them to send off to 'The Caretaker, Leytonstone Cemetery' with the note 'Give these plague bones decent burial.'³² It is a sign of his humanity and a sign of his doom, for he is an ailing publican also. In such a manner the novel uses the pub to uncover the picture of a cosmopolitan London seething with less than civil behaviour in a time of unacknowledged crisis.

'Darts, innit': Martin Amis's *London Fields*

> Though fond of bars and boozing in hotels, I'm not a lover of that gloomiest of English institutions the public house. There is a legend of the gaiety, the heart-warming homeliness of these 'friendly inns' – a legend unshakeable; but all a dispassionate eye can see in them is the

> grim spectacle of 'regulars' at their belching back-slapping beside the counter or, as is more often, sitting morosely eyeing one another, in private silence, before their half-drained gassy pints. (There is also, of course, that game called darts.)
>
> Colin MacInnes, *City of Spades*[33]

> 'Whilst darts is basically a twentieth-century sport, darts go way back into the English folk Heritage. Those famed English archers are said to have played a form of darts prior to defeating the French at the proverbial Battle of Agincourt in 1415.'
>
> Martin Amis, *London Fields*[34]

I end my history of English literature as seen through the bottom of a glass with Martin Amis's *London Fields* (1989). The novel itself is dealing with 'ending', preparing itself and the reader for the Millennium, and as such its whole trajectory is onwards to the cataclysmic. As with O'Neill's *Duffy is Dead*, a London pub is the touchstone of human nature under stress. There are three or four main characters (the novel gives us the choice): Keith Talent, Guy Clinch, Nicola Six and Samson Young, the narrator. Keith is definitively lower class, into promiscuity, darts, pornography and the pub; Guy is very rich, and has to cope with a monstrous child and a passionless wife. Nicola is a fantasy female acting out the role of whore to Keith, innocent maiden to Guy, and 'subject' to/for the narrator. The novel is in the self-reflexive (meta-fictional) mould of postmodern fiction, as the narrator appears to write the novel we are reading as we read it, drawing material from the 'real' world of the characters to construct the story, since, as he says, he has no imagination of his own. The first three chapters set up the book as a 'thriller' with the titles of 'Murderer', 'Murderee' and 'Foil', placing the characters in the role of narrative function rather than purely psychological entities. As the story proceeds it becomes apparent that Nicola has experienced everything that there is to experience in life (except perhaps love, and the novel flirts with the idea of the Death of Love) and so plans her own death (reminiscent of Muriel Spark's *The Driver's Seat* (1970)[35]). Hence she plays psychological desire games with both Keith and Guy, building them up into a frenzy where, when it comes to the end, either one is capable of murdering her. At the meta-fictional level there is only one person who can 'end' Nicola, and that is the author-narrator. The novel also flits around this idea until at the death, of the number of possible endings, this is the most suitable, although the narrator can still claim that Nicola 'outwrote' him. The expected ending is that Keith will be the murderer. The surprise ending is that Guy will do it. The actual ending is the 'meta-fictional' murder of Nicola Six.

The other key element in the novel is the pub, and Amis uses it in many ways. At the start of the novel the narrator has returned from America and comments: 'Things have changed, things have remained the same, over the past ten years. London's pub aura, that's certainly intensified.'[36] The pub becomes the place where all the characters will meet. It is where the narrator, Guy, and Nicola first meet Keith. Keith thus plays the pivotal role. He gives his address as 'The Black Cross, Portobello Road' as people used to do before street numbering was introduced. Thus Keith is both a link to the past and anachronistic. The narrator proceeds to make the pub central to the ideas of the novel: 'If London's a pub and you want the whole story, then where do you go? You go to a London pub. And that single instant in the Black Cross set the whole story in motion.'[37] The moment is when Nicola Six walks into the pub and enchants all three men: Keith drops his dart onto his big toe, Guy freezes at the pinball table, and the narrator 'melts' into 'the background': 'This moment in the public house, this pub moment, I'm going to have to keep on coming back to it.'[38]

The novel knows that there is something atypical involved in bringing together these four characters. Their social range is too conveniently broad for this type of pub as Amis uses it to introduce class and gender issues. Both Guy and Nicola, the novel proffers, are 'outsiders' to this environment. After all, this is Keith's home. In addition, the lives of both Guy and Nicola are deemed dead or sterile, and so the pub represents 'life', or 'real life' to them, an echo of Eliot's 'Game of Chess'. There is something of an ambivalence in that the novel explores the relationship between art and 'real life', but, self-consciously or not, can only centre 'real life' in a lower-class pub. It is the pub that brings these two characters to 'life'. It is also the foil for judging the anaemic self-satisfied lives of the monied classes, and for exploring the sexism inherent in overtly male environments. Again, evidently, only the lower class exhibit 'aggressive' sexism. Guy's adoration of Nicola as virginal is sexism of a different kind. Yet for all the novel tries to forestall criticism of Nicola as a fantasy figure by making her knowingly complicit in her configuration – '"Nicola, I'm worried about you, as usual … I'm worried they're going to say you're a male fantasy figure" – "I *am* a male fantasy figure. I've been one for fifteen years. It really takes it out of a girl,"'[39] this hardly answers the accusation.

The novel conditionally offers the pub up as the microcosm of London (and by extension, England, since the novel also works as a 'state-of-the-nation' adventure). It shows how England is 'multicultural' by peopling it with 'blacks' and telling us how Keith is helplessly 'multiracial' because he sleeps with anyone, regardless of race, colour or creed.[40] In fact, it is his redeeming feature, the narrator quips. We find Shakespeare to be 'one of the black guys' in the pub, as if no literary pub is complete without a reference to the Bard.[41] That this is the name he gives himself suggests self-publicity in an unresponsive world, and the joke is continued when the narrator remarks that he is the least successful of 'the brothers'.[42]

As to the pub name, the Black Cross[43], this is central to the narrative structure and the novel's symbolism. In general terms it is a sign of the dark side of Christianity, or the demise of Christianity. There is something of this in relation to Guy, who rather than being the bad boy of religion in his association with Guy Fawkes is too 'good' for his own good, or for the present world. More pertinently the narrator opines: 'The Black Cross. A good name, I always thought, sent my way by reality. The cross, darkly cruciform, the meeting place of Nicola and Keith and Guy. A cross has three points. Depending on how you look at it, though, it might be said to have four.'[44] The uncertainty about the number of points is also the uncertainty about the narrative structure and interpretation. It later materialises that the fourth point could be the narrator. The symbolism comes heavy, with cross suggesting both a meeting place and a place on which to suffer, as all the characters do. 'Black' in 'Black Cross' at the least suggests something uneasy, and at the most something evil,[45] and if the reader is in any doubt of the religious thematic Keith's other favourite place is a drinking club called The Golgotha.

As with the reduction of Shakespeare to a mere secondary character in a pub, God too is reduced. When Keith has spent some time with Nicola he feels the need to talk to someone about its bizarreness (nothing has happened): 'The conversation Keith wanted and needed would be with God the barman or with Shakespeare, both of whom, like Keith, had a peculiar difficulty with girls.'[46] In the postmodern era, both God and Shakespeare are defunct absolutes, questionable as ultimate founts of knowledge and artistic achievement, and so they can only appear in the guise of characters in a public house. But ultimately the Black Cross provides an emblem for the difficulty of interpretation. Should the narrator/observer/author be included as an element in fictional calculations? Or are they outside the story? In this instance the author-narrator figure works so hard at putting himself into the narrative there is little real doubt, and the novel ends with a letter from the narrator to Kim Talent, the angelic child of Keith and Kath. The last words are 'Always me. It was me. It was me.'[47]

Keith's talent is darts, and the novel uses this game and its role within popular culture to signify the state of the nation. Keith is venerated in the Black Cross for his darts prowess, which, as the narrator notes, is quite limited. He is therefore something of a false idol. His goal is to be in competition on television, and the novel makes it plain that the game and the esteem with which it and its players are held is a sure sign of reduced circumstances for the nation. The main manner in which this is achieved is by taking quotations from Keith's bible, *Darts: Master the Discipline*, which shows all English history to be a result of darts (probably):

> What is a definite historical fact is that early English cavemen played a form of darts. This is definite from certain markings on the cave walls, thought to resemble a dartboard. Many top darters believe that darts skill goes back to cavemen times. The top caveman would be the guy who brought back the meat every time, employing his darts skills. So in a way, everything goes back to darts. If you think about it, the whole world is darts.[48]

Even Stonehenge might be explained by the fact that it resembles a dartboard. The words of wisdom from *Darts: Master the Discipline* are contrasted with Keith's own thoughts on the subject. Some of it plagiarises the book, as in 'Remember you are a machine. Delivring the dart the same way every time', and some of it is Keith's own thinking, as in 'Clear ideas from your head. You do'nt want nothing in your fukcing head.'⁴⁹ But the relationship between darts and the state of the English nation is made clear when the narrator gives the opinion of Keith and the country at large: 'I don't know why I say Keith isn't good at darts. Keith *is* good at darts. Very often, the darts go where he throws them. His darts genius shines, and brightly. But he is no better at darts than practically everyone else in England. This is a darts culture here: darts is what the Brits do best, in the afterglow of empire.'⁵⁰

England's place in the world as a lesser power trading on its darts ability also places it in the global context. *London Fields* deals with both the national and the universal, as *Darts: Master the Discipline* confidently tells us: 'If you think about it, the whole world is darts,' and the novel offers this postmodern context, not just as it writes itself in a postmodern form, but in some of its observations. The sense of Millennium and apocalypse, enhanced by the odd passage on black holes, is a shared telos. For the drinker, Amis shows it in another fashion. Nicola has been watching darts on television and has noticed that the players only ever drink lager. Why should this be so?

> 'Intelligent question. Good talking point. It's like this. Your top darter is travelling the land, from pub to pub. Now beers vary. Some of them local brews, couple pints and you're well pissed. But lager …'
> 'Yes?'
> 'But lager's *kegged*. It's *kegged*. Standard. You know what you're getting. Now the darter has to drink. Has to. To loosen the throwing arm. Part of his job. But within reason. You know like you set yourself a limit. Like ten pints. Pacing it out over an evening.'⁵⁰

This is the argument about globalisation brought out at the level of the pub. Like fast food and McDonaldisation, the aim is for things to be the same wherever you are in the world. Rather than seeing this as a consequence of supranational power and inherently bad, as the cultural context might normally see it, Keith, unaware of the argument that the artificial (kegged) is undesirable, proudly boasts of the need for standardisation and its use for the darter who has to travel around the country. As Keith expands his horizons to other pubs he becomes corrupted away from the 'values' of the 'local' (community etc.) towards a global community which has little regard for the local (or what might be 'different'). This becomes evident towards the end of the novel when he is due to give a pre-match interview for television. Class prejudice returns in full strength in the studio. The producer's pseudo-French name marks him out as of a higher class order than Keith.

> Keith said, 'Where's the pub then?'
> 'Pub? What pub?' Tony de Taunton looked at Keith curiously.
> 'The venue. The -' Keith snapped his darting finger – 'the Chuckling Sparrow.'
> 'There's no *pub*. Don't you think we have enough grief already, Keith. Without wheeling a couple of hundred pissers in and out of here four nights a week.'[52]

The pub will be dubbed in later from library pictures. In the other world, the world of the media, the mediated world that fakes 'the real', there is no room for the real 'real'. Once again, 'the pub' is real life, here too real for television.

Ultimately, however, the rhetorical 'If London's a pub …' is a red herring, because London/the nation/the world cannot be so neatly compressed. It competes with other spaces, most notably Keith's flat, Guy's house, Nicola's flat and the narrator's alter ego's flat. These are dystopic domestic spaces. The male characters, in time-honoured fashion, escape the home space into the pub, Keith so much so that on television he denies he has a wife or home life at all (although the narrator himself prefers surrogate fatherhood of Kim Talent, suggesting an ultimate distaste for pub-life, and a trajectory away from the pub for author-narrator). What connects 'London Fields' and 'The Black Cross' is their plausible implausibility. There *is* such a place as London Fields marked on the map (Hackney), when no one would expect the capital to play host to its opposite, the rural, but even if this is the case, at the same time the narrator knows that London Fields is 'an escape'. The idea of such an 'escape' in the middle of London mirrors the idea of the Black Cross, a pub that is defiantly 'local' in its atmosphere, 'historical' in its embedded associations, both inside and outside global culture – kegged yet outside mediation.

Doors closing

'Time please' has shouted the end of pub time for most of the twentieth century. But time, as we have seen throughout the book, has been the weft of understanding since at least the Anglo-Saxon riddle whose answer was 'ale', tied to the agricultural cycle of John Barleycorn. By limiting 'time' spent in a public house or similar hostelry (two hours at any one sitting in Jacobean legislation – anything longer was 'idle tippling'), the time of the lower classes has always been circumscribed by those who deemed them untrustworthy, from the religious leaders of the seventeenth century, to the temperance reformers of the nineteenth, and the political leaders during World War I. The licensing legislation that came out of that war dominated much of twentieth-century pub-drinking, and it was not until as late as 1988 that pubs in England (and Wales) were allowed to open weekday afternoons. It was not until 1995 that Sunday afternoon drinking was allowed in England. Pub time had expanded.

London Fields, published in 1989, showed itself aware of the relaxation of hours from the year before, although not in a way likely to endear it to advocates of the change: 'Even though pubs were now open more or less round the clock (there was one near the entrance to the dead-end street), they still exploded at the old closing times: coded memories deep in the genes of pubs.'[53] Amis's novel wrestles with 'time' as a theme, unsure what to do with the conundrum other than describe its complexity in flights of poesy. Originally the novel was to be called *Time's Arrow*, which was indeed to be the title of his next work. It is an allusion to the philosophical problem of which way time flows. *Time's Arrow* picked up on the use of 'time' as an uncertain entity from a passage in Kurt Vonnegut's *Slaughterhouse Five* (1969) in which time runs backwards. *London Fields*, in its preordained outcome, mimics the narrative construction of Vonnegut's novel as a whole, which tells the reader from the outset what the ending will be. Everything has already happened and is about to happen. In *London Fields* the reader always knows that Nicola Six will die.

'It was all about *time*. Time was everywhere present, was massively operational, in the life Keith moved through.'[54] The same could be said of the whole book. Pub time mirrors one of the complexities of time: it is meant to have a beginning and an end, an early doors and a closing time, yet it still contrives to be eternally open (and compare *Happy Birthday, Mister Deka D*, above). Time is finite and time is infinite. When the narrator of *London Fields* keeps returning to 'this pub moment' there is the myth of Nietzsche's 'eternal return' underwriting it, where time moves cyclically, re-presenting the same events, rather than advancing in an irreversible straight line. Although the governance of the public house will no doubt always be prey to the vicissitudes of the great and the good, the pub 'genes' linger on, culturally crucial, continuing to provide fertile material for the literary imagination, the pub moment to which England keeps returning.

Notes

1. Introductory Note to Mass Observation, *The Pub and the People: A Worktown Study by Mass Observation* (London, Victor Gollancz, 1943).
2. George Orwell, 'The Moon under Water', in *The Collected Essays, Journalism and Letters of George Orwell*, vol. 3 (Harmondsworth, Penguin, 1971 [1946]), pp. 63–5, p. 63.
3. George Orwell, *Keep the Aspidistra Flying* (1936), in *The Penguin Complete Novels of George Orwell* (Harmondsworth, Penguin, 1983, p. 619). Ravelston goes to buy a whisky in the pub, but the place is too poor to afford a spirits licence, another sign of the social difference between Ravelston and Gordon.
4. Review, '*The Pub and the People* by Mass Observation', in Orwell, *Collected*

Essays, pp. 61–2, p. 61.
5 Until a recent chain of pubs started up under that name, I don't believe it was an actual sign. Larwood and Hotten do not list one: Jacob Larwood and John Camden Hotten, *English Inn Signs*, revised and modernised (London, Chatto and Windus, 1951 [1866]).
6 William Cooper, *Scenes from Provincial Life* (London, Macmillan, 1969 [1950]).
7 Kingsley Amis, *Lucky Jim* (Harmondsworth, Penguin, 1962 [1954]), p. 54.
8 John Osborne, *The Entertainer* (London, Faber, 1995 [1957]), Scene 8.
9 John Braine, *Room at the Top* (Harmondsworth, Penguin, 1967 [1957]), p. 72.
10 John Hampson, *Saturday Night at The Greyhound* (London, Penguin, 1937 [1931]), p. 249.
11 Alan Sillitoe, *Saturday Night and Sunday Morning* (London, Flamingo, 1994 [1958]).
12 John Wain, *Hurry on Down* (Harmondsworth, Penguin, 1969 [1953]), p. 25.
13 *Ibid*, p. 27.
14 *Ibid*.
15 Doris Lessing, *In Pursuit of the English* (St Albans, Herts, Granada/Panther, 1980 [1960]).
16 Edinburgh Festival, August 1999. At that time it had been running for four years. It went on to win the prestigious Perrier Award.
17 Robert Rankin, *The Antipope* (London, Corgi, 1998 [1981]).
18 Seen by the author at the Crucible Theatre, Sheffield, 16 October 1999.
19 Michael Curtin, *The League Against Christmas* (London, Fourth Estate, 1997 [1989]), p. 47.
20 *Ibid*., p. 44.
21 J. M. O'Neill, *Duffy is Dead* (London, Heinemann, 1987), p. 4.
22 *Ibid*., p. 67.
23 *Ibid*., p. 11.
24 *Ibid*., p. 62.
25 *Ibid*., p. 6.
26 *Ibid*., p. 7.
27 *Ibid*., p. 9.
28 *Ibid*., p. 98.
29 *Ibid*., p. 13.
30 *Ibid*., p.16
31 *Ibid*., p. 145.
32 *Ibid*., p. 146.
33 Colin MacInnes, *City of Spades* (Harmondsworth, Penguin, 1964 [1957]), p. 48.
34 Martin Amis, *London Fields* (London, Penguin, 1990 [1989]), p. 180.
35 Muriel Spark, *The Driver's Seat* (Harmondsworth, Penguin, 1974 [1970]). There may also be an element of Spark's first novel *The Comforters* (1957) involved, since Nicola 'always knew what was going to happen next', p. 15. In Spark's novel the character 'hears' what is going to happen next.
36 Amis, *London*, p. 3.
37 *Ibid*., p. 14.
38 *Ibid*., p. 23.
39 *Ibid*., p. 260.
40 *Ibid*., p. 4.

41　In Curtin's *The League Against Christmas*, Shakespeare is 'decentred' when he becomes the name for the pub in Ireland the motley crew drink in.
42　Amis puts these terms into a comparative framework of America and Britain, and it is not clear whether he intends 'brothers' to signify American slang.
43　'The Black Cross' is the sign of the Teutonic Knights, but the novel does not appear to use this (Larwood, *Signs*, p. 91).
44　Amis, *London*, p. 209. The observation about three or four points does not really make sense, since most crosses have at least four points (and the one that *London Fields* conjures up would be classed as having four points). Symbolically 'four points' is important – 'the cross of the crucifixion is said to have been made of palm, cedar, olive, and cypress, to signify the four quarters of the globe' (*Brewer's Dictionary of Phrase and Fable*). The only cross that could be said to have three points is the 'tau' cross, or 'crux commissa', in the shape of a 'T', from ancient Egyptian culture, but there is nothing to suggest that this is the kind of cross involved in the pub sign.
45　Although not as a racial element. Elsewhere in the novel there is a hint of play on 'blackness' as a cultural force, in racial and other terms such as 'black hole', but this is not developed.
46　*Ibid.*, p. 168.
47　*Ibid.*, p. 470.
48　*Ibid.*, p. 396.
49　*Ibid.*
50　*Ibid.*, p. 208.
51　*Ibid.*, p. 174.
52　*Ibid.*, p. 457.
53　*Ibid.*, p. 66.
54　*Ibid.*, p. 172.

Bibliography

Ames, Richard, *A Search after Wit; Or a Visitation of the Authors: In Answer to the late Search After Claret, Or visitation of Vintners, 'By an Under-Drawer at the —'s Head Tavern in Gate-Street'*, London, 1691.
Amis, Kingsley, *Lucky Jim*, Harmondsworth, Penguin, 1962 [1954].
Amis, Martin, *London Fields*, London, Penguin, 1990 [1989].
—— *Time's Arrow*, London, QPD [Quality Paperbacks Direct], 1992 [1991].
Amussen, Susan Dwyer, 'The Gendering of Popular Culture in Early Modern England', in Harris, ed., *Culture*, 1995, pp. 48–68.
Annual Register, 1763, pp. 35–8.
Ashton, Robert, 'Popular Entertainment and Social Control in Later Elizabethan and Early Stuart London', *London Journal*, 9 (1983), 3–19.
Askwith, Lord, *British Taverns: Their History and Laws*, London, Routledge, 1928.
Assheton, William, *A Discourse Against 1. Drunkenness. 2. Swearing and Cursing …*, London, 1692.
Baggott, Rob, *Alcohol, Politics and Social Policy*, Aldershot, Hants, Gower Publishing, 1990.
Bamford, Samuel, *The Autobiography of Samuel Bamford*, 2 vols; vol. I: *Early Days* [1848–49]; vol. 2: *Passages in the Life of a Radical* [1839–41], ed. W. H. Chaloner, London, Frank Cass, 1967.
Bandele, Biyi and 'Told by an Idiot', *Happy Birthday, Mister Deka D*, Crucible Theatre, Sheffield, 16 October 1999.
Barker, Francis, *The Tremulous Private Body: Essays on Subjection*, London, Methuen, 1984.
Barr, Andrew, *Drink: An Informal Social History*, London, Bantam, 1995.
Barry, Jonathan, 'Literacy and Literature in Popular Culture: Reading and Writing in Historical Perspective', in Harris, ed., *Culture*, 1995, pp. 69–94.
Batchelor, Denzil, *The English Inn*, London, Batsford, 1964.
Beaumont, Francis and John Fletcher, *The Knight of the Burning Pestle*, in C. B. Wheeler (ed.), *Six Plays by Contemporaries of Shakespeare*, London, Oxford University Press, 1964.
Bennett, Judith M., *Ale, Beer, and Brewsters in England: Women's Work in a Changing World, 1300–1600*, New York, Oxford University Press, 1996.
Bickerdyke, John, *The Curiosities of Ale and Beer: An Entertaining History*, London, Swan Sonnenschein, 1889.

Boardman, Kay, '"The Glass of Gin": Renegade Reading Possibilities in the Classic Realist Text', in *Gendering the Reader*, ed. Sara Mills, New York, Harvester Wheatsheaf, 1994, pp. 199–216.

Boorde, Andrew, *Regiment of Health*, London, 1542.

Boswell, James, *Boswell's London Journal 1762–3*, ed. Frederick A. Pottle, London, Heinemann, 1951.

—— *The Life of Johnson*, 3rd edition, R. W. Chapman, corrected by J. D. Fleeman, London, Oxford University Press, 1970.

Bottomley, Maurice, 'Insiders, Outsiders and Taxpayers: Sub-cultural Drinking Spaces in Colin MacInnes' *London Trilogy*', paper given at 'Drink, Drinkers and Drinking Places', University of Sheffield, 15/16 November, 1997.

Bradley, S. A. J., ed. and trans., *Anglo-Saxon Poetry*, London, Dent, 1997.

Braine, John, *Room at the Top*, Harmondsworth, Penguin, 1967 [1954].

Bretherton, R. F., 'Country Inns and Alehouses', in *Englishmen at Rest and Play: Some Phases of English Leisure 1558–1714*, ed. Reginald Lennard, Oxford, Clarendon Press, 1931.

Brewer's Dictionary of Phrase and Fable, centenary edition, revised by Ivor H. Evans, London, Cassell, 1970.

Bribery at Elections, British Parliamentary Papers (Report from the Select Committee on Bribery at Elections Together with Minutes of Evidence Appendix and Index), Shannon (Ireland), Irish University Press, 1968 [1835].

Brome, Vincent, *The Other Pepys*, London, Weidenfeld and Nicolson, 1992.

Brontë, Anne, *The Tenant of Wildfell Hall*, Edinburgh, Thomas Nelson, n.d. [1848].

Browne, Dr Peter, *A Discourse of Drinking Healths …*, Dublin, 1716.

Burke, Thomas, *The English Inn*, London, Longmans, Green and Co., 1931.

—— *English Inns*, London, Collins, 1944.

—— *The Winsome Wench: The Story of a London Inn 1825–1900*, London, Routledge, 1938.

Burns, Robert, *Poems and Songs*, Edinburgh, Gordon Wright Publishing, 1987.

Bushaway, Bob, *By Rite: Custom, Ceremony and Community in England 1700–1880*, London, Junction Books, 1982.

Carter, Henry, *The English Temperance Movement: A Study in Objectives*, London, Hogarth Press, 1933.

Centlivre, Susanna, *The Man's Bewitch'd; or The Devil to do About Her*, Chadwyck-Healey English Prose Drama Full-Text Database, 1996 [1709].

Cervantes, Miguel de, *Don Quixote*, Harmondsworth, Penguin, 1986 [1605].

Chaucer, Geoffrey, *The Canterbury Tales*, in *The Complete Works of Geoffrey Chaucer*, ed. F. N. Robinson, London, Oxford University Press, 1976.

Chesterton, G. K., *The Flying Inn*, London, Methuen, 1954 [1914].

Cheyne, George, *An Essay on Health and Long Life*, London, 1724.

Child, Samuel, *Every Man His Own Brewer*, London, n.d. [1795].

Cippola, Carlo M., *Clocks and Culture 1300–1700*, London, Collins, 1967.

Clark, Peter, 'The Alehouse and the Alternative Society', in *Puritans and Revolutionaries: Essays in Seventeenth-Century History Presented to Christopher Hill*, ed. Donald Pennington and Keith Thomas, Oxford, Oxford University Press, 1976.

—— *The English Alehouse: A Social History 1200–1830*, Harlow, Longman, 1983.

Clavell, John, *A Recantation of an ill led Life. Or A discoverie of the High-way Law*, London, 1628.

Coates, Neil, *Best Pub Walks in the Lake District*, Wilmslow, Cheshire, Sigma, 1998.
—— *Parliamentary History*, vol. 15, 1763, pp. 1307–14.
Cobbett, William, *Cottage Economy: Containing Information relative to the brewing of BEER, making of BREAD ...*, London, Peter Davies, 1926, reprint, 1966 [1822].
Coghill, Nevill, trans. *The Canterbury Tales*, London, Penguin, 1977.
Coleridge, Samuel Taylor, *Biographia Literaria or Biographical Sketches of My Literary Life and Opinions*, ed. George Watson, London, Dent, 1982 [1817].
Colquhoun, Patrick, *Observations and Facts Relative to Licensed Ale-Houses, in the City of London and its Environs*, London, 1794.
Combe, William, *Doctor Syntax's Three Tours: In Search of the Picturesque, Consolation, and a Wife*, London, James Camden Hotten, Piccadilly, n.d. [1809; 1820; 1821].
Cooper, William, *Scenes from Provincial Life*, London, Macmillan, 1969 [1950].
Coppard, A. E., *The Black Dog and Other Stories*, London, Jonathan Cape, 1923.
Cowper, William, *The Task and Other Poems*, ed. James Sambrook, London, Longman, 1994.
Crabbe, George, *The Complete Poetical Works*, ed. Norma Dalrymple-Champneys and Arthur Pollard, 3 vols, Oxford, Clarendon Press, 1988.
Creighton, Charles, *A History of Epidemics in Britain from A. D. 664 to the Extinction of Plague*, London, Cambridge University Press, 1891.
Curtin, Michael, *The League Against Christmas*, London, Fourth Estate, 1997 [1989].
Day, Gary, ed., *Varieties of Victorianism: The Uses of a Past*, Basingstoke, Macmillan, 1998.
Dekker, Thomas, *The Non-Dramatic Works of Thomas Dekker*, ed. Alexander B. Grosart, 5 vols, London, 1884–5.
—— *The Seven Deadly Sinnes of London: Drawne in Severall Coaches Through the Seven Severall Gates of the Citie Bringing the Plague with Them*, London, 1606.
Delderfield, Eric R., *Introduction to Inn Signs*, Newton Abbot, David and Charles, 1969.
De Quincey, Thomas, *Confessions of an English Opium-Eater*, Oxford, Oxford University Press, 1998 [1821].
Dickens, Cedric, *Drinking with Dickens*, Goring-on-Thames, England, Elvendon Press, 1980.
Dickens, Charles, *Barnaby Rudge*, London, Penguin, 1997 [1841].
—— *Bleak House*, Ware, Herts., Wordsworth, 1996 [1853].
—— *David Copperfield*, London, Penguin, 1996 [1849–50].
—— *Dombey and Son*, London, Penguin, 1985 [1846–48].
—— *Great Expectations*, Harmondsworth, Penguin, 1980 [1860-61].
—— *Hard Times*, Harmondsworth, Penguin, 1982 [1854].
—— *Martin Chuzzlewit*, London, Penguin, 1986 [1843–44].
—— *Nicholas Nickleby*, London, Penguin, 1986 [1838–39].
—— *The Old Curiosity Shop*, London, Penguin, 1985 [1840–41].
—— *Oliver Twist [or, the Parish Boy's Progress]*, London, Penguin, 1985 [1837–39].
—— *Our Mutual Friend*, London, Penguin, 1985 [1864–65].
—— *The Pickwick Papers*, London, Penguin, 1986 [1836–37].
—— *Sketches by Boz*, London, Penguin, 1995 [1836; 1839].
Dixon, John Henry, ed., *Ancient Ballads, and Songs of the Peasantry of England, Taken down from Oral Recitation From Private Manuscripts, Rare Broadsides, and*

Scarce Publications, Wakefield, Yorks., EP Publishing Limited, 1973 [London, 1846].

Dogget, Thomas, *The Country-Wake*, London, 1692.

Dollimore, Jonathon, 'Transgression and Surveillance in Measure for Measure', in *Political Shakespeare: New Essays in Cultural Materialism*, ed. Jonathon Dollimore and Alan Sinfield, Manchester, Manchester University Press, 1985, pp. 72–87.

Dorn, Nicholas, *Alcohol, Youth and the State*, London, Croom Helm, 1983.

Duckworth, Alistair M., 'Gardens, Houses, and the Rhetoric of Description in the English Novel', in *The Fashioning and Functioning of the British Country House*, ed. Gervase Jackson-Stops *et al.*, Hanover, University Press of New England, 1989, pp. 395–413.

Dunlop, John, *The Philosophy of Artificial and Compulsory Drinking Usage in Great Britain and Northern Ireland*, London, Houlston and Stoneman, 1839.

Earle, Peter, *The Making of the English Middle Class: Business, Society and Family Life in London, 1660–1730*, London, Methuen, 1989.

Earnshaw, Steven, 'The Reason for Drinking in Hardy's *The Mayor of Casterbridge*', in Day, ed., *Varieties of Victorianism*, 1988, pp. 142–60.

Eliot, George, *Felix Holt: The Radical*, London, Penguin, 1995 [1866].

—— *Scenes of Clerical Life*, London, Penguin, 1998 [1857].

—— *Silas Marner*, London, Penguin, 1996 [1861].

Eliot, T. S., *Collected Poems 1909–1962*, London, Faber, 1974.

Eliot, Valerie, ed., *The Waste Land: A Facsimile and Transcript of the Original Drafts Including the Annotations of Ezra Pound*, London, Faber, 1971.

Emmison, F. G., *Elizabethan Life*, Chelmsford, 1970.

Everitt, Alan, ed., *Perspectives in English Urban History*, London, Macmillan, 1973.

The Exeter Book Riddles, translated and introduced by Kevin Crossley-Holland, Harmondsworth, Penguin, 1979.

Farquhar, George, *The Works of George Farquhar*, ed. Shirley Strum Kenny, 2 vols, Oxford, Clarendon Press, 1988.

Federico, Annette, '"I must have drink": Addiction, Angst, and Victorian Realism', *Dionysos*, 2:2 (Fall 1990), 11–25.

Fielding, Henry, *Amelia*, ed. A. R. Humphreys, 2 vols, London, Dent, 1968 [1755].

—— *An Enquiry into the Causes of the Late Increase of Robbers and Related Writings*, ed. Malvin R. Zirker, Oxford, Clarendon Press, 1988.

—— *An Enquiry into the Causes ...*, facsimile edition, AMS Press, New York, 1975.

—— *Joseph Andrews*, London, Penguin, 1977 [1742].

—— *Journal of a Voyage to Lisbon*, London, Chiswick Press, 1892 [1755].

—— *Tom Jones*, ed. R. P. C. Mutter, London, Penguin, 1985 [1749].

Finch, Anne, [Countess of Winchilsea], *Miscellany Poems, on Several Occasions*, London, 1713.

Findlay, Alison. 'Theatres of Truth: Drinking and Drama in Early Modern England', paper delivered to English Staff Seminar, Sheffield Hallam University, 1996.

Fletcher, Anthony and John Stevenson, eds, *Order and Disorder in Early Modern England*, Cambridge, Cambridge University Press, 1985. Introduction by Fletcher and Stevenson, pp. 1–40.

Fothergill, John, *An Innkeeper's Diary*, London, Faber, 1987 [1931].

Fowler, Alastair, *The Country House Poem: A Cabinet of Seventeenth-Century Estate*

Poems and Related Items, Edinburgh, Edinburgh University Press, 1994.

French, R. V., *Nineteen Centuries of Drink in England: A History*, 2nd edition – enlarged and revised, London, National Temperance Publication Depot, n.d. [1st edition 1884].

Gascoyne, George, *A Delicate Diet, for daintie mouthde droonkards. Wherein the fowle abuse of common Carowsing, and Quaffing with hartie draughtes, is honestlie admonished*, London, 1576, reprint, 1789.

Gay, John, *The Beggar's Opera*, ed. Bryan Loughrey and T. O. Treadwell, Harmondsworth, Penguin, 1986.

—— 'Wine. A Poem', Chadwyck-Healey Poetry Full-Text Database, 1996–98 [1708].

George, Dorothy M., *London Life in the Eighteenth Century*, Harmondsworth, Penguin (Peregrine), 1966 [1925].

Gervais, David, *Literary Englands: Versions of 'Englishness' in Modern Writing*, Cambridge, Cambridge University Press, 1993.

Gillespie, Stuart, '"The Worst Inn's Worst Room": Pope's Setting for Buckingham's Death', *Notes and Queries*, 37.3 (1990), 306–8.

Gilmour, Ian, *Riot, Risings and Revolution: Governance and Violence in Eighteenth-Century England*, London, Hutchinson, 1992.

Gilmour, Robin, *The Victorian Period: The Intellectual and Cultural Context of English Literature 1830–1890*, London, Longman, 1993.

Gissing, George, *The Nether World*, London, Dent, 1973 [1889].

Gittings, Robert, *John Keats*, London, Heinemann, 1970.

Goddard, Eileen, *Drinking in England and Wales in the Late 1980s*, London, HMSO, 1991.

Goldsmith, Oliver, *Collected Works of Oliver Goldsmith*, ed. Arthur Friedman, 5 vols, Oxford, Clarendon Press, 1966.

Goodridge, J. F., trans., *Piers the Ploughman*, Harmondsworth, Penguin, 1966.

Gould, Tony, *Inside Outsider: The Life and Times of Colin MacInness*, London, Allison and Busby, 1993.

Greene, Richard Leighton, ed., *A Selection of English Carols*, Oxford, Clarendon Press, 1962.

Grove, John, (?) *Wine, Beer, Ale, and Tobacco, Contending for Superiority: A Dialogue*, London, 1658.

Hackwood, Frederick W., *Inns, Ales, and Drinking Customs of Old England*, London, T. Fisher Unwin, 1910.

Hadfield, Andrew, *Literature, Politics and National Identity: Reformation to Renaissance*, Cambridge, Cambridge University Press, 1994.

Haig, Stirling, '"By the Rivers of Babylon": Water and Exile in *The Mayor of Casterbridge*', *The Thomas Hardy Yearbook*, 11 (1984), 55–62.

Haley, K. H. D., *The First Earl of Shaftesbury*, Oxford, Clarendon Press, 1968.

Hamilton, Patrick, *Hangover Square: A Story of Darkest Earl's Court*, London, Penguin, 1974 [1941].

—— *Money with Menaces* and *To the Public Danger* (radio plays), London, Constable, 1939.

—— *Twenty Thousand Streets under the Sky: A London Trilogy* (*The Midnight Bell*, *The Siege of Pleasure*, *The Plains of Cement*), London, Constable, 1935.

Hampson, John, *Saturday Night at The Greyhound*, London, Penguin, 1937 [1931].

Hanna, Ralph, 'Brewing Trouble: On Literature and History – and Ale-Wives', in

Bodies and Disciplines: Intersections of Literature and History in Fifteenth-Century England, ed. Barbara Hanawalt and David Wallace, Minneapolis, University of Minnesota Press, pp. 1–17.
—— 'Pilate's Voice/Shirley's Case', *South Atlantic Quarterly*, 91 (1992), 793–812.
Hardy, Thomas, *Jude the Obscure*, Ware, Herts., Wordsworth, 1995 [1895].
—— *The Mayor of Casterbridge*, London, Penguin, 1994 [1886].
Harris, Tim, ed., *Popular Culture in England, c. 1500–1850*, Houndmills, Basingstoke, Macmillan, 1995.
Harrison, Brian, *Drink and the Victorians: The Temperance Question in England 1815–1872*, 2nd edition, Keele, Staffordshire, Keele University Press, 1994 [1971].
Haydon, Benjamin Robert, *The Autobiography and Memoirs of Benjamin Robert Haydon (1786–1846)*, ed. from his Journals by Tom Taylor, London, Peter Davies, 1926.
Healy, Thomas, ed., *Andrew Marvell*, Harlow, Addison Wesley Longman, 1998.
Helgerson, Richard, *Forms of Nationhood: The Elizabethan Writing of England*, Chicago, The University of Chicago Press, 1992.
Heywood, Thomas, *Philocothonista, or, the Drunkard, Opened, Dissected, and Anatomized*, London, 1635.
—— *A Preparative to Studie: Or, The Vertue of Sack*, London, 1641.
Hibbert, Christopher, ed., *Captain Gronow: His Reminiscences of Regency and Victorian Life 1810–60*, London, Kyle Cathie, 1991.
Hill, Christopher, *Reformation to Industrial Revolution: British Economy and Society 1530/1780*, London, Weidenfeld and Nicholson, 1968.
Hindle, Steve, 'Custom, Festival and Protest in Early Modern England: The Little Budworth Wakes, St. Peter's Day, 1596', *Rural History*, 6:2 (1995), 155–78.
Hoccleve, Thomas, *La Male Regle De T. Hoccleve*, [1405], in *Selections from Hoccleve*, ed. M. C. Seymour, Oxford, Clarendon Press, 1981, pp. 12–23.
Homans, G. C., *English Villagers of the Thirteenth Century*, Cambridge, Massachusetts, Harvard University Press, 1942.
Hunt, Leigh, 'Pleasant Memories Connected with Various Parts of the Metropolis', *Essays of Leigh Hunt*, ed. Arthur Symons, London, Walter Scott, 1887.
Hunter, J. Paul, *Before Novels: The Cultural Contexts of Eighteenth-Century English Fiction*, London, Norton, 1990.
Hussey, Maurice, *The World of Shakespeare and his Contemporaries: A Visual Approach*, London, Heinemann, 1971.
Hussey, Maurice, A. C. Spearing and James Winny, *An Introduction to Chaucer*, London, Cambridge University Press, 1965.
Irving, Washington, 'The Boar's Head Tavern, Eastcheap', in *The Sketch-Book of Geoffrey Crayon, Gent.* [1820], London, Cassell, n.d.
Jenner, Charles, *Town Eclogues*, London, 1772.
'Joan's Ale is New; Or: A new merry Medly, shewing the power, the strength, the operation, and the vertue that remains in good Ale, which is accounted the Mother-drink of England', 1670, in a collection of English Ballads, British Library.
Jonson, Ben, *Bartholomew Fair*, ed. Maurice Hussey, London, Ernest Benn, 1964 [1614].
—— *The New Inn*, ed. Michael Hattaway, Manchester, Manchester University Press, 1984 [1629].

Judges, A. V., *The Elizabethan Underworld*, London, Routledge and Kegan Paul, 1965 [1930].

Kantorowicz, Ernst H., *The King's Two Bodies: A Study in Mediaeval Political Theology*, Princeton, New Jersey, Princeton University Press, 1981 [1957].

Keating, P. J., *The Working-Classes in Victorian Fiction*, London, Routledge, 1971.

Keats, John, *Letters of John Keats to his Family and Friends*, ed. Sidney Colvin, London, Macmillan, 1925.

—— *The Works of John Keats*, Ware, Herts., Wordsworth Editions, 1994.

Kee, Robert, *Munich: The Eleventh Hour*, London, Hamilton, 1988.

Kandall, Monica, 'The Archpoet's "Estuans intrinsicus ira vehementi" and manuscripts in England', MA diss., University College London, 1997.

Kennedy, Philip F., *The Wine Song in Classical Arabic Poetry: Abū Nuwās and the Literary Tradition*, Oxford, Clarendon Press, 1997.

Kermode, Jenny, and Garthine Walker, eds, *Women, Crime and the Courts in Early Modern England*, London, UCL Press, 1994.

Kerrigan, John, ed., *William Shakespeare, 'The Sonnets' and 'A Lover's Complaint'*, Harmondsworth, Penguin, 1986.

King, Bruce, *Seventeenth-Century English Literature*, Houndmills, Basingstoke, Macmillan, 1992.

Kingsley, Charles, *Alton Locke*, London, Collins, n.d. [1850].

Kinney, Arthur F., *John Skelton: Priest as Poet*, Chapel Hill, University of California Press, 1987.

Kinsman, Robert S., ed., *John Skelton: Poems*, Oxford, Clarendon Press, 1969.

Lamb, Charles, *John Woodvil*, London, 1802.

Landes, David S., *Revolution in Time: Clocks and the Making of the Modern World*, Cambridge, Massachusetts, Harvard University Press, 1983.

Langland, William, *The Vision of William Concerning Piers the Plowman in Three Parallel Texts*, ed. Walter W. Skeat, vol. 1, London, Oxford University Press, 1968 [1886].

Larwood, Jacob, and John Camden Hotten, *English Inn Signs*, revised and modernised, London, Chatto and Windus, 1951 [1866].

Leclerq, Jean, 'Experience and Interpretation of Time in the Early Middle Ages', *Studies in Medieval Culture*, ed. John R. Sommerfeldt, Larry Syndergaard and E. Rozanne Elder, vol. 5, Western Michigan University, 1975, pp. 9–19.

Le Goff, Jacques, *Time, Work and Culture in the Middle Ages*, trans. Arthur Goldhammer, Chicago, University of Chicago Press, 1980.

Legouis, Emile, 'The Bacchic Element in Shakespeare's Plays', in *Aspects of Shakespeare's Plays*, London, Abercrombie, 1933, pp. 84–107.

Lehmann, Hartmut and Guenther Roth, eds, *Weber's Protestant Ethic: Origins, Evidence, Contexts*, Cambridge, Cambridge University Press, 1993.

Leinwand, Theodore B., 'Spongy Plebs, Mighty Lords, and the Dynamics of the Alehouse', *Journal of Medieval and Renaissance Studies*, 19:2 (1989), 159–84.

Lessing, Doris, *In Pursuit of the English*, St Albans, Herts., 1980 [1960].

Lewis, Terrance L., *A Climate for Appeasement*, New York, Peter Lang, 1991.

Lister, Joseph, *The Autobiography of Joseph Lister, of Bradford in Yorkshire, to which is added a contemporary account of the defence of Bradford and the Capture of Leeds by the Parliamentarians in 1642*, ed. Thomas Wright, London, John Russell Smith, 1842.

London, Jack, *John Barleycorn or Alcoholic Memoirs*, London, Mills and Boon, 1914.
—— *The People of the Abyss*, London, Journeyman Press, 1980 [1903].
Lowe, Roger, *The Diary of Roger Lowe of Ashton-in-Makerfield, Lancashire, 1663–74*, ed. William L. Sachse, Foreword by Wallace Notestein, n.d., Preface dated 1938.
Lydgate, John, *The Minor Poems of John Lydgate edited from all available mss. with an attempt to establish the Lydgate Canon*, by Henry Noble MacCracken, London, published for The Early English Text Society by Humphrey Milford, Oxford University Press, 1910–34.
McCandless, Peter, '"Curses of Civilization": Insanity and Drunkenness in Victorian Britain', *British Journal of Addiction*, 79 (1984), 49–58.
McCormick, Mairi, 'First Representations of the Gamma Alcoholic in the English Novel', *Quarterly Journal of Studies on Alcoholism*, 30 (1969), 957–80.
MacInnes, Colin, *Absolute Beginners*, London, MacGibbon and Kee, 1959.
—— *City of Spades*, Harmondsworth, Penguin, 1964 [1957].
McKenna, Brian, 'Confessions of a Heavy-Drinking Marxist: Addiction in the Work of Patrick Hamilton', in *Beyond the Pleasure Dome: Writing and Addiction from the Romantics*, ed. Sue Vice, Matthew Campbell and Tim Armstrong, Sheffield, Sheffield Academic Press, 1994, pp. 231–44.
Marcus, Leah S., *Puzzling Shakespeare: Local Reading and its Discontents*, Berkeley, California, University of California Press, 1988.
—— 'Pastimes with a Court', in *Andrew Marvell*, ed. Thomas Healy, Harlow, Addison Wesley Longman, 1988.
Marrs, Jr., Edwin W., ed., *The Letters of Charles and Mary Anne Lamb*, 3 vols, Ithaca, Cornell University Press, 1975.
Marshall, Roderick, *Falstaff: The Archetypal Myth*, Element Books, Shaftesbury, Dorset, 1989.
Marston, John, *The Dutch Courtesan*, ed. M. L. Wine, London, Edward Arnold, 1965.
Mass Observation, *The Pub and the People: A Worktown Study by Mass Observation*, London, Victor Gollancz, 1943.
Matz, B. W., *Dickensian Inns and Taverns*, London, Cecil Palmer, 1922.
—— *The Inns and Taverns of 'Pickwick' with Some Observations on their Other Associations*, London, Cecil Palmer, 1921.
Meriton, George, *A Guide for Constables, Churchwardens, Overseers of the Poor ...*, London, 1669.
Middleton, Thomas, and Thomas Dekker, *The Roaring Girl*, Manchester, Manchester University Press, 1987 [?1611].
Miles, Dudley, *Francis Place: The Life of a Remarkable Radical, 1771–1854*, Brighton, Sussex, The Harvester Press, 1988.
Monckton, H. A., *A History of English Ale and Beer*, London, Bodley Head, 1966.
—— *A History of the English Public House*, London, Bodley Head, 1969.
Montagu, Basil, *Some Enquiries into the Effects of Fermented Liquors*, 2nd edition, London, 1818.
Morrison, Arthur, *A Child of the Jago*, Woodbridge, Suffolk, The Boydell Press, 1982 [1896].
—— *The Hole in the Wall*, London, Methuen, 1902.
—— *Tales of Mean Streets*, London, Methuen, 1896 [1894].

Muilenburg, James, 'The Biblical View of Time', *Harvard Theological Review*, 45:4 (October 1961), 225–52.
Nashe, Thomas, *A Pleasant Comedie, called Summers Last Will and* Testament, London, 1600.
—— *The Unfortunate Traveller and Other Works*, ed. J. B. Steane, Harmondsworth, Penguin, 1972.
Newey, Vincent, *Cowper's Poetry: A Critical Study and Reassessment*, Liverpool, Liverpool University Press, 1982.
North Briton, The, issues XLI, XLIII and XLVI (1763).
O'Brien, Flann, *The Best of Myles*, London, Paladin, 1990.
—— *Myles before Myles*, London, Paladin, 1989.
O'Brien, J. M., 'Attributes of Alcohol in the Old Testament', *Drinking and Drug Practices Surveyor*, 18 (1982), 18–24.
Ollard, Richard, *Pepys: A Biography*, London, Hodder and Stoughton, 1974.
O'Neill, J. M., *Duffy is Dead*, London, Heinemann, 1987.
Orwell, George, 'The Moon under Water', in *The Collected Essays, Journalism and Letters of George Orwell*, vol. 3, Harmondsworth, Penguin, 1971 [1946], pp. 63–5.
—— *The Penguin Complete Novels of George Orwell*, Harmondsworth, Penguin, 1983.
Osborn, Francis, 'A Character of an Host', in *A Miscellany of Sundry Essayes, Paradoxes ...*, London, 1659, pp. 197–9.
Osborne, John, *The Entertainer*, London, Faber, 1995 [1957].
Owst, G. R., *Literature and Pulpit in Medieval England: A Neglected Chapter in the History of English Letters and of the English People*, Oxford, Blackwell, 1966 [1933].
Palmer, Roy, ed., *Everyman's Book of English Country Songs*, London, Dent, 1979.
Parkes, Joan, *Travel in England in the Seventeenth Century*, London, Oxford University Press, 1925.
Parliamentary Debates. Commons. 1915.
Peck, John, 'Thackerary and Drink: *Vanity Fair* and *The Newcomes*', *Dionysos*, 4:1 (1992), 14–18.
Pepys, Samuel, *The Diary of Samuel Pepys*, ed. Robert Latham and William Matthews, 11 vols, London, G. Bell and Sons/Bell and Hyman, 1970–83.
Pink, Matthew, *Field and Pink: Liquor Licensing Law and Practice*, 2nd edition, London, Sweet and Maxwell, 1991.
Pinkus, Philip, *Grub St. Stripped Bare*, London, Constable, 1968.
—— *Improvement of the Working People: Drunkenness – Education*, London, 1834.
Place, Francis, *The Autobiography of Francis Place (1771–1854)*, ed. Mary Thrale, London, Cambridge University Press, 1972.
Plumb, J. H., *The Commercialisation of Leisure in Eighteenth-Century England* (Pamphlet – The Stenton Lecture, 1972), University of Reading, 1973.
Pollett, Maurice, *John Skelton: Poet of Tudor England*, trans. John Warrington, London, Dent, 1971.
Popham, H. E., *The Taverns of London Topographically Arranged*, 2nd edition, London, Cecil Palmer, 1928 [1927].
Potter, Lois, *Secret Rites and Secret Writing: Royalist iterature 1641–1660*, Cambridge, Cambridge University Press, 1989.

Powys, T. F., *Mr Weston's Good Wine*, Penguin, Harmondsworth, 1976 [1927].
Priestman, Martin, *Cowper's* Task: *Structure and Influence*, Cambridge, Cambridge University Press, 1983.
Protz, Roger, ed., (CAMRA) *Good Beer Guide 2000/Millennium edition*, St Albans, Herts., CAMRA Books, 1999.
Rankin, Robert, *The Antipope*, London, Corgi, 1998 [1981].
Rawlidge, Richard, *A Monster late found out and discovered. A discourse against Tipling and the Tipling Houses of the Citie of London*, [London] 1606.
Ray, John, ed., *A Collection of English Proverbs*, Cambridge, 1678.
Reay, Barry, ed., *Popular Culture in Seventeenth-Century England*, London, Croom Helm, 1985.
Restoration Plays, ed. Robert G. Lawrence, London, Dent, 1985.
Richardson, A. E. and H. Donaldson Eberlein, *The English Inn Past and Present: A Review of its History and Social Life*, London, Batsford, 1925.
Richardson, Samuel, *Pamela*, Harmondsworth, Penguin, 1985 [1740–41].
Rochester, Earl of [John Wilmot], *Love Poems*, Chadwyck-Healey Poetry Full-Text Database, 1996–98.
Rogers, Pat, ed., *Alexander Pope: A Selection of his Finest Poems*, Oxford, Oxford University Press, 1994.
—— *Grub Street: Studies in a Subculture*, London, Methuen, 1972.
Rollins, Hyder Edward, ed., *The Letters of John Keats 1814–21*, 2 vols, London, Cambridge University Press, 1958.
Roulstone, Michael, *Taverns in Town*, St Ives, Huntingdon, Balfour/Traveller's Rest, 1973.
The Roxburghe Ballads, vols I–III ed. William Chappell: vol. I, London, Taylor and Co., 1871, vols II–III, Hertford, Stephen Austin and Sons, 1874–80; vols IV–IX ed. J. Woodfall Ebsworth, Hertford, Stephen Austin and Sons, 1883–99.
Royal College of Psychologists, *Alcohol: Our Favourite Drug*, London, Tavistock Publications, 1986.
Rudé, George, *Hanoverian London 1714–1808*, London, Secker and Warburg, 1971.
Rush, Benjamin, *An Inquiry into the Effects of Ardent Spirits upon the Human Body and Mind ...*, 7th edition, Boston, 1812.
Salem, Frederick William, *Beer, Its History and Its Economic Value as a National Beverage*, reprint of 1880s edition, New York, Arno Press, 1972.
Sambrook, Pamela, *Country House Brewing in England 1500–1900*, London, The Hambledon Press, 1996.
Samuelson, James, *The History of Drink: A Review, Social, Scientific, and Political*, London, Trübner and Co., 1878.
Scheindlin, Raymond, *Wine, Women and Death: Medieval Hebrew Poems on the Good Life*, Philadelphia, Jewish Publication Society, 1986.
Sekora, John, *Luxury: The Concept in Western Thought, Eden to Smollett*, Baltimore, The Johns Hopkins University Press, 1977.
Shadwell, Arthur, *Drink in 1914–1922: A Lesson in Control*, London, Longmans, Green and Co., 1923.
—— *Drink, Temperance and Legislation*, London, Longmans, Green and Co., 1903.
Shadwell, Thomas, *The Squire of Alsatia*, London, 1688.
Shakespeare, William, *Henry IV Part One*, ed. P. H. Davison, London, Penguin, 1968.
—— *Henry IV Part Two*, ed. P. H. Davison, London, Penguin, 1977.

—— *Henry V*, ed. A. R. Humphries, London, Penguin, 1968.
—— *Measure for Measure*, ed. J. M. Nosworthy, London, Penguin, 1969.
—— *The Merry Wives of Windsor*, in *The Complete Oxford Shakespeare*, ed. Stanley Wells; Gary Taylor, John Jowett and William Montgomery, London, Guild Publishing (in association with Oxford University Press), 1987.
—— *Othello*, ed. Kenneth Muir, Penguin, London, 1996 [1968].
—— *Richard II (King Richard the Second)*, ed. Stanley Wells, London, Penguin, 1969.
—— *Taming of the Shrew*, in *The Complete Oxford Shakespeare*, ed. Stanley Wells, Gary Taylor, John Jowett and William Montgomery, London, Guild Publishing (in association with Oxford University Press), 1987.
—— *Timon of Athens*, ed. J. C. Maxwell, Cambridge, Cambridge University Press, 1968.
—— *Twelfth Night*, ed. Herschel Baker, New York, Signet, 1965.
Shepard, Leslie, *The History of Street Literature*, Newton Abbot, 1973.
Shiman, Lilian Lewis, *Crusade against Drink in Victorian England*, New York, St. Martin's Press, 1988.
Shorter Oxford English Dictionary, Oxford, Clarendon Press, 1993.
Sillitoe, Alan, *Saturday Night and Sunday Morning*, London, Flamingo, 1994 [1958].
Simon, André L., *Bottlescrew Days: Wine Drinking in England During the Eighteenth Century*, London, Duckworth, 1926.
'Sir John Barleycorn', in Dixon, ed., *Ancient Ballads*, 1973 [1846], pp. 120–2.
Smith, Peter, *Social Shakespeare: Aspects of Renaissance Dramaturgy and Contemporary Society*, Basingstoke, Macmillan, 1995.
Smollett, Tobias, *The Life and Adventures of Sir Launcelot Greaves*, London, Oxford University Press, 1973 [1760–61].
—— *Roderick Random*, London, Penguin, 1995 [1748].
Spark, Muriel, *The Driver's Seat*, Harmondsworth, Penguin, 1974 [1970].
Spufford, M., 'Puritanism and Social Control?', in Fletcher and Stevenson, eds, *Order*, 1985, pp. 41–57.
Sturt, George ('George Bourne'), *The Wheelwright's Shop*, London, Cambridge University Press, 1923.
Tale of Beryn (anon.), Chadwyck-Healey Poetry Full-Text Database, 1996–98.
The Taming of a Shrew: The 1594 Quarto, ed. Stephen Roy Miller, Cambridge, Cambridge University Press, 1998.
The Tavern Scuffle (1725) with 'The Report of the Committee appointed to Enquire out the Number of Publick Shops that sell Geneva in the Out-Parishes of London. To his Majesty's Justices of the Peace for the County of Middlesex, in their General Quarter Sessions assembled', London, 1726. ['Anon. No trace.' – written in pencil, inside front board, copy in the British Library.]
Taylor, Anya, *Bacchus in Romantic England: Writers and Drink, 1780–1830*, Houndmills, Basingstoke, Macmillan, 1999.
—— 'Coleridge, Keats, Lamb, and Seventeenth-Century Drinking Songs', in *Milton, the Metaphysicals and Romanticism*, ed. Lisa Low and Anthony John Harding, Cambridge, Cambridge University Press, 1994.
Taylor, John, *Ale Alevated into the Ale-titude: Or, A Learned Oration before a Civill Assembly of ALE-Drinkers* …, London, 1651.
—— *Drinke and welcome: or the Famous Historie of the most part of Drinks, in use now in the Kingdomes of* Great Brittaine *and* Ireland, London, 1637.

—— *The Pennyles Pilgrimage, or The Money-less perambulation, of John Taylor*, Alias the Kings Majesties Water Poet …, London, 1618.
—— *Taylors Travels and Circular Perambulation, through, and by more then thirty times twelve Signes of the Zodiack, of the Famous Cities of London and Westminster, Works not in the volume of 1630* (1870), Chadwyck-Healey Poetry Full-Text Database, 1996–98.
Taylor, Mark, 'Falstaff and the Origins of Private Life', *Shakespeare Yearbook* (1992), 63–83.
Taylor, William B., *Drinking, Homicide and Rebellion in Colonial Mexican Villages*, Stanford, California, Stanford University Press, 1979.
Thompson, E. P., *Customs in Common*, London, Penguin, 1993.
—— *The Making of the English Working Class*, London, Penguin, 1991.
—— 'Time, Work-Discipline and Industrial Capitalism', *Past and Present*, 35 (1967).
Thrift, Nigel, *Spatial Formations*, London, Sage, 1996.
Tolman, Albert H., 'Drunkenness in Shakespeare's Plays', in *Falstaff and other Shakespearean Topics*, New York, Macmillan, 1925, pp. 44-52.
Tourneur, Cyril, *The Revenger's Tragedy*, ed. R. A. Foakes, Manchester, Manchester University Press, 1990 [?1605–06].
Trotter, Thomas, *An Essay Medical, Philosophical, and Chemical on Drunkenness and its Effects on the Human Body*, ed. Roy Porter, London, Routledge, 1988 [1804].
Troyer, Howard William, *Ned Ward of Grubstreet: A Study of Sub-Literary London in the Eighteenth Century*, Cambridge, Massachusetts, Harvard University Press, 1946.
Tucker, Josiah, *An Impartial Inquiry into the Benefits and Damages Arising to the Nation from the present very great Use of* Low-priced *Spirituous Liquors* …, London, 1751.
Underdown, David, *Revel, Riot, and Rebellion: Popular Politics and Culture in England 1603–1660*, Oxford, Clarendon Press, 1985.
Vonnegut, Kurt, *Slaughterhouse Five*, London, Triad/Panther Books, 1979 [1969].
Wain, John, *Hurry on Down*, Harmondsworth, Penguin, 1969 [1953].
Ward, Ned, *Apollo's Maggot in His Cups: Or, the Whimsical Creation of a Little Satyrical Poet*, Chadwyck-Healey English Poetry Full-Text Database, 1992 [1729].
—— *A Compleat and Humorous Account of all the Remarkable Clubs and Societies in the Cities of London and Westminster*, London, J. Wren, 1756 [1709].
—— *The Compleat Vintner: Or, the Delights of the Bottle*, Chadwyck-Healey English Poetry Full-Text Database, 1992 [1720].
—— *The Hudibrastick Brewer: Or, a Preposterous Union Between Malt and Meter*, Chadwyck-Healey English Poetry Full-Text Database, 1992 [1714].
—— *The London Spy*, ed. Paul Hyland from the 4th edition of 1709, East Lansing, Colleagues Press, 1993.
—— *Nuptial Dialogues and Debates*, Dialogue XVIII, 'Between a teazing Husband, and his vexatious tipling Wife', Chadwyck-Healey English Poetry Full-Text Database, 1992 [1723].
—— *The Rambling Fuddle-Caps: Or, A Tavern-Struggle For a Kiss*, London, 1709.
—— *The Rise and Fall of Madam Coming-Sir: Or, An Unfortunate Slip from the Tavern-Bar, Into the Surgeon's Powdering-Tub*, Stamford, Lincolnshire, 1720 [1703].
Watney, John, *Mother's Ruin: A History of Gin*, London, Peter Owen, 1976.

Webb, Sidney and Beatrice Webb, *The History of Liquor Licensing in England: Principally from 1700 to 1830*, London, Frank Cass, 1963 (reprint) [1903].

Weber, Max, *The Protestant Work Ethic and the Spirit of Capitalism*, Introduction by Anthony Giddens, London, George Allen and Unwin, 1976 [1930].

Wells, H. G., *A Modern Utopia*, London, Collins, n.d. [1905].

Wheeler, C. B., ed., *Six Plays by Contemporaries of Shakespeare*, London, Oxford University Press, 1964.

Whicher, George F., *The Goliard Poets: Medieval Latin Songs and Satires*, Westport, Connecticut, Greenwood Press, 1979.

Widdowson, P. J., 'The Saloon Bar Society: Patrick Hamilton's Fiction in the 1930s', in *The 1930s: A Challenge to Orthodoxy*, ed. John Lucas, Sussex, Harvester Press, 1978, pp. 117–37.

Wightman, Mrs Charles, *Haste to the Rescue; or, Work While it is Day*, London, James Nisbet, 1860.

Williams, Raymond, *The Country and the City*, St Albans, Herts., Granada/Paladin, 1975.

Wilson, F. P., ed., *The Plague Pamphlets of Thomas Dekker*, Oxford, Clarendon Press, 1925.

Winny, James, 'Chaucer Himself', in Hussey *et al.*, *Chaucer*, 1965, pp. 1–27.

—— 'Chaucer's Science', in Hussey *et al.*, *Chaucer*, 1965, pp. 153–84.

Wood, Nigel, ed., *Henry IV Parts One and Two*, Buckingham, Open University Press, 1995.

Woodland, Patrick, 'Extra-Parliamentary Political Organization in the Making: Benjamin Heath and the Opposition to the 1763 Cider Excise', *Parliamentary History*, 4 (1985), 115–36.

—— 'The House of Lords, The City of London and Political Controversy in the Mid-1760s: The Opposition to the Cider Excise Further Considered', *Parliamentary History*, 11:1 (1992), 57–87.

—— 'Political Atomization and Regional Interests in the 1761 Parliament: The Impact of the Cider Debates 1763–1766', *Parliamentary History*, 8:1 (1989), 63–89.

Wordsworth, Dorothy, *Journals of Dorothy Wordsworth*, ed. E. de Selincourt, vol. 1, London, Macmillan, 1941.

Wordsworth, William, *Benjamin the Waggoner*, ed. Paul F. Betz, Ithaca, New York, Cornell University Press, 1981.

—— *The Prelude*, in Wu, ed., *Romanticism*, 1994.

—— *The Waggoner*, from *The Poetical Works* (1849–50), Chadwick-Healey Full-Text Poetry Database, 1996–99 [1805].

Wrightson, Keith, 'Alehouses, Order and Reformation in Rural England, 1590–1660', in *Popular Culture and Class Conflict 1590–1914*, ed. Eileen and Stephen Yeo, Sussex, Harvester Press, 1981, pp. 1–27.

—— 'Two Concepts of Order: Justices, Constables and Jurymen in Seventeenth-Century England', in *An Ungovernable People: The English and their Law in the Seventeenth and Eighteenth Centuries*, ed. John Brewer and John Styles, London, Hutchinson, 1980, pp. 21–46.

Wrightson, Keith and David Levine, *Poverty and Piety in an English Village: Terling, 1525–1700*, New York, Academic Press, 1979.

Wu, Duncan, ed., *Romanticism An Anthology*, Oxford, Blackwell, 1994.

Wycherley, William, *The Country Wife*, in *Restoration Plays*, Notes and Introduction by Robert G. Lawrence, London, Dent, 1985.
Young, Thomas, *Englands Bane: or, the Description of Drunkennesse*, London, 1617.
Zall, P. M., ed., *A Nest of Ninnies and Other English Jestbooks of the Seventeenth Century*, Lincoln, University of Nebraska Press, 1970.

Index

Note: literary works can be found under authors' names; 'n' after a page reference indicates a note on that page.

abstinence 92–3, 95, 222–3, 224–7
Acts: 11 Henry VII, c.2 (1496) 45–6; 5+6 Edward VI, c.25 (1552) 45, 46, 47; 7 Edward 6, c.5 (1553) 46–7; 2(1) Jac. I, c.9 (1604) 5, 48; 2 Geo. 2, c.28 (1729) 134; 6 Geo. 2, c.17 (1733) 134; 9 Geo.2, c.23 (1736) 8, 135; 4 Geo. 3, c.7 (1763) 8; (1830) Beerhouse Act 197, 218–19; (1832) Reform Act 212–14; (1915) Defence of the Realm (Amendment No. 3) Bill 241; (1921) Licensing Act 246; (1988) 270; (1995) 270–1
addiction 170, 173, 196, 208, 222, 236, 249, 250–1, 253
Addison, Joseph 190
adulteration 22, 75
agriculture 31–3, 50, 82–3, 134, 135, 219, 222, 223
alcoholics 3, 220, 222, 236, 248–54
 see also drunkards
ale 13, 28–33, 64, 75, 81, 90–9 *passim*, 135, 139, 169
alewives 13, 22–8, 72, 136, 155
Alexander the Great 59–60, 81
Alfric's Colloquy 28
'A Litany from Geneva' 92
Amis, Kingsley
 Lucky Jim 259, 260
Amis, Martin
 London Fields 13, 265–71
Anacreontics 3
Angry Young Men 258, 260
Arabic wine poem (*khamriyya*) 4
architecture 57, 160, 191, 258

Archpoet of Cologne 4
Aristotle 147, 148
authority 8, 45, 48–51, 75, 115, 116, 117, 120–1, 144, 152–3

Bacchus 3, 4, 29, 79, 82, 120, 129, 168
ballads 6, 26, 90, 173
Bamford, Samuel 215, 230n.17
Bandele, Biyi
 Happy Birthday, Mister Deka D. 262, 271
barmaids 13, 127, 141, 143, 246–7
Bartholomew Fair 123, 124
bawdy houses *see* brothels
Beaumont, Francis
 The Knight of the Burning Pestle 74
beer, 9, 12–13, 28–33, 75, 80, 82, 90, 91, 94, 99, 100, 135, 169, 179, 262, 269
beggars 75–6
Bennett, Judith M. 11, 22, 26–7
bible 48–9, 43n.72
blasphemy 13
Boar's Head, 14, 45, 48, 54, 56–7, 60, 73, 160, 163, 168, 171
Boorde, Andrew 30
boozing-kens 117, 119
Boswell, James 160–1, 181
Braine, John
 Room at the Top 259
brawling 105–6
Bretherton, R. F. 8
breweries 194–5
brewing 8, 22, 27, 31
brewsters 11, 22
bribery 103

Index

Brontë, Anne
  The Tenant of Wildfell Hall 220
brothels 59, 70, 74, 75, 79, 81, 84, 96, 116, 122, 128, 146
Brown, Tom 111
'Bryng Us in Good Ale' 30
Burns, Robert 3, 168, 178
  'Tam O'Shanter' 173, 176

Campaign For Real Ale (CAMRA) 262
'Canary's Coronation' 91
canon, the 3, 6, 145
capitalism 9, 12, 27, 140, 223, 228
Carlile, Richard 9
'Catalogue of Contented Cuckolds, The' 23
Cavaliers 90–1
Centlivre, Mrs [Susanna]
  The Man's Bewitch'd 140–1
Chamberlain, Neville 248, 251–2, 253
Chartists 199, 201, 219, 220
Chaucer, Geoffrey
  The Canterbury Tales 2, 6, 14, 18–21, 34–5, 37–9, 54, 79, 165, 242, 243
Chester Mystery Play 22
Chesterton, G. K.
  The Flying Inn 234, 235
Christianity 80–1
church 10, 21, 35, 39, 115, 228, 244
Cider Riots 16n.19
Clark, Peter 6, 10, 23, 56, 135, 161, 206n.42
class 134, 135, 169, 221, 226, 242, 257, 259, 269
  see also lower orders; middle class; middling classes; upper orders; working class(es)
clergy 10, 35, 76, 163
closing time 2, 270–1
clubs 90, 127–9
coaching inns 133, 151–2, 189–213
Cobbett, William 9
coffee 122–3
coffee-houses 94, 100, 113, 116, 121, 122–3, 124, 126
Coleridge, S. T. 168–9, 171–2, 173, 175
  Biographia Literaria 179
commerce 46, 55–6, 95–106 passim, 141, 163, 218–19, 222
community 228, 240, 250, 258, 262, 269
  see also organic community
Conrad, Joseph
  The Secret Agent 236, 255n.14

constitution
  legal 2, 13, 60, 146
  national 51, 52–4, 60, 62, 77, 86–7, 146, 153–6, 166
  physical 52–4, 86–7, 166
'Content's a Treasure' 92
conviviality 6, 39, 58, 70, 82, 92, 95, 123, 126, 135, 144, 165, 227
  see also sodality
Cooper, Anthony Ashley (1st Earl of Shaftesbury) 91–2
Cooper, William
  Scenes from Provincial Life 258–9, 260
Copland, Robert
  'The Highway to the Spital-House' 28, 36–7, 74–5
Coppard, A. E.
  'The Black Dog' 243–5, 247, 258
country pubs 243–5, 260
Court 106, 133, 134
Cowper, William
  The Task 14, 163–6, 184
cozeners 75–7
Crabbe, George 178–84
  The Borough 180–4
  'Inebriety' 179
  The Village 180
crime 1, 50–8 *passim*, 74–9, 137, 138–9, 140, 144–7, 151, 152–3, 164, 228
Cromwell, Oliver 91, 106, 123
Crowch, Humfrey
  'The Industrious Smith' 26
Cruikshank, George 197
cuckoldry 23, 136
Curtin, Michael
  The League Against Christmas 262–3
customary society 12, 133, 137, 139, 142, 146, 202, 209–10, 213, 214, 246–7

darts 265–70
day of misrule 8, 61, 83
death 37–8, 79, 81–2, 263–5
Defoe, Daniel 111, 127, 134, 167
Dekker, Thomas 82, 112
  The Bellman of London 76
  The Dead Tearme 77–8, 82
  The Gul's Horne-book 78
  Lantern and Candlelight 37, 76–7
  The Seven Deadly Sins 112
  The Wonderfull yeare 79–82
De Quincey, Thomas 173, 175
  Confessions of an English Opium-Eater 170–1

dicing houses *see* gambling houses
Dickens, Charles 111, 188–205, 234, 235
  Barnaby Rudge 190–1, 193, 199–205, 208–9, 211, 212, 216
  David Copperfield 196
  Dombey and Son 189
  Great Expectations 194–5, 196
  Hard Times 195, 232n.45
  Martin Chuzzlewit 190, 191, 193, 195
  The Old Curiosity Shop 193, 194, 197, 198
  Oliver Twist 193–4, 195, 234
  Our Mutual Friend 220, 235
  Pickwick papers 13, 188–9, 192, 195–6, 198–9, 218
  Sketches by Boz 197
Dionysus 4
Dogget, Thomas
  The Country Wake 30–1
dram shops 135, 161
Drayton, Michael
  Polyolbion 212–13
drink 3, 79, 90
  as inspiration 3, 14, 120
  symbolic nature of, 28–33, 61–4, 70, 118, 139
  as transformative 10
drink-driving 250, 252–3
drinking place
  alternative to church 11, 12, 13, 21, 23, 75, 95, 116
  hierarchy 5–6, 54–7, 133, 169, 179, 181, 216, 226
drinking songs 3, 4, 90–2, 144–5
drunkards 10–11, 13, 70, 76–7, 81, 84, 115, 136–7, 195–6, 220, 236
  see also alcoholics
drunkenness 4, 6, 10–11, 20, 34–8, 48–9, 70, 71, 79, 81, 103, 106, 117, 134, 135, 147–8, 153, 164, 167, 179, 196, 217, 220, 222, 236, 237, 250, 259
Dryden, John
  Absalom and Achitophel 91, 126
dts (*delirium tremens*) 196, 236

Earle, John 27–8, 56–7
East End 237–9
education 215
elections 198–9, 212, 214–17, 219
Eliot, George 234, 235
  Felix Holt 212–17, 221, 223, 233n.77, 234, 239
  'Janet's Repentance' 212, 216, 220, 235

Silas Marner 208–12, 216, 235
Eliot, T. S.
  The Waste Land 236, 240–3, 267
elite culture 9
elitism 242
Empire 163, 251–2, 269
English Civil War 76, 90, 94
English literature 2–7, 12, 115
Englishness 2–3, 12, 14, 71, 153, 202, 209, 226, 239
estates 50, 55, 77, 83–7, 133, 137, 139–41, 151, 152, 246–7
  see also mansions
Exeter Book, The 42

Falstaff 45–64, 135, 161, 163, 165
Farquhar, George 135
  The Beaux' Stratagem 136–7, 138–40, 141
  Love and a Bottle 135–6
  The Stage Coach 28, 137–8
Fascism 250, 253
Fennor, William
  The Counter's Commonwealth 77–8
festival culture 8, 45, 50, 175, 200, 246, 260
festivals 82–3
feudalism 9, 140
Fielding, Henry 145–8, 152
  Amelia 153
  A Charge Delivered to the Grand Jury 146–7, 151
  An Enquiry into the Cause of the Late Increase of Robbers 14, 135, 146–7, 148, 151, 163
  Joseph Andrews 13, 14, 148
  Journal of a Voyage to Lisbon 151, 153–6
  Tom Jones 13, 14, 127, 145, 147, 148, 162, 194, 202
Finch, Anne (Countess of Winchilsea)
  'The Prevalence of Custom' 137
Fletcher, John
  The Knight of the Burning Pestle 74
friendship *see* sodality
Fuller, Isaac 120

gallants 75, 77–9, 86, 113, 123
gambling 74, 77, 106, 146
gaol *see* prison
Gascoyne, George 37
Gay, John
  The Beggar's Opera 13, 135, 144–5, 160–1
  'Wine' 158n.43, 179

gender 1, 11–12, 22–8 *passim*, 71, 84, 86, 105, 176–7, 263, 267
  see also women
genre 2, 38, 53, 149, 150–1, 169
gentility 19–20, 51, 154, 169
gentlemen 51, 74, 77, 112, 137–43, 144, 229, 244
gentry 10, 58, 113, 124, 133, 141
George, Lloyd 241
gin 8, 134–5, 147, 169, 197–8
gin palaces 197–8
gin shops 135
Gladstone, William 219
gluttony 13, 19–21, 34–5, 83
golden age 12, 148, 155, 161, 162, 165
Goldsmith, Oliver 104, 185n.10
  The Deserted Village 162, 163, 165
  'Happiness' 157n.37
  'A Reverie at the *Boar's-head-tavern* in Eastcheap' 160, 161
  She Stoops to Conquer 13, 14, 133, 141–4, 162, 163, 171, 198, 243
Goliardic poetry 4, 20, 92
goodfellowship *see* sodality
Gordon Riots 199–205, 208
'Gossip's Meeting, The' 23
Great Exhibition 221
Great Fire of London 104
Grove, John 30, 134
Grub Street 110–12
gulls 75, 77–9

hack writing 6, 110, 111–12
Hamilton, Patrick 6, 236–7
  Hangover Square 13, 248–54, 257
  To the Public Danger 252–3
  Twenty Thousand Streets under the Skies 249–50
Hampson, John
  Saturday Night at the Greyhound 236, 246–7, 259–60, 264
hangovers 97–9
Hardy, Thomas 234
  The Mayor of Casterbridge 173, 218–30
Harman, Thomas
  A Caveat for Common Cursitors 75–6, 112
Haydon, Benjamin 166, 169–70
health 30, 52, 53, 77–9, 91, 95, 97–8, 102, 107–8
healths *see* toasting
Heywood, Thomas
  'A Preparative to Studie' 29–30

Philocothonista 37
Higden, Henry
  The Wary Widow 135
highwaymen 137, 138–9, 144–5, 151, 153
historiography 209
Hoccleve, Thomas
  La Male Regle 35
Hogarth, William 135, 147, 197, 198
hostesses 27, 57, 70, 71, 72, 76, 80–1
  see also landladies
hosts 2, 39, 57, 80–1, 84–6, 104, 150, 194
  see also landlords
house mistaken for inn 14, 85, 133, 140–3, 202
humours 37, 79, 83, 85
Hunt, Leigh 160

idleness 13, 48–51, 55–6, 99, 134, 164, 213, 217
'immortal dinner party' *see* Haydon, Benjamin
impotence 136
industrialisation 210, 213–14, 220, 221, 223
infrastructure 46, 55–6, 133, 140, 151
inheritance 77–9, 83–7, 105, 138–40, 212, 217
Irving, Washington
  'The Boar's Head Tavern, Eastcheap' 160, 161

'Joan's Ale is New' 23
'John Barleycorn' 6, 31–3, 82
Johnson, Samuel 167, 181
Jonson, Ben 29, 69
  Bartholomew Fayre 97
  The New Inn 38, 83–7
Joyce, James 3, 236

Keats, John 14, 166, 170
  Hyperion 29
Kingsley, Charles
  Alton Locke 220

lager 13, 262, 269
Lamb, Charles 14, 167, 168, 169–70
  Confessions of a Drunkard 168
  Letters 171–2
  The Old Familiar Faces 168
landladies 22, 105, 107, 125, 151, 152, 154–5, 162, 192–3, 246–7
  see also hostesses
landlords 13, 74, 75, 104–5, 110–11, 135,

138–43 passim, 151, 152, 182–4, 200, 203, 214, 246–7, 263–5
see also hosts
Langland, William
    Piers the Plowman 6, 18–21, 22, 25, 33, 34, 38, 71, 165
language 3, 11, 57, 84, 102, 116–17, 119, 179
last orders see closing time
Last Will and Testament of Anthony 92
law, the 5, 46, 53, 60, 70, 71, 144, 222
legislation 8, 47, 56, 79, 95, 99, 134, 241–2, 270–1
    see also Acts; law
lewdness 39, 44, 55, 75, 84, 106, 125
literary traditions 3–4
literature
    and decorum 3, 6–7, 14, 19–21, 38–9, 115, 172, 178–9, 180–1, 183, 243
    'working class' 237
    see also canon; English literature; hack writing
Livesey, Joseph 219
lock-ins 8
London 3, 13, 57, 70, 74–82 passim, 93, 111–27, 133–41 passim, 152, 201, 236–9, 245–7, 265–70
    see also East End
London, Jack
    The People of the Abyss 237
Lowe, Roger 93, 95
lower orders 10, 39, 50, 51, 57, 70, 75, 76, 84–5, 119, 134, 140, 146–7, 152, 163–5, 169–71, 178–9, 180, 210, 216, 221, 228, 229, 239, 240–2, 259, 267, 270
    see also working classes
low-life 13, 135, 178–9, 180
Lydgate, John
    'Ballad on an Ale-Seller' 22, 25–6
    'Nine Properties of Wine' 28
luxury 163, 213

'Madam Geneva' 8
madness 34, 79, 80, 219, 221
'Mad Tom of Bedlam' 131n.40
'Man in the Moon Drinks Claret, The' 23
mansions 137, 139, 140–3, 202, 246
marriage 136–7, 139, 151, 172, 182–3, 211–12, 220, 223, 238, 244, 247, 260, 270
Marston, John
    The Dutch Courtesan 74

Marvell, Andrew
    'Upon Appleton House' 137
Massinger, Philip
    A New Way to Pay Old Debts 74, 89n.64
Mass Observation
    The Pub and the People 234, 254n.3, 255n.32, 257, 258, 259
medicine 219, 220, 236
merrie England 12–13, 14, 45, 59, 64, 70 71, 101, 163, 165, 200–2
metadrama 61, 70–1, 72–3, 83, 85–6, 89n.68
metafiction 115
middle class 169, 171, 215, 221, 226, 258, 260, 261
    see also middling classes
middling classes 9–10, 50, 57, 77, 114, 133, 135, 229
    see also middle class
Milton, John 167, 175
misogyny 22–8
mob (the 'mobility') 92, 121, 124, 165, 203–4, 216
modernism 235, 236
Mompesson, Sir Giles 74
monarchy 95–6, 120, 121, 226
Morrison, Arthur 6, 236, 237, 240, 243
    A Child of the Jago 237
    The Hole in the Wall 237
    Tales of Mean Streets 237–9
MPs 166
multiculture 262, 264, 266
Munich 248–54
Murray, Al (Pub Landlord) 262

narrative structure 2, 13–14, 38–9, 120, 127, 144, 147, 148–50, 192, 200–1, 210–11, 218–23 passim, 250, 260, 268, 271
narrative voice 39, 112, 122, 148, 149–51, 175, 184, 237, 242, 243, 250, 259, 266
Nashe, Thomas 112
    Pierce Penniless 37, 112
    Summer's Last Will 82–3
nation 1–3, 8, 12, 45, 47–64, 77–82, 91, 93, 146, 154–5, 163–6, 177, 209, 268–70
nature 174, 176, 177, 178, 227
nobility 50, 57, 58, 71–2, 77
North–South divide 5, 15n.14, 259
'Nottingham Ale' 29
novel, the 189
Nuwās, Abū 4

oaths 99, 100, 101, 103, 222, 223, 224–7

Index

O'Neill, J. M.
   Duffy is Dead 262, 263–5
opening hours 2, 8, 95, 241–2, 270–1
ordinaries 74–9, 88n.34, 94, 105, 106, 113, 123, 150, 151
organic community 9, 12, 163, 211–12, 257
Orwell, George
   Keep the Aspidistra Flying 257
   'The Moon under Water' 257, 258
Osborne, John
   The Entertainer 259

pastoral 178–9
patrician culture 9, 50
Pepys, Samuel 92–108, 122, 171
picaresque 13–14, 148
Place, Francis 166, 215, 230n.19
plague 79–82, 264–5
plebeian culture 9, 49, 50, 90, 91, 124, 216
pledging 63
poetry 14
politics 90, 96, 123, 128, 239
Pope, Alexander 5, 7, 110
   Dunciad 7, 111
   Dunciad Variorum 111, 130n.6
   'Epistle to Bathurst' 5
   Peri Bathous 130n.6
   Rape of the Lock 184
postmodern fiction 266
poverty 135, 136, 147, 163–4, 197–8, 219, 237–9
prison 78, 119, 121, 144–5
Prohibition 243
prostitutes 102, 114, 116, 144
prostitution 111, 127, 135
Protestantism 9, 10, 12, 46, 49, 118, 223
Protestant work ethic 11, 50, 93, 128
provinces 133, 259
Prynne, William 101
psychology 36, 37, 173, 218, 225, 235, 249, 266
Puritanism 10, 50, 69, 91–106 *passim*, 175, 209–10, 217

Quakers 118, 126, 151

racism 264
Radical movement 9, 212, 215, 216–17
railways 234
Rankin, Robert
   The Antipope 262
realism 19, 20–1, 38–9, 58, 111–13, 148–9, 179, 180–1, 189, 234–7, 261

reason 221, 229
rebellion 8, 13, 45, 60, 70, 91, 92
   see also riots
Reformation 10, 11, 12, 80, 220
respectability 5, 9, 20, 152, 184, 226, 227, 228
Restoration 90, 97, 135–7
Richardson, Samuel 141
   Pamela 149, 150, 151
riots 8, 135, 146, 165, 199–205, 212, 216
Rochester, Earl of (John Wilmot) 136
Romanticism 14, 161, 167–78
Roundheads 90, 106
rounds 97, 256
rowdiness 69, 71, 72, 85
Roxburghe Ballads, The 22, 26, 90
Royalists 91, 94
Rump Parliament 90, 91

sack 61–4, 71, 92, 98, 99
'Sack for my Money' 90–1
sailors 125, 126, 176
Saturday night 170
schizophrenia 250, 254
self 100, 101, 102, 168, 224–5
sexism 267
sexual activity 13, 97, 101–7, 116, 117, 151, 152, 260
Shaftesbury, 1st Earl of, *see* Cooper, Anthony Ashley
Shakespeare, William 2, 7, 26, 69, 110, 161, 170, 267, 273n.41
   1 Henry IV 11, 14, 28, 45–64, 82, 168, 243
   2 Henry IV 14, 27, 45–64, 82, 168, 243
   Henry V 45–64, 243
   Macbeth 70, 136
   Measure for Measure 36, 64, 70
   The Merry Wives of Windsor 57
   Othello 36, 70
   Richard II 5, 44, 45–64 passim
   The Taming of the Shrew 70–3, 79, 83
   The Tempest 70
   Timon of Athens 63
   Twelfth Night 69–70, 91
Shenstone, William
   'Written at an Inn at Henley' 134
signs 120, 182, 189–91, 200, 226, 245, 247, 267–8, 273n.44
Sillitoe, Alan
   Saturday Night and Sunday Morning 246, 259–60

Skelton, John 7
  'The Tunnyng of Elynour Rummyng' 22, 23–5, 35, 38, 117
small beer 100–1
soaps 261–2
sobriety 8, 12, 48, 91, 93, 95, 98, 100, 106, 123, 128, 164, 175, 180, 217
socialism 219, 223
social range 13, 18–19, 24, 38, 50, 54, 57, 70, 71, 75, 84–5, 121, 151–2, 164–5, 211, 227–8, 239, 263, 267
sodality 4, 13, 57–8, 80, 82, 90, 144, 172
space 51, 52–64, 71, 83, 101, 107, 122, 133, 144, 151, 165, 204, 242, 270
  domestic 71, 151, 164–5, 204, 216, 217, 260, 270
  dramatic 13–14, 61
spirits 135, 152
squirearchy 151, 246–7
State, the 5, 8–9, 11, 45–64, 152, 165–6, 221, 226, 242, 243
stews *see* brothels
Sunday opening 95, 97, 103, 125, 270–1
swearing 103, 106, 113

Tabard, the 2, 5, 18–20, 39
Tale of Beryn (Anon.) 22
Taming of a Shrew, The (Anon.) 38, 71, 79, 83
Tavern Scuffle, The 134
taxation 8, 91, 94, 167, 219
Taylor, John, 'The Water Poet' 30, 189–90, 264
teetotalism 226, 227
temperance movement 165, 197, 198, 218, 219, 221, 230
Thackeray, William Makepeace 220
theatre 13–14, 74, 97, 99, 100, 102, 117
Thomson, James
  The Seasons 179
time 47–51, 82, 164, 217, 218, 222–9 *passim*, 240–2, 243, 270–1
toasting 81, 90, 95–6, 97, 101, 105, 106, 108, 113
treating 198–9, 215–16
Trotter, Thomas 186n.32, 220

United Kingdom Alliance (UKA) 219

upper orders 10, 56, 77, 146, 210, 211, 217, 221, 229, 240, 242

vagrancy acts 155

Wain, John
  Hurry on Down 260–1
Ward, Ned 3, 7, 110–29, 135, 171
  Apollo's Maggot in His Cups 111
  The Compleat Vintner 129
  Durgen, or a Plain Satyr upon a Pompous Satyrist 111
  The History of London Clubs 127–9
  The Hudibrastick Brewer 111
  The London Spy 3, 110, 111–26
  Nuptial Dialogues and Debates 129
  The Rambling Fuddle-Caps 127
  The Rise and Fall of Madam Coming-Sir 127
  The Tippling Philosophers 112
  A Trip to Jamaica 110, 130n.13
Wells, H. G.
  The History of Mr. Polly 235
'whoring' 106, 111
wine 4, 28, 29, 46, 61–4, 70, 75, 90, 94, 96, 99–105 *passim*, 114, 118, 129, 135, 136, 169, 170, 179, 262
women 11–12, 22–8 *passim*, 75, 84, 96–7, 106, 107, 114–15, 121–2, 127, 129, 131n.45, 136–7, 179–80, 220, 247, 266
  see also alewives; barmaids; brewsters; hostesses; landladies; misogyny
Wordsworth, William 169, 171, 209
  The Prelude 167, 175, 179
  The Waggoner 167, 173–8, 200
work discipline 8, 12, 46–51, 218, 220, 246
working class(es) 9, 165, 217, 219, 221, 237, 239
  see also lower orders
World War I 241
World War II 248–54, 258
Wycherley, William
  The Country Wife 136

Young, Thomas 10, 34, 37
Younge, Robert 48